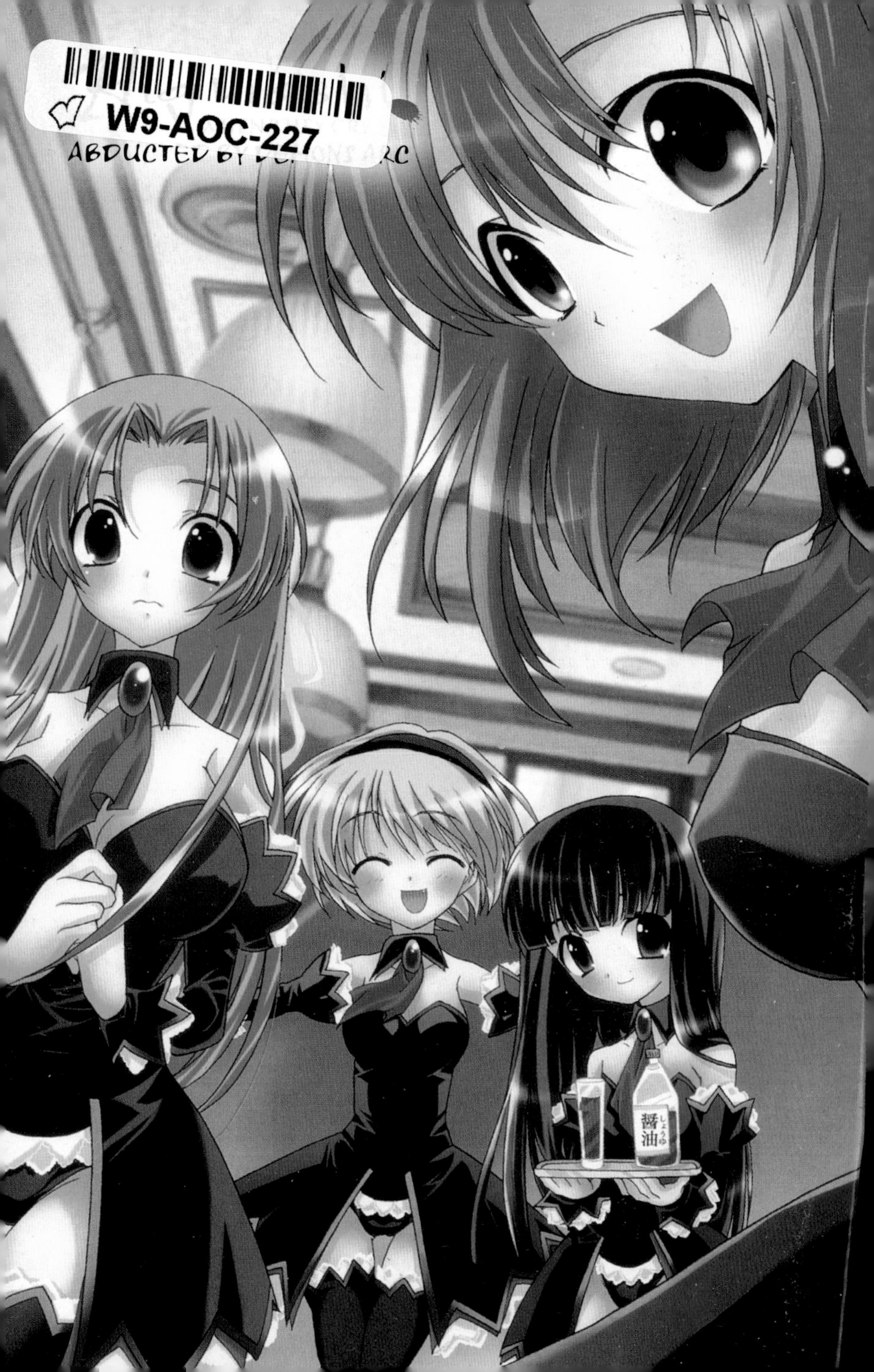
ABDUCTED BY
醤油
しょうゆ

Higurashi
WHEN THEY CRY
ABDUCTED BY DEMONS ARC

1

CONTENTS

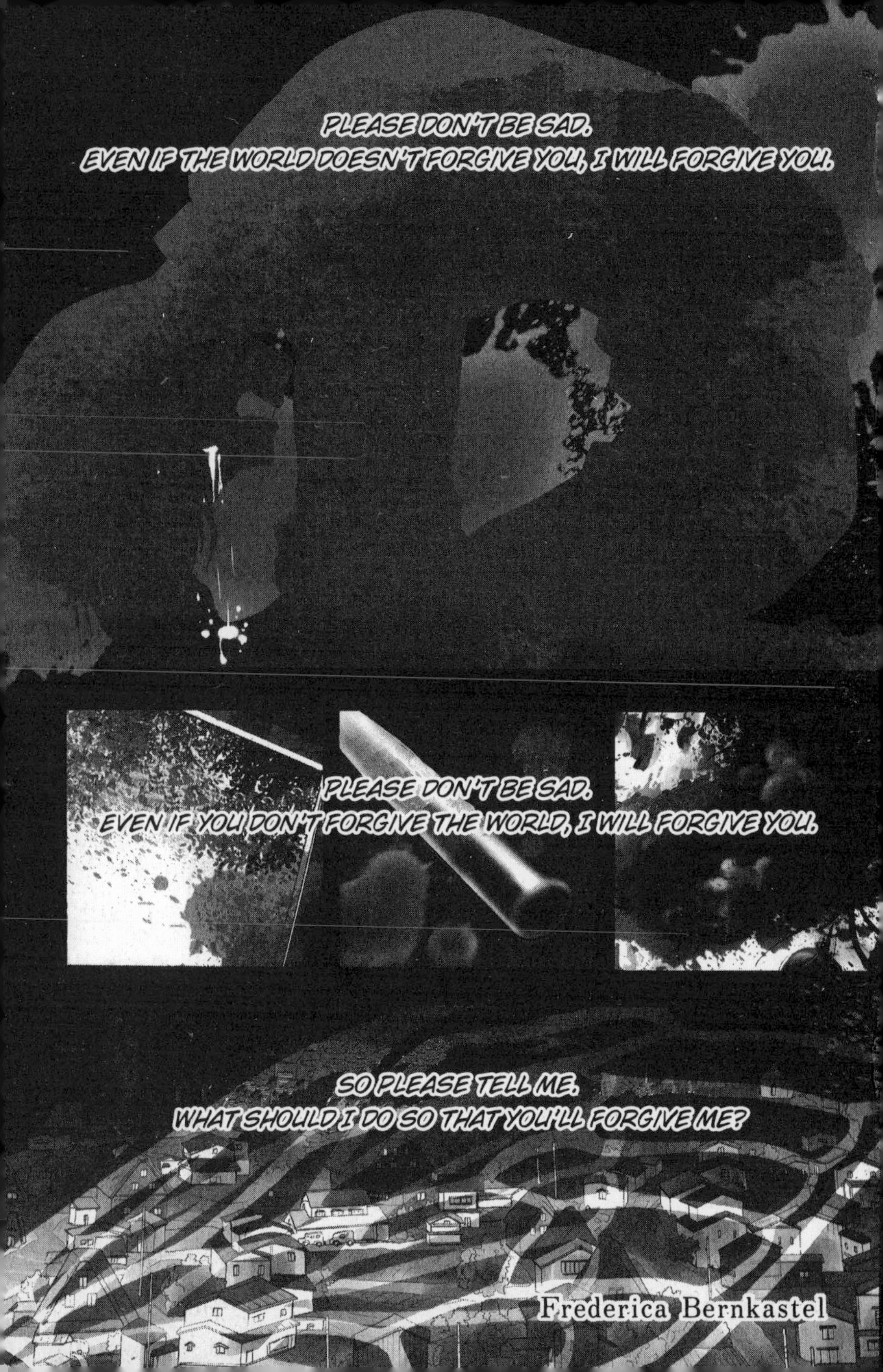
PLEASE DON'T BE SAD.
EVEN IF THE WORLD DOESN'T FORGIVE YOU, I WILL FORGIVE YOU.
PLEASE DON'T BE SAD.
EVEN IF YOU DON'T FORGIVE THE WORLD, I WILL FORGIVE YOU.
SO PLEASE TELL ME.
WHAT SHOULD I DO SO THAT YOU'LL FORGIVE ME?
Frederica Bernkastel

CHAPTER 1: HINAMIZAWA VILLAGE

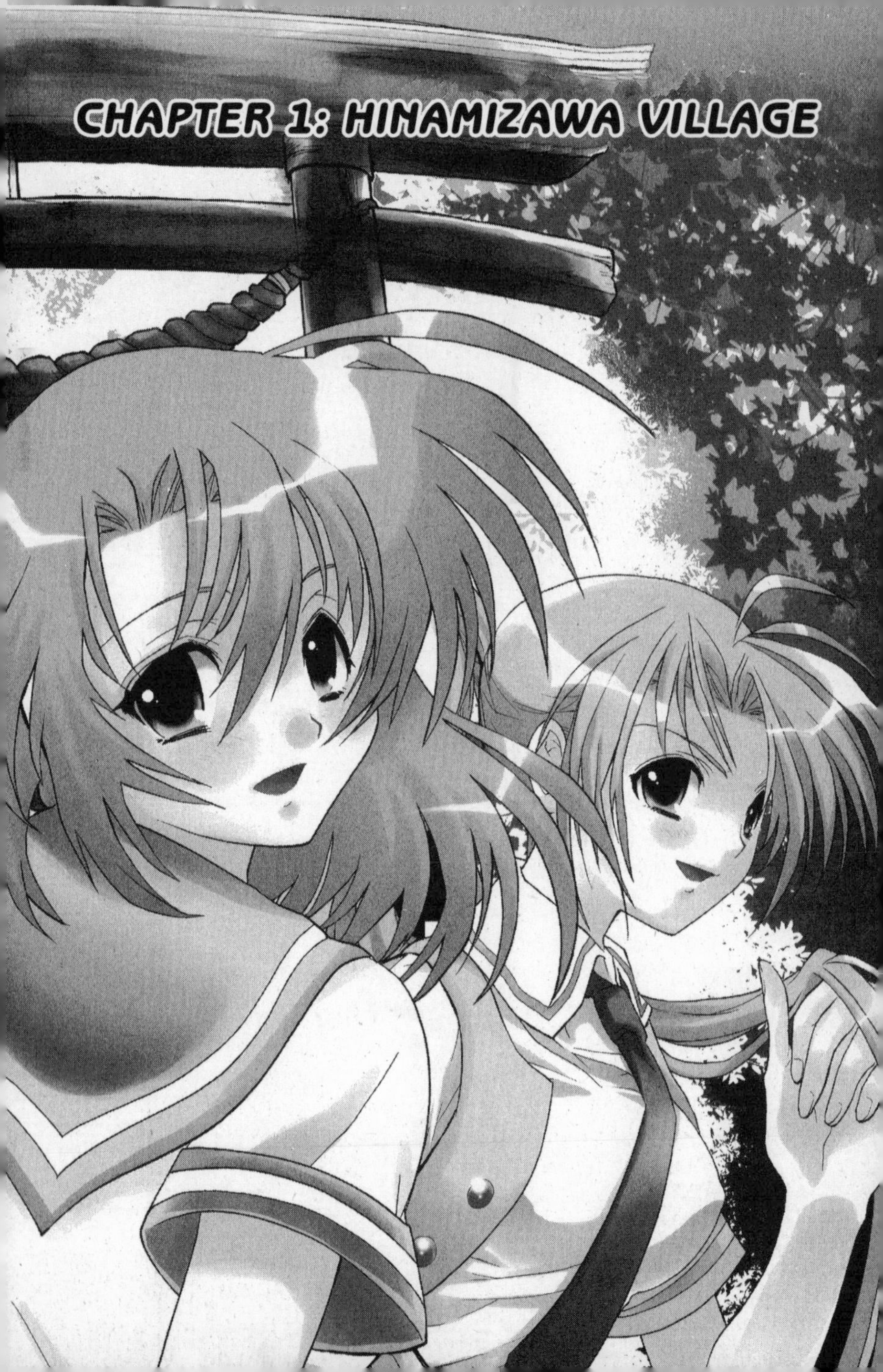

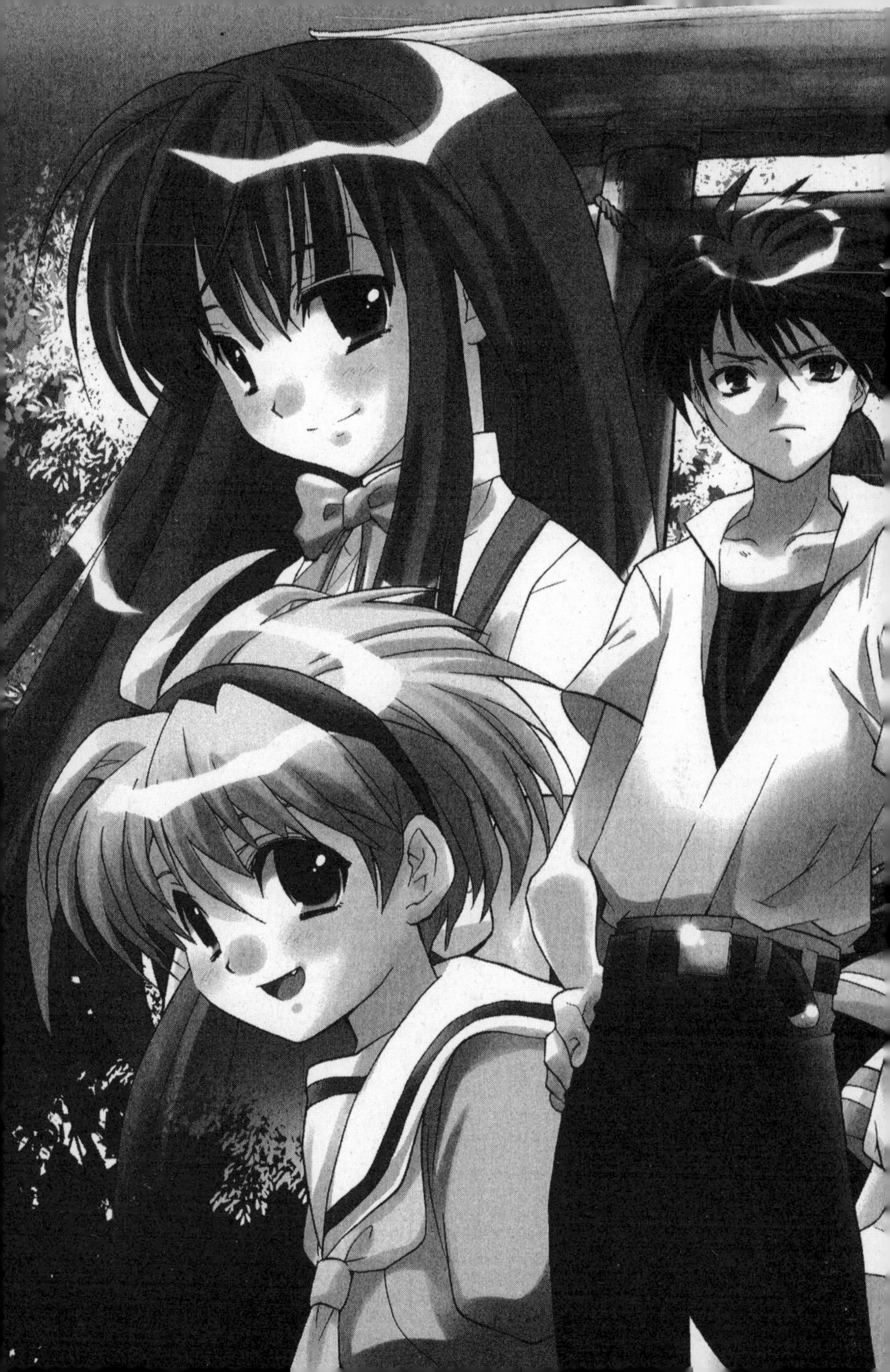

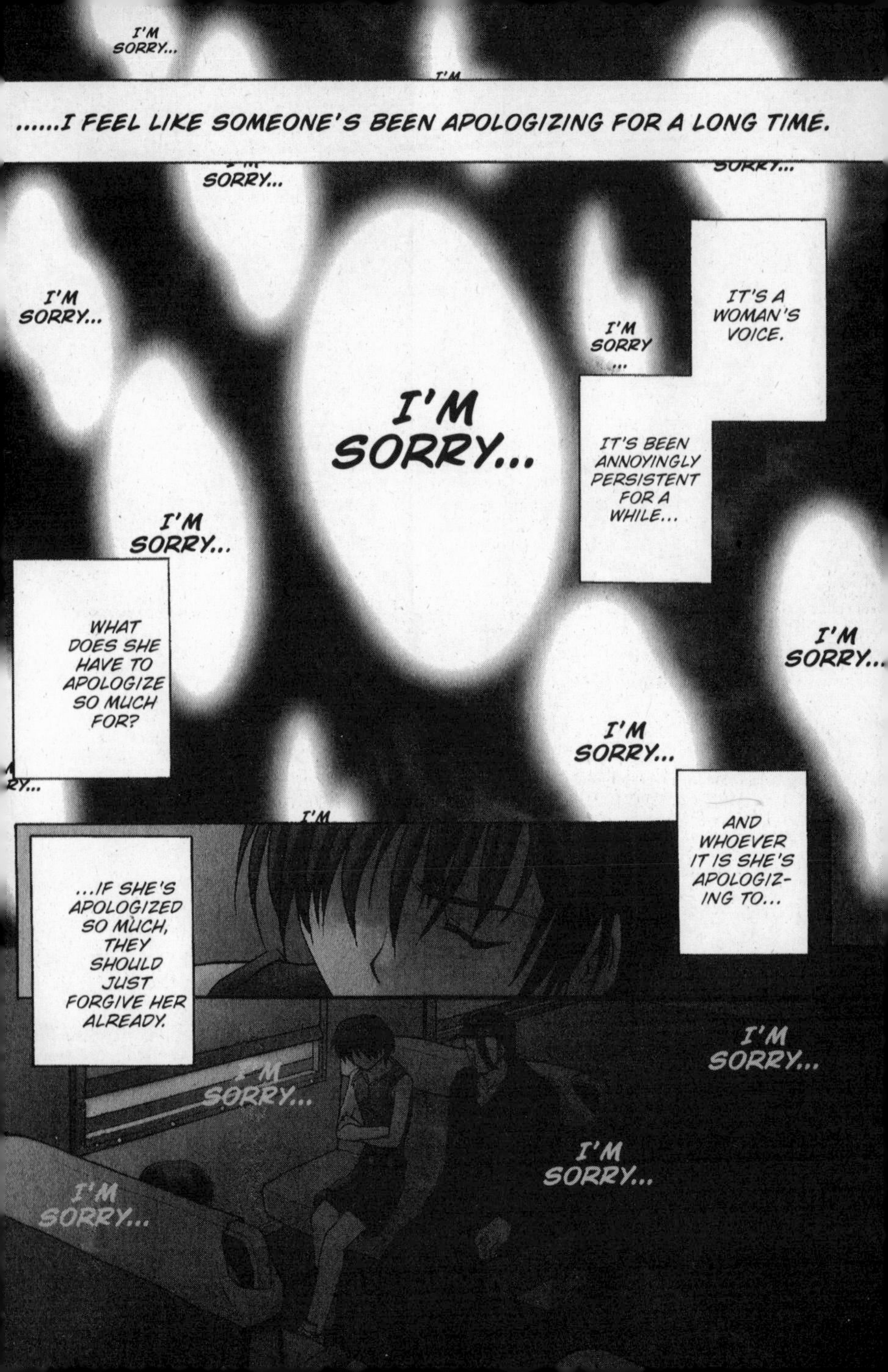
I'M SORRY...
......I FEEL LIKE SOMEONE'S BEEN APOLOGIZING FOR A LONG TIME.
IT'S A WOMAN'S VOICE.
I'M SORRY...
IT'S BEEN ANNOYINGLY PERSISTENT FOR A WHILE...
I'M SORRY...
SORRY...
I'M SORRY...
I'M SORRY...
I'M SORRY...
I'M SORRY...
WHAT DOES SHE HAVE TO APOLOGIZE SO MUCH FOR?
AND WHOEVER IT IS SHE'S APOLOGIZING TO...
...IF SHE'S APOLOGIZED SO MUCH, THEY SHOULD JUST FORGIVE HER ALREADY.
I'M SORRY...
I'M SORRY...
I'M SORRY...
I'M SORRY...

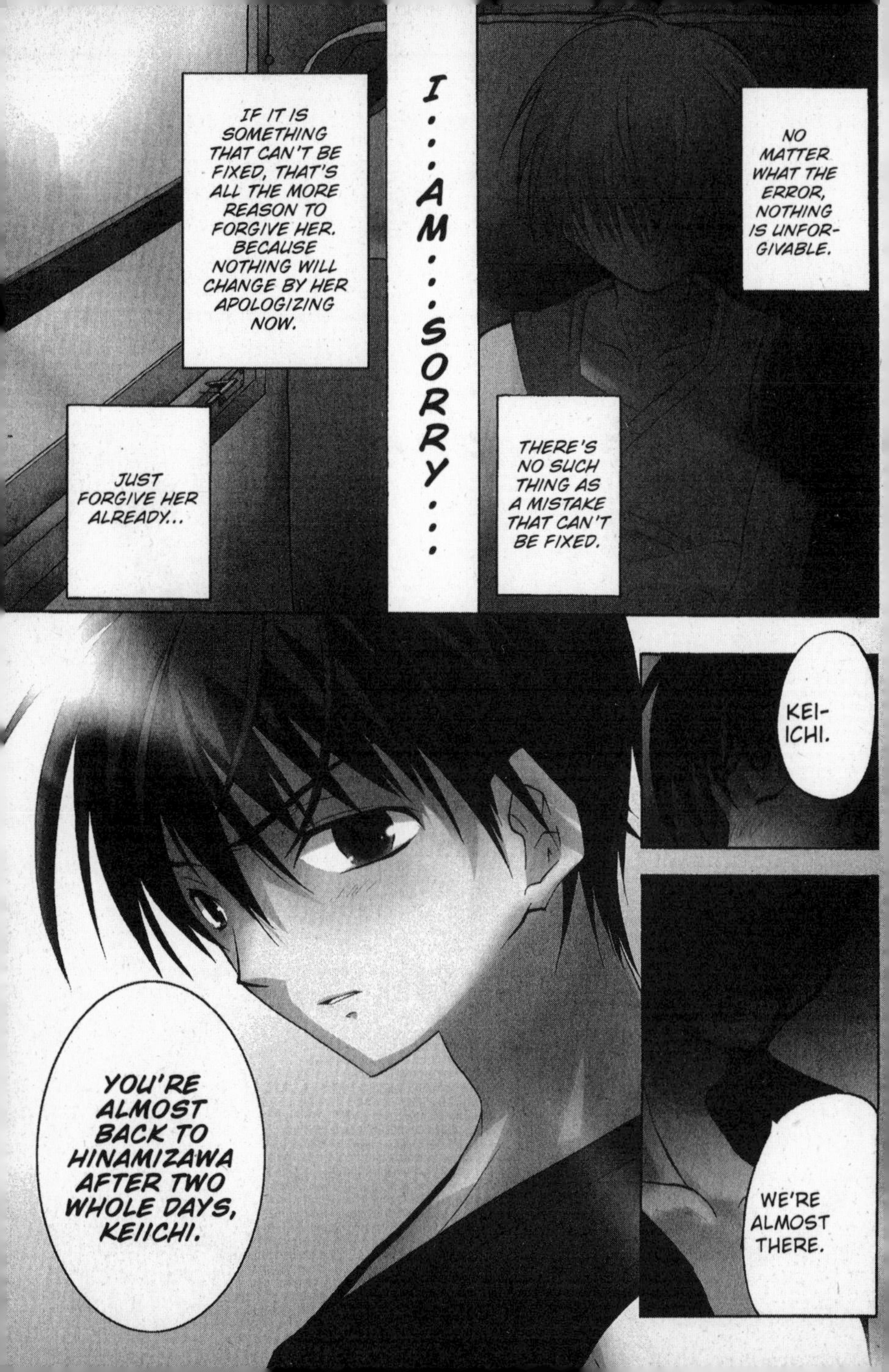
NO MATTER WHAT THE ERROR, NOTHING IS UNFORGIVABLE.
THERE'S NO SUCH THING AS A MISTAKE THAT CAN'T BE FIXED.
I...AM...SORRY...
IF IT IS SOMETHING THAT CAN'T BE FIXED, THAT'S ALL THE MORE REASON TO FORGIVE HER. BECAUSE NOTHING WILL CHANGE BY HER APOLOGIZING NOW.
JUST FORGIVE HER ALREADY...
KEI-ICHI.
WE'RE ALMOST THERE.
YOU'RE ALMOST BACK TO HINAMIZAWA AFTER TWO WHOLE DAYS, KEIICHI.

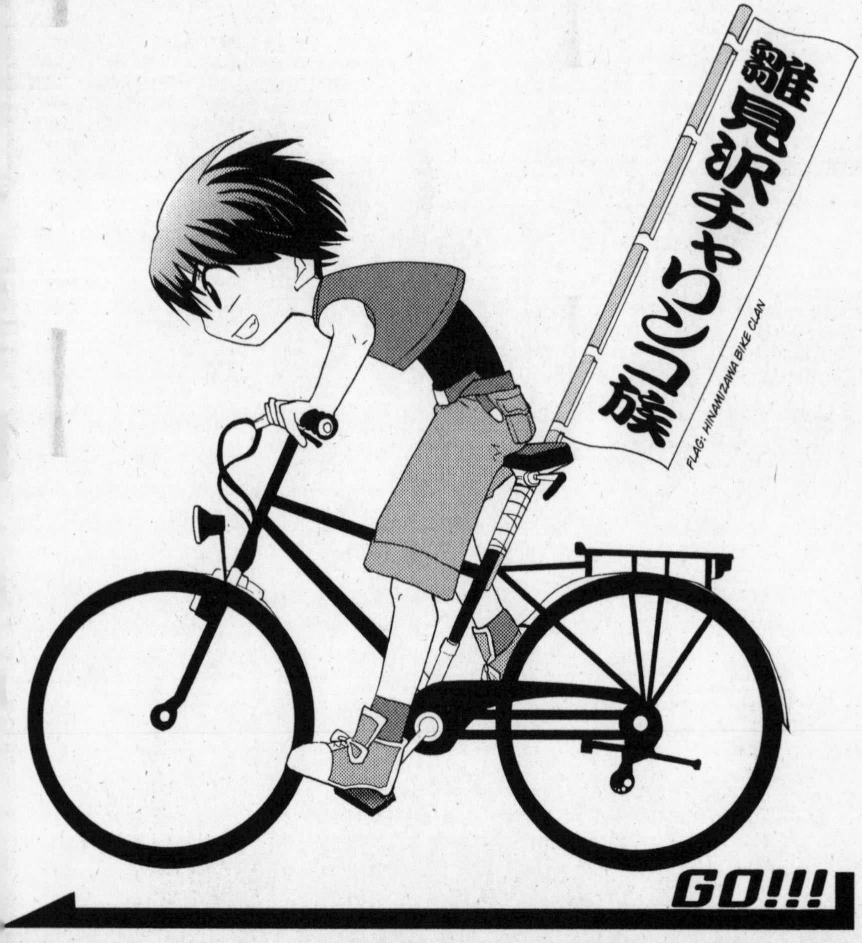
雛見沢チャりんコ族
FLAG: HINAMIZAWA BIKE CLAN
GO!!!

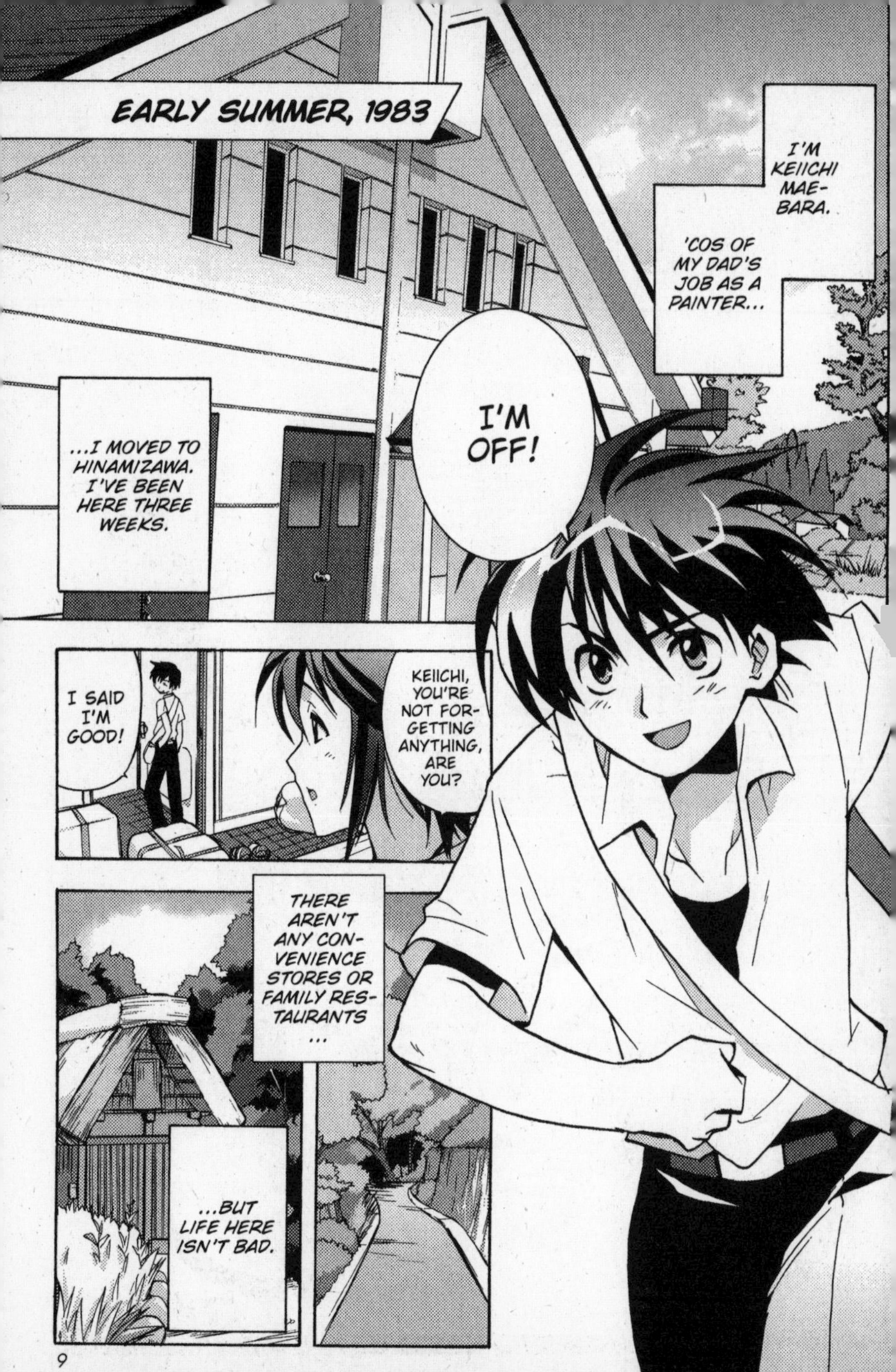
EARLY SUMMER, 1983
I'M KEIICHI MAEBARA.
'COS OF MY DAD'S JOB AS A PAINTER...
...I MOVED TO HINAMIZAWA. I'VE BEEN HERE THREE WEEKS.
I'M OFF!
KEIICHI, YOU'RE NOT FORGETTING ANYTHING, ARE YOU?
I SAID I'M GOOD!
THERE AREN'T ANY CONVENIENCE STORES OR FAMILY RESTAURANTS...
...BUT LIFE HERE ISN'T BAD.

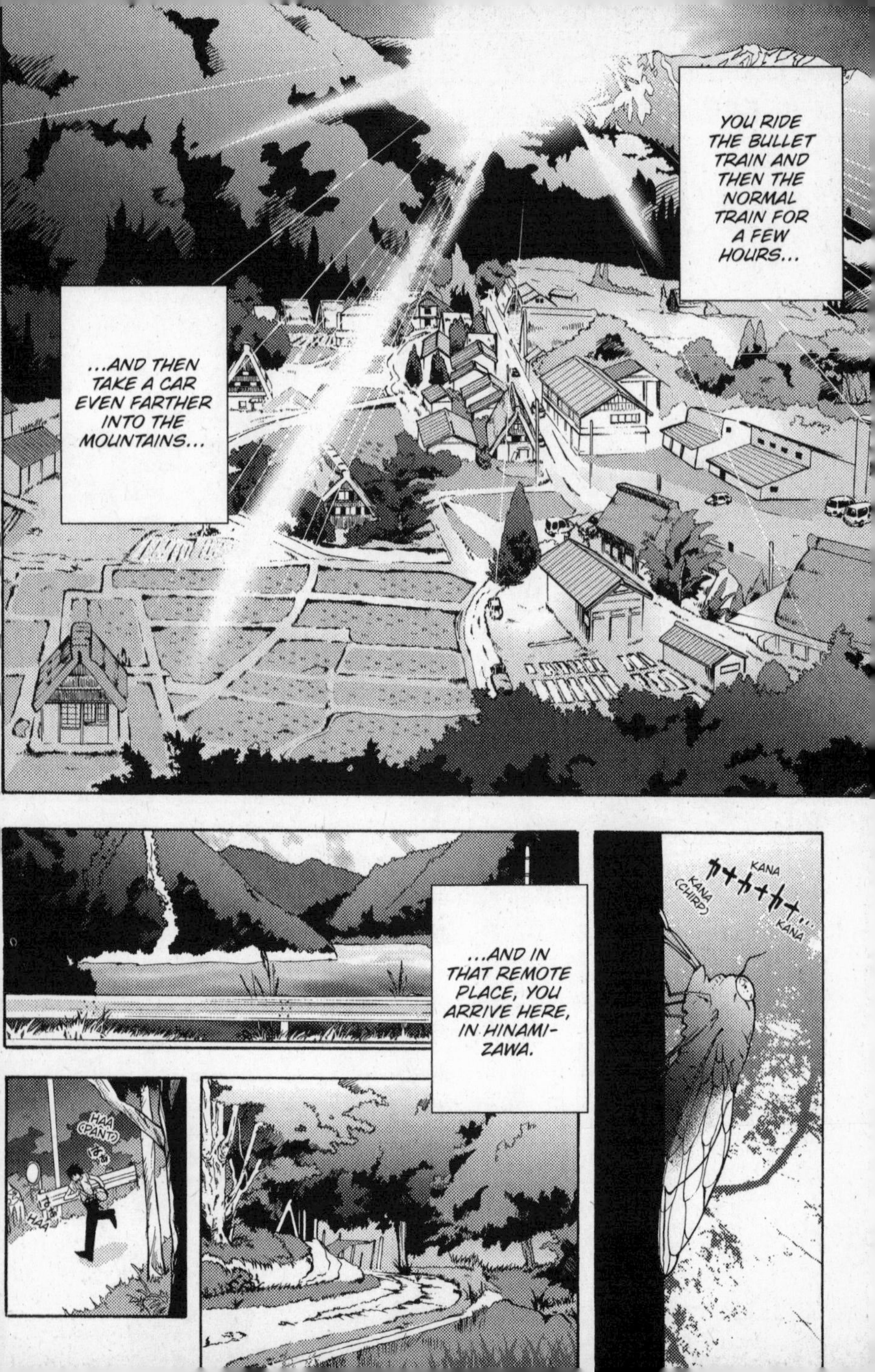
YOU RIDE THE BULLET TRAIN AND THEN THE NORMAL TRAIN FOR A FEW HOURS...
...AND THEN TAKE A CAR EVEN FARTHER INTO THE MOUNTAINS...
カナカナカナ…
KANA KANA (CHIRP) KANA
...AND IN THAT REMOTE PLACE, YOU ARRIVE HERE, IN HINAMI-ZAWA.
HAA (PANT)
HAA

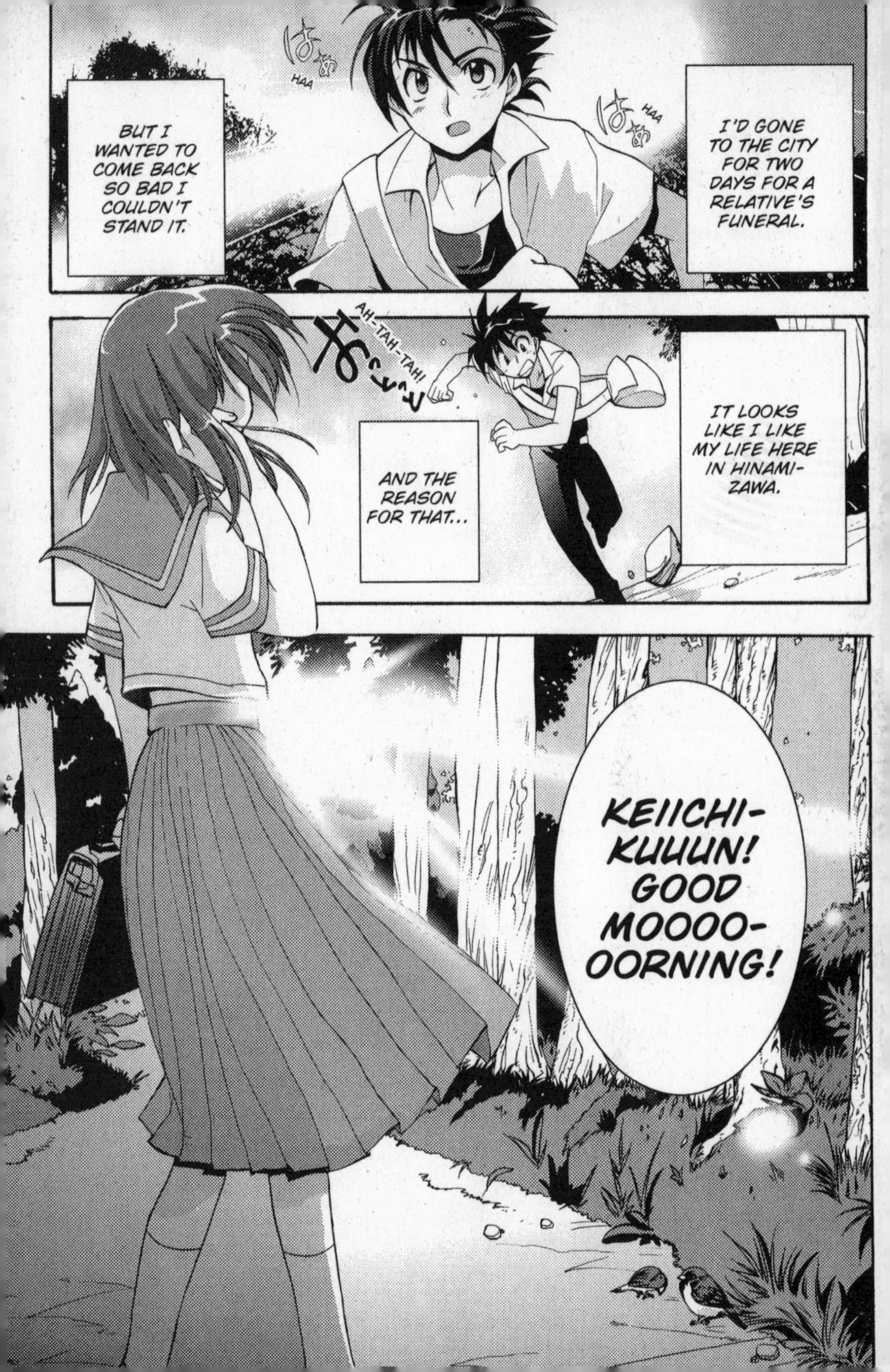
I'D GONE TO THE CITY FOR TWO DAYS FOR A RELATIVE'S FUNERAL.
HAA
HAA
BUT I WANTED TO COME BACK SO BAD I COULDN'T STAND IT.
IT LOOKS LIKE I LIKE MY LIFE HERE IN HINAMI-ZAWA.
AND THE REASON FOR THAT...
AH-TAH-TAH!
KEIICHI-KUUUN! GOOD MOOOO-OORNING!

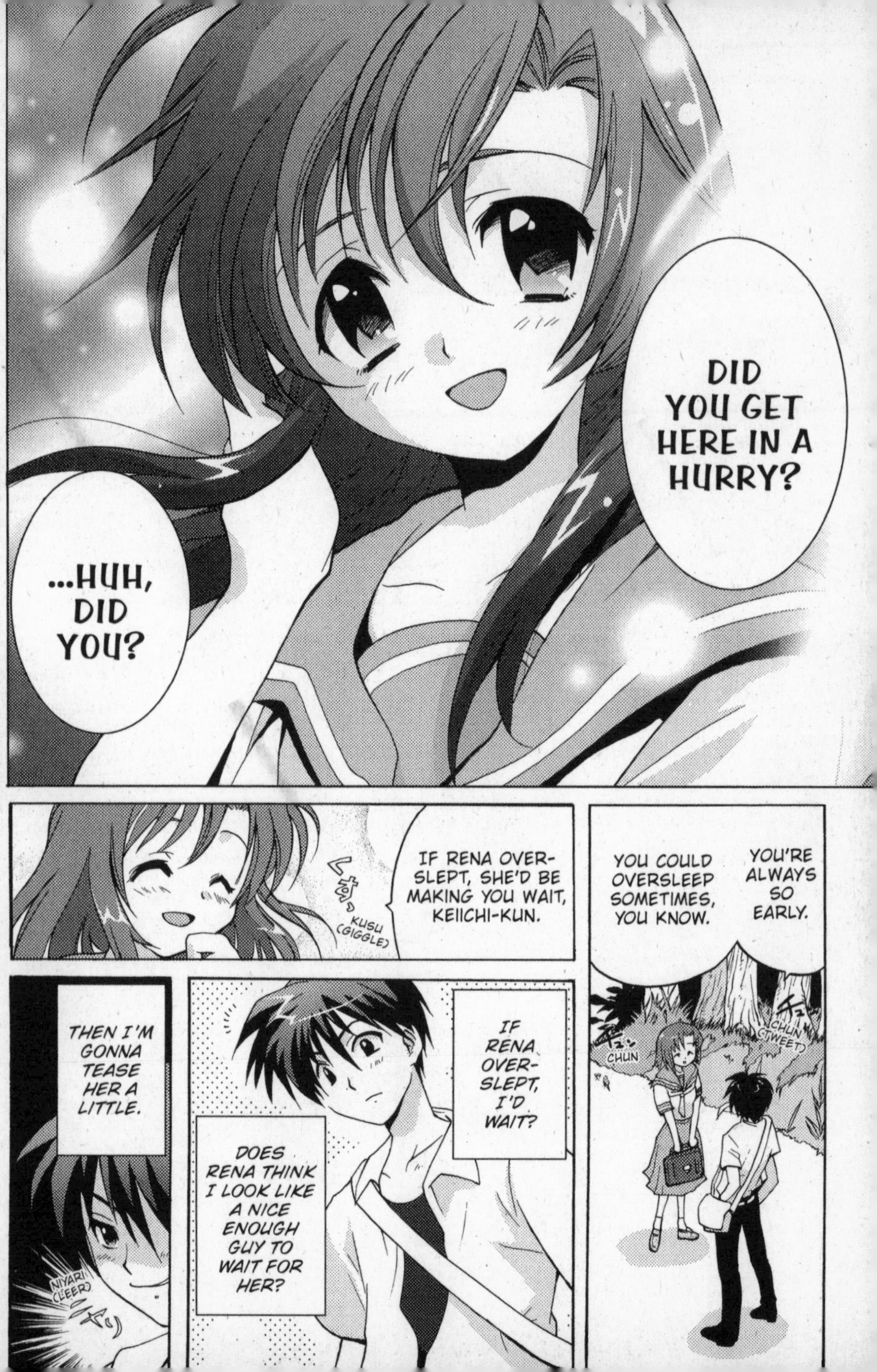

DID YOU GET HERE IN A HURRY?
...HUH, DID YOU?
YOU'RE ALWAYS SO EARLY.
YOU COULD OVERSLEEP SOMETIMES, YOU KNOW.
IF RENA OVER-SLEPT, SHE'D BE MAKING YOU WAIT, KEIICHI-KUN.
KUSU (GIGGLE)
CHUN (TWEET)
CHUN
IF RENA OVER-SLEPT, I'D WAIT?
DOES RENA THINK I LOOK LIKE A NICE ENOUGH GUY TO WAIT FOR HER?
THEN I'M GONNA TEASE HER A LITTLE.
NIYARI (LEER)

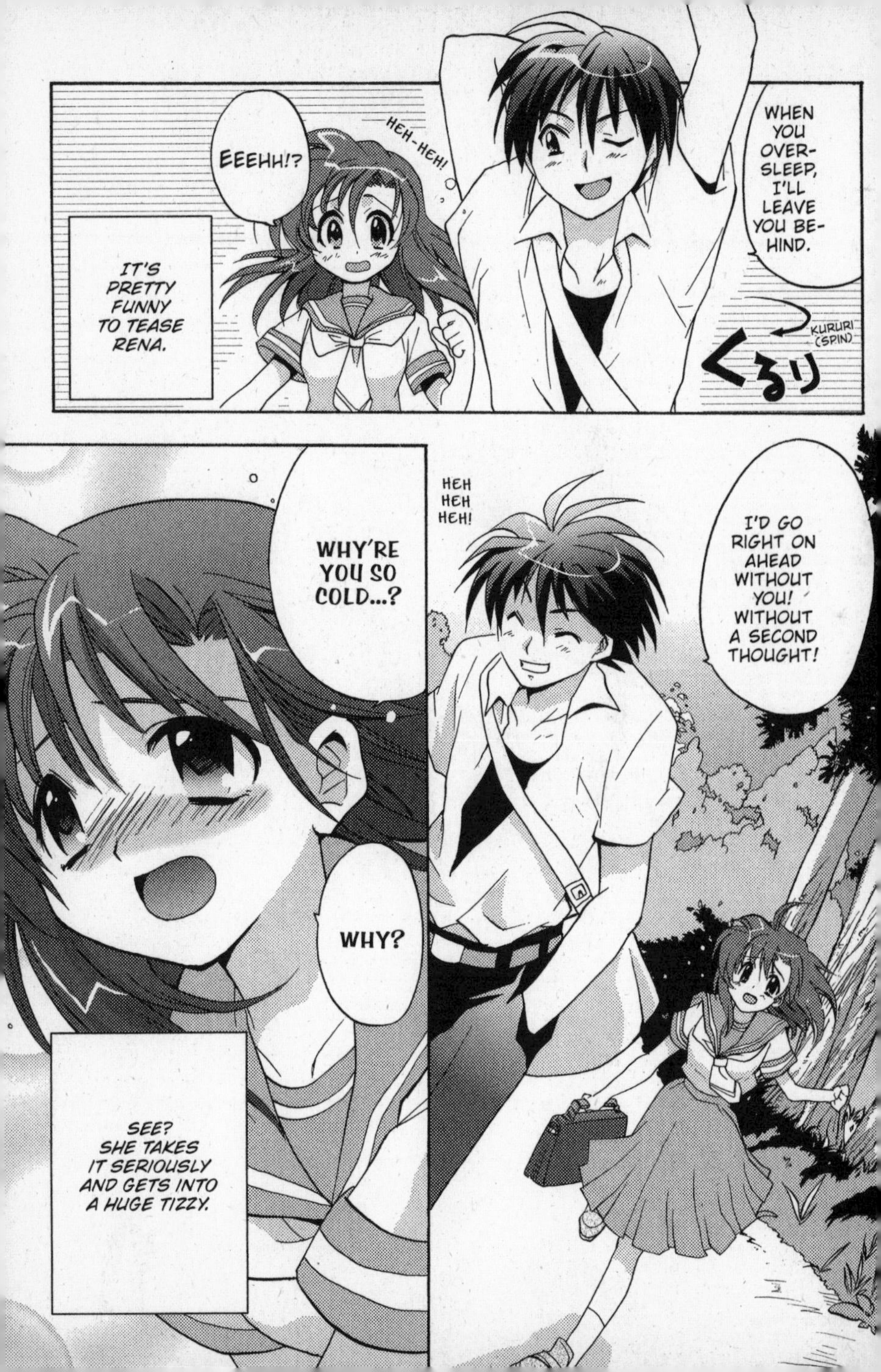
WHEN YOU OVER-SLEEP, I'LL LEAVE YOU BE-HIND.
くるり
KURURI (SPIN)
HEH-HEH!
EEEHH!?
IT'S PRETTY FUNNY TO TEASE RENA.
I'D GO RIGHT ON AHEAD WITHOUT YOU! WITHOUT A SECOND THOUGHT!
HEH HEH HEH!
WHY'RE YOU SO COLD...?
WHY?
SEE? SHE TAKES IT SERIOUSLY AND GETS INTO A HUGE TIZZY.

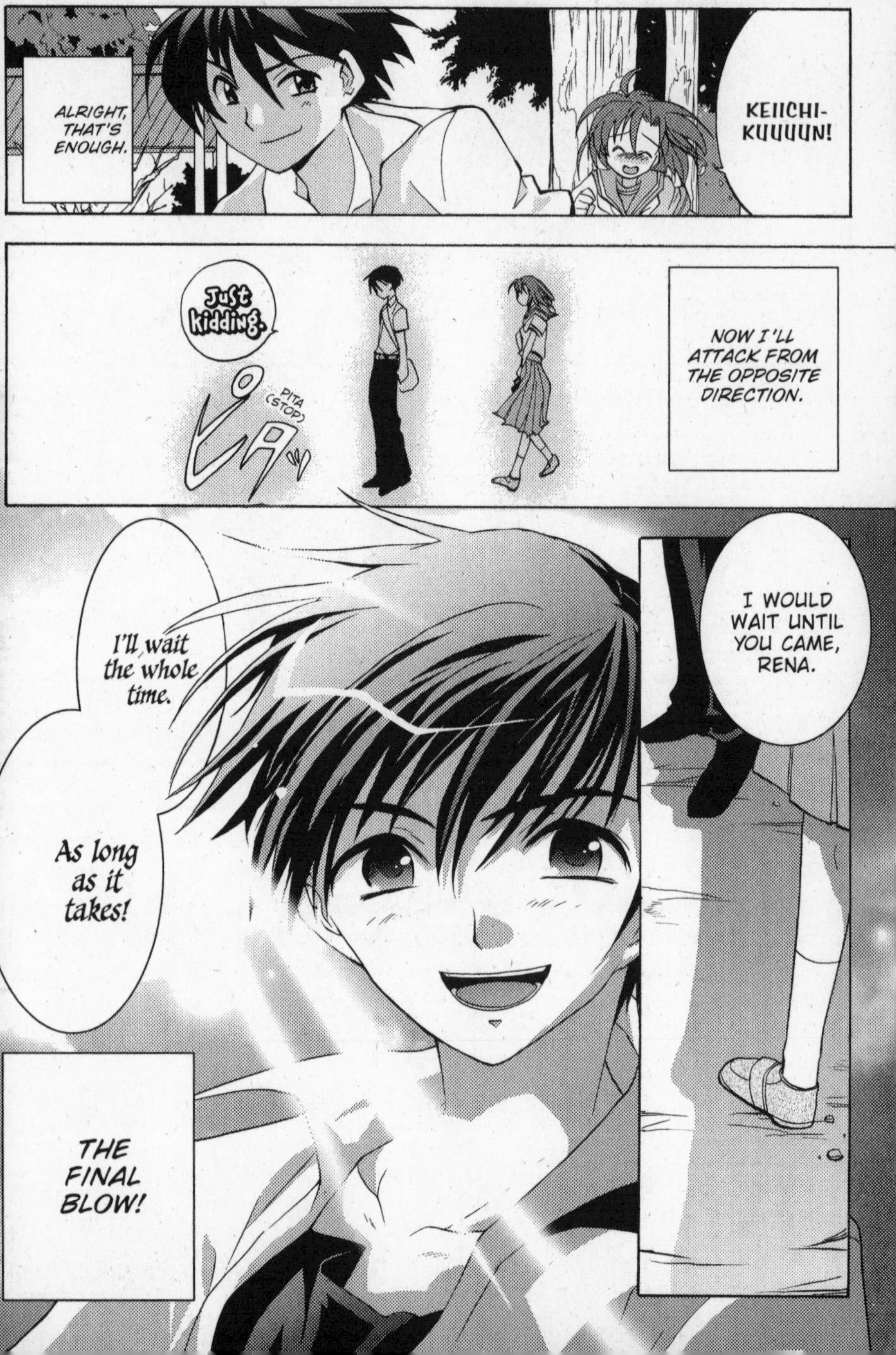
KEIICHI-KUUUUN!
ALRIGHT, THAT'S ENOUGH.
NOW I'LL ATTACK FROM THE OPPOSITE DIRECTION.
Just kidding.
PITA (STOP)
I WOULD WAIT UNTIL YOU CAME, RENA.
I'll wait the whole time.
As long as it takes!
THE FINAL BLOW!

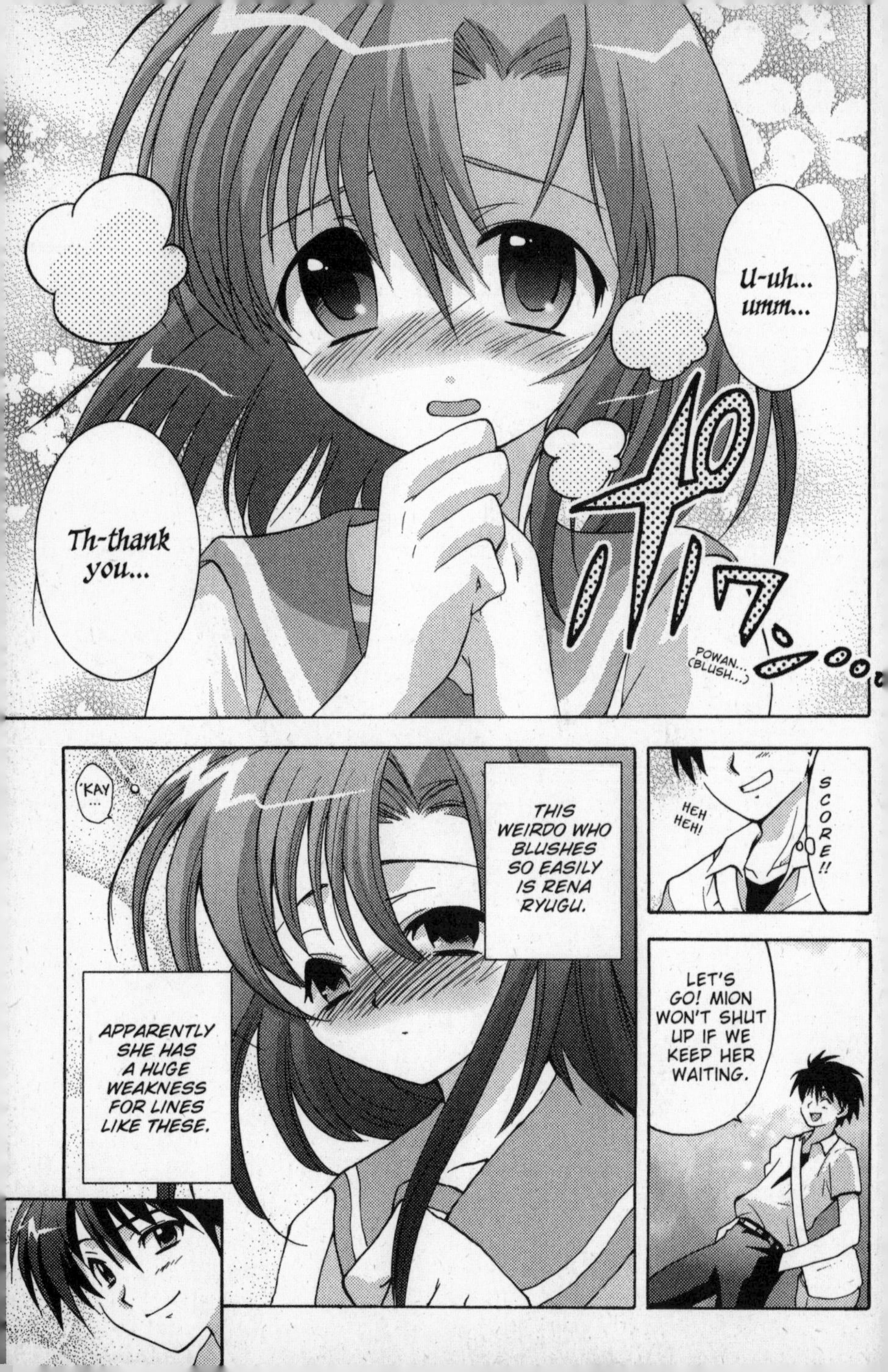
U-uh... umm...
Th-thank you...
POWAN... (BLUSH...)
SCORE!!
HEH HEH!
LET'S GO! MION WON'T SHUT UP IF WE KEEP HER WAITING.
THIS WEIRDO WHO BLUSHES SO EASILY IS RENA RYUGU.
'KAY...
APPARENTLY SHE HAS A HUGE WEAKNESS FOR LINES LIKE THESE.

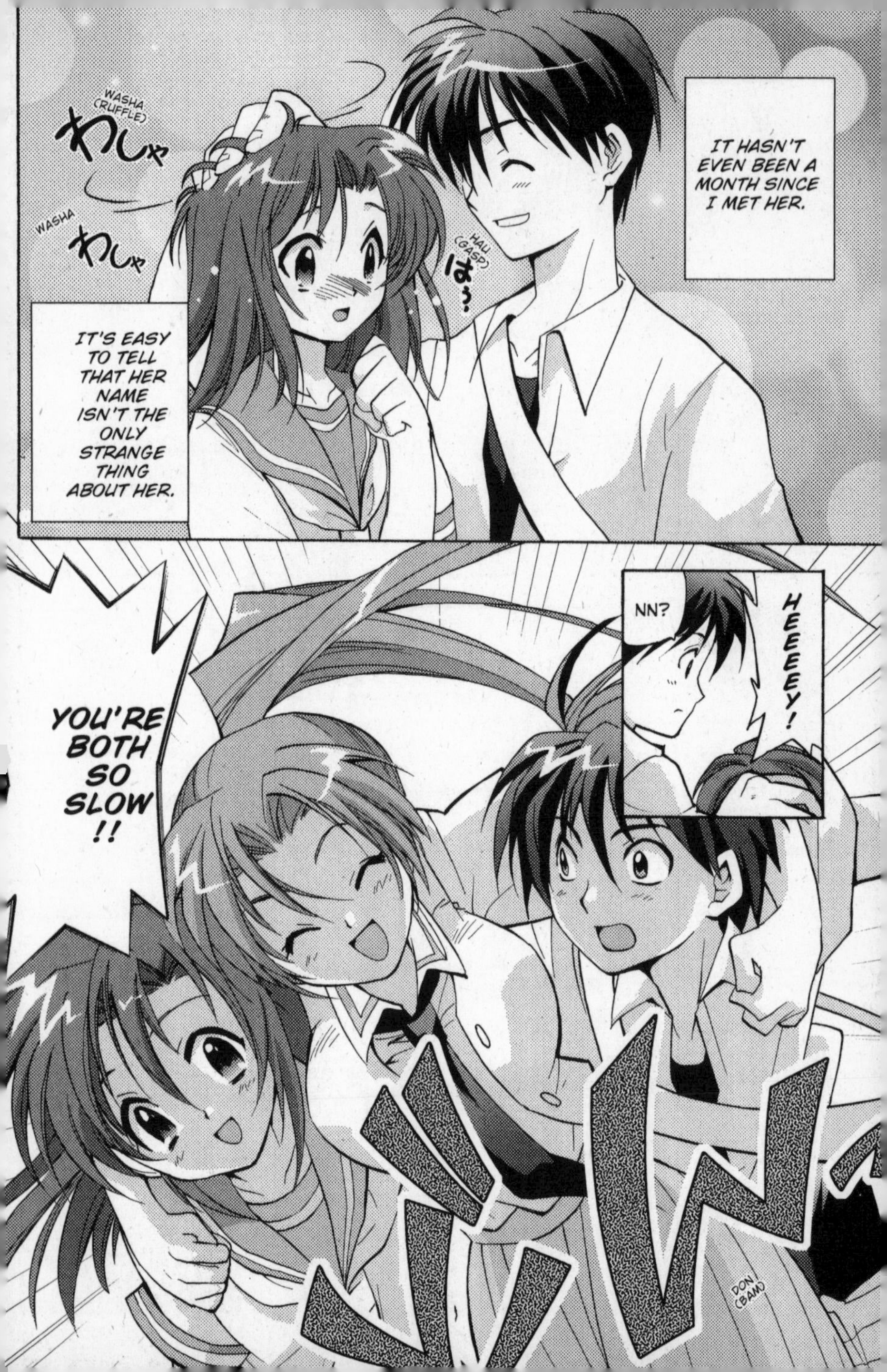
IT HASN'T EVEN BEEN A MONTH SINCE I MET HER.
WASHA (RUFFLE)
わしゃ
WASHA
わしゃ
HAU (GASP)
はっ
IT'S EASY TO TELL THAT HER NAME ISN'T THE ONLY STRANGE THING ABOUT HER.
HEEEEY!
NN?
YOU'RE BOTH SO SLOW!!
DON (BAM)

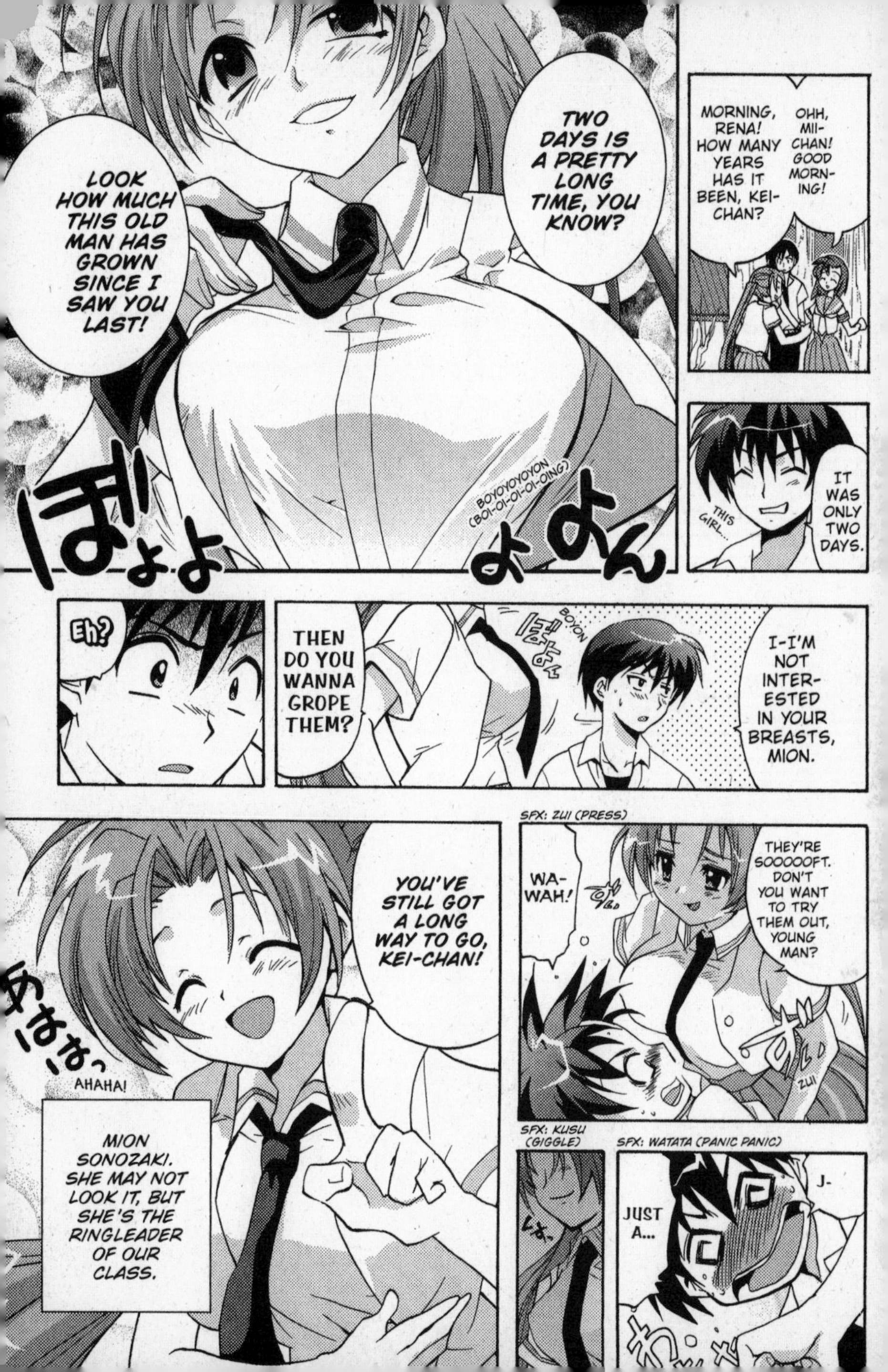
OHH, MII-CHAN! GOOD MORNING!
MORNING, RENA! HOW MANY YEARS HAS IT BEEN, KEI-CHAN?
IT WAS ONLY TWO DAYS.
THIS GIRL...
TWO DAYS IS A PRETTY LONG TIME, YOU KNOW?
LOOK HOW MUCH THIS OLD MAN HAS GROWN SINCE I SAW YOU LAST!
ぼよよよん
BOYOYOYOYON (BOI-OI-OI-OI-OING)
I-I'M NOT INTERESTED IN YOUR BREASTS, MION.
ぼよん
BOYON
THEN DO YOU WANNA GROPE THEM?
Eh?
SFX: ZUI (PRESS)
THEY'RE SOOOOOFT. DON'T YOU WANT TO TRY THEM OUT, YOUNG MAN?
WA-WAH!
ZUI
SFX: WATATA (PANIC PANIC)
J-
JUST A...
SFX: KUSU (GIGGLE)
YOU'VE STILL GOT A LONG WAY TO GO, KEI-CHAN!
あははっ
AHAHA!
MION SONOZAKI. SHE MAY NOT LOOK IT, BUT SHE'S THE RINGLEADER OF OUR CLASS.

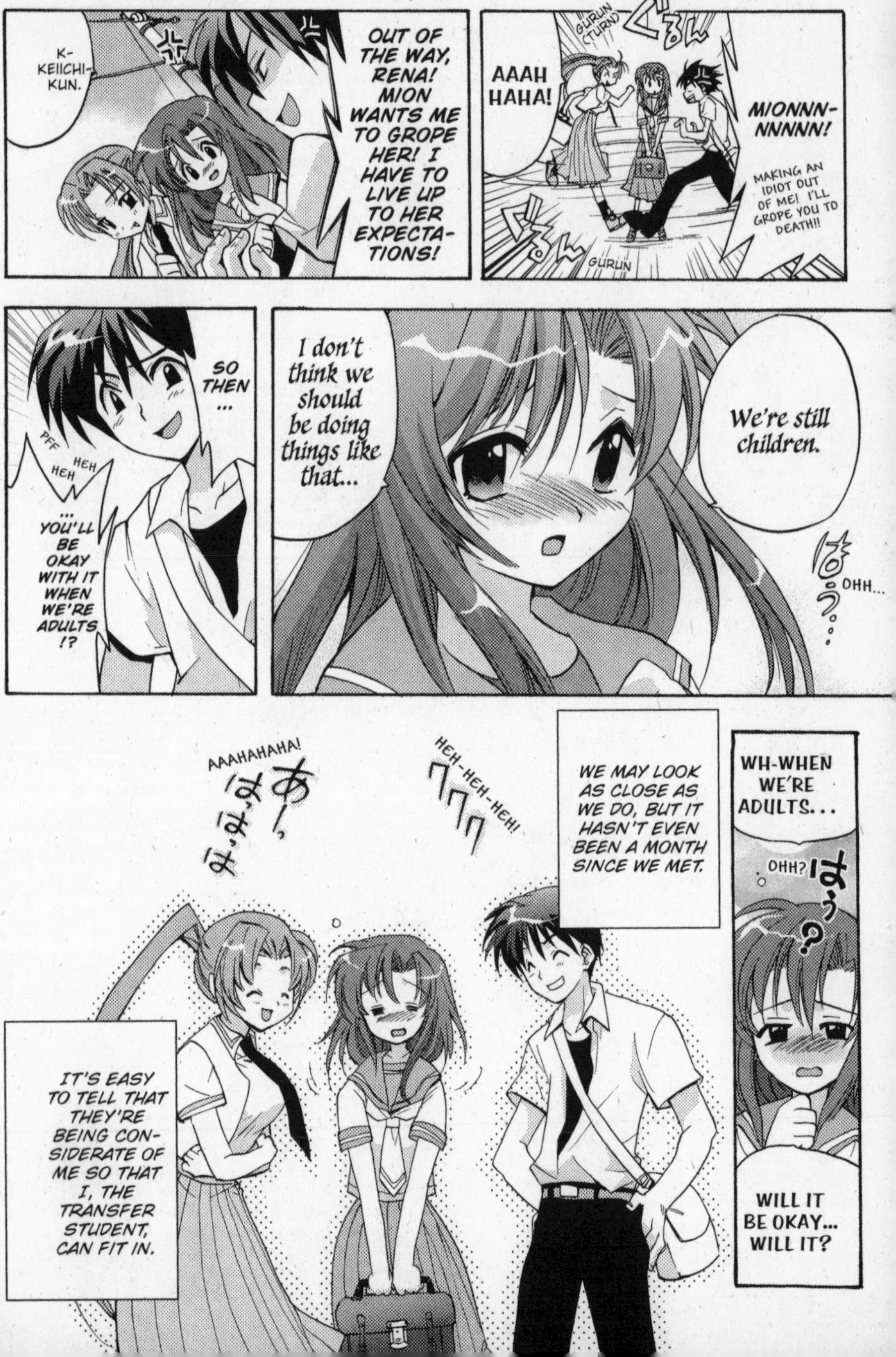
GURUN (TURN)
ぐるん
AAAH HAHA!
MIONNN-NNNNN!
MAKING AN IDIOT OUT OF ME! I'LL GROPE YOU TO DEATH!!
ぐるん
GURUN
OUT OF THE WAY, RENA! MION WANTS ME TO GROPE HER! I HAVE TO LIVE UP TO HER EXPECTATIONS!
K-KEIICHI-KUN.
We're still children.
I don't think we should be doing things like that...
はうっ。。。
OHH...
SO THEN ...
PFF HEH HEH
... YOU'LL BE OKAY WITH IT WHEN WE'RE ADULTS !?
WH-WHEN WE'RE ADULTS...
はぅ?
OHH?
WILL IT BE OKAY... WILL IT?
WE MAY LOOK AS CLOSE AS WE DO, BUT IT HASN'T EVEN BEEN A MONTH SINCE WE MET.
ククク
HEH-HEH-HEH!
あー、ははは
AAAHAHAHA!
IT'S EASY TO TELL THAT THEY'RE BEING CON-SIDERATE OF ME SO THAT I, THE TRANSFER STUDENT, CAN FIT IN.

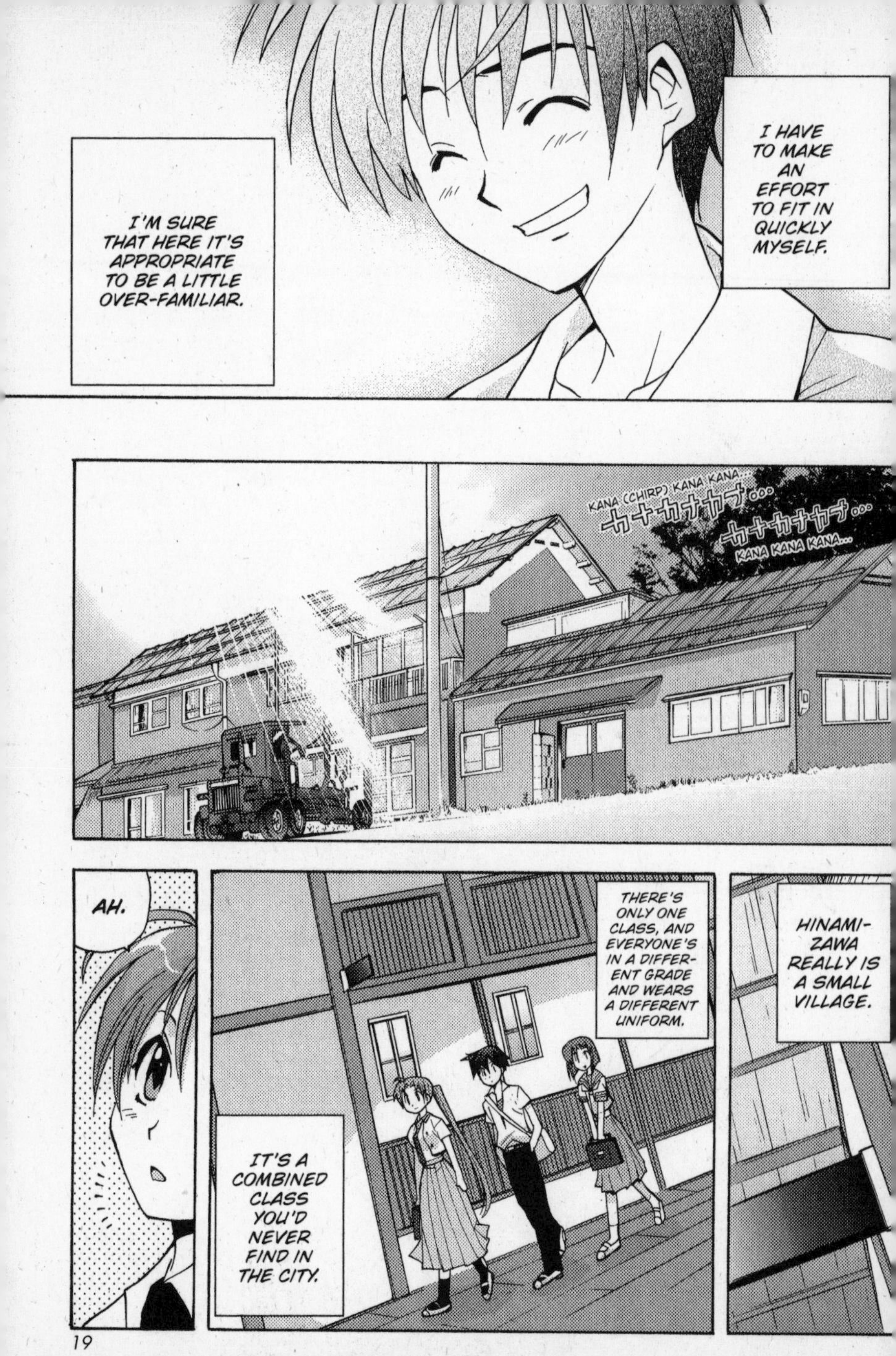
I HAVE TO MAKE AN EFFORT TO FIT IN QUICKLY MYSELF.
I'M SURE THAT HERE IT'S APPROPRIATE TO BE A LITTLE OVER-FAMILIAR.
KANA (CHIRP) KANA KANA...
カナカナカナ...
カナカナカナ...
KANA KANA KANA...
HINAMI-ZAWA REALLY IS A SMALL VILLAGE.
THERE'S ONLY ONE CLASS, AND EVERYONE'S IN A DIFFER-ENT GRADE AND WEARS A DIFFERENT UNIFORM.
IT'S A COMBINED CLASS YOU'D NEVER FIND IN THE CITY.
AH.

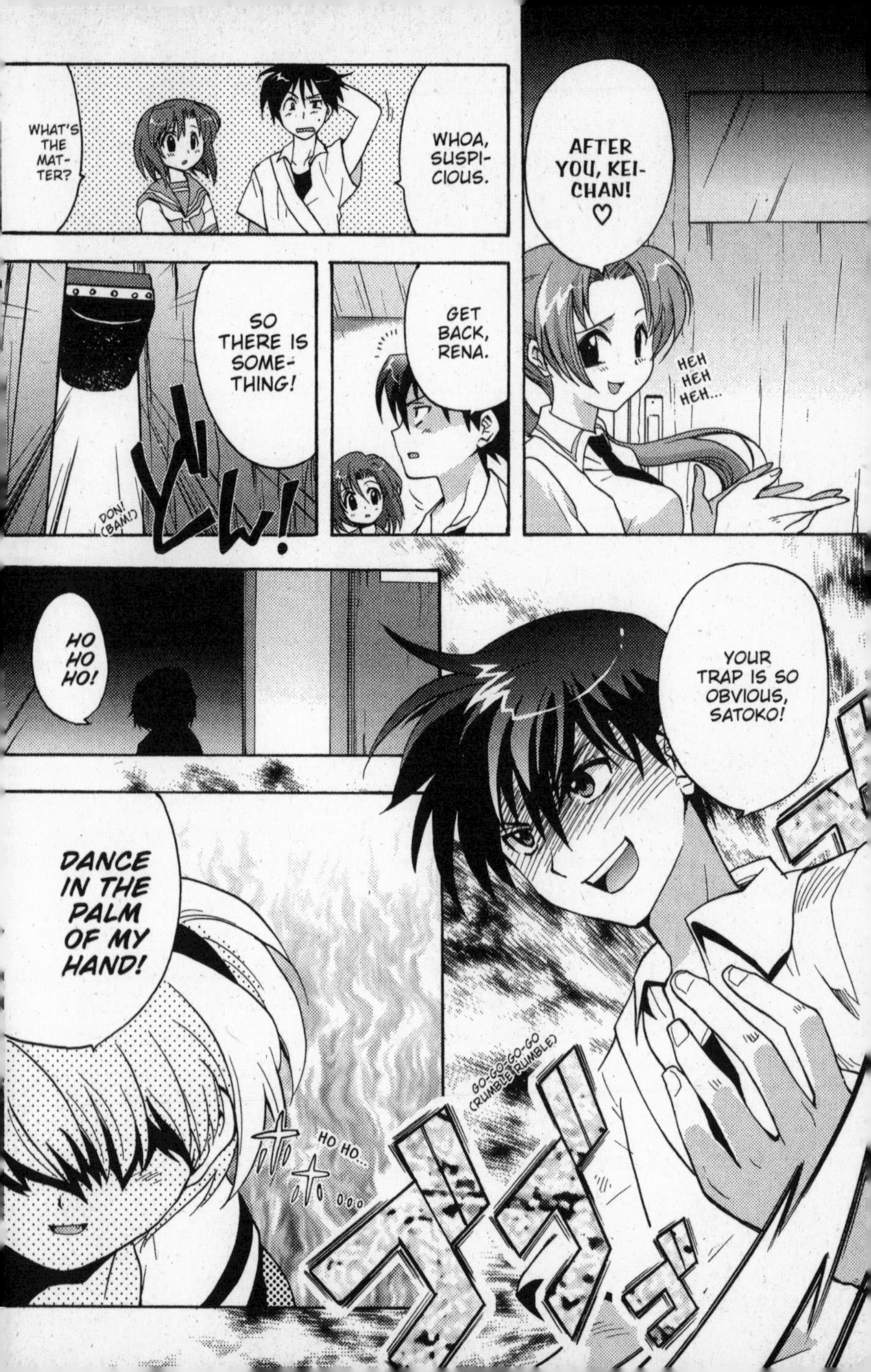
AFTER YOU, KEI-CHAN! ♡
HEH HEH HEH...
WHOA, SUSPICIOUS.
WHAT'S THE MATTER?
GET BACK, RENA.
SO THERE IS SOMETHING!
DON! (BAM!)
YOUR TRAP IS SO OBVIOUS, SATOKO!
GO-GO-GO-GO (RUMBLE RUMBLE)
HO HO HO!
DANCE IN THE PALM OF MY HAND!
HO HO...

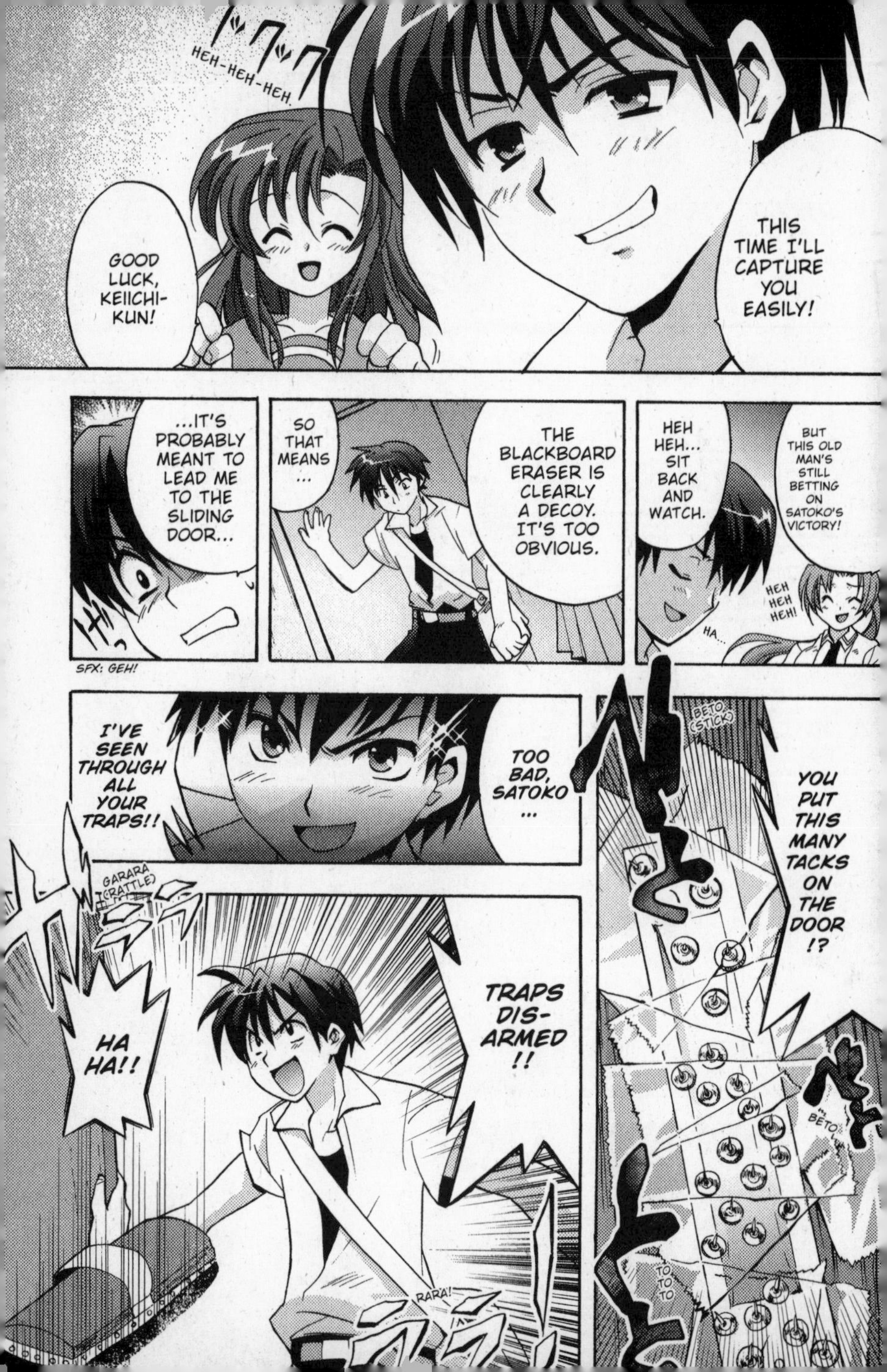
HEH-HEH-HEH.
THIS TIME I'LL CAPTURE YOU EASILY!
GOOD LUCK, KEIICHI-KUN!
BUT THIS OLD MAN'S STILL BETTING ON SATOKO'S VICTORY!
HEH HEH HEH!
HEH HEH... SIT BACK AND WATCH.
HA...
THE BLACKBOARD ERASER IS CLEARLY A DECOY. IT'S TOO OBVIOUS.
SO THAT MEANS...
...IT'S PROBABLY MEANT TO LEAD ME TO THE SLIDING DOOR...
SFX: GEH!
BETO (STICK)
YOU PUT THIS MANY TACKS ON THE DOOR!?
BETO
TO TO TO
TOO BAD, SATOKO...
I'VE SEEN THROUGH ALL YOUR TRAPS!!
TRAPS DIS-ARMED!!
HA HA!!
GARARA (RATTLE)
RARA!

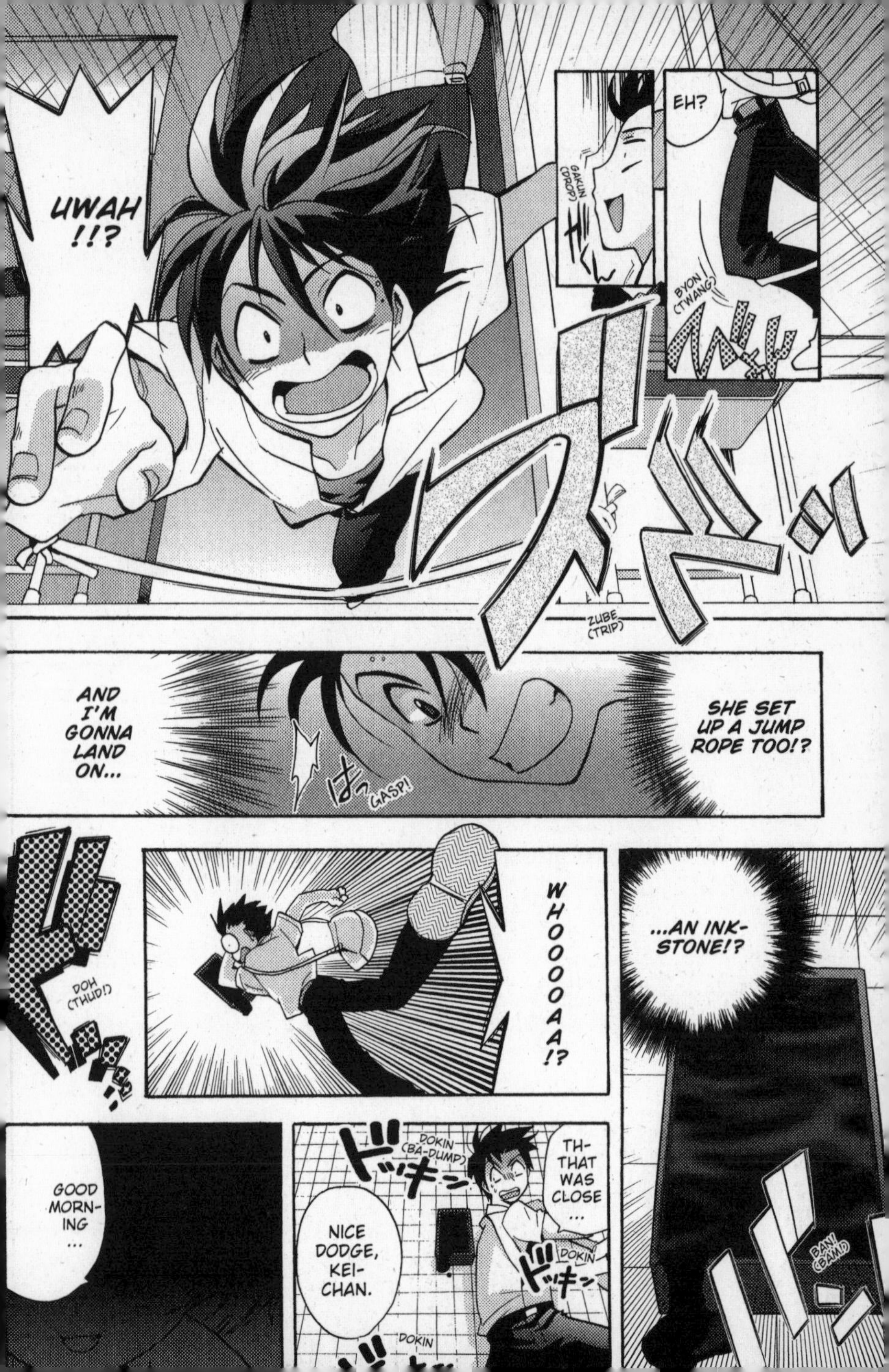
EH?
BYON (TWANG)
GAKUN (DROP)
UWAH!!?
ZUBE (TRIP)
SHE SET UP A JUMP ROPE TOO!?
GASP!
AND I'M GONNA LAND ON...
...AN INK-STONE!?
BAN! (BAM!)
WHOOOOOAA!?
DOH (THUD!)
TH-THAT WAS CLOSE...
DOKIN (BA-DUMP)
DOKIN
NICE DODGE, KEI-CHAN.
DOKIN
GOOD MORNING...

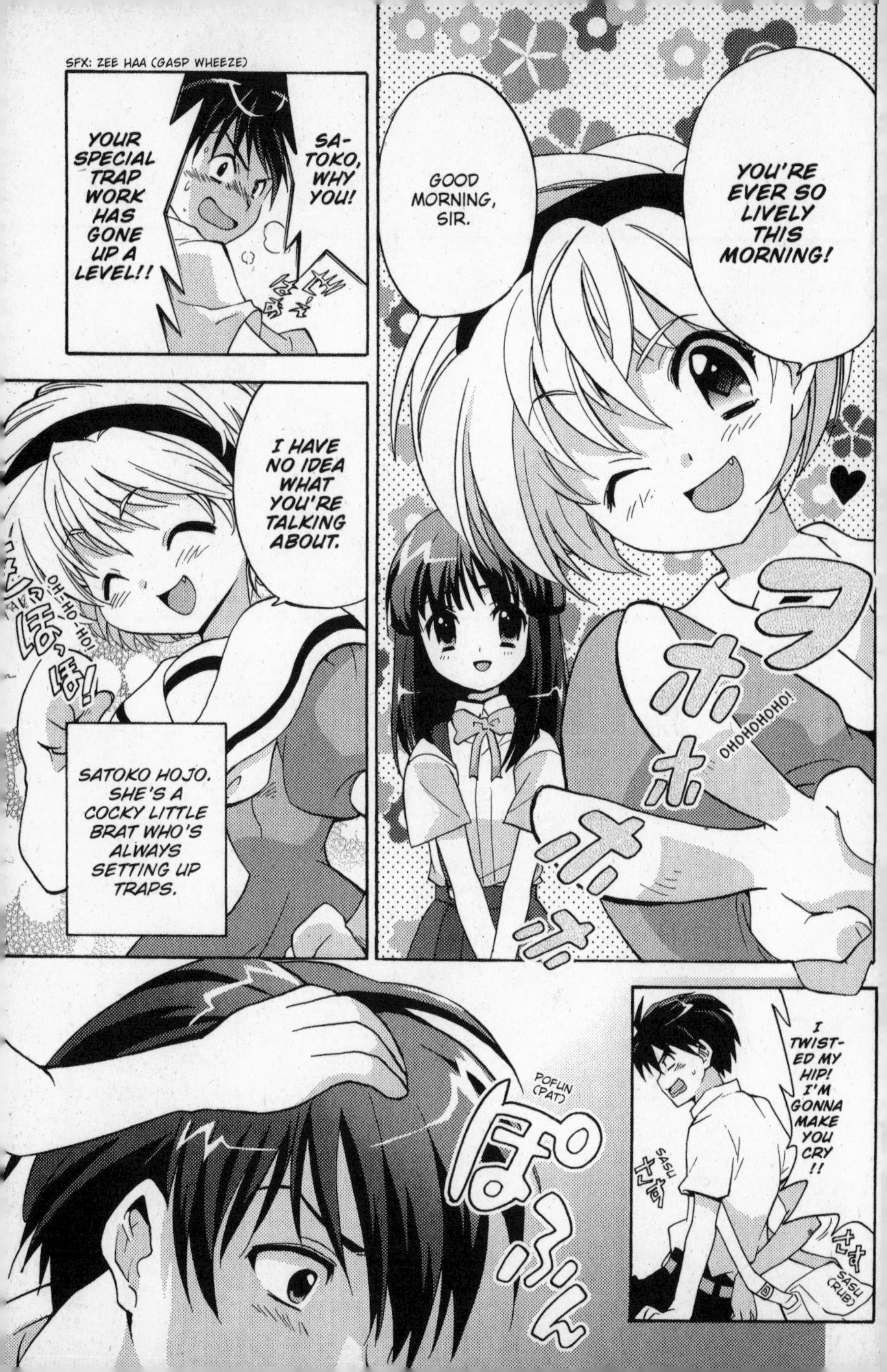
YOU'RE EVER SO LIVELY THIS MORNING!
GOOD MORNING, SIR.
OHOHOHOHO!
SFX: ZEE HAA (GASP WHEEZE)
SA-TOKO, WHY YOU!
YOUR SPECIAL TRAP WORK HAS GONE UP A LEVEL!!
I HAVE NO IDEA WHAT YOU'RE TALKING ABOUT.
OH-HO-HO!
SATOKO HOJO. SHE'S A COCKY LITTLE BRAT WHO'S ALWAYS SETTING UP TRAPS.
I TWIST-ED MY HIP! I'M GONNA MAKE YOU CRY!!
SASU
SASU (RUB)
POFUN (PAT)

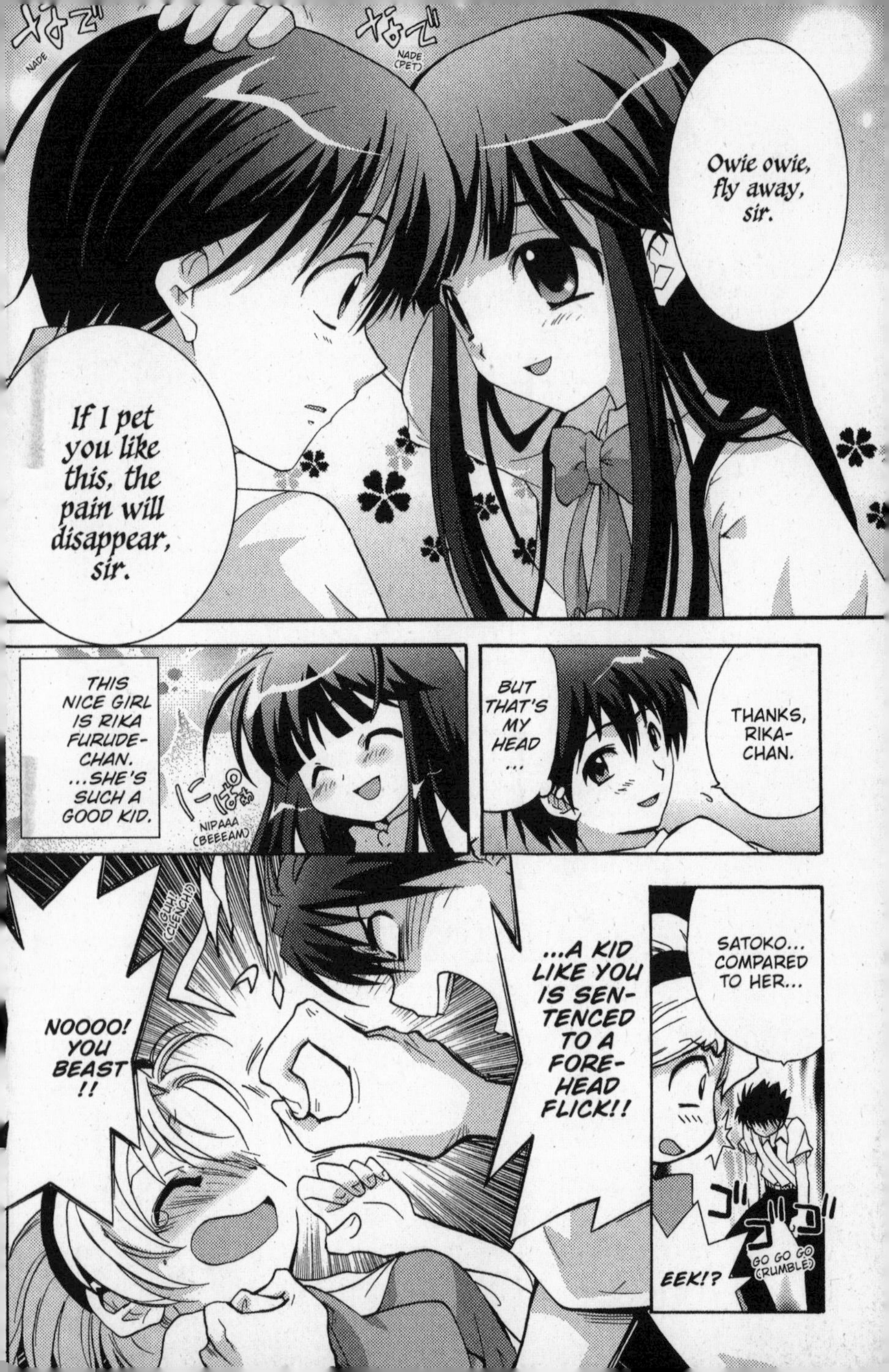
なで
NADE (PET)
なで
NADE
Owie owie, fly away, sir.
If I pet you like this, the pain will disappear, sir.
THANKS, RIKA-CHAN.
BUT THAT'S MY HEAD ...
にぱぁ
NIPAAA (BEEEAM)
THIS NICE GIRL IS RIKA FURUDE-CHAN. ...SHE'S SUCH A GOOD KID.
SATOKO... COMPARED TO HER...
ゴゴゴ
GO GO GO (RUMBLE)
EEK!?
...A KID LIKE YOU IS SEN-TENCED TO A FORE-HEAD FLICK!!
GUH! (CLENCH!)
NOOOO! YOU BEAST !!

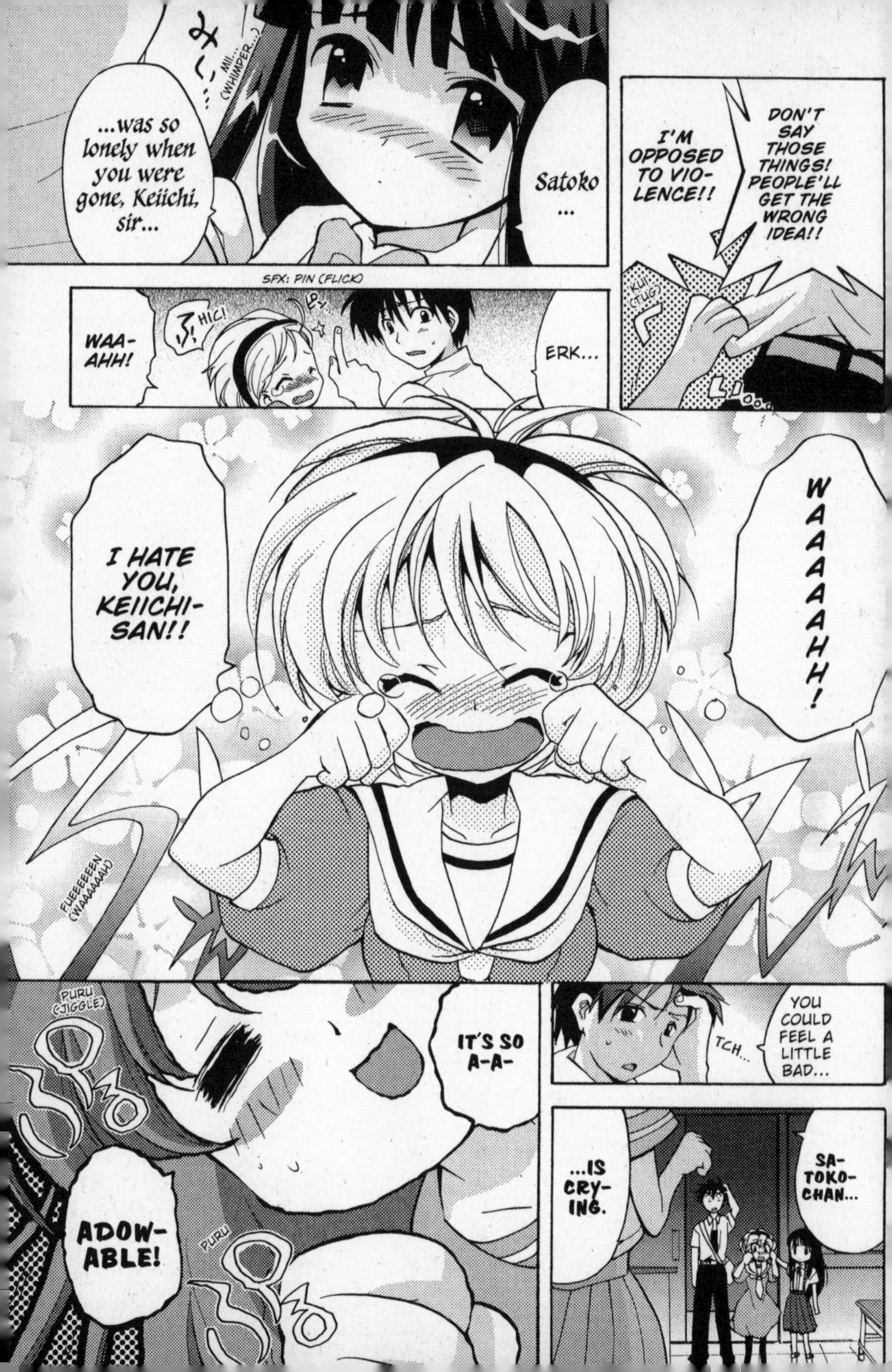
DON'T SAY THOSE THINGS! PEOPLE'LL GET THE WRONG IDEA!!
I'M OPPOSED TO VIO-LENCE!!
KUI (TUG)
Satoko ...
MII... (WHIMPER...)
...was so lonely when you were gone, Keiichi, sir...
SFX: PIN (FLICK)
ERK...
HIC!
WAA-AHH!
WAAAAAAAHH!
I HATE YOU, KEIICHI-SAN!!
FUEEEEEEN (WAAAAAAH)
YOU COULD FEEL A LITTLE BAD...
TCH...
SA-TOKO-CHAN...
...IS CRY-ING.
IT'S SO A-A-
PURU (JIGGLE)
ADOW-ABLE!
PURU

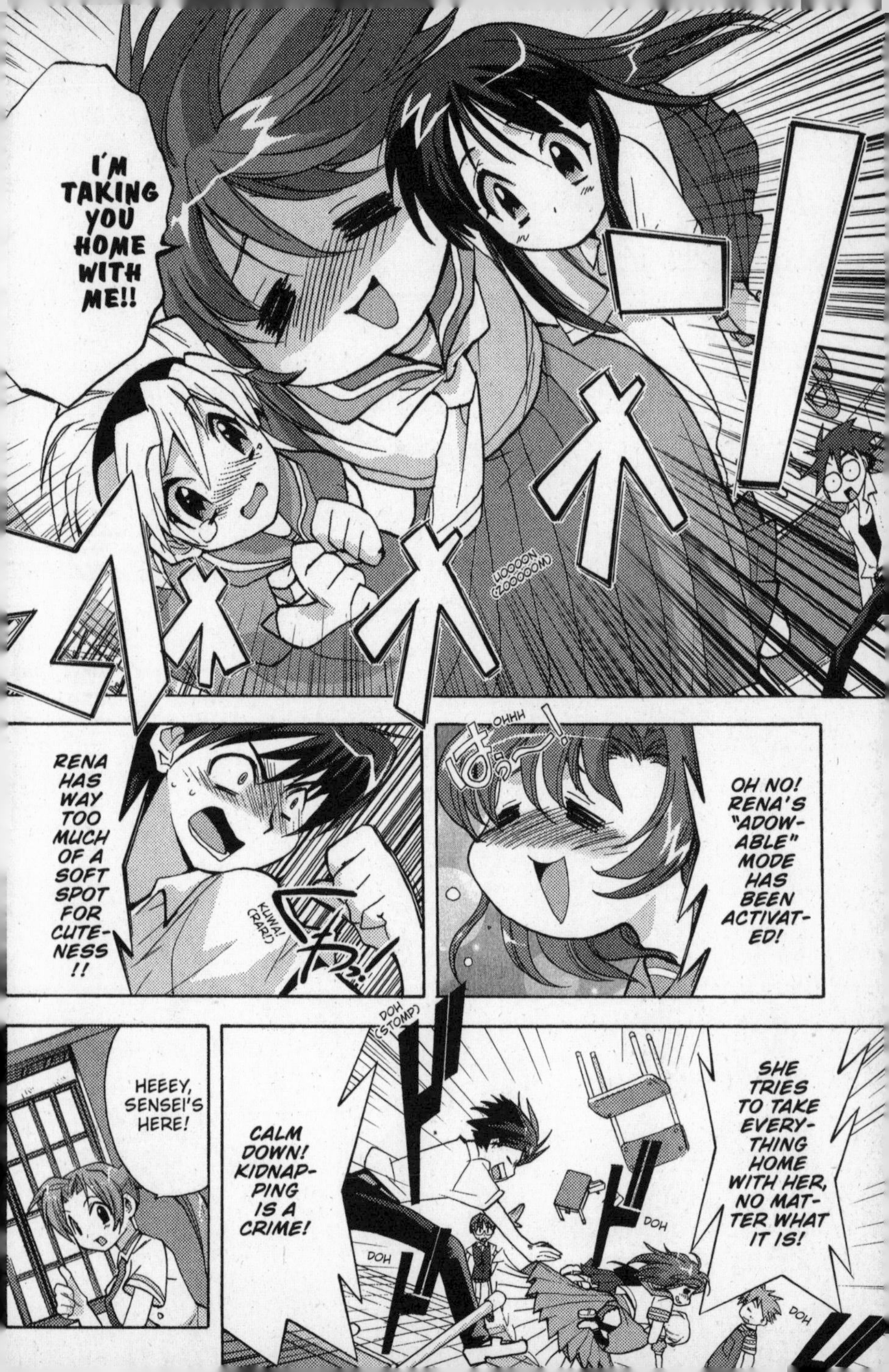
I'M TAKING YOU HOME WITH ME!!
NOOOOH (ZOOOOOOM)
OHHH
OH NO! RENA'S "ADOWABLE" MODE HAS BEEN ACTIVATED!
KUWA! (RAR!)
RENA HAS WAY TOO MUCH OF A SOFT SPOT FOR CUTENESS!!
SHE TRIES TO TAKE EVERYTHING HOME WITH HER, NO MATTER WHAT IT IS!
DOH
DOH
DOH (STOMP)
CALM DOWN! KIDNAPPING IS A CRIME!
DOH
HEEEY, SENSEI'S HERE!

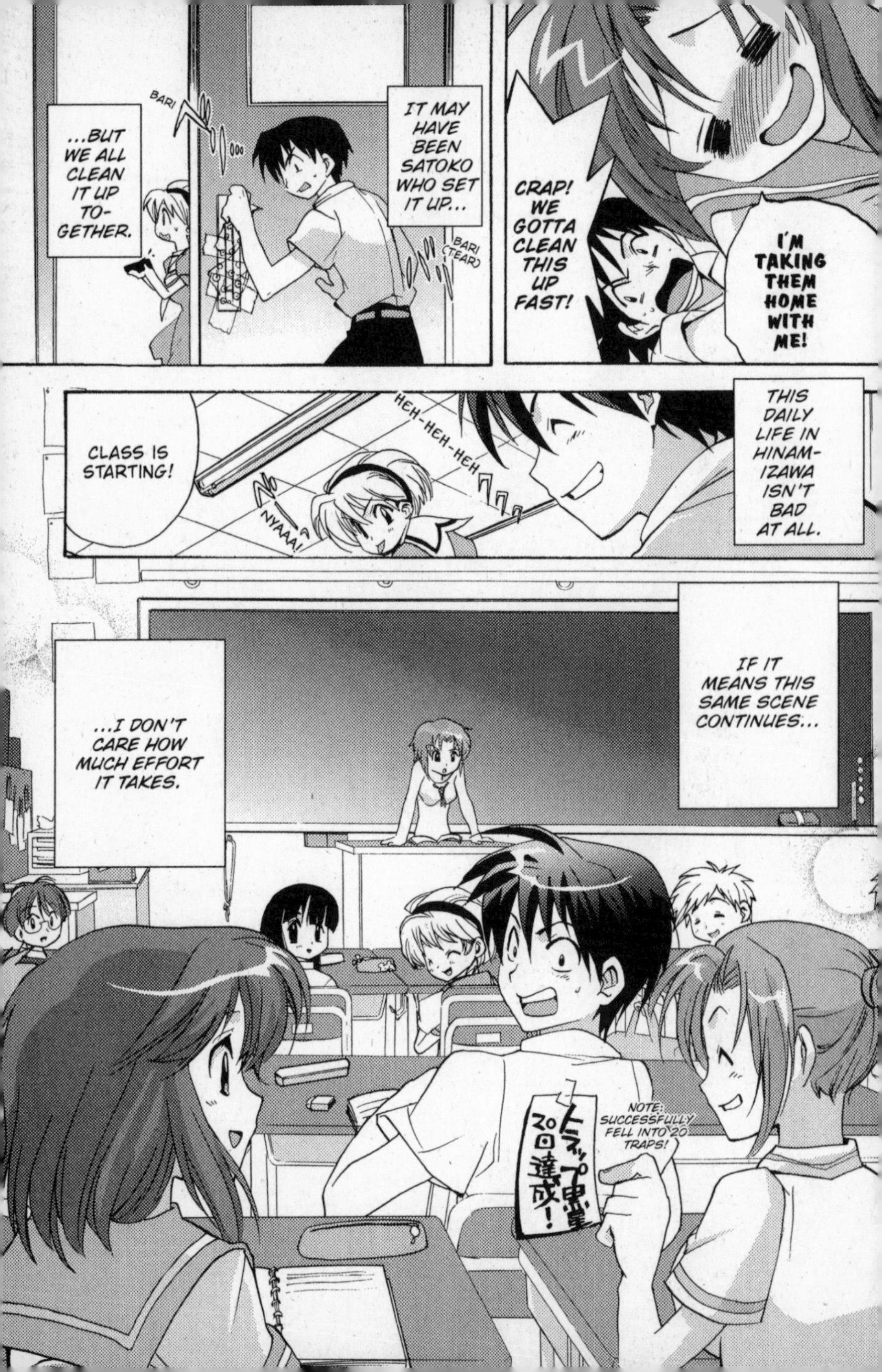
I'M TAKING THEM HOME WITH ME!
CRAP! WE GOTTA CLEAN THIS UP FAST!
IT MAY HAVE BEEN SATOKO WHO SET IT UP...
BARI (TEAR)
BARI!
...BUT WE ALL CLEAN IT UP TO-GETHER.
THIS DAILY LIFE IN HINAMI-IZAWA ISN'T BAD AT ALL.
HEH-HEH-HEH
NYAAA!
CLASS IS STARTING!
IF IT MEANS THIS SAME SCENE CONTINUES...
...I DON'T CARE HOW MUCH EFFORT IT TAKES.
NOTE: SUCCESSFULLY FELL INTO 20 TRAPS!

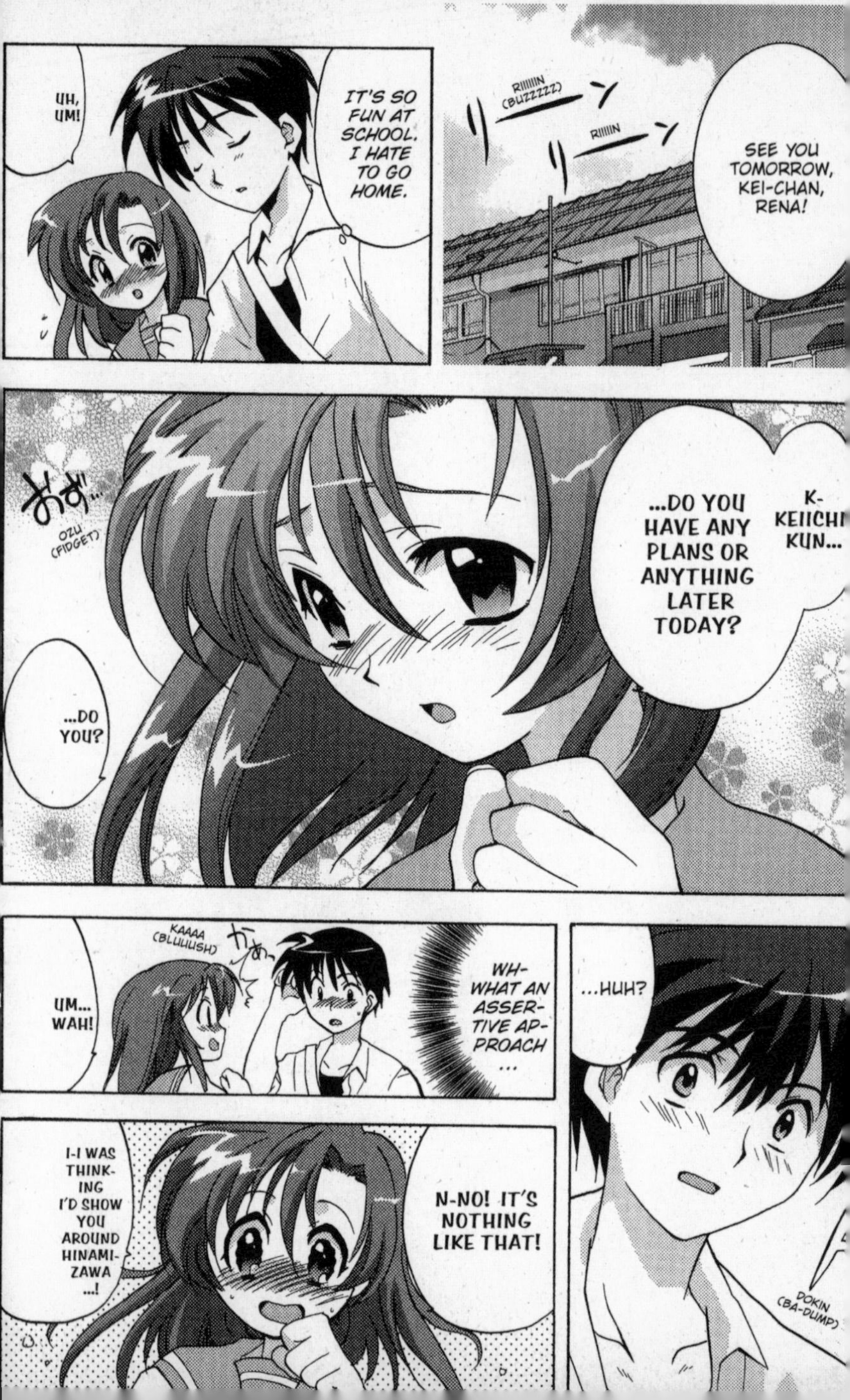
RIIIIIN (BUZZZZZ)
RIIIIN
SEE YOU TOMORROW, KEI-CHAN, RENA!
IT'S SO FUN AT SCHOOL. I HATE TO GO HOME.
UH, UM!
K- KEIICH KUN...
...DO YOU HAVE ANY PLANS OR ANYTHING LATER TODAY?
おず...
OZU (FIDGET)
...DO YOU?
...HUH?
DOKIN (BA-DUMP)
WH- WHAT AN ASSERTIVE APPROACH ...
かあっ
KAAAA (BLUUUSH)
UM... WAH!
N-NO! IT'S NOTHING LIKE THAT!
I-I WAS THINKING I'D SHOW YOU AROUND HINAMIZAWA ...!

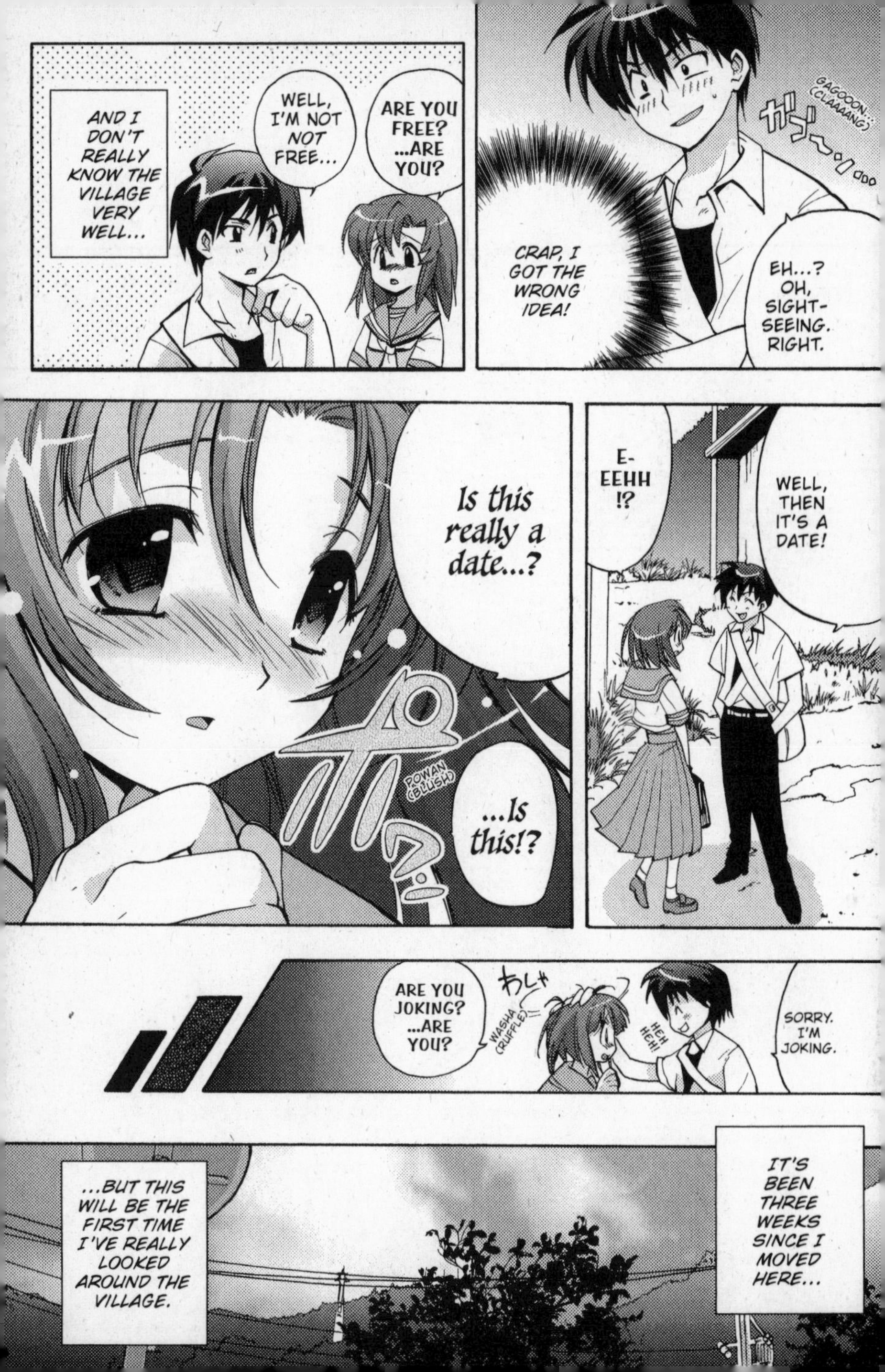
GAGOOON... (CLAAAANG)
EH...? OH, SIGHT-SEEING. RIGHT.
CRAP, I GOT THE WRONG IDEA!
ARE YOU FREE? ...ARE YOU?
WELL, I'M NOT NOT FREE...
AND I DON'T REALLY KNOW THE VILLAGE VERY WELL...
WELL, THEN IT'S A DATE!
E-EEHH!?
Is this really a date...?
POWAN (BLUSH)
...Is this!?
SORRY. I'M JOKING.
HEH HEH!
わしゃ
WASHA (RUFFLE)
ARE YOU JOKING? ...ARE YOU?
IT'S BEEN THREE WEEKS SINCE I MOVED HERE...
...BUT THIS WILL BE THE FIRST TIME I'VE REALLY LOOKED AROUND THE VILLAGE.

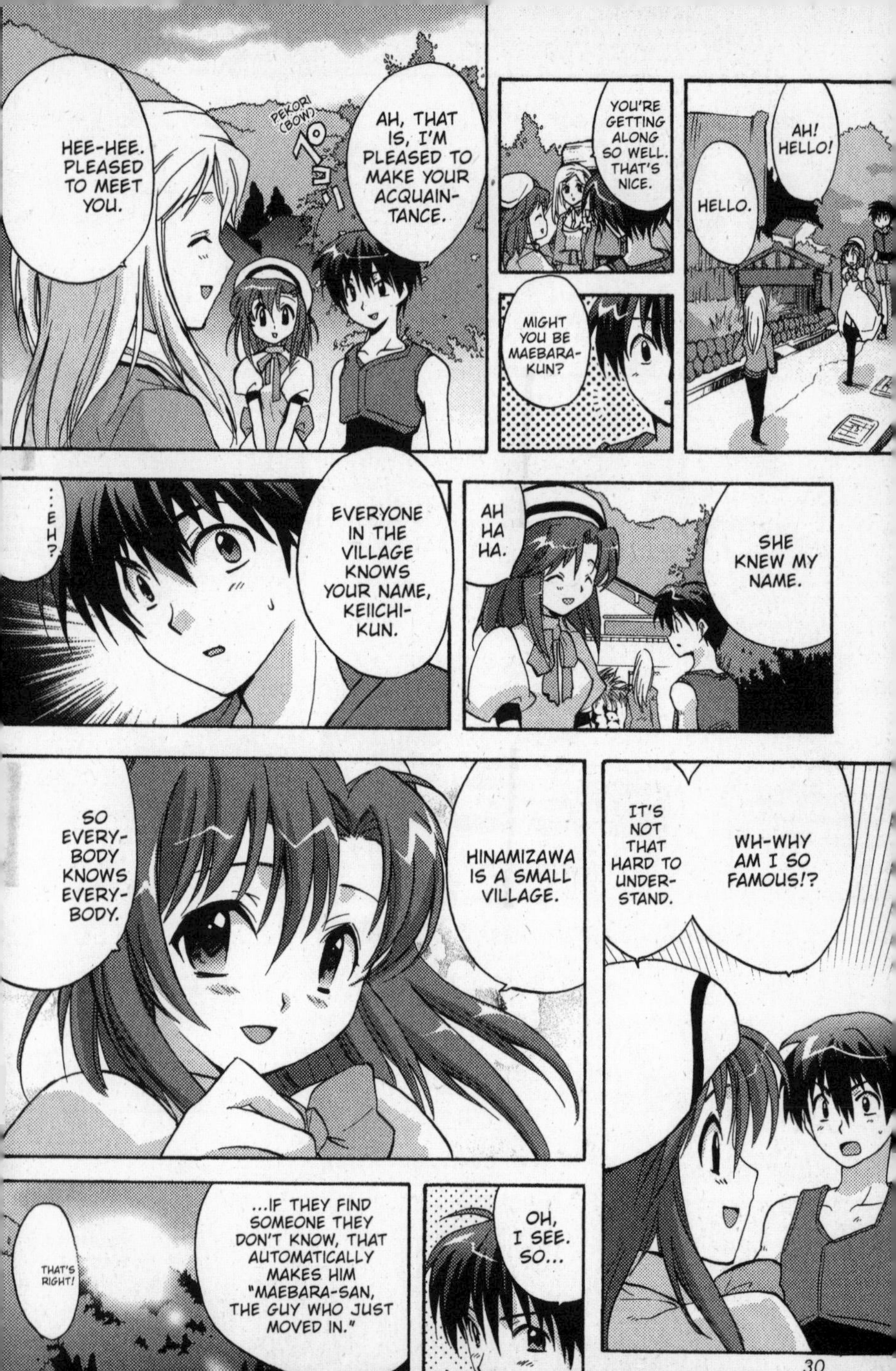
AH! HELLO!
HELLO.
YOU'RE GETTING ALONG SO WELL. THAT'S NICE.
MIGHT YOU BE MAEBARA-KUN?
PEKORI (BOW)
AH, THAT IS, I'M PLEASED TO MAKE YOUR ACQUAIN-TANCE.
HEE-HEE. PLEASED TO MEET YOU.
SHE KNEW MY NAME.
AH HA HA.
EVERYONE IN THE VILLAGE KNOWS YOUR NAME, KEIICHI-KUN.
...EH?
WH-WHY AM I SO FAMOUS!?
IT'S NOT THAT HARD TO UNDER-STAND.
HINAMIZAWA IS A SMALL VILLAGE.
SO EVERY-BODY KNOWS EVERY-BODY.
OH, I SEE. SO...
...IF THEY FIND SOMEONE THEY DON'T KNOW, THAT AUTOMATICALLY MAKES HIM "MAEBARA-SAN, THE GUY WHO JUST MOVED IN."
THAT'S RIGHT!

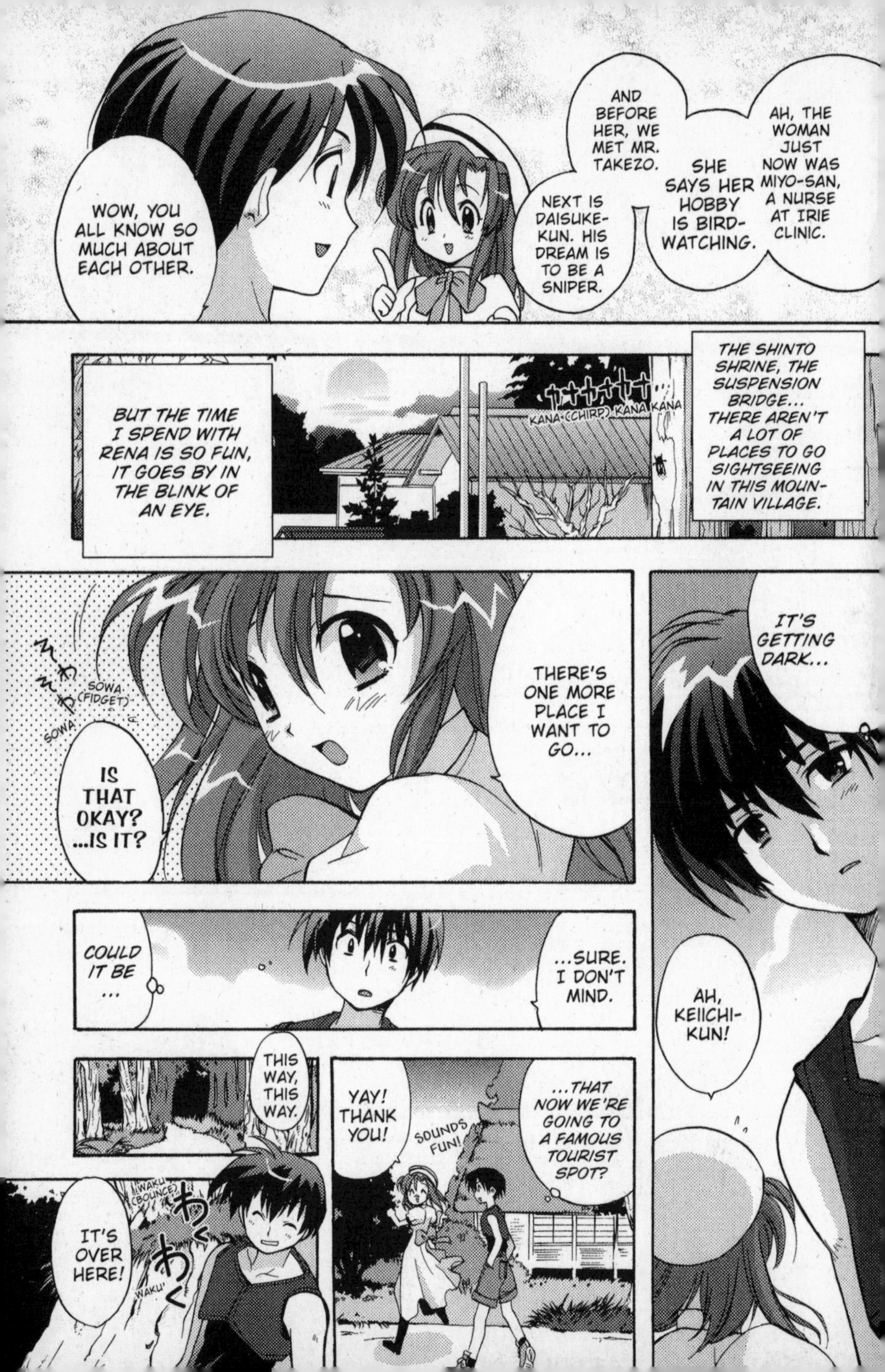
AH, THE WOMAN JUST NOW WAS MIYO-SAN, A NURSE AT IRIE CLINIC.
SHE SAYS HER HOBBY IS BIRD-WATCHING.
AND BEFORE HER, WE MET MR. TAKEZO.
NEXT IS DAISUKE-KUN. HIS DREAM IS TO BE A SNIPER.
WOW, YOU ALL KNOW SO MUCH ABOUT EACH OTHER.
THE SHINTO SHRINE, THE SUSPENSION BRIDGE... THERE AREN'T A LOT OF PLACES TO GO SIGHTSEEING IN THIS MOUNTAIN VILLAGE.
KANA (CHIRP) KANA KANA
BUT THE TIME I SPEND WITH RENA IS SO FUN, IT GOES BY IN THE BLINK OF AN EYE.
IT'S GETTING DARK...
AH, KEIICHI-KUN!
THERE'S ONE MORE PLACE I WANT TO GO...
SOWA (FIDGET) SOWA
IS THAT OKAY? ...IS IT?
...SURE. I DON'T MIND.
COULD IT BE ...
...THAT NOW WE'RE GOING TO A FAMOUS TOURIST SPOT?
SOUNDS FUN!
YAY! THANK YOU!
THIS WAY, THIS WAY.
WAKU (BOUNCE) WAKU
IT'S OVER HERE!

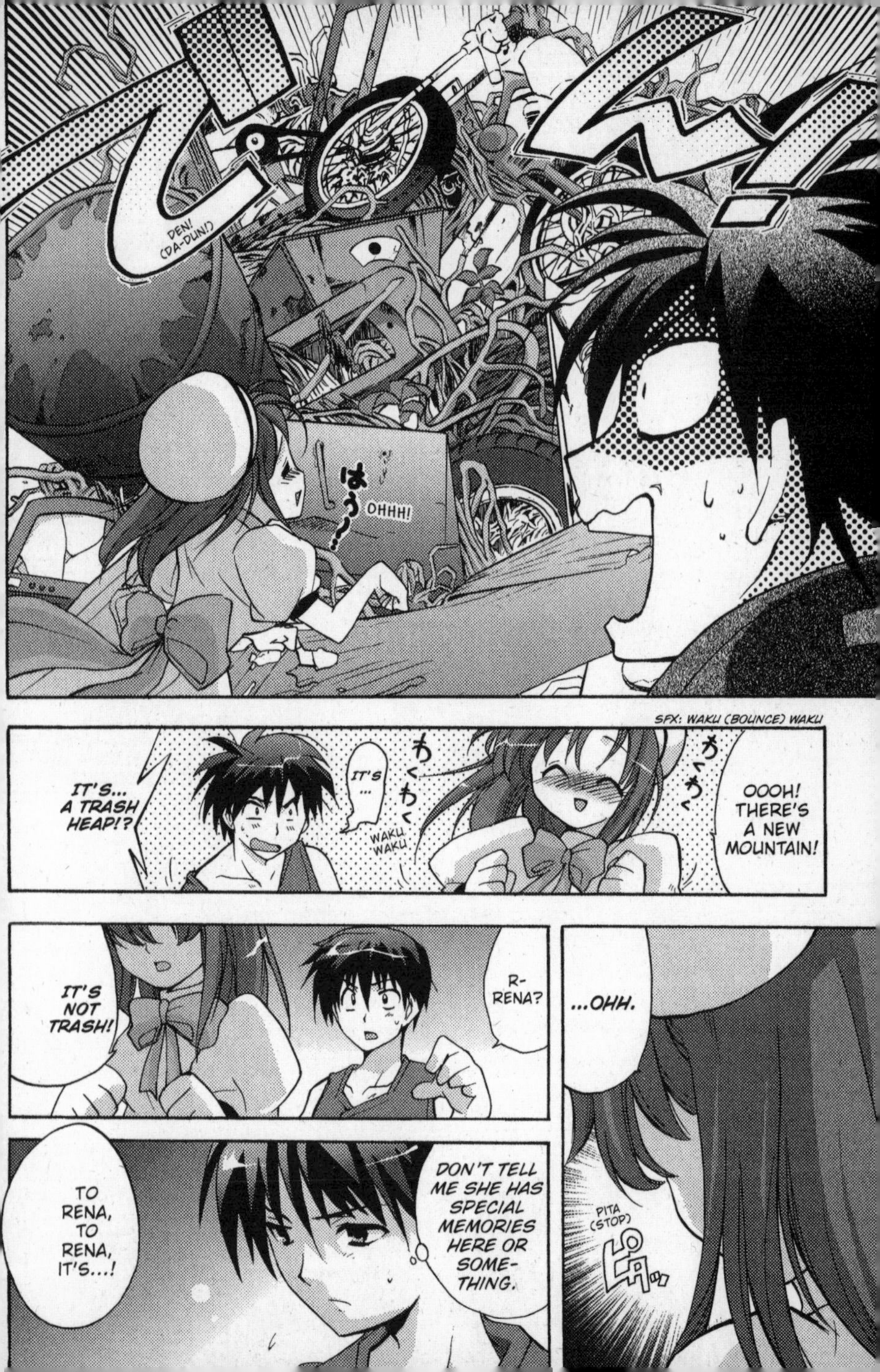
DEN! (DA-DUN!)
はう～・・
OHHH!
SFX: WAKU (BOUNCE) WAKU
OOOH! THERE'S A NEW MOUNTAIN!
わくわく
WAKU WAKU
わくわく
IT'S ...
IT'S... A TRASH HEAP!?
...OHH.
PITA (STOP)
ピタッ
R-RENA?
IT'S NOT TRASH!
DON'T TELL ME SHE HAS SPECIAL MEMORIES HERE OR SOMETHING.
TO RENA, TO RENA, IT'S...!

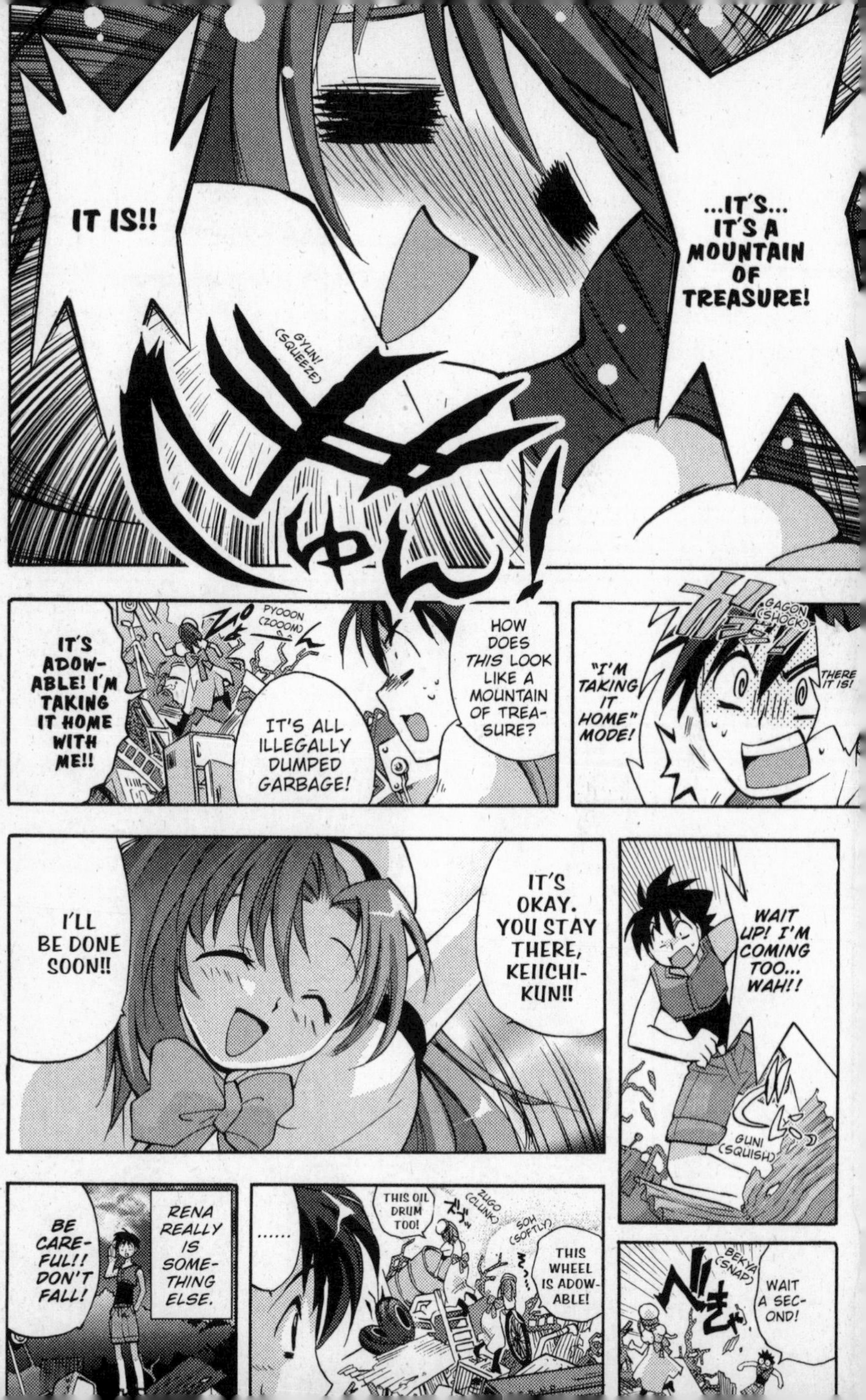

...IT'S... IT'S A MOUNTAIN OF TREASURE!
IT IS!!
GYUN! (SQUEEZE)
GAGON (SHOCK)
THERE IT IS!
"I'M TAKING IT HOME" MODE!
HOW DOES THIS LOOK LIKE A MOUNTAIN OF TREA-SURE?
IT'S ALL ILLEGALLY DUMPED GARBAGE!
PYOOON (ZOOOM)
IT'S ADOW-ABLE! I'M TAKING IT HOME WITH ME!!
WAIT UP! I'M COMING TOO... WAH!!
GUNI (SQUISH)
IT'S OKAY. YOU STAY THERE, KEIICHI-KUN!!
I'LL BE DONE SOON!!
BEKYA (SNAP)
WAIT A SEC-OND!
THIS OIL DRUM TOO!
ZUGO (CLUNK)
SOH (SOFTLY)
THIS WHEEL IS ADOW-ABLE!
......
RENA REALLY IS SOME-THING ELSE.
BE CARE-FUL!! DON'T FALL!

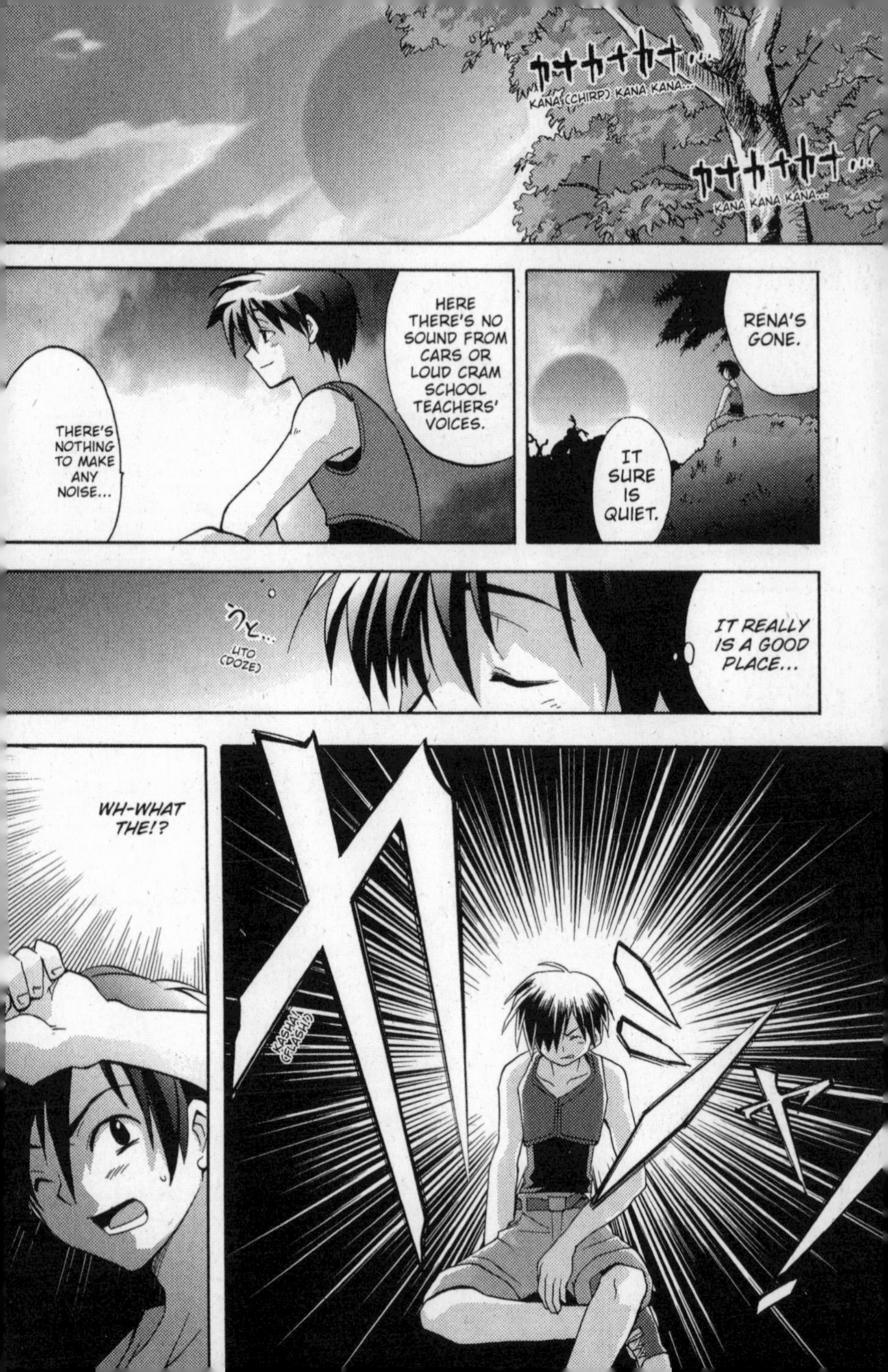

カナカナカナ…
KANA (CHIRP) KANA KANA...
カナカナカナ…
KANA KANA KANA...
RENA'S GONE.
IT SURE IS QUIET.
HERE THERE'S NO SOUND FROM CARS OR LOUD CRAM SCHOOL TEACHERS' VOICES.
THERE'S NOTHING TO MAKE ANY NOISE...
IT REALLY IS A GOOD PLACE...
うと…
UTO (DOZE)
KASHA! (FLASH!)
WH-WHAT THE!?

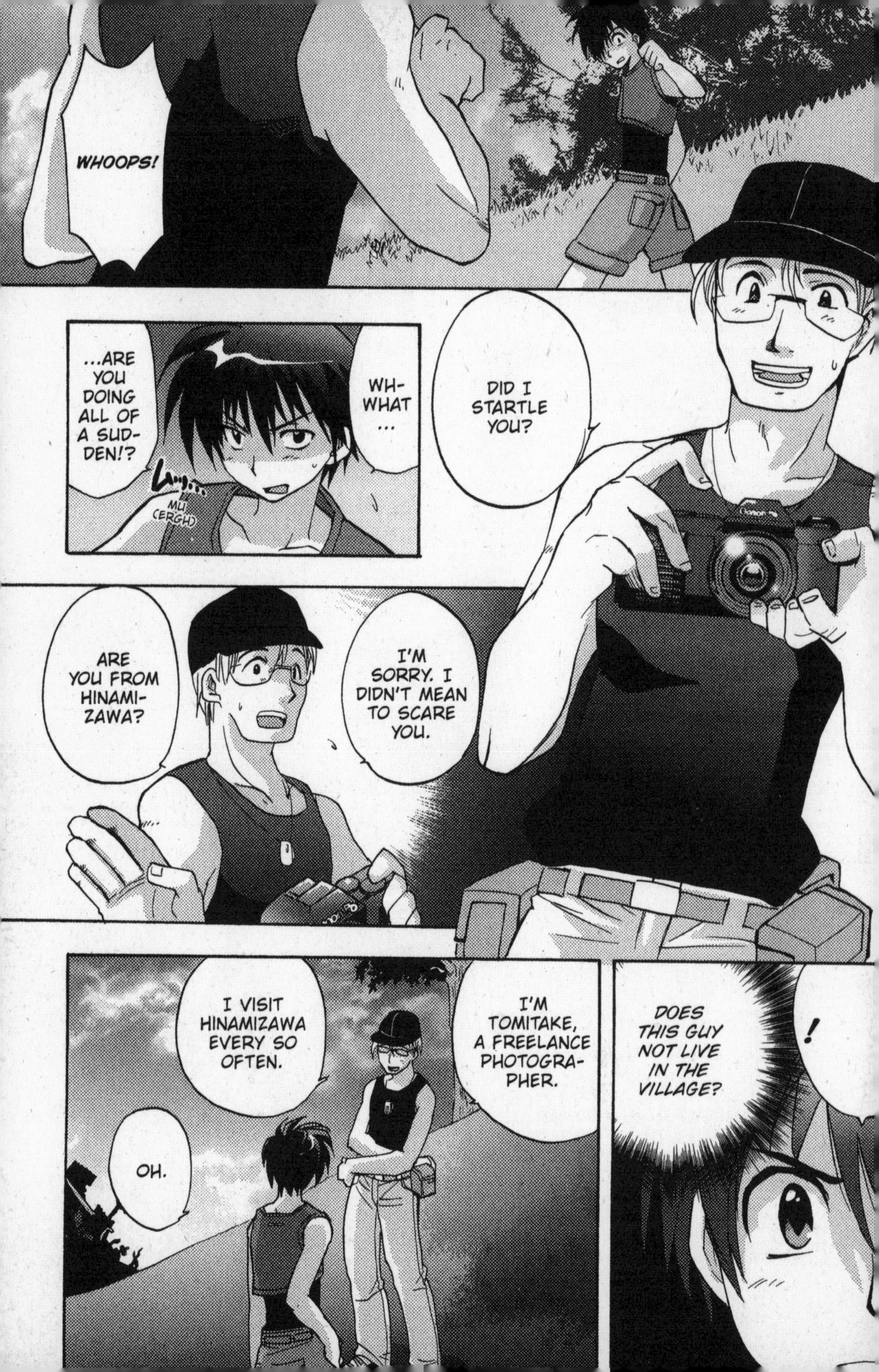
WHOOPS!
DID I STARTLE YOU?
WH-WHAT ...
...ARE YOU DOING ALL OF A SUD-DEN!?
MU (ERGH)
I'M SORRY. I DIDN'T MEAN TO SCARE YOU.
ARE YOU FROM HINAMI-ZAWA?
!
DOES THIS GUY NOT LIVE IN THE VILLAGE?
I'M TOMITAKE, A FREELANCE PHOTOGRA-PHER.
I VISIT HINAMIZAWA EVERY SO OFTEN.
OH.

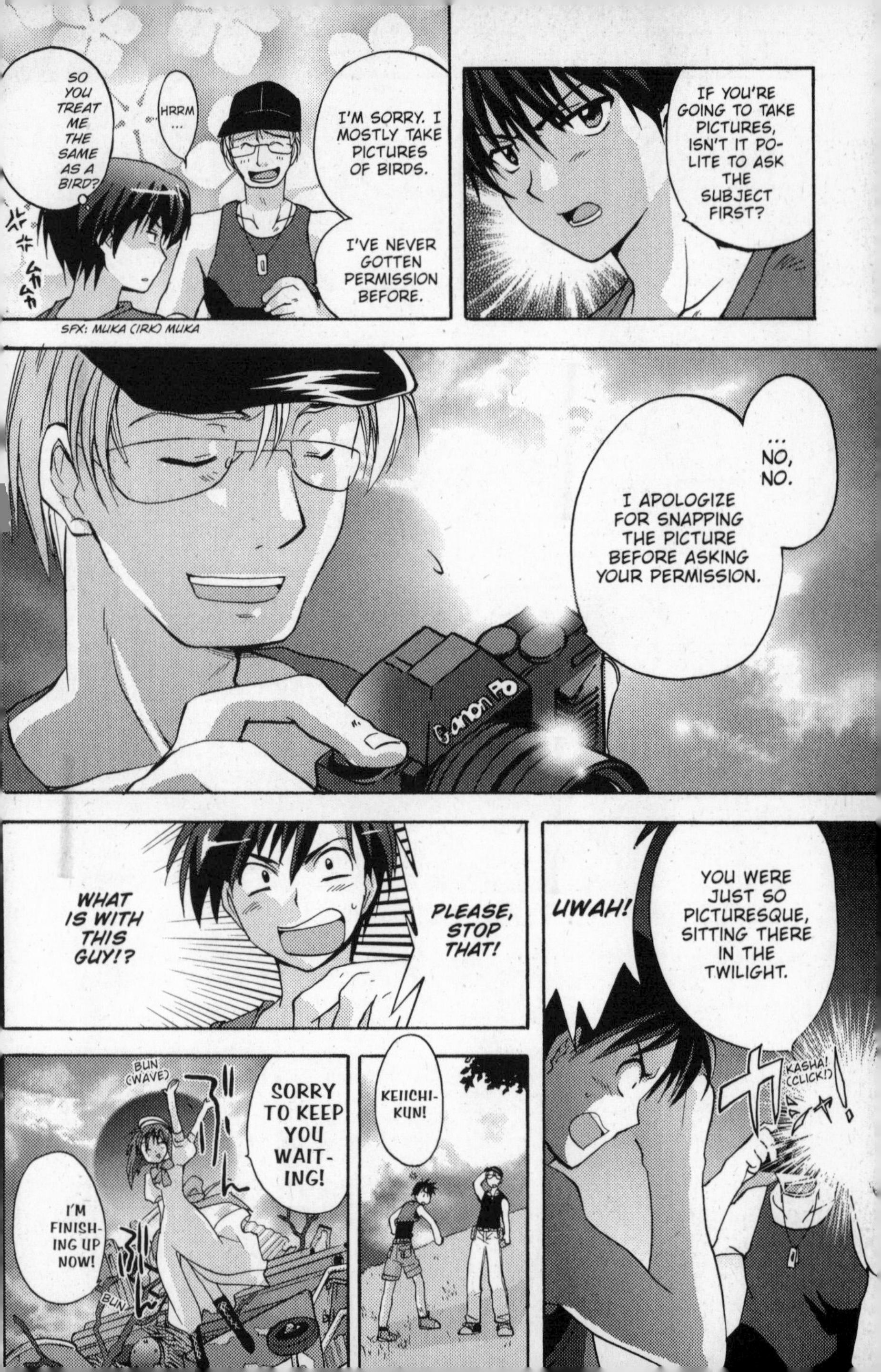
IF YOU'RE GOING TO TAKE PICTURES, ISN'T IT PO-LITE TO ASK THE SUBJECT FIRST?
I'M SORRY. I MOSTLY TAKE PICTURES OF BIRDS.
I'VE NEVER GOTTEN PERMISSION BEFORE.
HRRM ...
SO YOU TREAT ME THE SAME AS A BIRD?
SFX: MUKA (IRK) MUKA
... NO, NO.
I APOLOGIZE FOR SNAPPING THE PICTURE BEFORE ASKING YOUR PERMISSION.
YOU WERE JUST SO PICTURESQUE, SITTING THERE IN THE TWILIGHT.
KASHA! (CLICK!)
UWAH!
PLEASE, STOP THAT!
WHAT IS WITH THIS GUY!?
KEIICHI-KUN!
SORRY TO KEEP YOU WAIT-ING!
BUN (WAVE)
I'M FINISH-ING UP NOW!
BUN

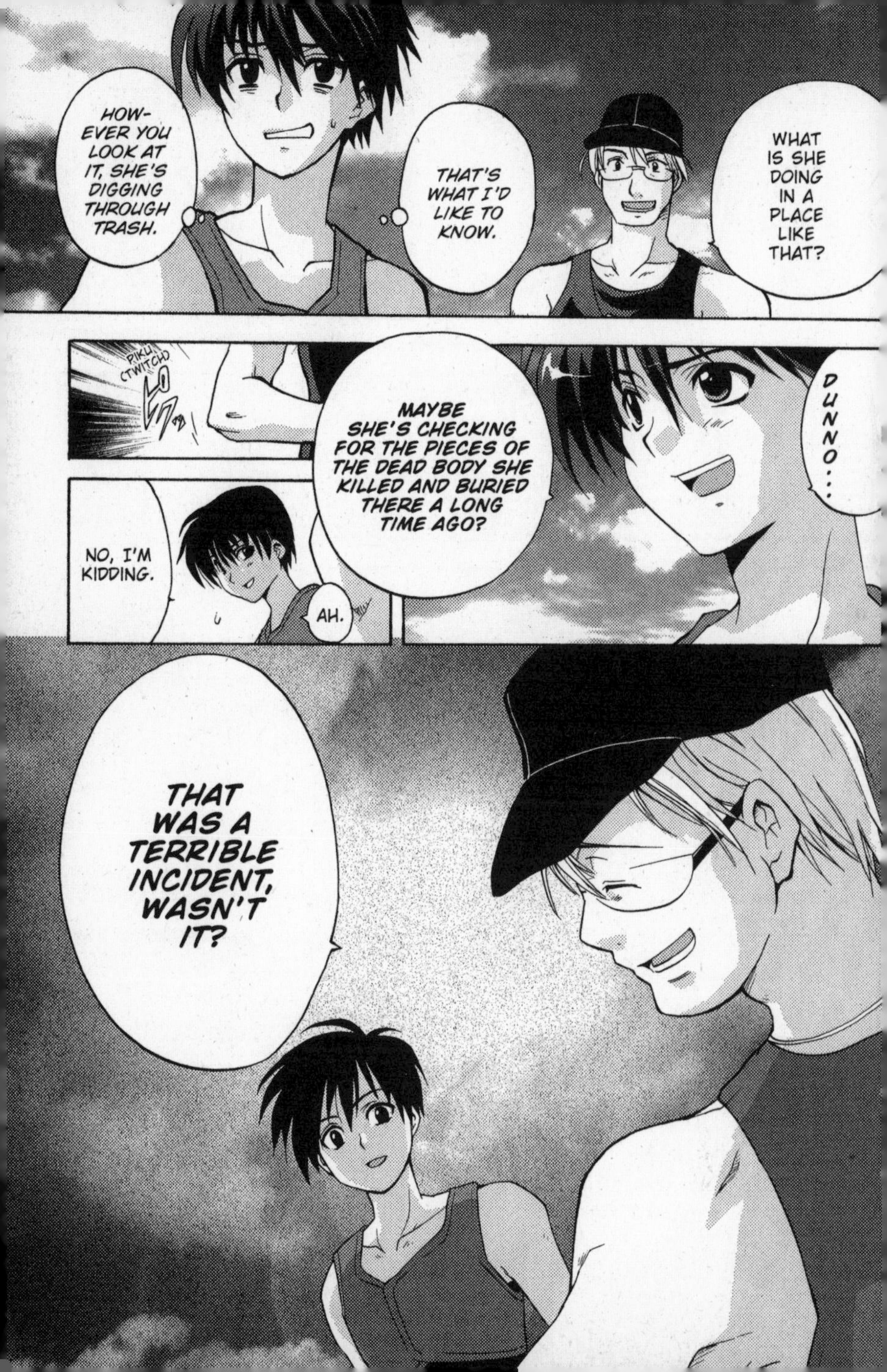
WHAT IS SHE DOING IN A PLACE LIKE THAT?
THAT'S WHAT I'D LIKE TO KNOW.
HOW-EVER YOU LOOK AT IT, SHE'S DIGGING THROUGH TRASH.
DUNNO...
MAYBE SHE'S CHECKING FOR THE PIECES OF THE DEAD BODY SHE KILLED AND BURIED THERE A LONG TIME AGO?
PIKU (TWITCH)
AH.
NO, I'M KIDDING.
THAT WAS A TERRIBLE INCIDENT, WASN'T IT?

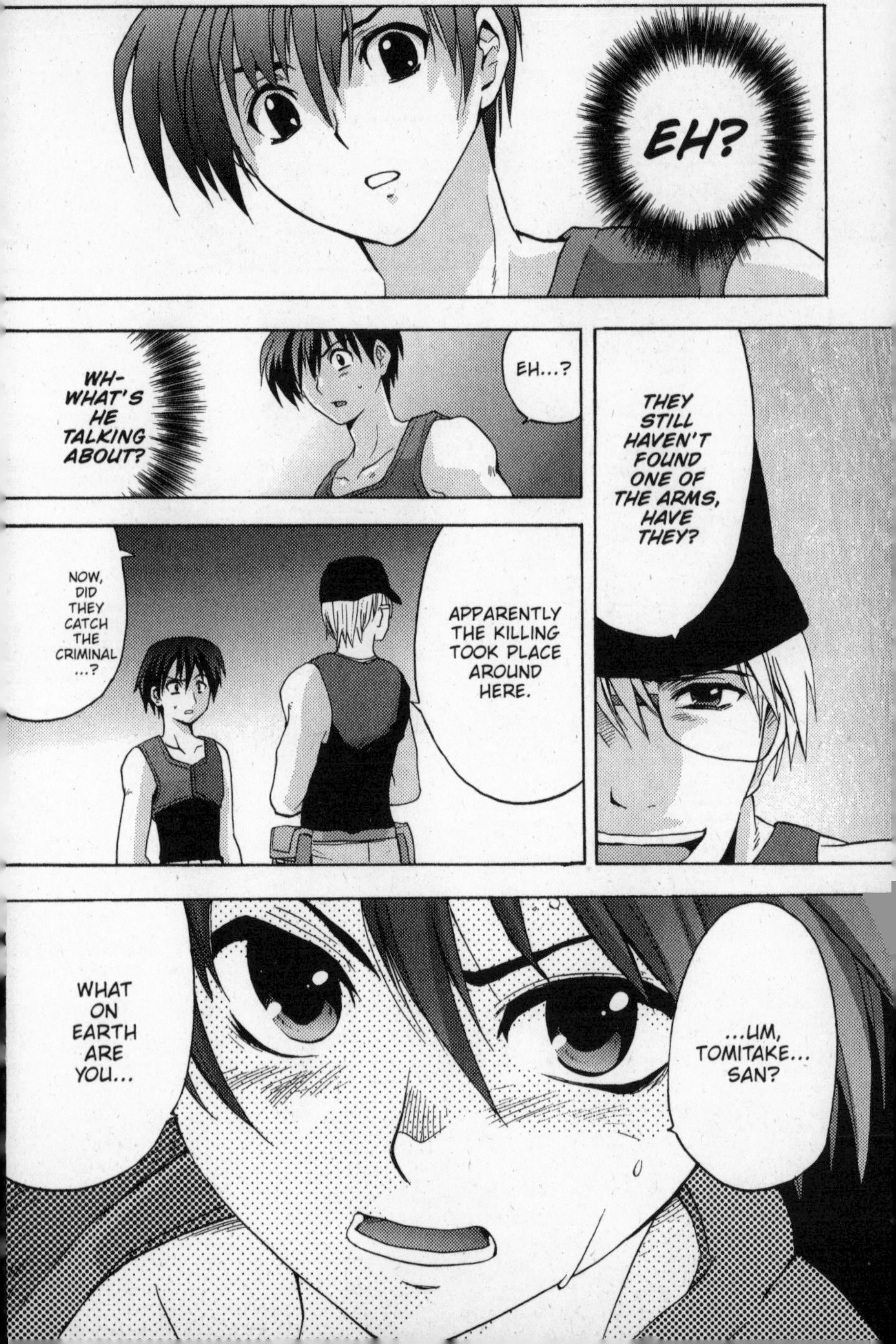
EH?
THEY STILL HAVEN'T FOUND ONE OF THE ARMS, HAVE THEY?
EH...?
WH-WHAT'S HE TALKING ABOUT?
APPARENTLY THE KILLING TOOK PLACE AROUND HERE.
NOW, DID THEY CATCH THE CRIMINAL...?
...UM, TOMITAKE... SAN?
WHAT ON EARTH ARE YOU...

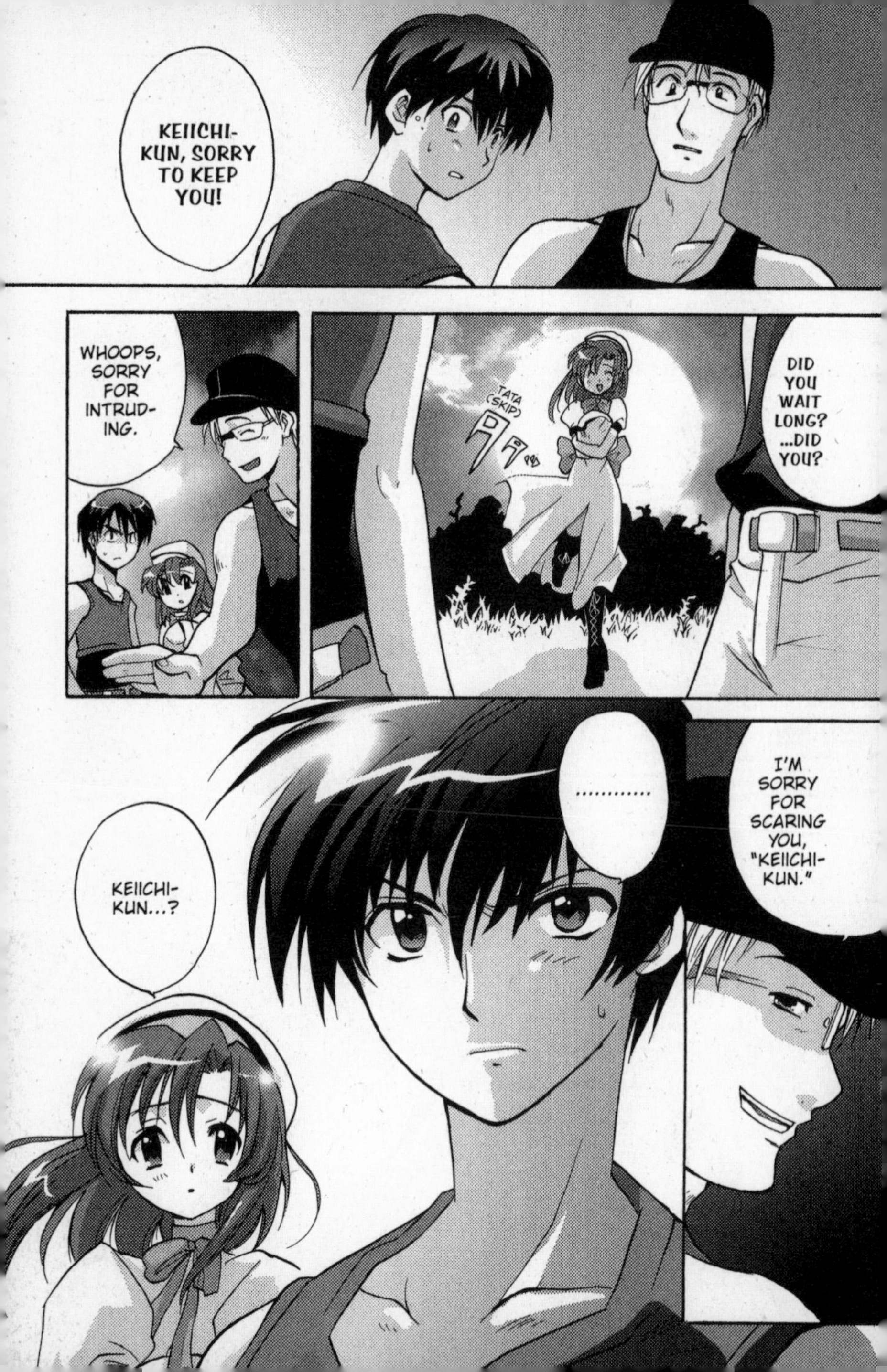
KEIICHI-KUN, SORRY TO KEEP YOU!
DID YOU WAIT LONG? ...DID YOU?
TATA (SKIP)
WHOOPS, SORRY FOR INTRUDING.
I'M SORRY FOR SCARING YOU, "KEIICHI-KUN."
....
KEIICHI-KUN...?

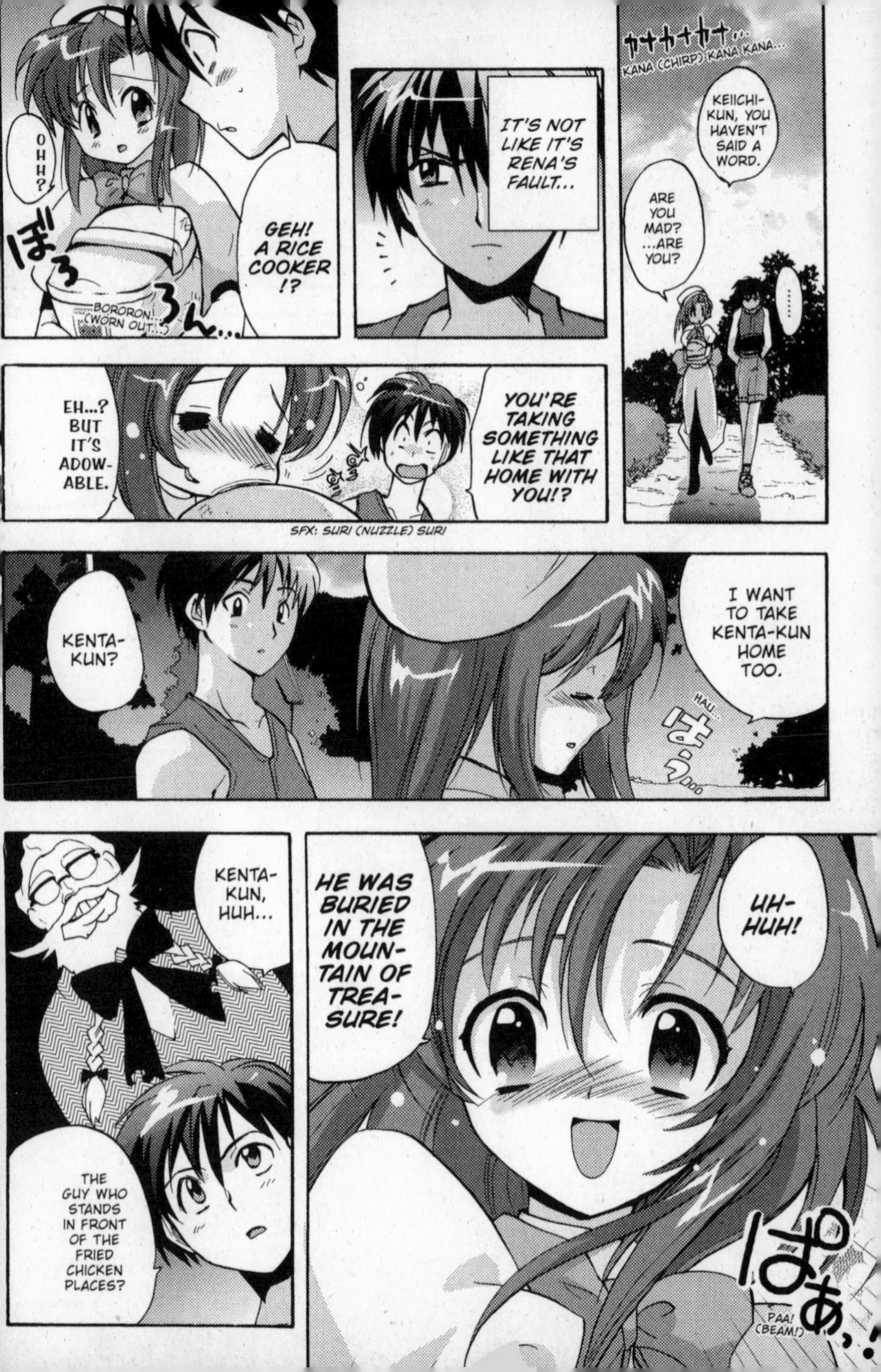
カナカナカナ…
KANA (CHIRP) KANA KANA...
KEIICHI-KUN, YOU HAVEN'T SAID A WORD.
ARE YOU MAD? ...ARE YOU?
......
IT'S NOT LIKE IT'S RENA'S FAULT...
GEH! A RICE COOKER!?
OHH?
ぼろろん…
BORORON (WORN OUT)
YOU'RE TAKING SOMETHING LIKE THAT HOME WITH YOU!?
EH...? BUT IT'S ADOWABLE.
SFX: SURI (NUZZLE) SURI
I WANT TO TAKE KENTA-KUN HOME TOO.
はう
HAU...
KENTA-KUN?
UH-HUH!
HE WAS BURIED IN THE MOUNTAIN OF TREASURE!
ぱぁっ
PAA! (BEAM!)
KENTA-KUN, HUH...
THE GUY WHO STANDS IN FRONT OF THE FRIED CHICKEN PLACES?

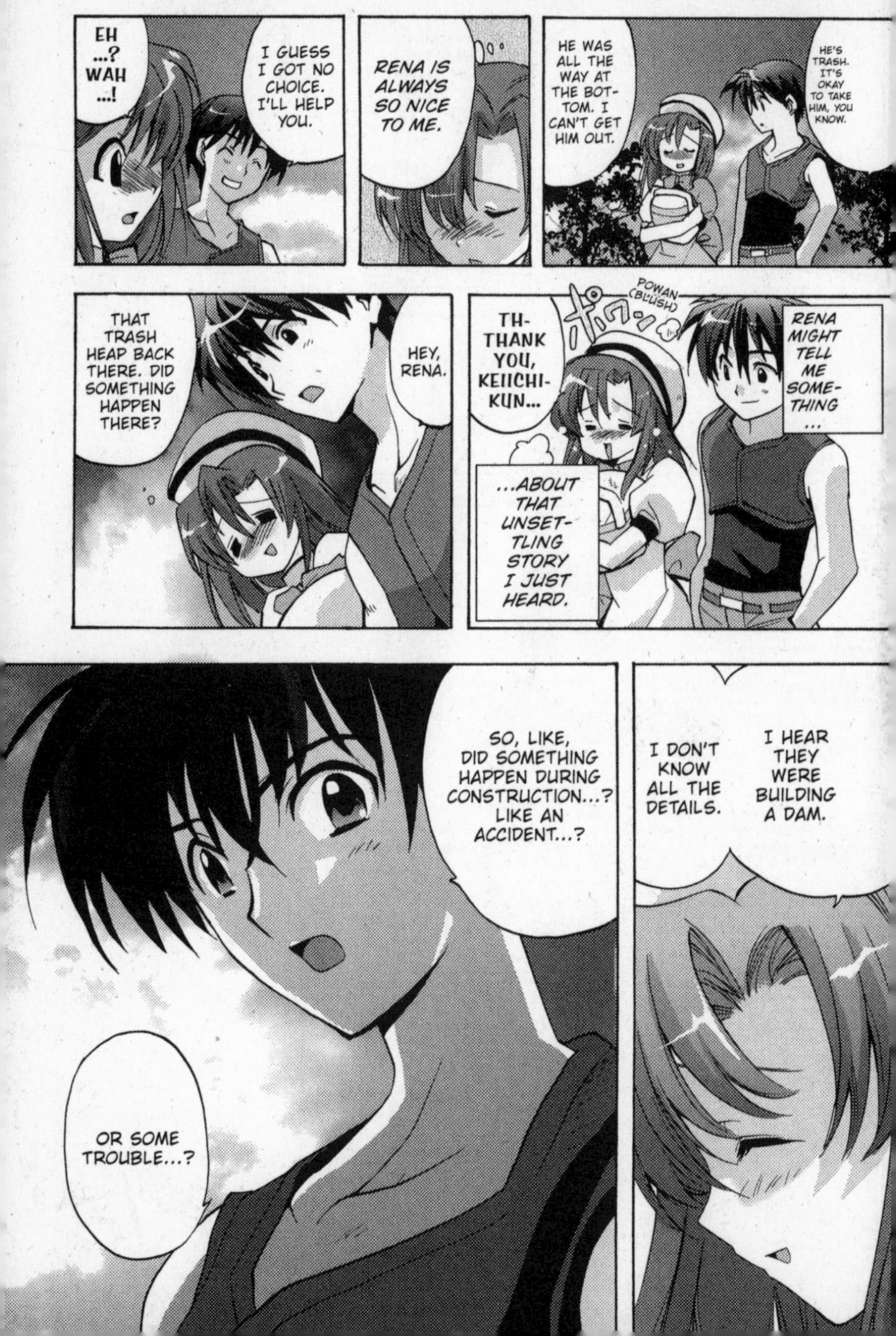
HE'S TRASH. IT'S OKAY TO TAKE HIM, YOU KNOW.
HE WAS ALL THE WAY AT THE BOT-TOM. I CAN'T GET HIM OUT.
RENA IS ALWAYS SO NICE TO ME.
I GUESS I GOT NO CHOICE. I'LL HELP YOU.
EH ...? WAH ...!
RENA MIGHT TELL ME SOMETHING ...
POWAN (BLUSH)
TH-THANK YOU, KEIICHI-KUN...
...ABOUT THAT UNSETTLING STORY I JUST HEARD.
HEY, RENA.
THAT TRASH HEAP BACK THERE. DID SOMETHING HAPPEN THERE?
I HEAR THEY WERE BUILDING A DAM.
I DON'T KNOW ALL THE DETAILS.
SO, LIKE, DID SOMETHING HAPPEN DURING CONSTRUCTION...? LIKE AN ACCIDENT...?
OR SOME TROUBLE...?

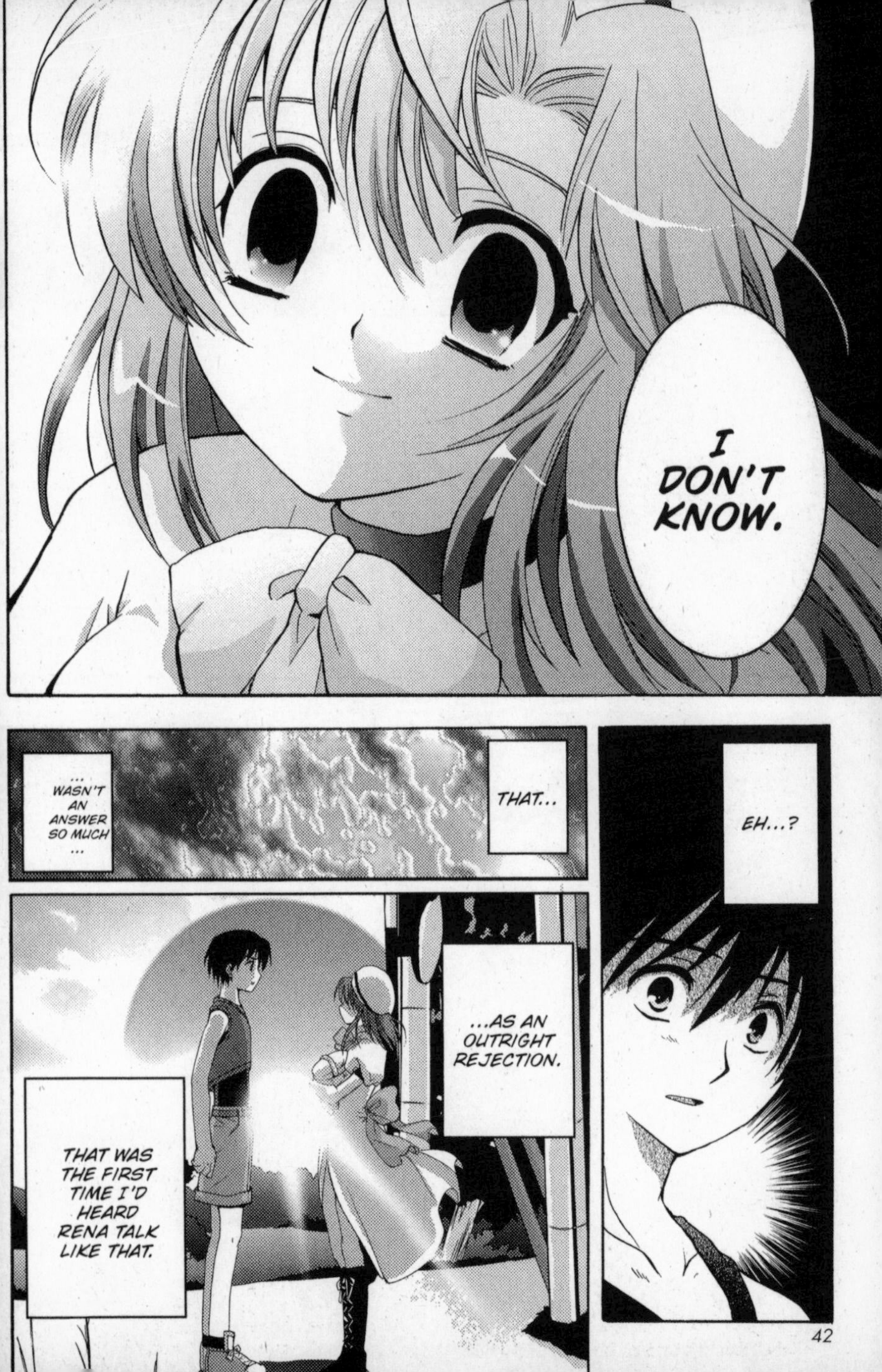
I DON'T KNOW.
EH...?
THAT...
...WASN'T AN ANSWER SO MUCH...
...AS AN OUTRIGHT REJECTION.
THAT WAS THE FIRST TIME I'D HEARD RENA TALK LIKE THAT.

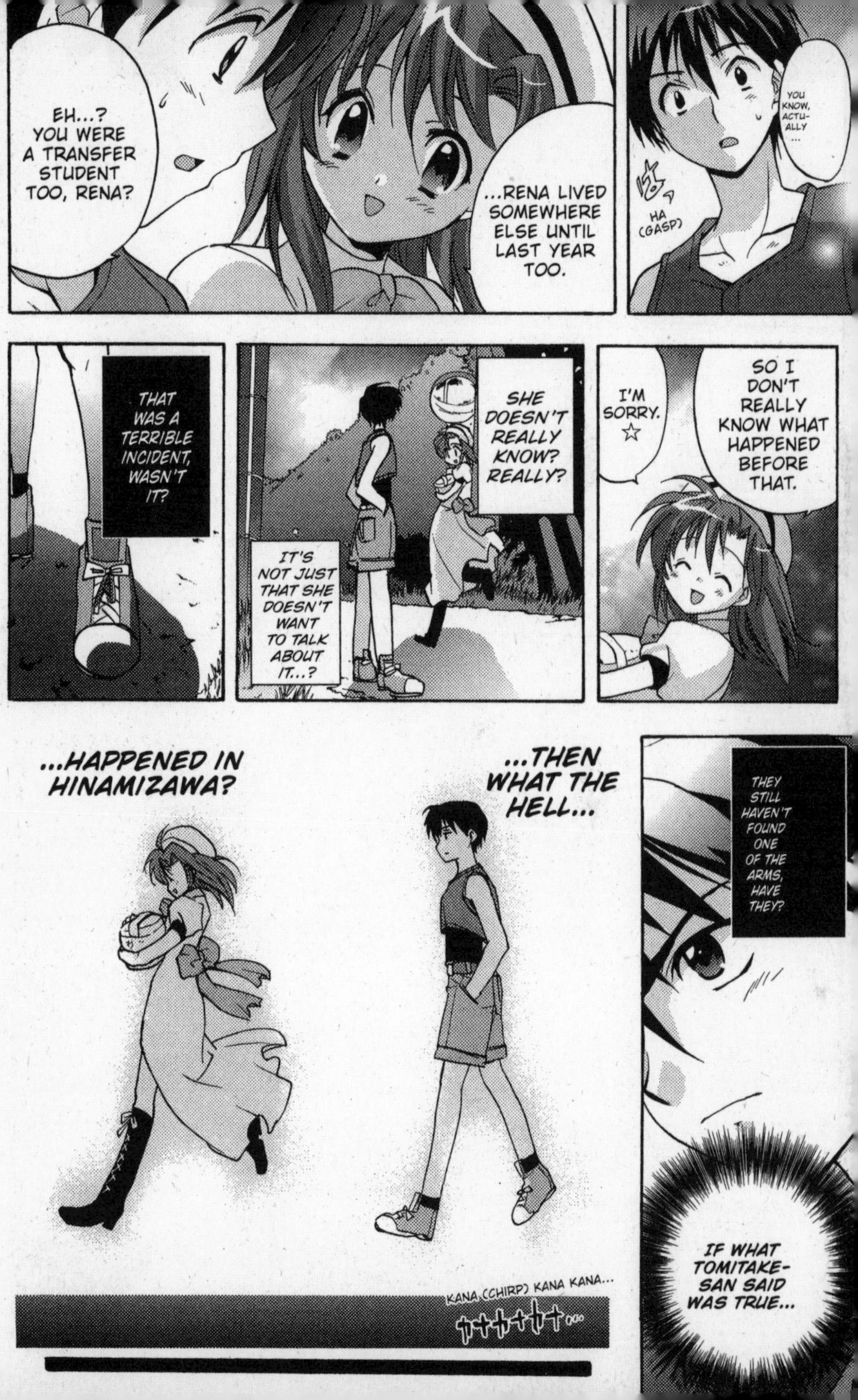
YOU KNOW, ACTUALLY ...
HA (GASP)
...RENA LIVED SOMEWHERE ELSE UNTIL LAST YEAR TOO.
EH...? YOU WERE A TRANSFER STUDENT TOO, RENA?
SO I DON'T REALLY KNOW WHAT HAPPENED BEFORE THAT.
I'M SORRY. ☆
SHE DOESN'T REALLY KNOW? REALLY?
IT'S NOT JUST THAT SHE DOESN'T WANT TO TALK ABOUT IT...?
THAT WAS A TERRIBLE INCIDENT, WASN'T IT?
THEY STILL HAVEN'T FOUND ONE OF THE ARMS, HAVE THEY?
IF WHAT TOMITAKE-SAN SAID WAS TRUE...
...THEN WHAT THE HELL...
...HAPPENED IN HINAMIZAWA?
KANA (CHIRP) KANA KANA...
カナカナカナ…

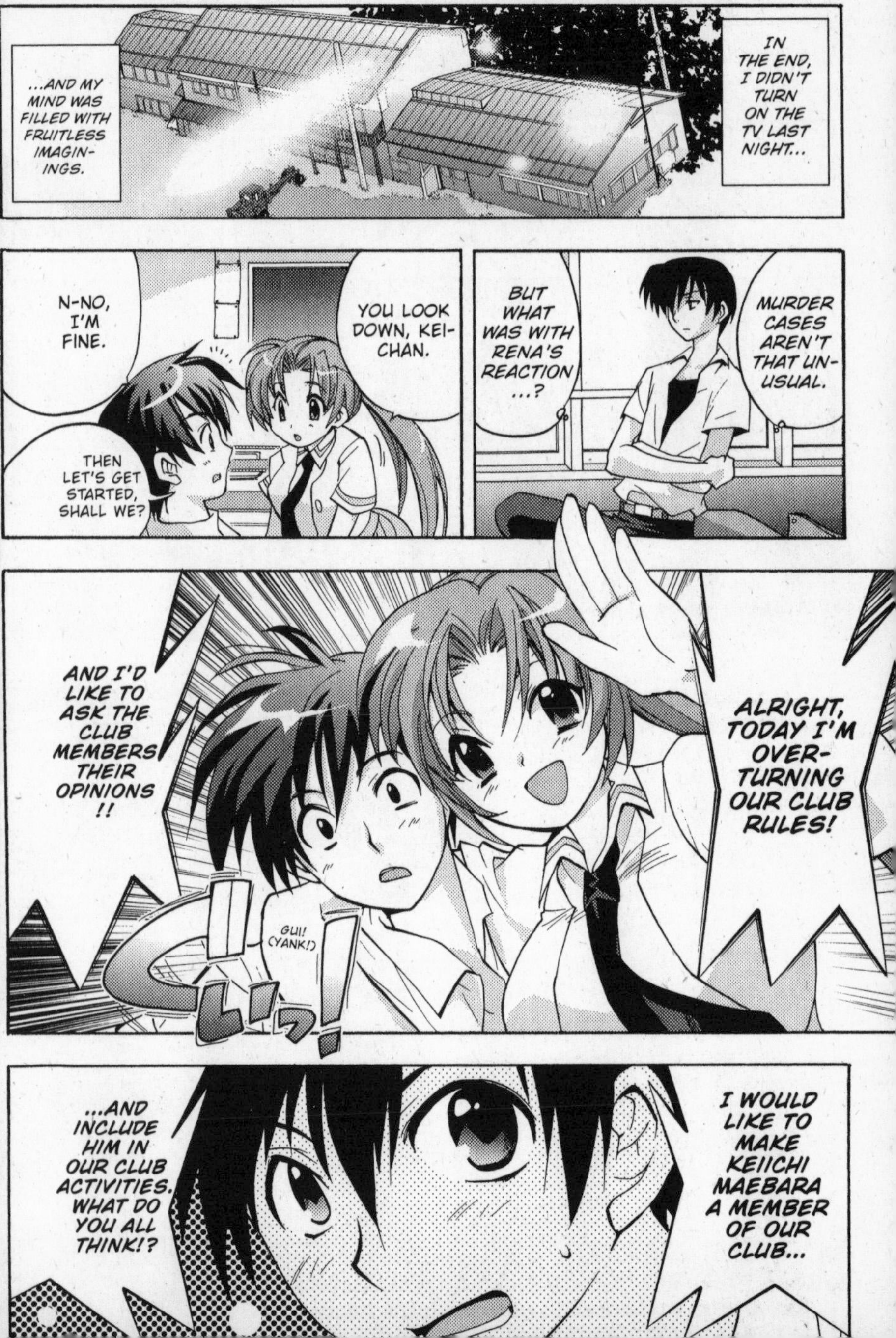
IN THE END, I DIDN'T TURN ON THE TV LAST NIGHT...
...AND MY MIND WAS FILLED WITH FRUITLESS IMAGININGS.
MURDER CASES AREN'T THAT UNUSUAL.
BUT WHAT WAS WITH RENA'S REACTION...?
YOU LOOK DOWN, KEI-CHAN.
N-NO, I'M FINE.
THEN LET'S GET STARTED, SHALL WE?
ALRIGHT, TODAY I'M OVERTURNING OUR CLUB RULES!
AND I'D LIKE TO ASK THE CLUB MEMBERS THEIR OPINIONS!!
GUI! (YANK!)
I WOULD LIKE TO MAKE KEIICHI MAEBARA A MEMBER OF OUR CLUB...
...AND INCLUDE HIM IN OUR CLUB ACTIVITIES. WHAT DO YOU ALL THINK!?

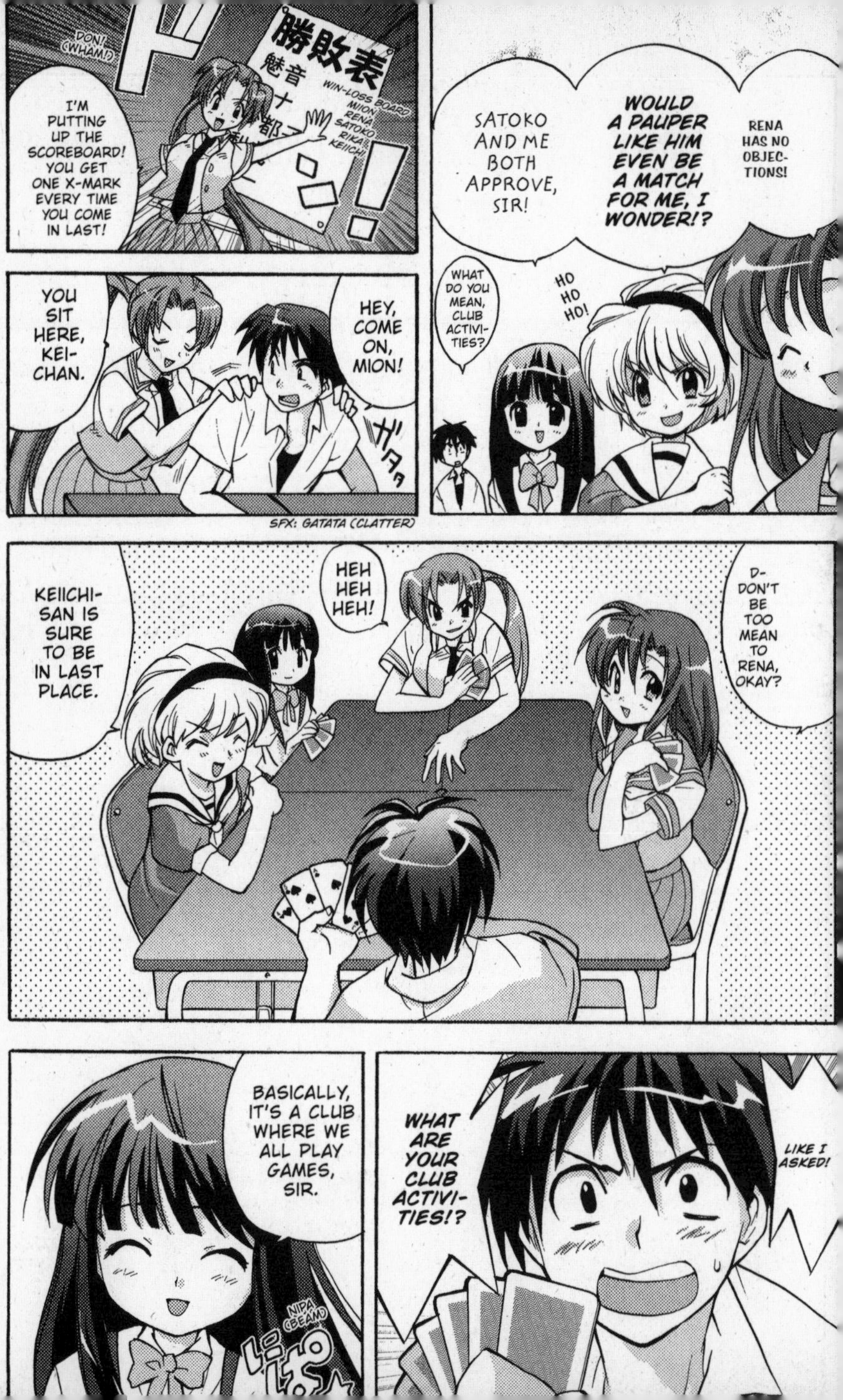
RENA HAS NO OBJECTIONS!
WOULD A PAUPER LIKE HIM EVEN BE A MATCH FOR ME, I WONDER!?
SATOKO AND ME BOTH APPROVE, SIR!
HO HO HO!
WHAT DO YOU MEAN, CLUB ACTIVITIES?
DON! (WHAM!)
勝敗表
魅音
WIN-LOSS BOARD
MION
RENA
SATOKO
RIKA
KEIICHI
I'M PUTTING UP THE SCOREBOARD! YOU GET ONE X-MARK EVERY TIME YOU COME IN LAST!
HEY, COME ON, MION!
YOU SIT HERE, KEI-CHAN.
ガタタ
SFX: GATATA (CLATTER)
D-DON'T BE TOO MEAN TO RENA, OKAY?
HEH HEH HEH!
KEIICHI-SAN IS SURE TO BE IN LAST PLACE.
LIKE I ASKED!
WHAT ARE YOUR CLUB ACTIVITIES!?
BASICALLY, IT'S A CLUB WHERE WE ALL PLAY GAMES, SIR.
NIPA (BEAM)
にぱ

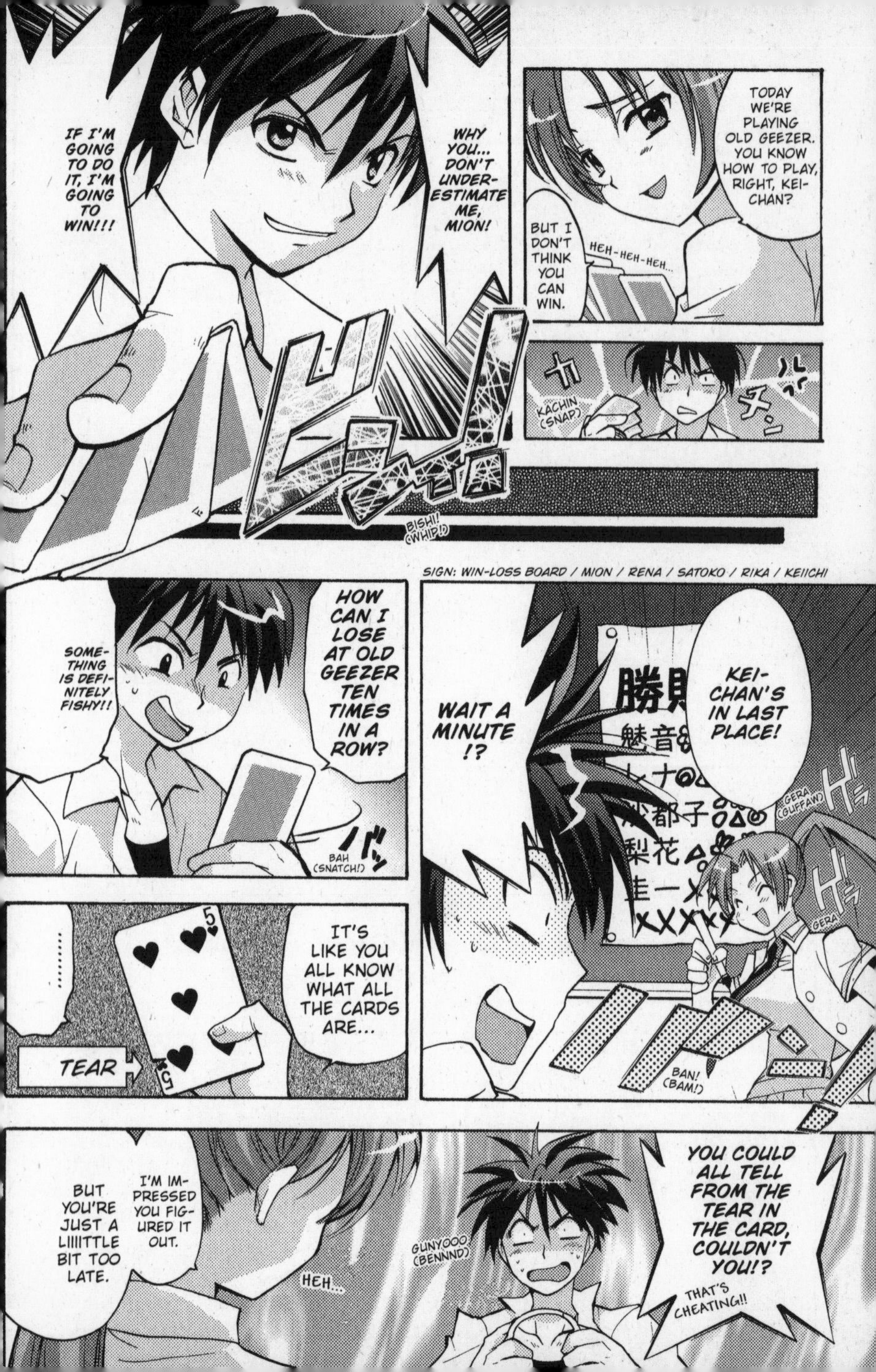
TODAY WE'RE PLAYING OLD GEEZER. YOU KNOW HOW TO PLAY, RIGHT, KEI-CHAN?
HEH-HEH-HEH...
BUT I DON'T THINK YOU CAN WIN.
KACHIN (SNAP)
WHY YOU... DON'T UNDER-ESTIMATE ME, MION!
IF I'M GOING TO DO IT, I'M GOING TO WIN!!!
BISHI! (WHIP!)
SIGN: WIN-LOSS BOARD / MION / RENA / SATOKO / RIKA / KEIICHI
KEI-CHAN'S IN LAST PLACE!
WAIT A MINUTE !?
GERA (GUFFAW)
GERA
BAN! (BAM!)
HOW CAN I LOSE AT OLD GEEZER TEN TIMES IN A ROW?
SOME-THING IS DEFI-NITELY FISHY!!
BAH (SNATCH!)
IT'S LIKE YOU ALL KNOW WHAT ALL THE CARDS ARE...
......
TEAR
YOU COULD ALL TELL FROM THE TEAR IN THE CARD, COULDN'T YOU!?
THAT'S CHEATING!!
GUNYOOO (BENNND)
HEH...
I'M IM-PRESSED YOU FIG-URED IT OUT.
BUT YOU'RE JUST A LIIIITTLE BIT TOO LATE.

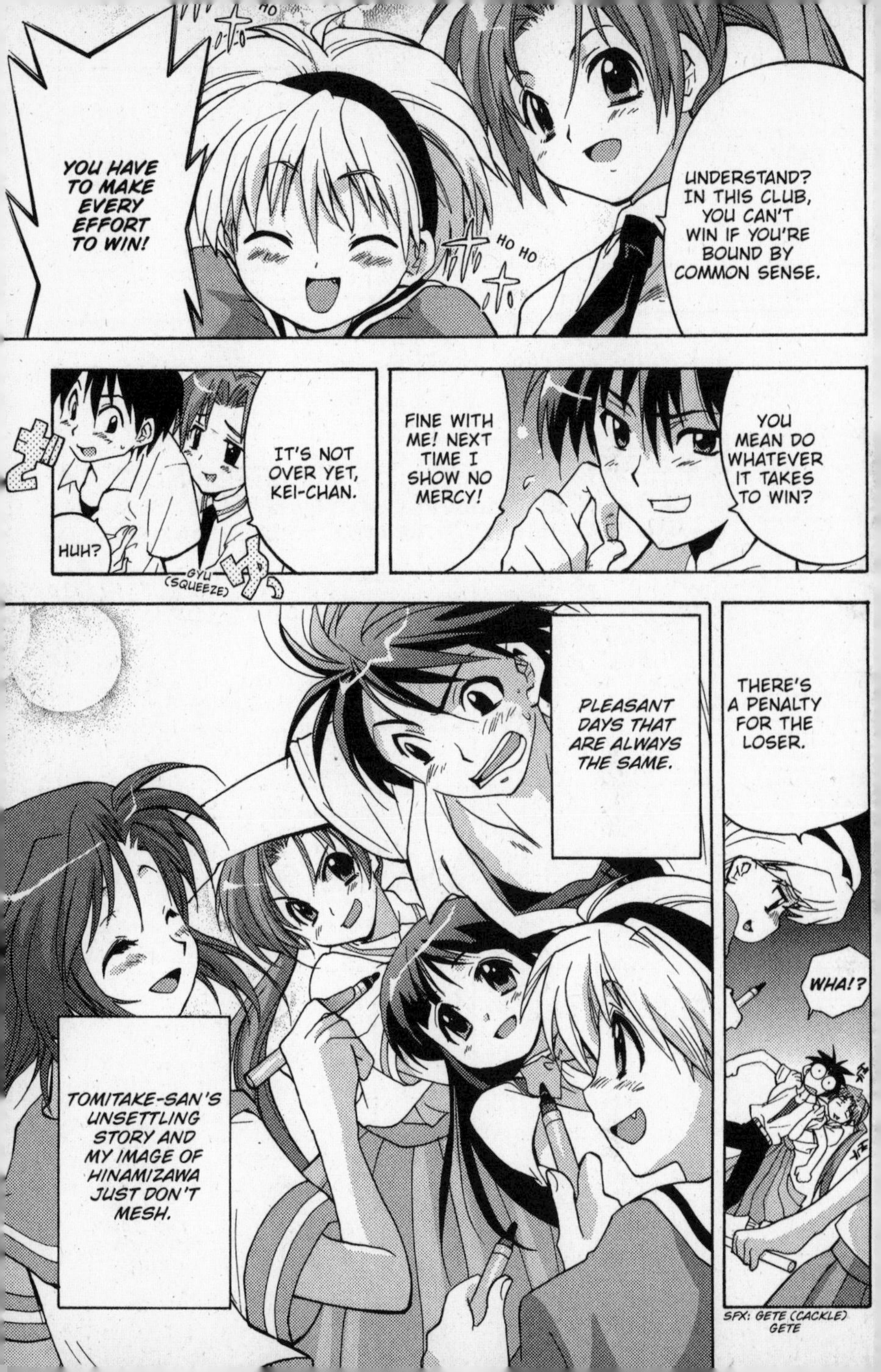
UNDERSTAND? IN THIS CLUB, YOU CAN'T WIN IF YOU'RE BOUND BY COMMON SENSE.
HO HO
YOU HAVE TO MAKE EVERY EFFORT TO WIN!
YOU MEAN DO WHATEVER IT TAKES TO WIN?
FINE WITH ME! NEXT TIME I SHOW NO MERCY!
IT'S NOT OVER YET, KEI-CHAN.
HUH?
GYU (SQUEEZE)
THERE'S A PENALTY FOR THE LOSER.
WHA!?
SFX: GETE (CACKLE) GETE
PLEASANT DAYS THAT ARE ALWAYS THE SAME.
TOMITAKE-SAN'S UNSETTLING STORY AND MY IMAGE OF HINAMIZAWA JUST DON'T MESH.

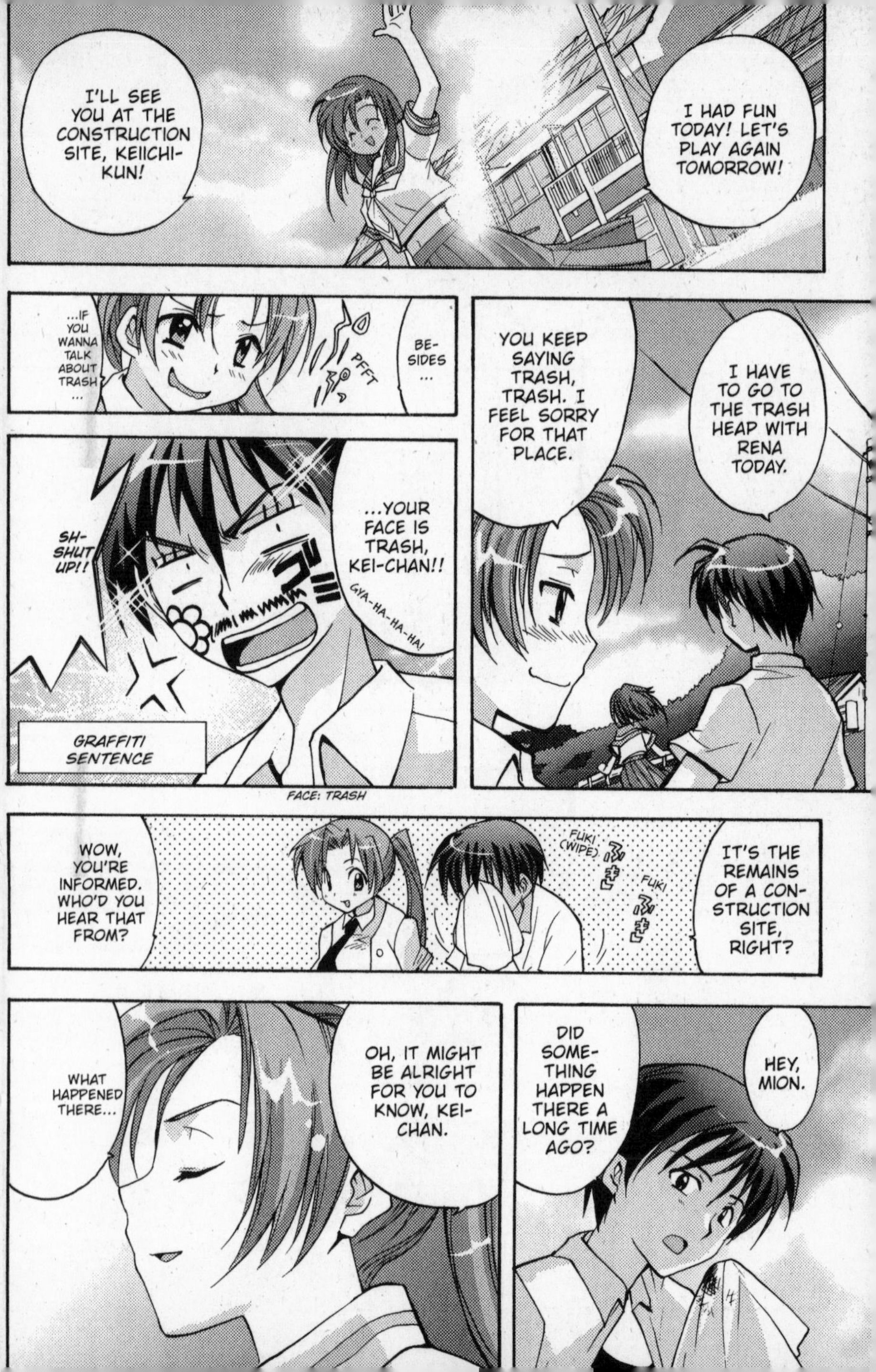
I HAD FUN TODAY! LET'S PLAY AGAIN TOMORROW!
I'LL SEE YOU AT THE CONSTRUCTION SITE, KEIICHI-KUN!
I HAVE TO GO TO THE TRASH HEAP WITH RENA TODAY.
YOU KEEP SAYING TRASH, TRASH. I FEEL SORRY FOR THAT PLACE.
BE-SIDES...
PFFT
...IF YOU WANNA TALK ABOUT TRASH...
...YOUR FACE IS TRASH, KEI-CHAN!!
GYA-HA-HA-HA!
SH-SHUT UP!!
GRAFFITI SENTENCE
FACE: TRASH
IT'S THE REMAINS OF A CON-STRUCTION SITE, RIGHT?
FUKI (WIPE)
FUKI
WOW, YOU'RE INFORMED. WHO'D YOU HEAR THAT FROM?
HEY, MION.
DID SOME-THING HAPPEN THERE A LONG TIME AGO?
OH, IT MIGHT BE ALRIGHT FOR YOU TO KNOW, KEI-CHAN.
WHAT HAPPENED THERE...

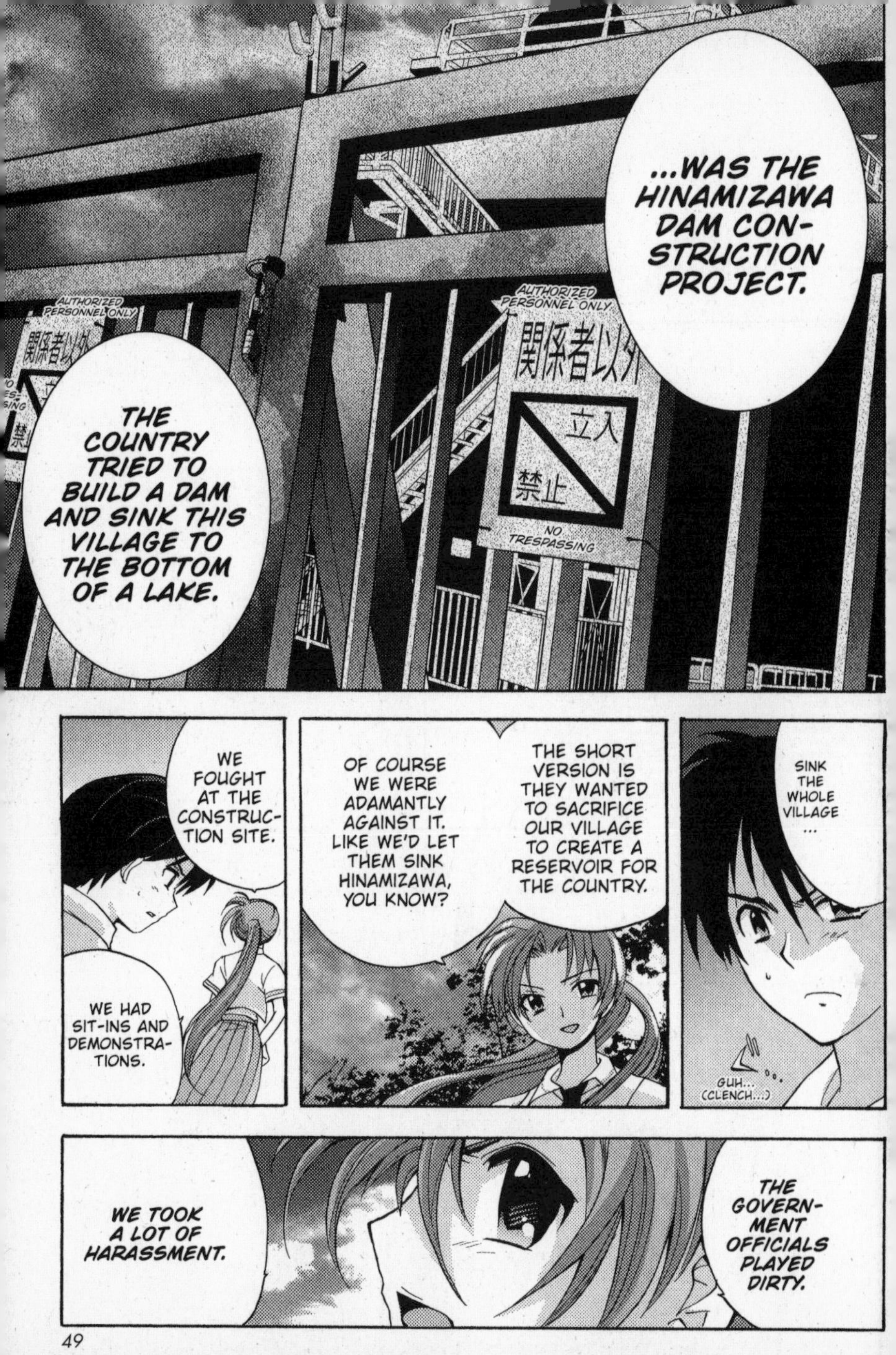
...WAS THE HINAMIZAWA DAM CONSTRUCTION PROJECT.
AUTHORIZED PERSONNEL ONLY
関係者以外
立入禁止
NO TRESPASSING
AUTHORIZED PERSONNEL ONLY
THE COUNTRY TRIED TO BUILD A DAM AND SINK THIS VILLAGE TO THE BOTTOM OF A LAKE.
SINK THE WHOLE VILLAGE ...
GUH... (CLENCH...)
THE SHORT VERSION IS THEY WANTED TO SACRIFICE OUR VILLAGE TO CREATE A RESERVOIR FOR THE COUNTRY.
OF COURSE WE WERE ADAMANTLY AGAINST IT. LIKE WE'D LET THEM SINK HINAMIZAWA, YOU KNOW?
WE FOUGHT AT THE CONSTRUCTION SITE.
WE HAD SIT-INS AND DEMONSTRATIONS.
THE GOVERNMENT OFFICIALS PLAYED DIRTY.
WE TOOK A LOT OF HARASSMENT.

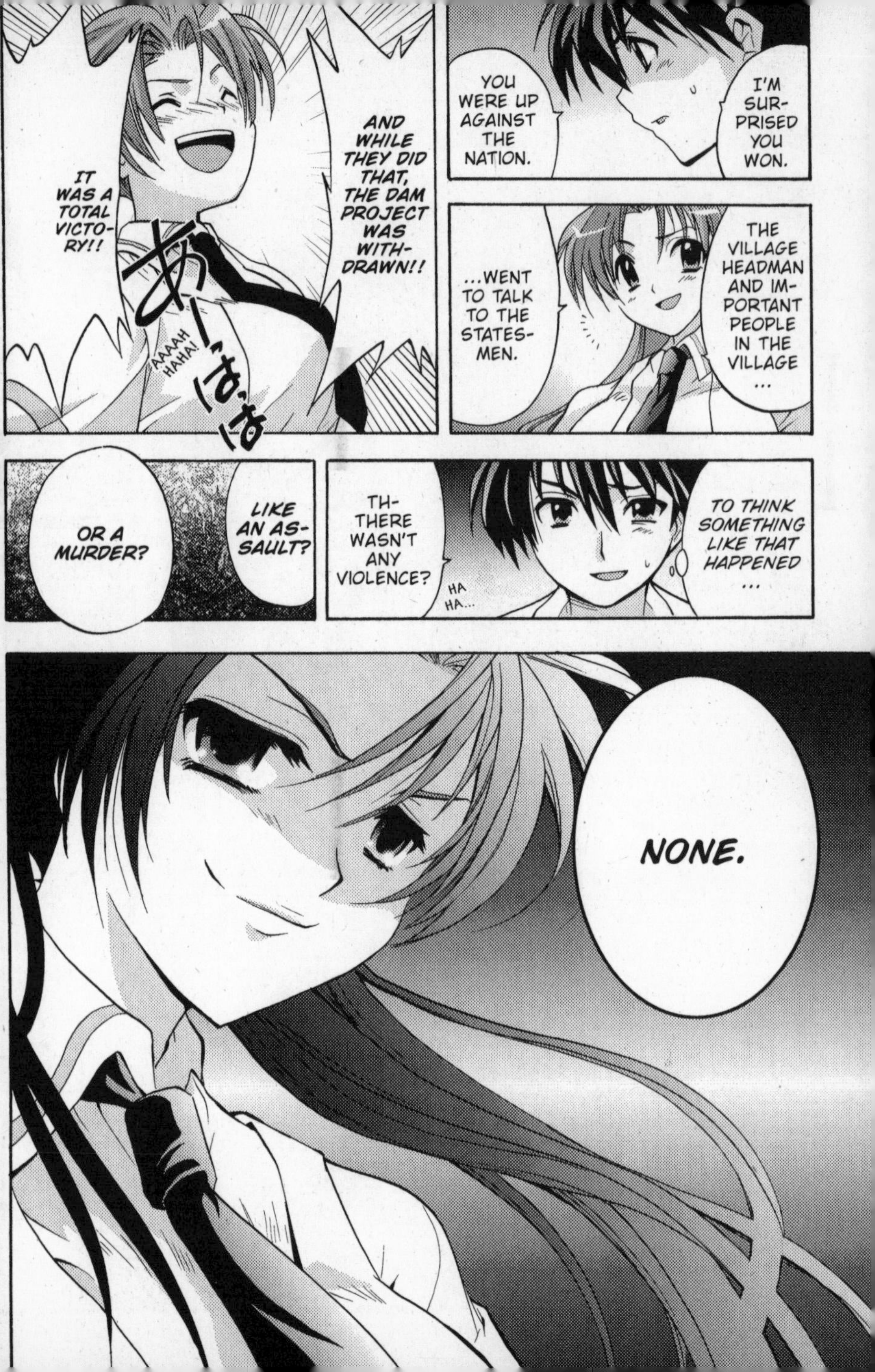
I'M SUR-PRISED YOU WON.
YOU WERE UP AGAINST THE NATION.
THE VILLAGE HEADMAN AND IM-PORTANT PEOPLE IN THE VILLAGE ...
...WENT TO TALK TO THE STATES-MEN.
AND WHILE THEY DID THAT, THE DAM PROJECT WAS WITH-DRAWN!!
IT WAS A TOTAL VICTO-RY!!
あーはっは
AAAAH HAHA!
TO THINK SOMETHING LIKE THAT HAPPENED ...
HA HA...
TH-THERE WASN'T ANY VIOLENCE?
LIKE AN AS-SAULT?
OR A MURDER?
NONE.

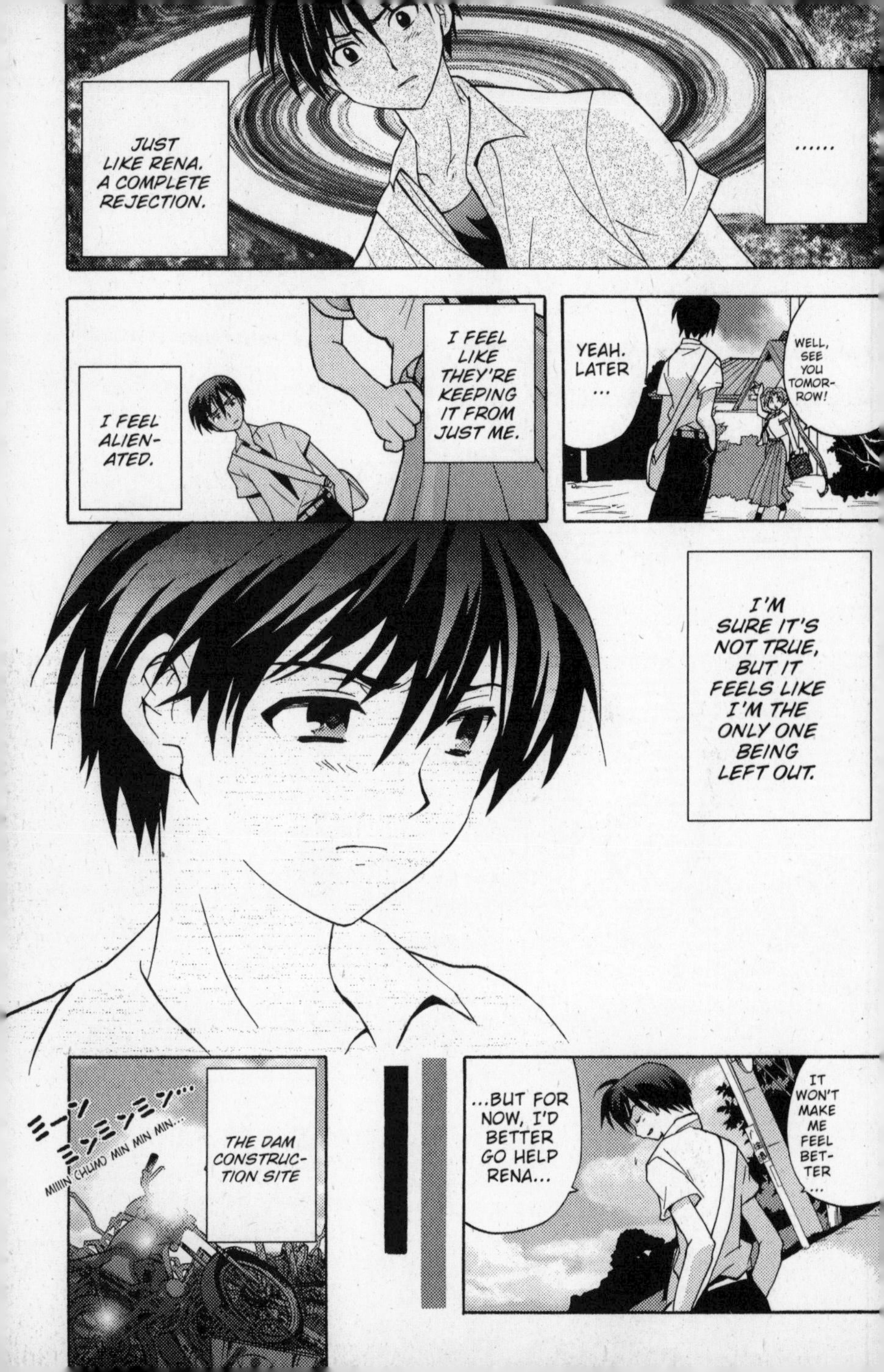
......
JUST LIKE RENA. A COMPLETE REJECTION.
WELL, SEE YOU TOMORROW!
YEAH. LATER...
I FEEL LIKE THEY'RE KEEPING IT FROM JUST ME.
I FEEL ALIENATED.
I'M SURE IT'S NOT TRUE, BUT IT FEELS LIKE I'M THE ONLY ONE BEING LEFT OUT.
IT WON'T MAKE ME FEEL BETTER...
...BUT FOR NOW, I'D BETTER GO HELP RENA...
THE DAM CONSTRUCTION SITE
ミーンミンミンミン…
MIIIIN CHUMD MIN MIN MIN...

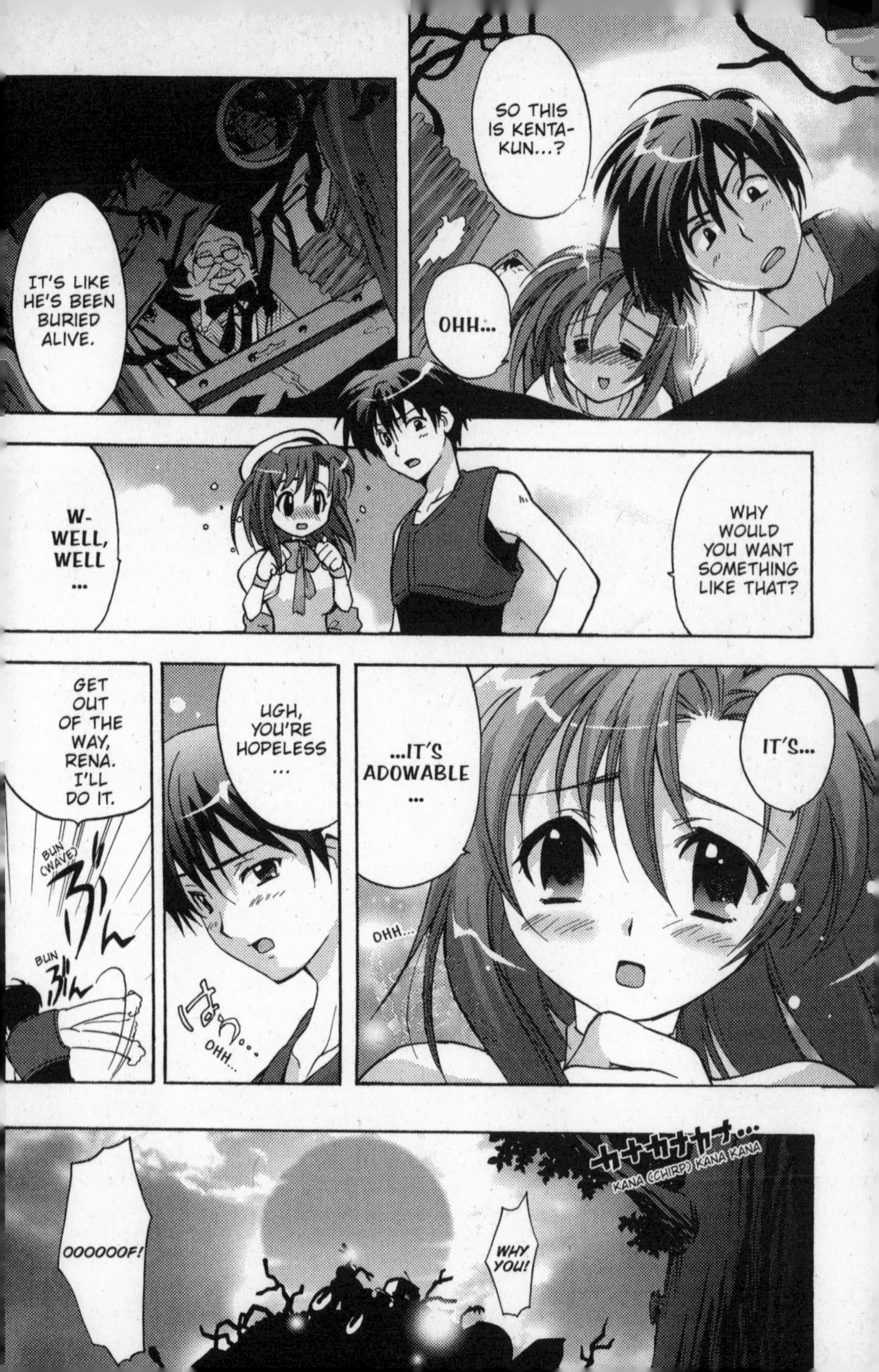
SO THIS IS KENTA-KUN...?
OHH...
IT'S LIKE HE'S BEEN BURIED ALIVE.
WHY WOULD YOU WANT SOMETHING LIKE THAT?
W-WELL, WELL ...
IT'S...
...IT'S ADOWABLE ...
OHH...
UGH, YOU'RE HOPELESS ...
OHH...
GET OUT OF THE WAY, RENA. I'LL DO IT.
BUN (WAVE)
BUN
KANA (CHIRP) KANA KANA
WHY YOU!
OOOOOOF!

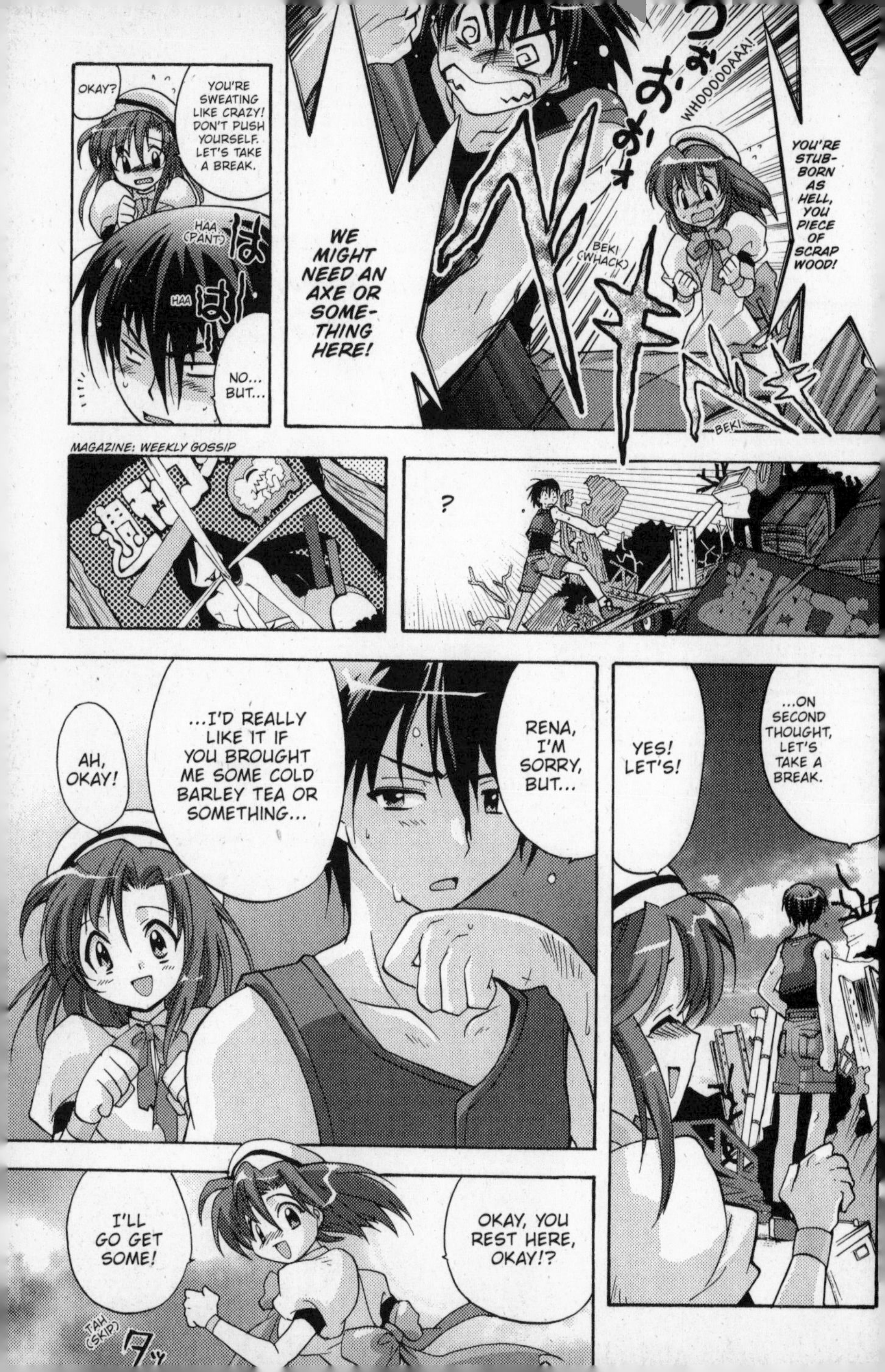
WHOOOOOAAA!
YOU'RE STUB- BORN AS HELL, YOU PIECE OF SCRAP WOOD!
BEKI (WHACK)
BEKI
WE MIGHT NEED AN AXE OR SOME- THING HERE!
YOU'RE SWEATING LIKE CRAZY! DON'T PUSH YOURSELF. LET'S TAKE A BREAK.
OKAY?
HAA (PANT)
HAA
NO... BUT...
?
MAGAZINE: WEEKLY GOSSIP
...ON SECOND THOUGHT, LET'S TAKE A BREAK.
YES! LET'S!
RENA, I'M SORRY, BUT...
...I'D REALLY LIKE IT IF YOU BROUGHT ME SOME COLD BARLEY TEA OR SOMETHING...
AH, OKAY!
OKAY, YOU REST HERE, OKAY!?
I'LL GO GET SOME!
TAH (SKIP)

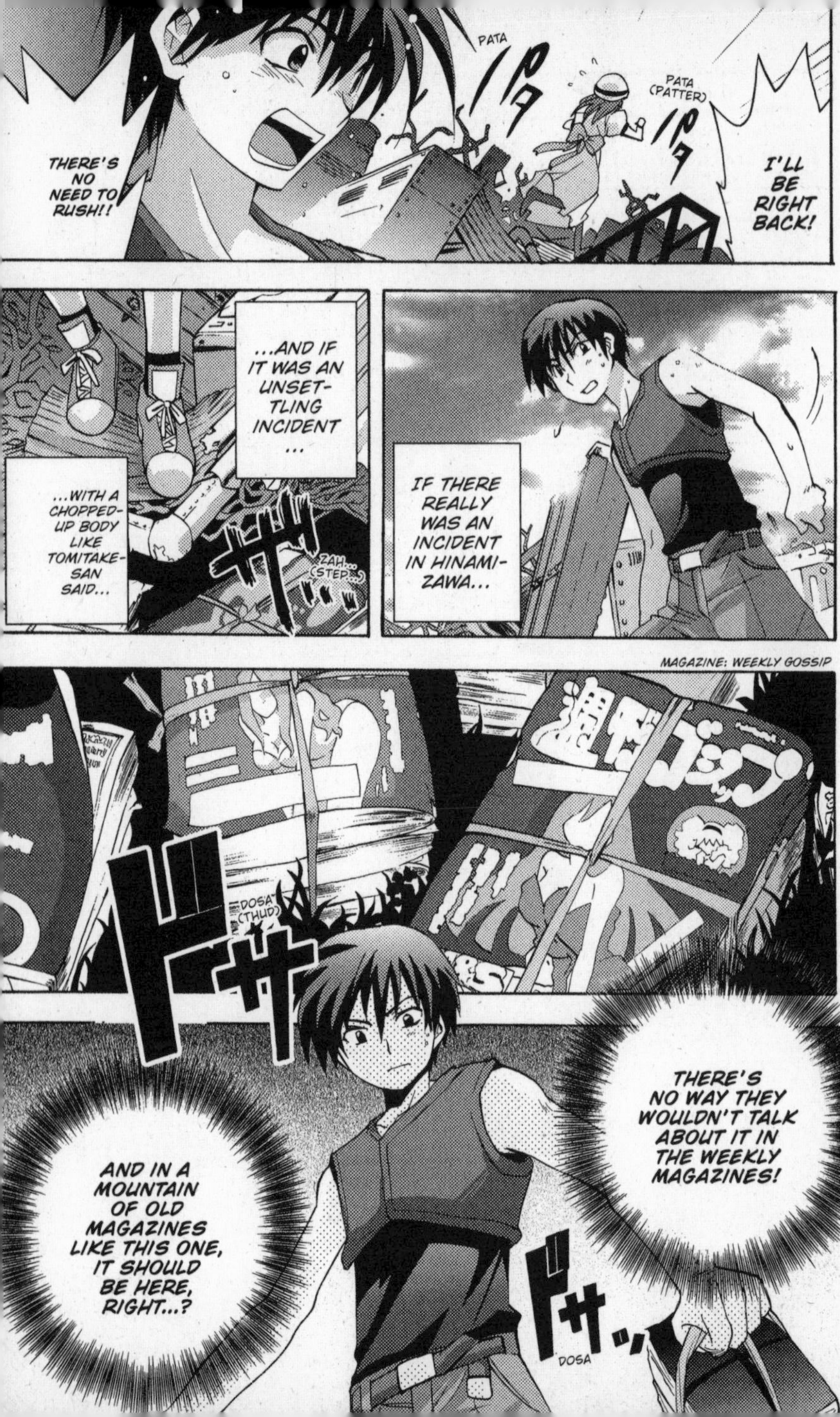
I'LL BE RIGHT BACK!
PATA (PATTER)
PATA
THERE'S NO NEED TO RUSH!!
IF THERE REALLY WAS AN INCIDENT IN HINAMI-ZAWA...
...AND IF IT WAS AN UNSET-TLING INCIDENT ...
ZAH... (STEP...)
...WITH A CHOPPED-UP BODY LIKE TOMITAKE-SAN SAID...
MAGAZINE: WEEKLY GOSSIP
DOSA (THUD)
THERE'S NO WAY THEY WOULDN'T TALK ABOUT IT IN THE WEEKLY MAGAZINES!
DOSA
AND IN A MOUNTAIN OF OLD MAGAZINES LIKE THIS ONE, IT SHOULD BE HERE, RIGHT...?

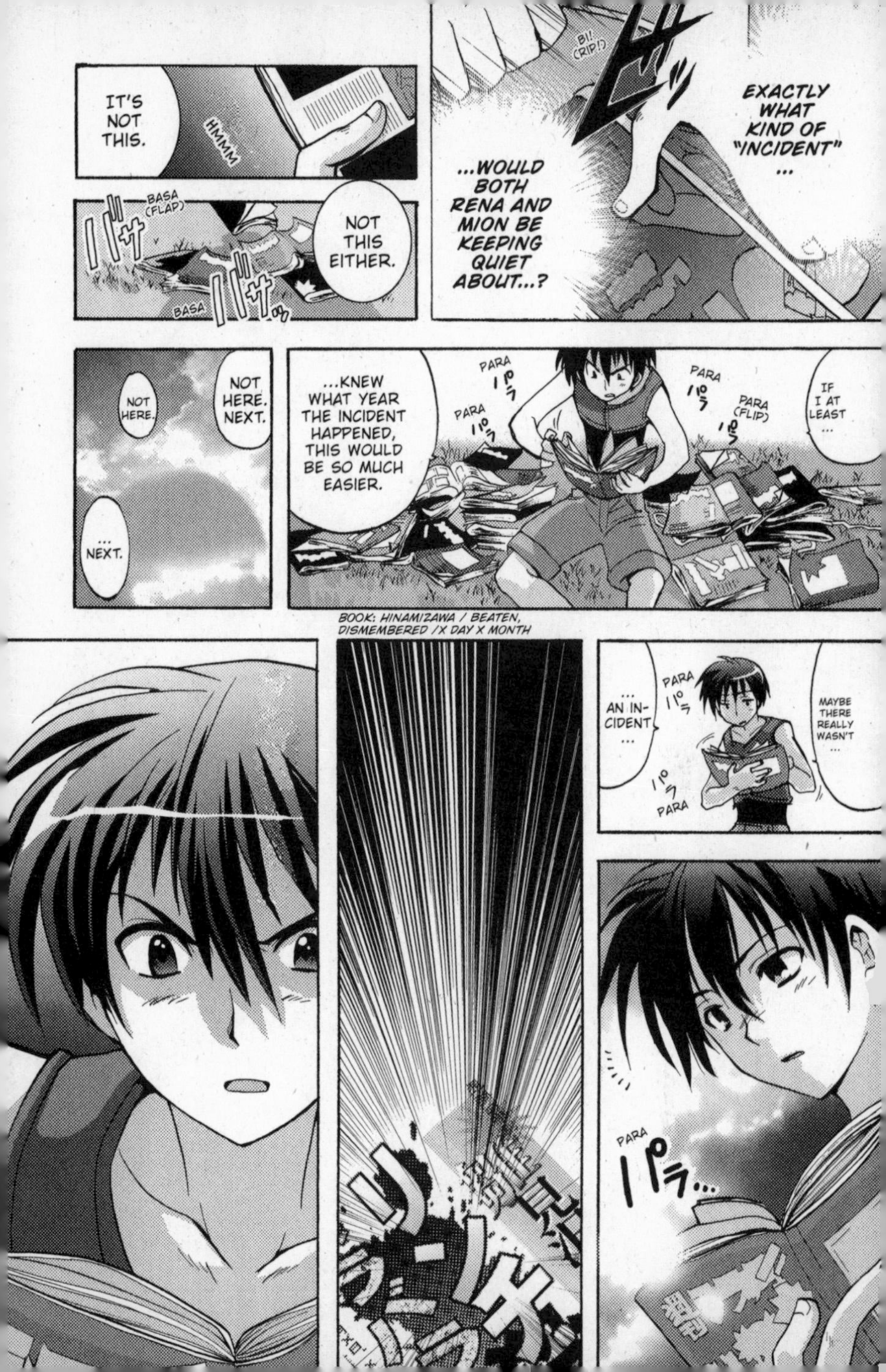
BI! (RIP!)
EXACTLY WHAT KIND OF "INCIDENT"...
...WOULD BOTH RENA AND MION BE KEEPING QUIET ABOUT...?
IT'S NOT THIS.
HMMM
BASA (FLAP)
NOT THIS EITHER.
BASA
IF I AT LEAST...
PARA
PARA (FLIP)
PARA
PARA
...KNEW WHAT YEAR THE INCIDENT HAPPENED, THIS WOULD BE SO MUCH EASIER.
NOT HERE. NEXT.
NOT HERE.
...NEXT.
BOOK: HINAMIZAWA / BEATEN, DISMEMBERED /X DAY X MONTH
MAYBE THERE REALLY WASN'T...
PARA
...AN INCIDENT...
PARA
PARA

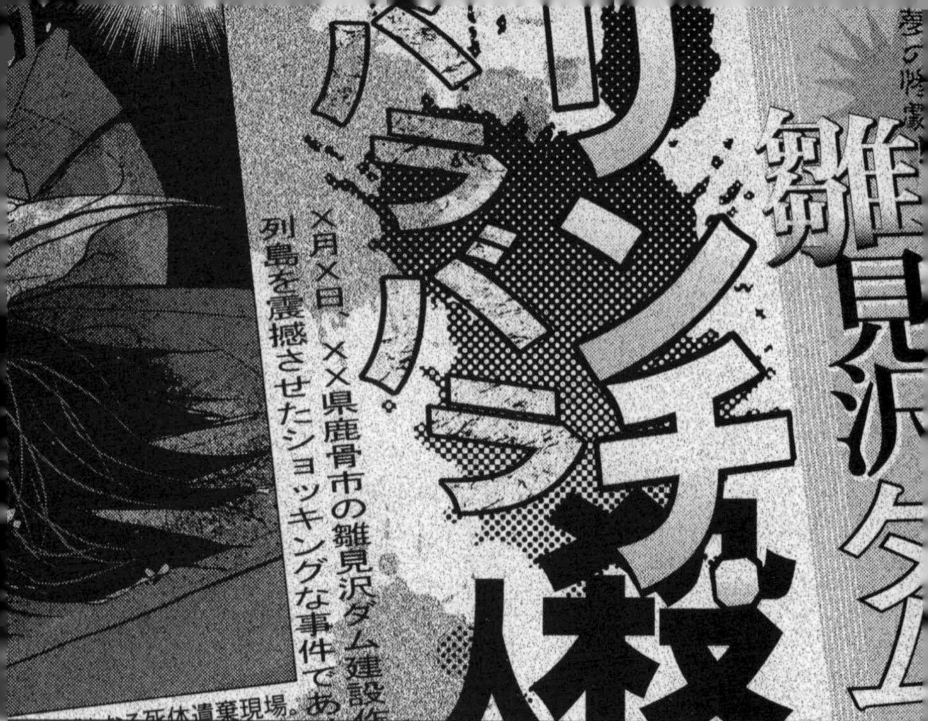
夢の惨劇
雛見沢ダム
撲殺
バラバラ殺人
×月×日、××県鹿骨市の雛見沢ダム建設作
列島を震撼させたショッキングな事件であ
死体遺棄現場。

BOOK: NIGHTMARISH TRAGEDY / HINAMIZAWA DAM / BEATEN, DISMEMBERED BODY / X MONTH, X DAY, XX PREFECTURE, SHISHIBONE CITY. THE HINAMIZAWA DAM PROJECT IS... / BY A SHOCKING INCIDENT THAT SHOOK UP THE ISLANDS... / WHERE THE BODY WAS LEFT...

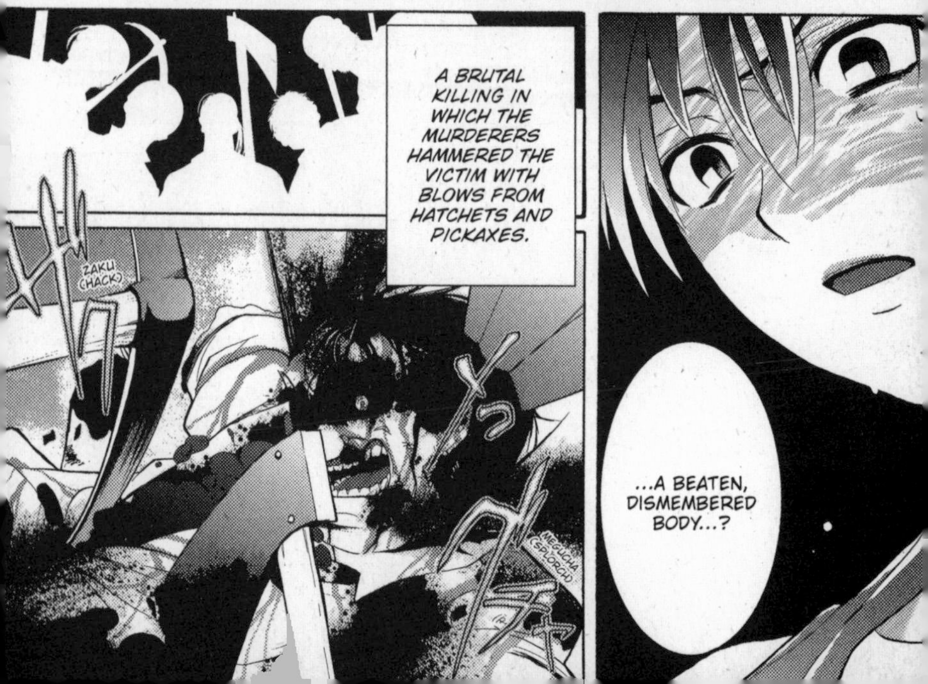
...A BEATEN, DISMEMBERED BODY...?
A BRUTAL KILLING IN WHICH THE MURDERERS HAMMERED THE VICTIM WITH BLOWS FROM HATCHETS AND PICKAXES.
ZAKU (HACK)
NEGUCHA (SPLORCH)

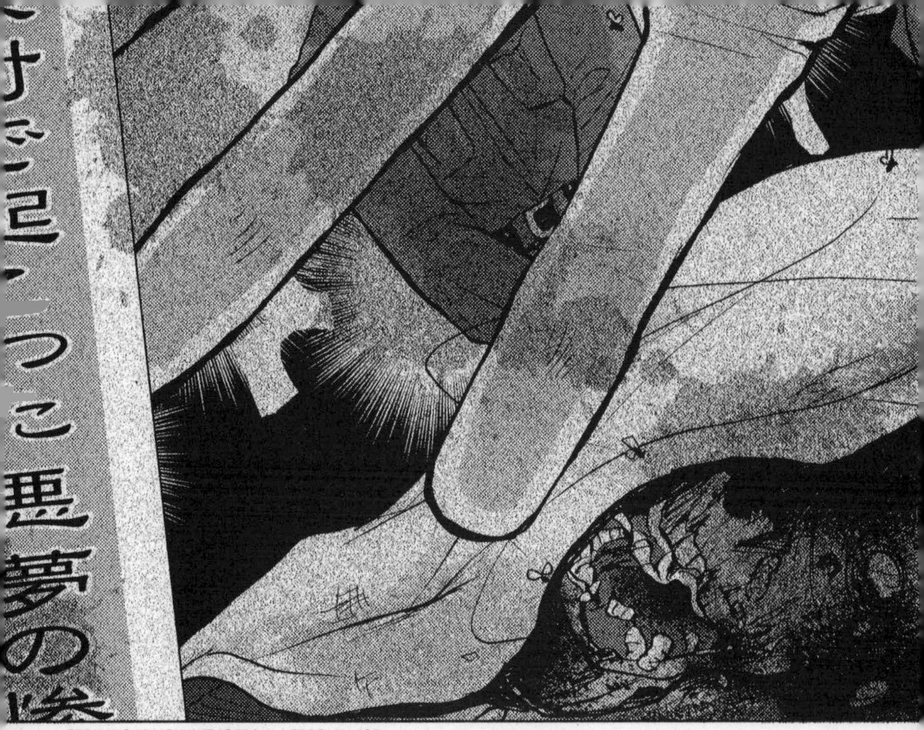

BOOK: NIGHTMARISH TRAGEDY IN A POOR VILLAGE

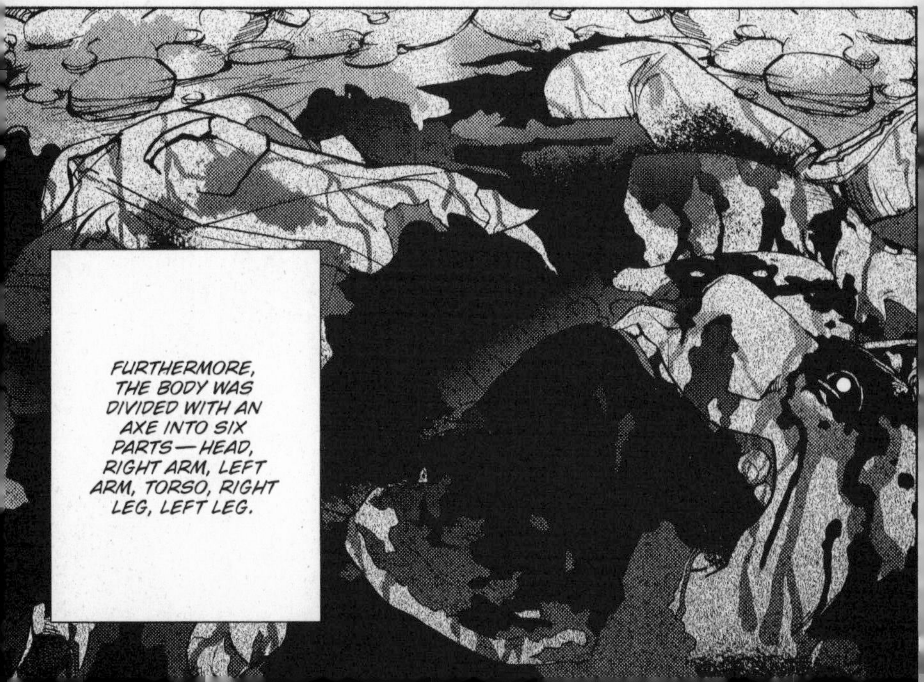
FURTHERMORE, THE BODY WAS DIVIDED WITH AN AXE INTO SIX PARTS—HEAD, RIGHT ARM, LEFT ARM, TORSO, RIGHT LEG, LEFT LEG.

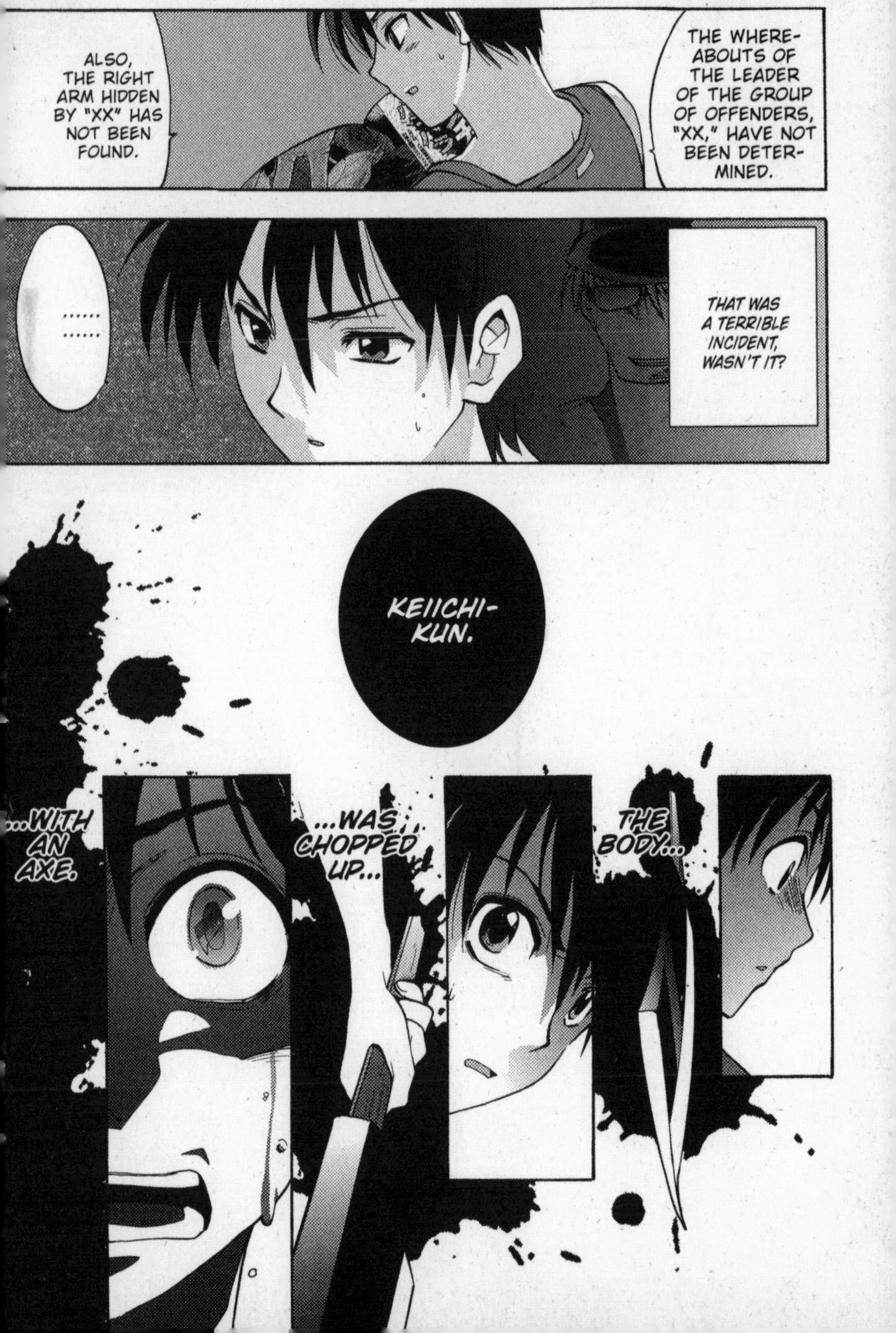
THE WHERE-ABOUTS OF THE LEADER OF THE GROUP OF OFFENDERS, "XX," HAVE NOT BEEN DETER-MINED.
ALSO, THE RIGHT ARM HIDDEN BY "XX" HAS NOT BEEN FOUND.
THAT WAS A TERRIBLE INCIDENT, WASN'T IT?
....
KEIICHI-KUN.
THE BODY...
...WAS CHOPPED UP...
...WITH AN AXE.

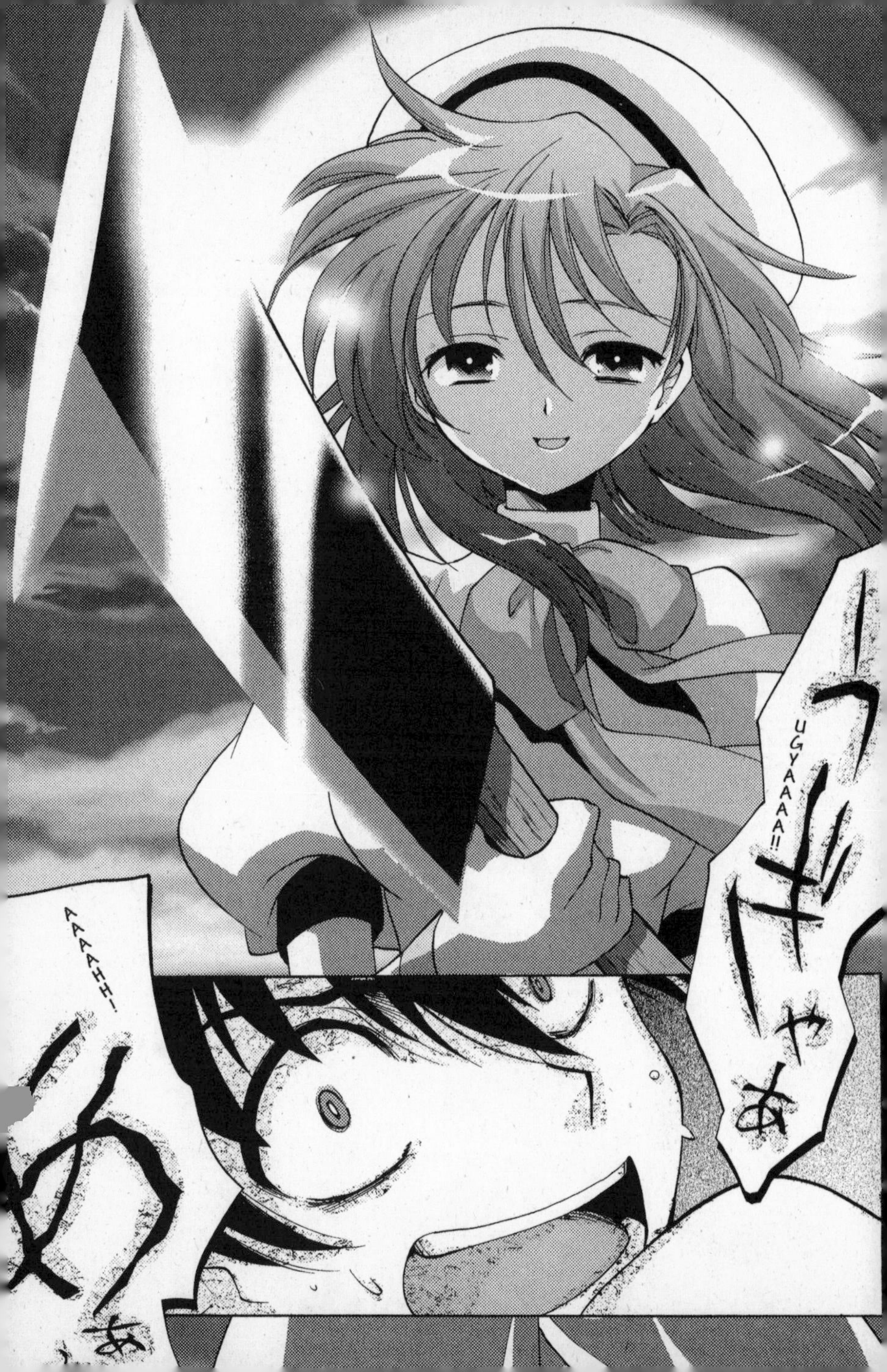
UGYAAAA!!
AAAAHH!

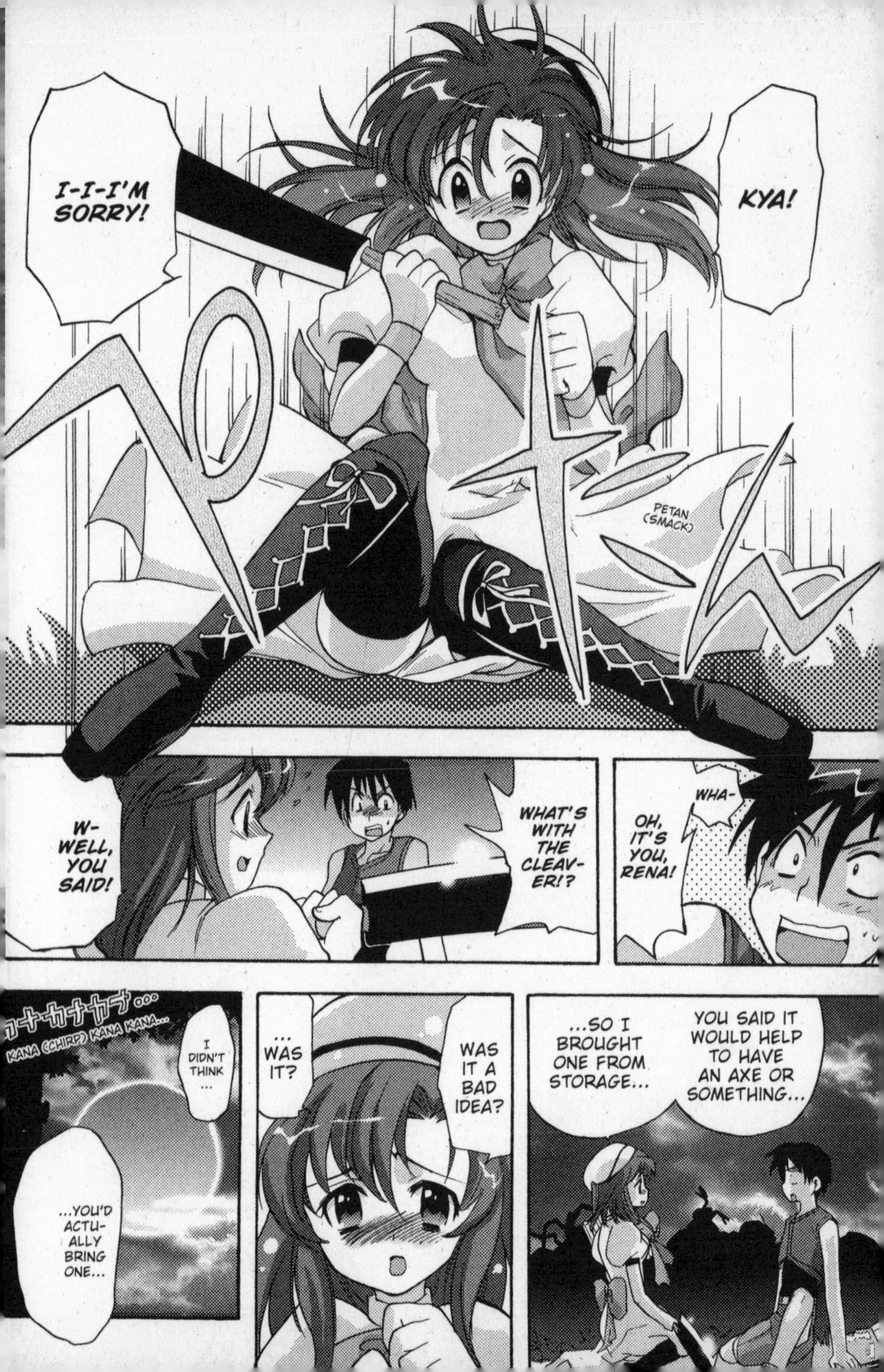
KYA!
I-I-I'M SORRY!
PETAN (SMACK)
WHA-
OH, IT'S YOU, RENA!
WHAT'S WITH THE CLEAVER!?
W-WELL, YOU SAID!
YOU SAID IT WOULD HELP TO HAVE AN AXE OR SOMETHING...
...SO I BROUGHT ONE FROM STORAGE...
WAS IT A BAD IDEA?
...WAS IT?
KANA (CHIRP) KANA KANA...
I DIDN'T THINK...
...YOU'D ACTUALLY BRING ONE...

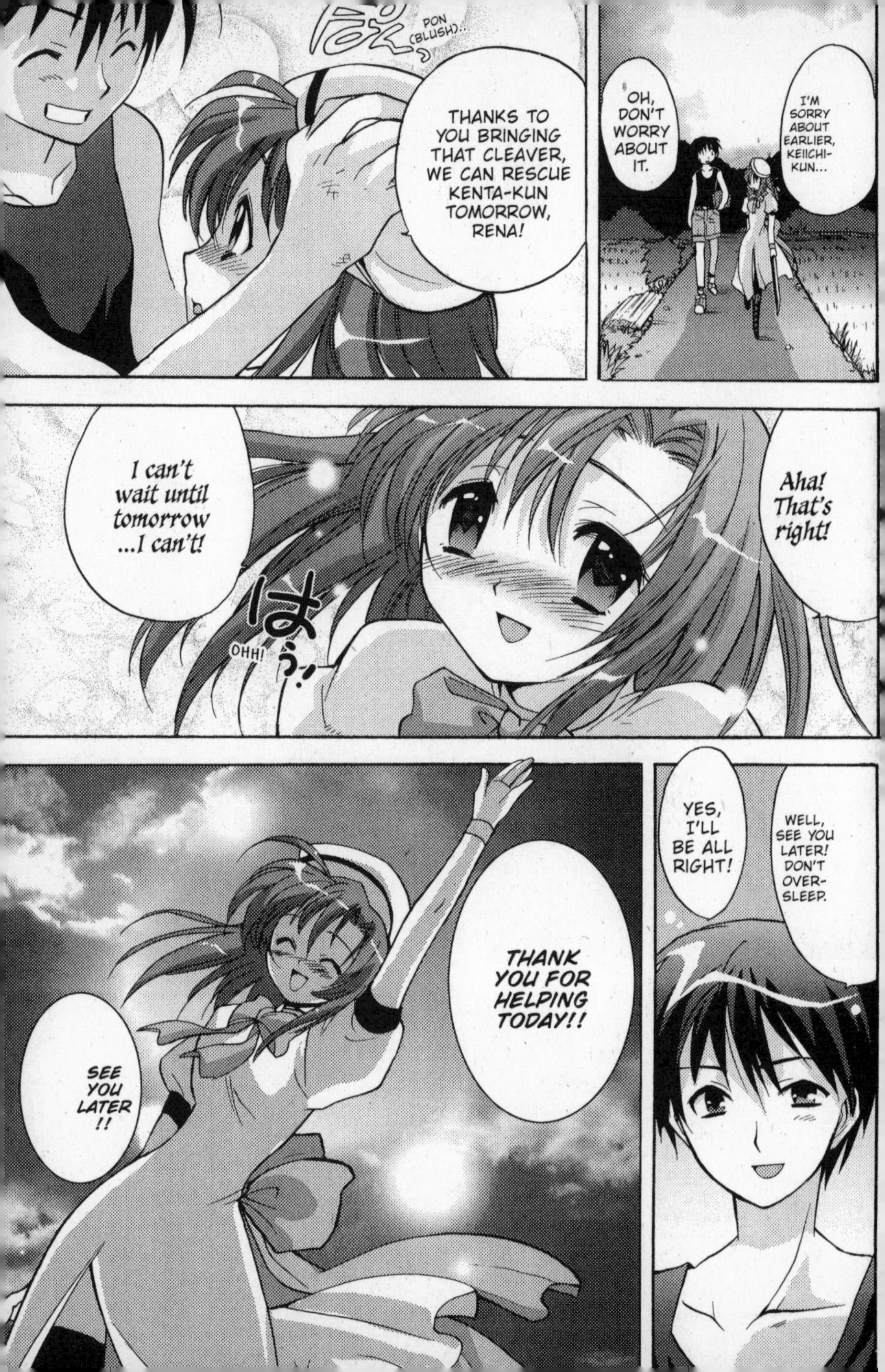
I'M SORRY ABOUT EARLIER, KEIICHI-KUN...
OH, DON'T WORRY ABOUT IT.
PON (BLUSH)...
THANKS TO YOU BRINGING THAT CLEAVER, WE CAN RESCUE KENTA-KUN TOMORROW, RENA!
Aha! That's right!
I can't wait until tomorrow ...I can't!
はぅ
OHH!
WELL, SEE YOU LATER! DON'T OVER-SLEEP.
YES, I'LL BE ALL RIGHT!
THANK YOU FOR HELPING TODAY!!
SEE YOU LATER!!

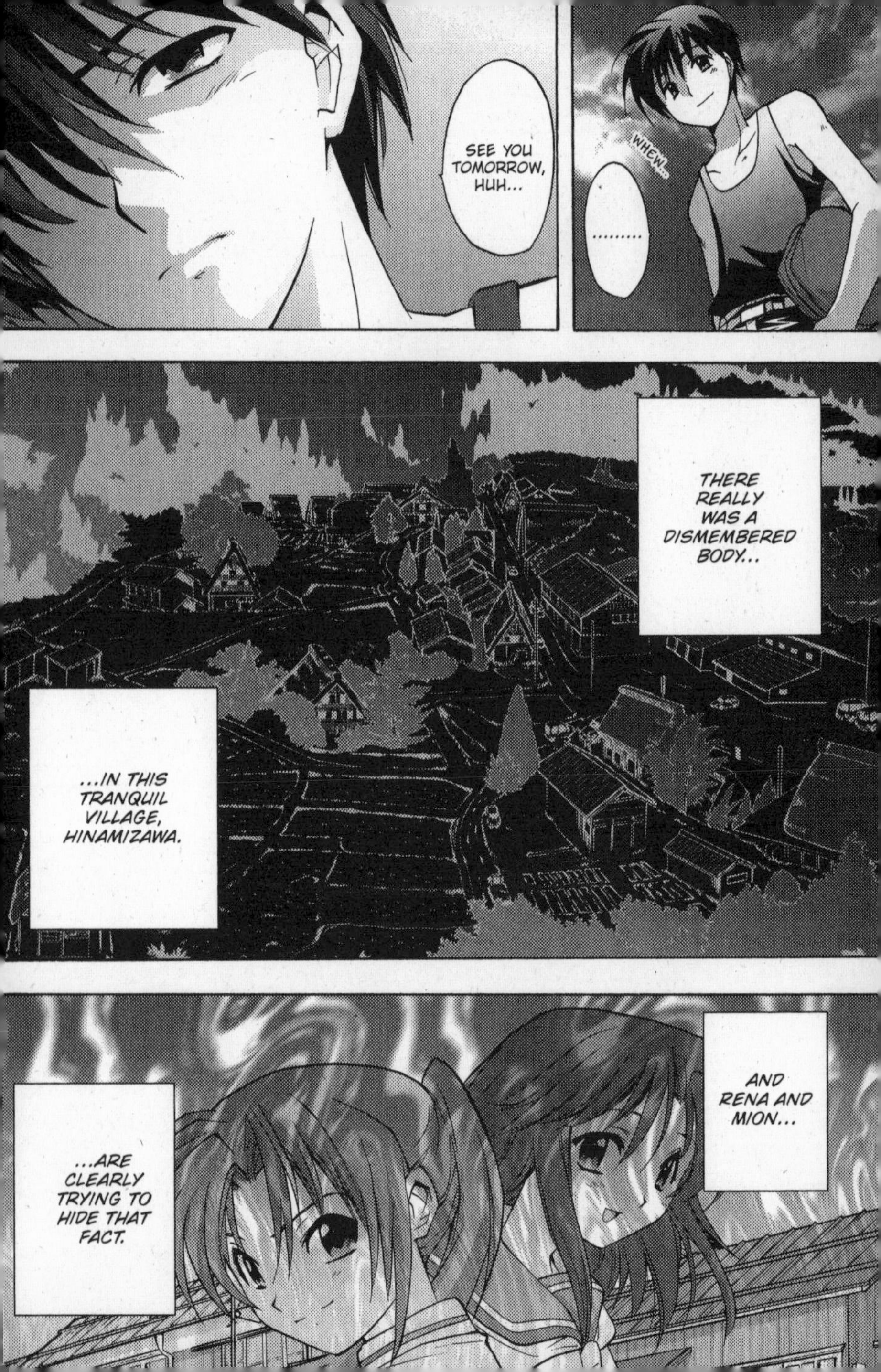
WHEW...
....
SEE YOU TOMORROW, HUH...
THERE REALLY WAS A DISMEMBERED BODY...
...IN THIS TRANQUIL VILLAGE, HINAMIZAWA.
AND RENA AND MION...
...ARE CLEARLY TRYING TO HIDE THAT FACT.

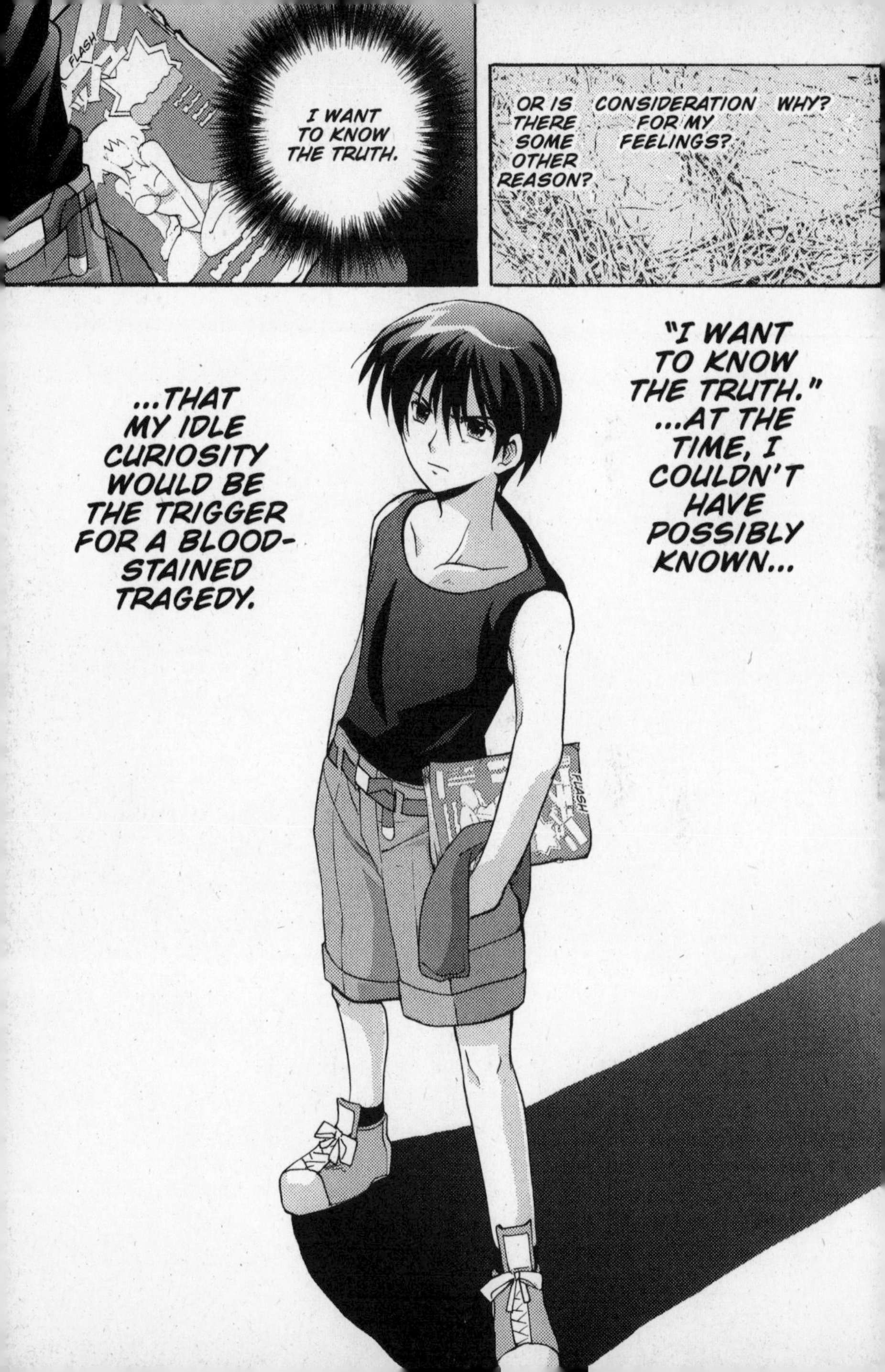
WHY?
CONSIDERATION FOR MY FEELINGS?
OR IS THERE SOME OTHER REASON?
FLASH
I WANT TO KNOW THE TRUTH.
"I WANT TO KNOW THE TRUTH." ...AT THE TIME, I COULDN'T HAVE POSSIBLY KNOWN...
...THAT MY IDLE CURIOSITY WOULD BE THE TRIGGER FOR A BLOOD-STAINED TRAGEDY.
FLASH

OMAKE ①

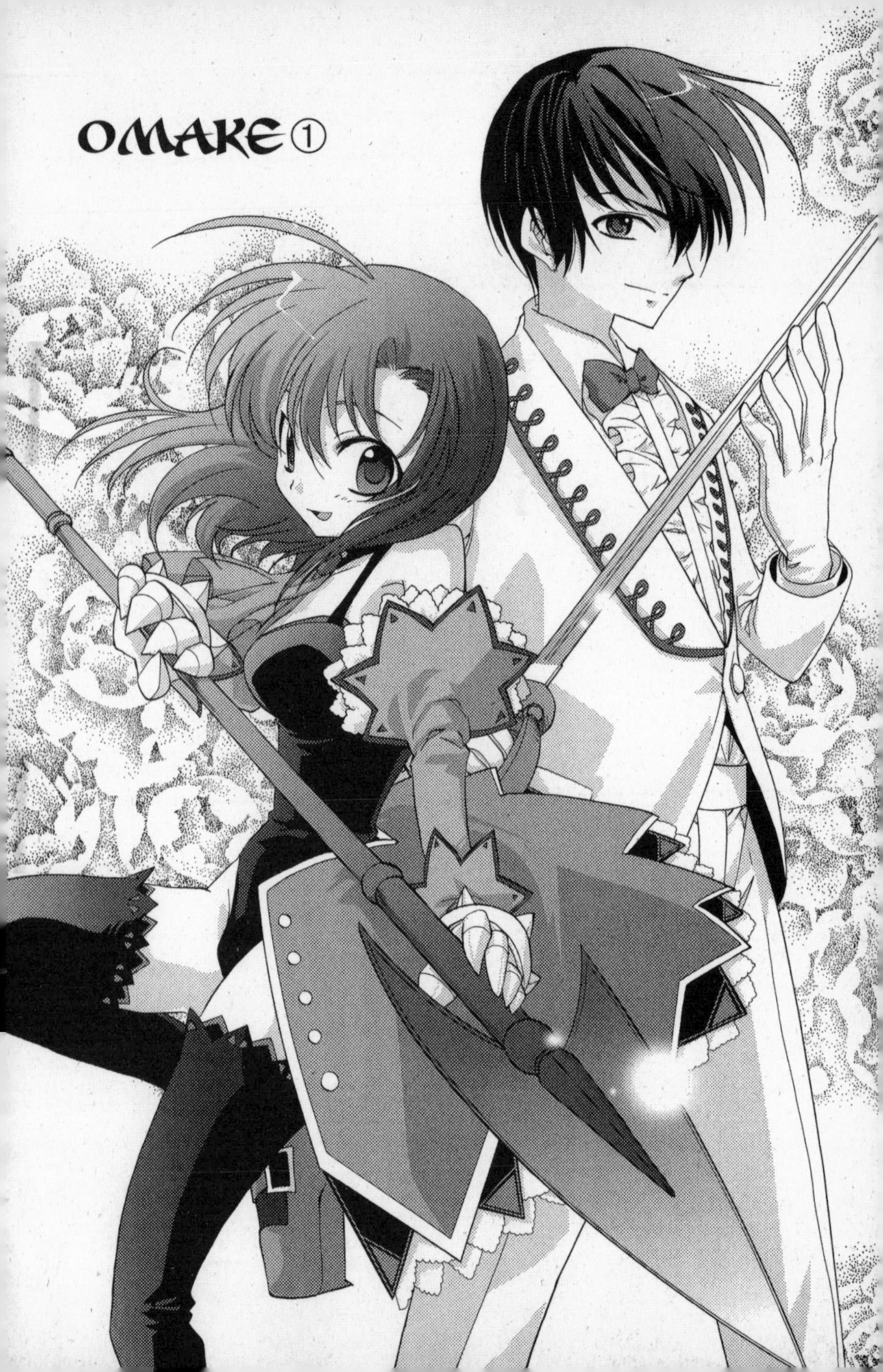

BONUS MANGA: "IT'S STUDY TIME"

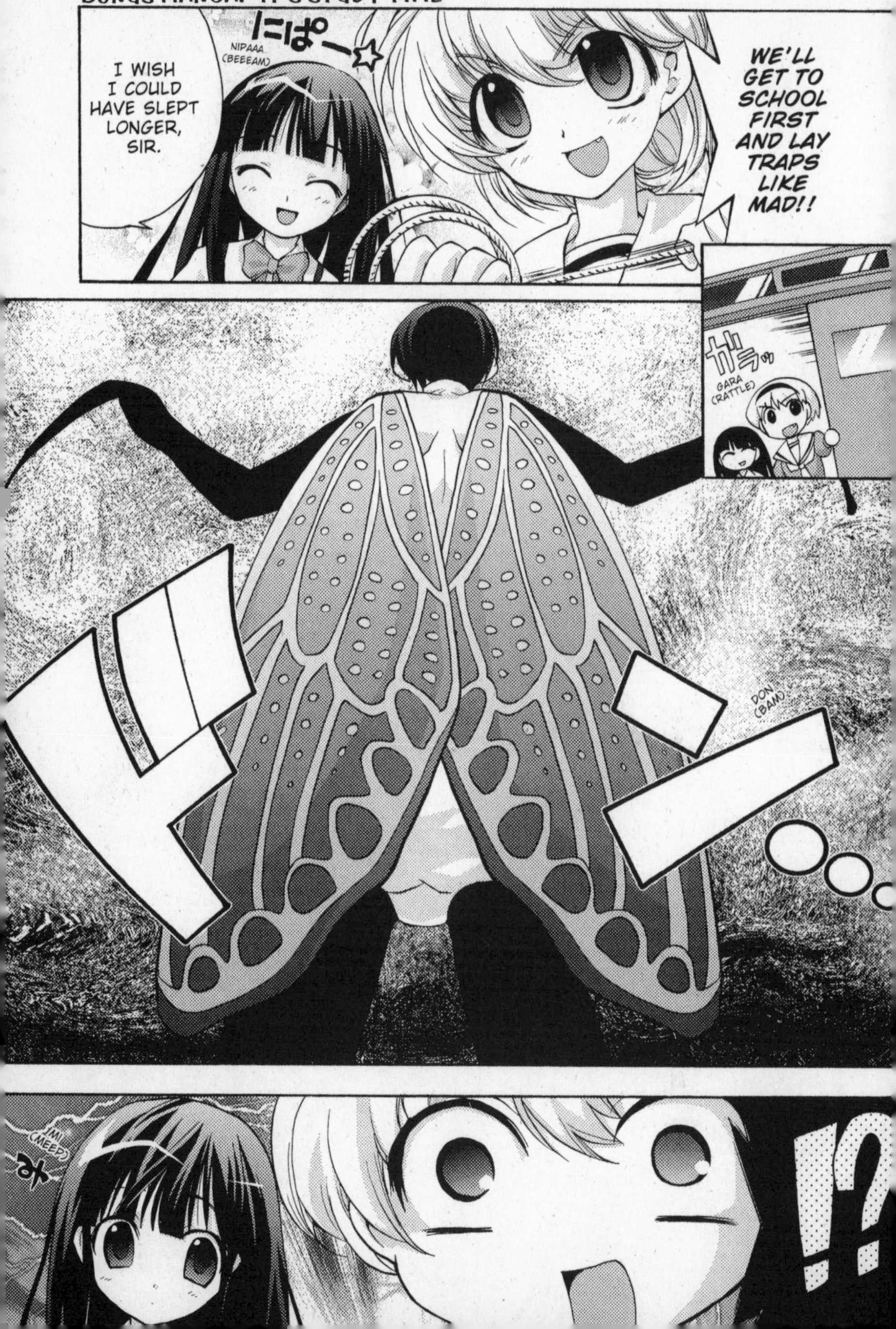
WE'LL GET TO SCHOOL FIRST AND LAY TRAPS LIKE MAD!!
にぱー☆
NIPAAA (BEEEAM)
I WISH I COULD HAVE SLEPT LONGER, SIR.
ガラッ
GARA (RATTLE)
DON (BAM)
...
!?
み
MI (MEEP)

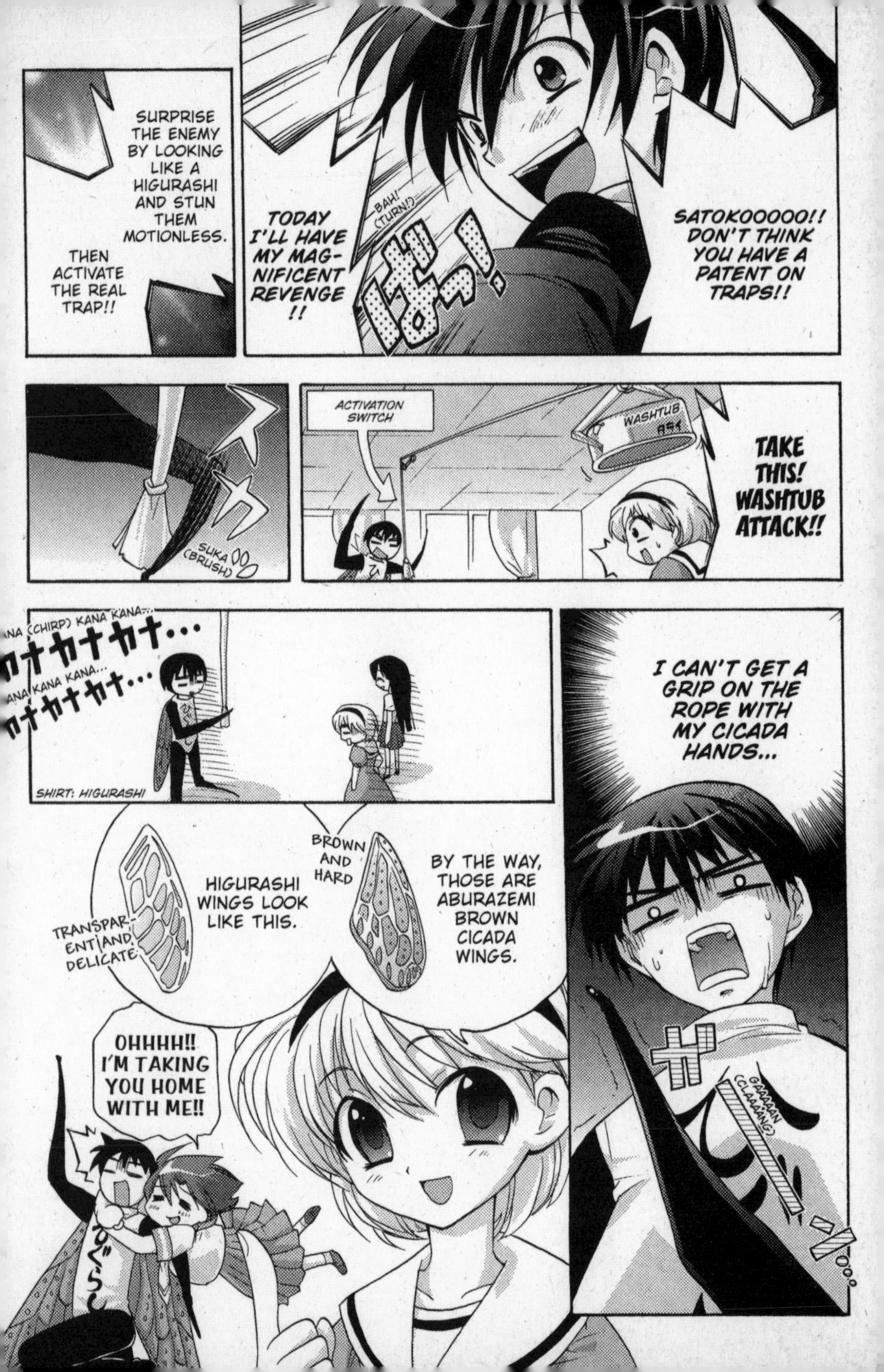
SATOKOOOOO!! DON'T THINK YOU HAVE A PATENT ON TRAPS!!
BAH! (TURN!)
TODAY I'LL HAVE MY MAGNIFICENT REVENGE!!
SURPRISE THE ENEMY BY LOOKING LIKE A HIGURASHI AND STUN THEM MOTIONLESS.
THEN ACTIVATE THE REAL TRAP!!
TAKE THIS! WASHTUB ATTACK!!
WASHTUB
ACTIVATION SWITCH
SUKA (BRUSH)
I CAN'T GET A GRIP ON THE ROPE WITH MY CICADA HANDS...
GAAAAAN (CLAAAANG)
ANA (CHIRP) KANA KANA...
ANA KANA KANA...
SHIRT: HIGURASHI
BY THE WAY, THOSE ARE ABURAZEMI BROWN CICADA WINGS.
BROWN AND HARD
HIGURASHI WINGS LOOK LIKE THIS.
TRANSPARENT AND DELICATE
OHHHH!! I'M TAKING YOU HOME WITH ME!!

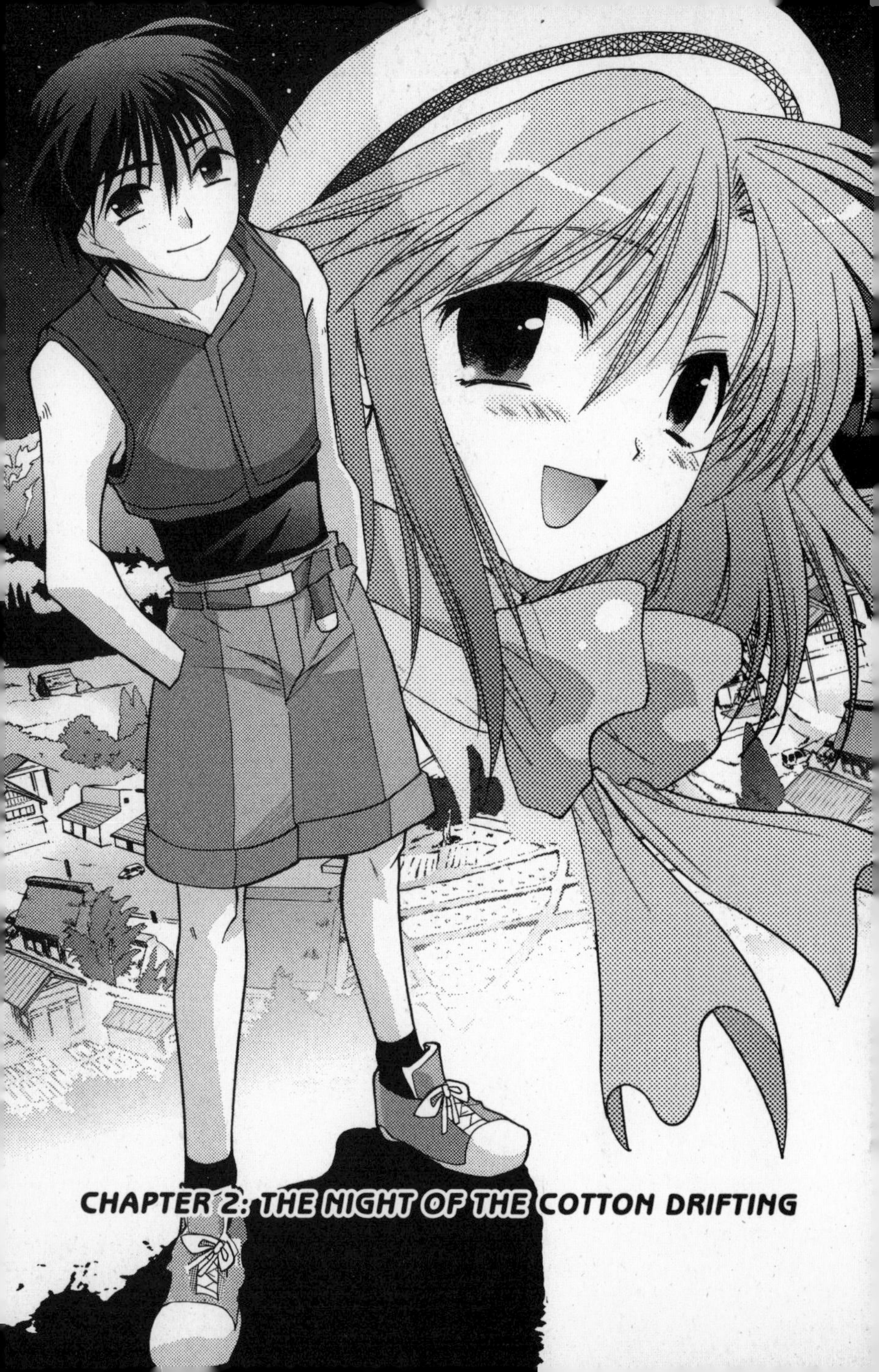

CHAPTER 2: THE NIGHT OF THE COTTON DRIFTING

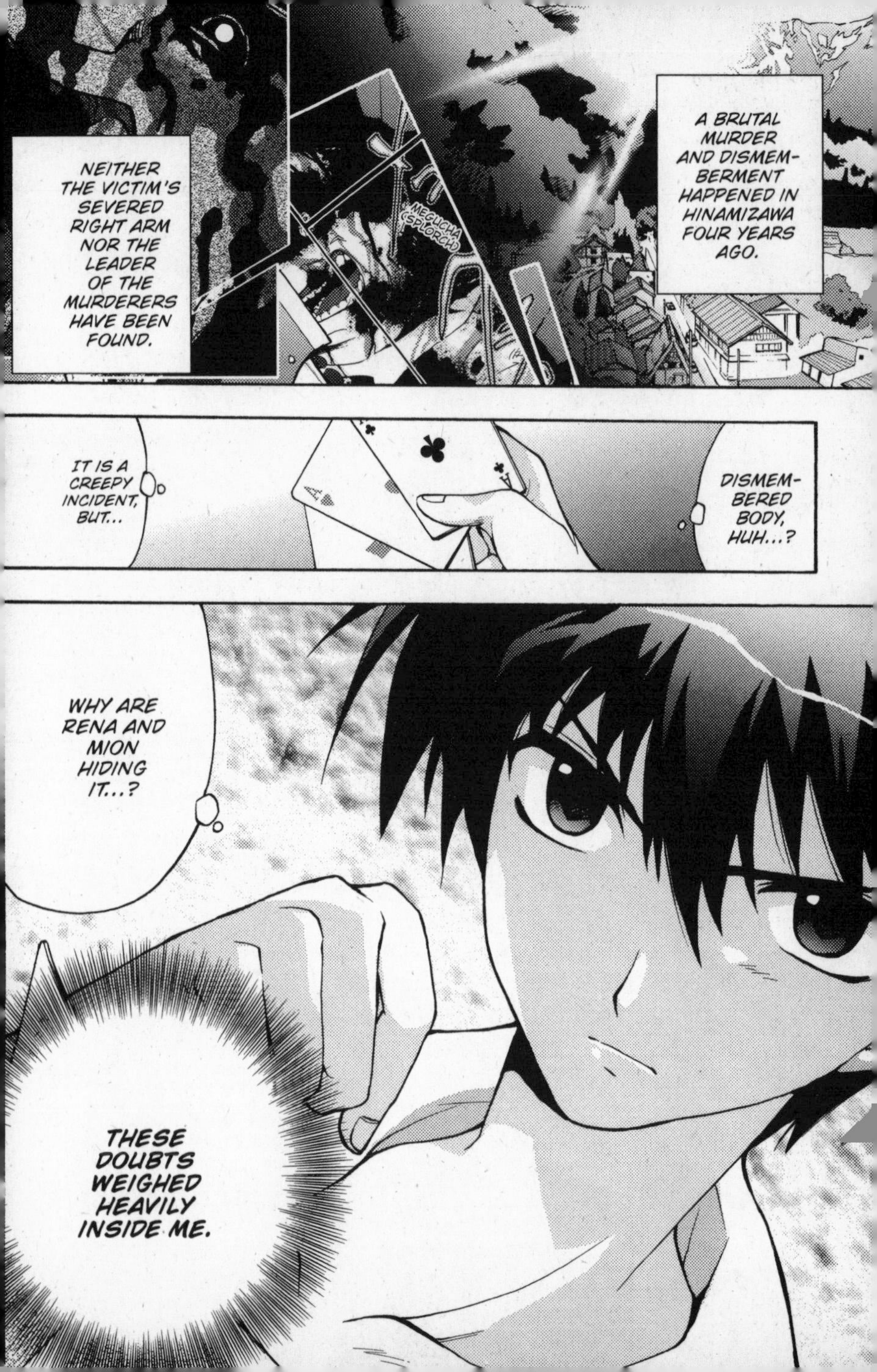
A BRUTAL MURDER AND DISMEMBERMENT HAPPENED IN HINAMIZAWA FOUR YEARS AGO.
MEGUCHA (SPLORCH)
NEITHER THE VICTIM'S SEVERED RIGHT ARM NOR THE LEADER OF THE MURDERERS HAVE BEEN FOUND.
DISMEMBERED BODY, HUH...?
IT IS A CREEPY INCIDENT, BUT...
WHY ARE RENA AND MION HIDING IT...?
THESE DOUBTS WEIGHED HEAVILY INSIDE ME.

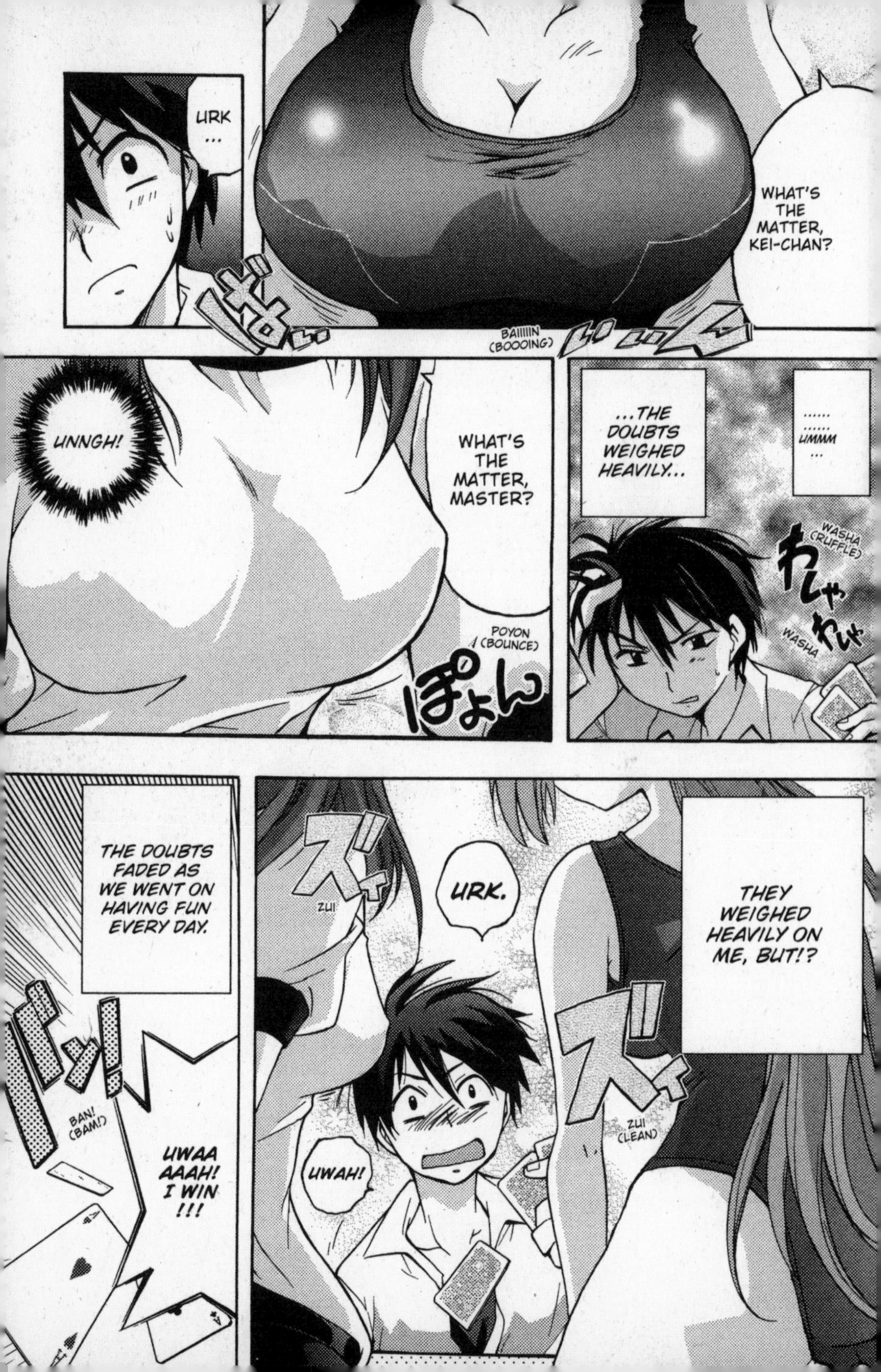
WHAT'S THE MATTER, KEI-CHAN?
BAIIIIN (BOOOING)
URK ...
.... UMMM ...
...THE DOUBTS WEIGHED HEAVILY...
WASHA (RUFFLE)
WASHA
WHAT'S THE MATTER, MASTER?
UNNGH!
POYON (BOUNCE)
THEY WEIGHED HEAVILY ON ME, BUT!?
ZUI (LEAN)
URK.
ZUI
UWAH!
THE DOUBTS FADED AS WE WENT ON HAVING FUN EVERY DAY.
BAN! (BAM!)
UWAA AAAH! I WIN !!!

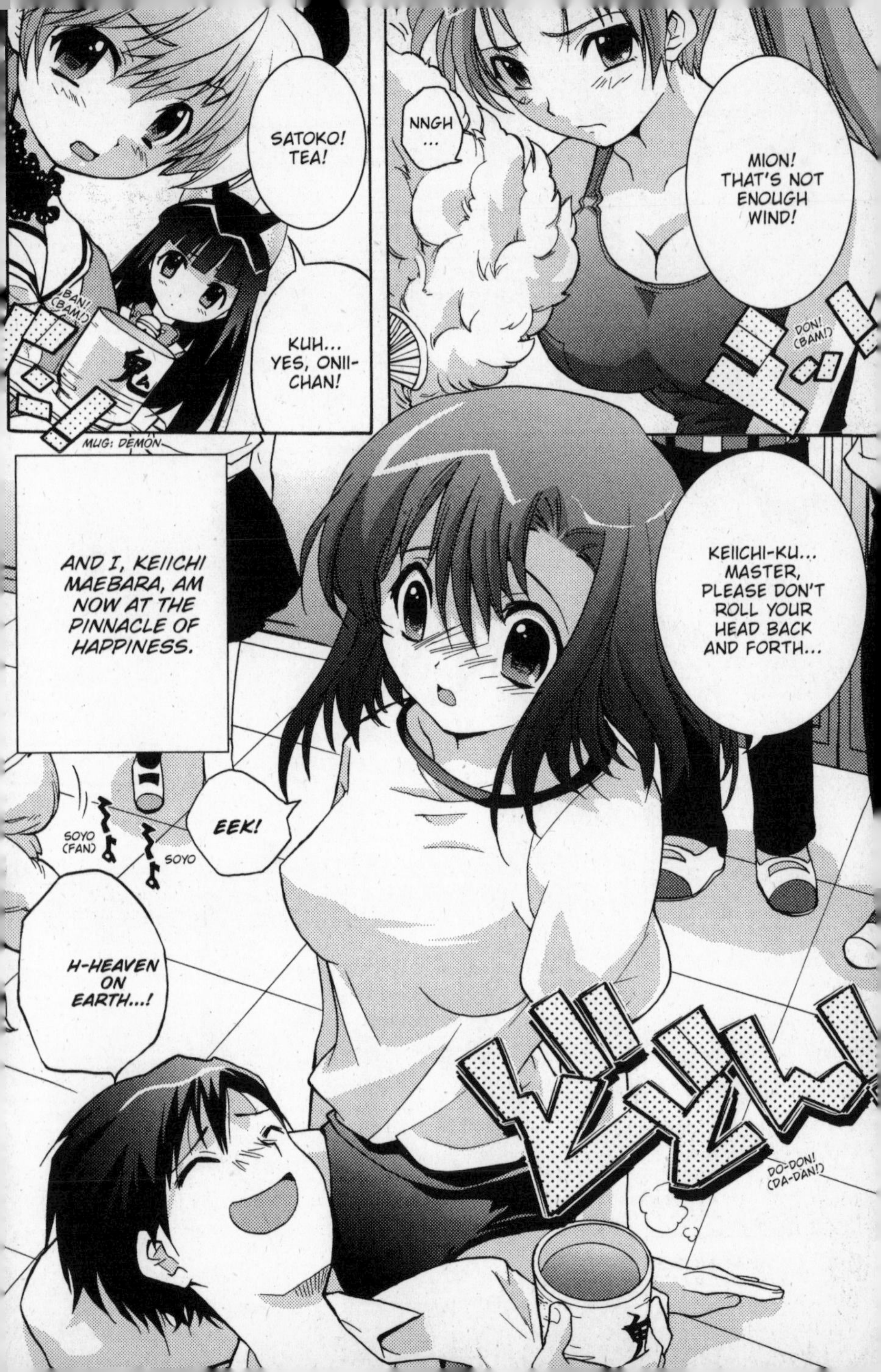
MION! THAT'S NOT ENOUGH WIND!
NNGH ...
DON! (BAM!)
SATOKO! TEA!
KUH... YES, ONII-CHAN!
BAN! (BAM!)
MUG: DEMON
KEIICHI-KU... MASTER, PLEASE DON'T ROLL YOUR HEAD BACK AND FORTH...
AND I, KEIICHI MAEBARA, AM NOW AT THE PINNACLE OF HAPPINESS.
EEK!
SOYO
SOYO (FAN)
H-HEAVEN ON EARTH...!
DO-DON! (DA-DAN!)

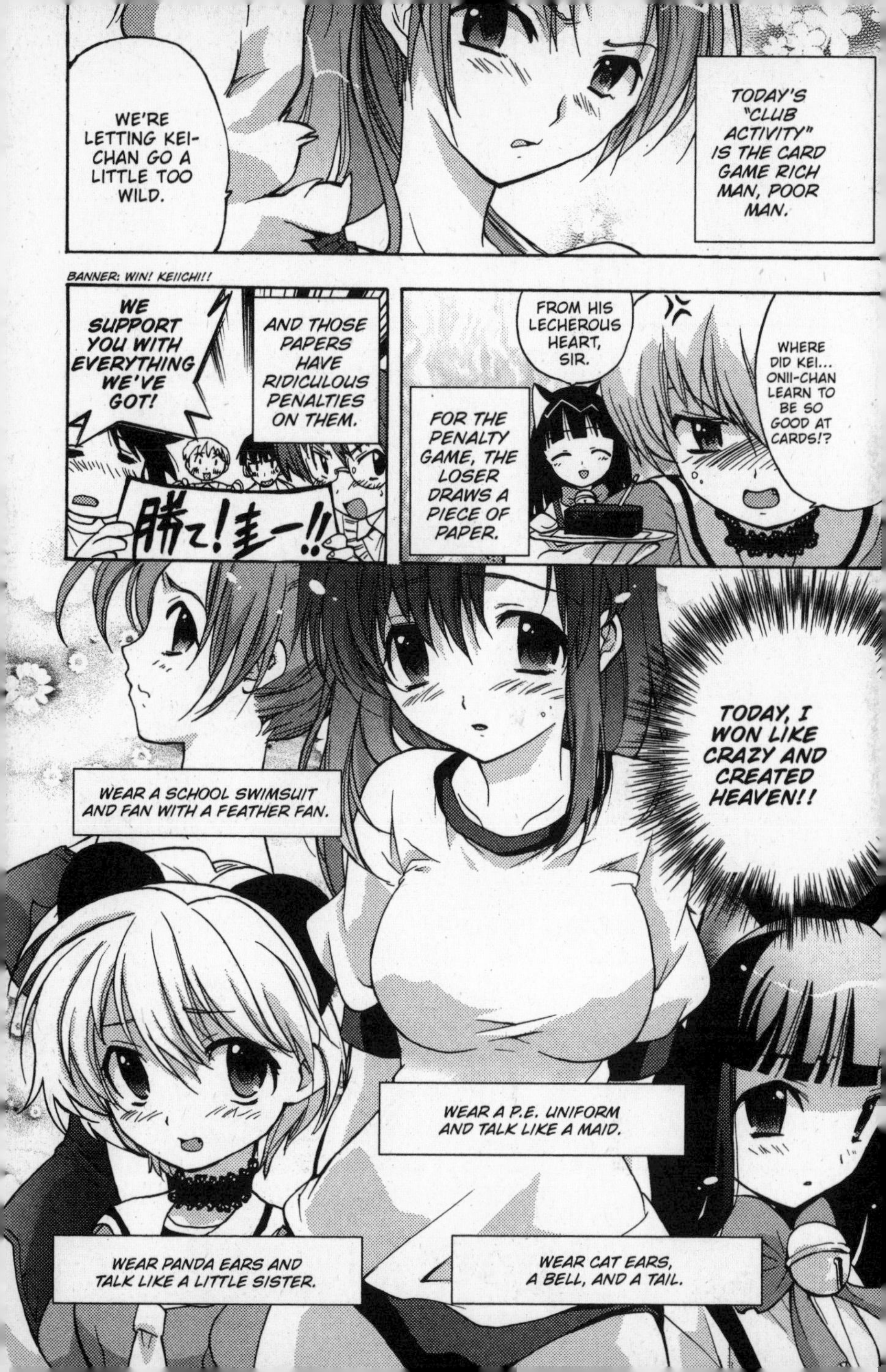
TODAY'S "CLUB ACTIVITY" IS THE CARD GAME RICH MAN, POOR MAN.
WE'RE LETTING KEI-CHAN GO A LITTLE TOO WILD.
WHERE DID KEI... ONII-CHAN LEARN TO BE SO GOOD AT CARDS!?
FROM HIS LECHEROUS HEART, SIR.
FOR THE PENALTY GAME, THE LOSER DRAWS A PIECE OF PAPER.
AND THOSE PAPERS HAVE RIDICULOUS PENALTIES ON THEM.
WE SUPPORT YOU WITH EVERYTHING WE'VE GOT!
勝て!圭一!!
BANNER: WIN! KEIICHI!!
TODAY, I WON LIKE CRAZY AND CREATED HEAVEN!!
WEAR A SCHOOL SWIMSUIT AND FAN WITH A FEATHER FAN.
WEAR A P.E. UNIFORM AND TALK LIKE A MAID.
WEAR CAT EARS, A BELL, AND A TAIL.
WEAR PANDA EARS AND TALK LIKE A LITTLE SISTER.

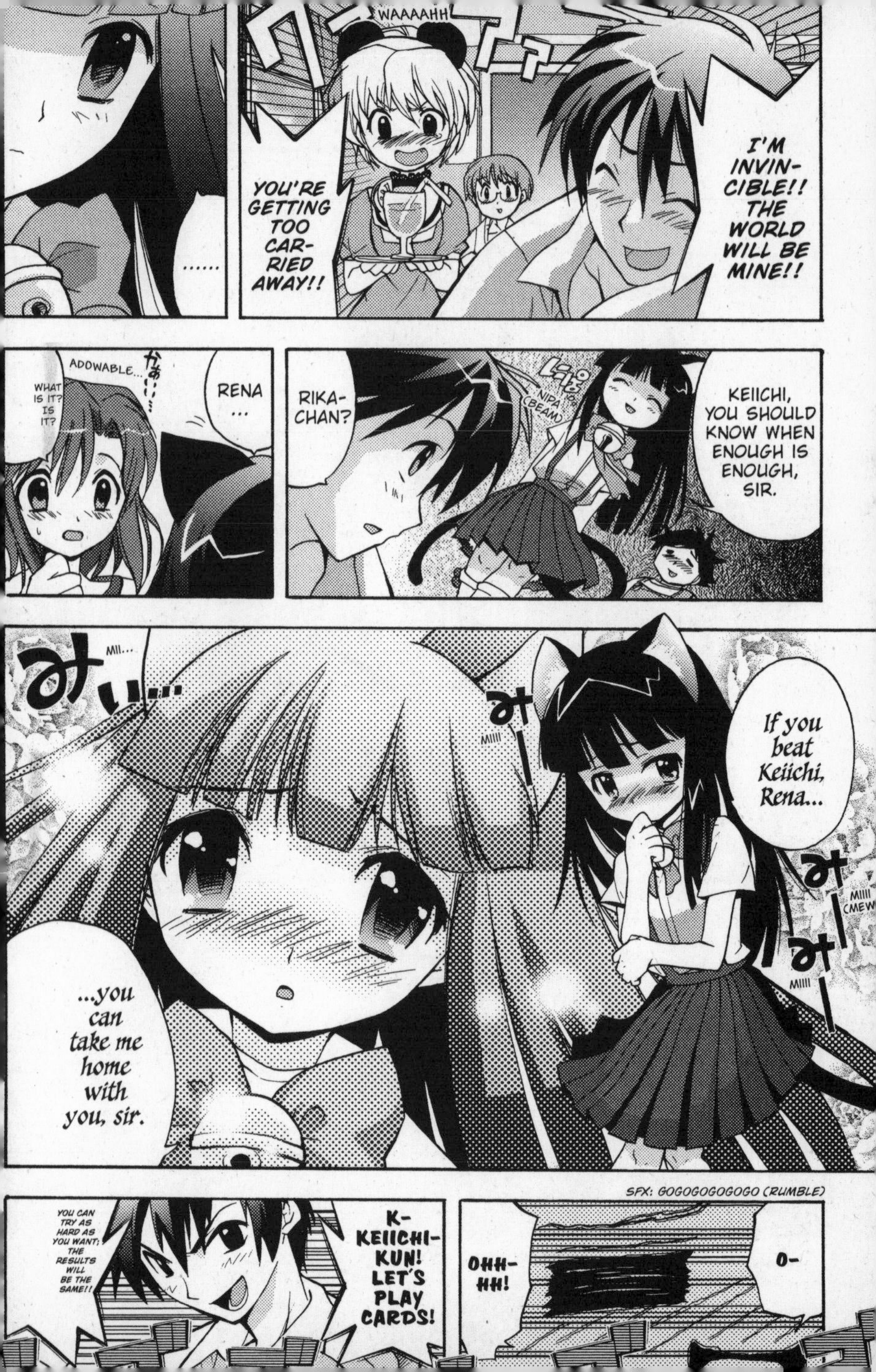
WAAAAHH
I'M INVINCIBLE!! THE WORLD WILL BE MINE!!
YOU'RE GETTING TOO CARRIED AWAY!!
......
KEIICHI, YOU SHOULD KNOW WHEN ENOUGH IS ENOUGH, SIR.
NIPA (BEAM)
RIKA-CHAN?
RENA ...
ADOWABLE...
WHAT IS IT? IS IT?
If you beat Keiichi, Rena...
MIIII CMEW
MIIII
MIIII
MII...
...you can take me home with you, sir.
SFX: GOGOGOGOGOGO (RUMBLE)
O-
OHHH-HH!
K-KEIICHI-KUN! LET'S PLAY CARDS!
YOU CAN TRY AS HARD AS YOU WANT; THE RESULTS WILL BE THE SAME!!

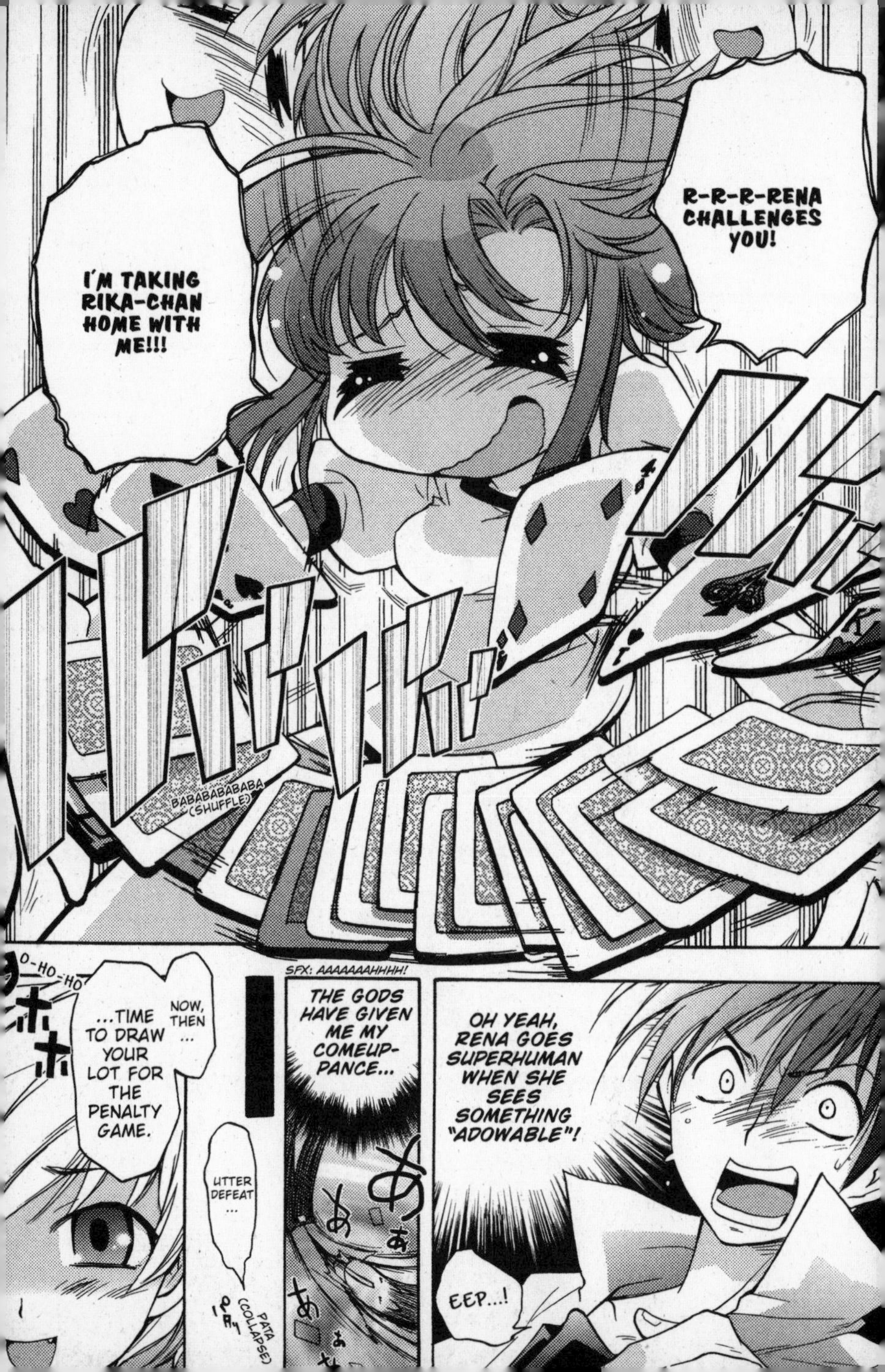
R-R-R-RENA CHALLENGES YOU!
I'M TAKING RIKA-CHAN HOME WITH ME!!!
BABABABABABA (SHUFFLE)
OH YEAH, RENA GOES SUPERHUMAN WHEN SHE SEES SOMETHING "ADOWABLE"!
EEP...!
SFX: AAAAAAAHHHH!
THE GODS HAVE GIVEN ME MY COMEUP-PANCE...
UTTER DEFEAT ...
PATA (COLLAPSE)
NOW, THEN ...
...TIME TO DRAW YOUR LOT FOR THE PENALTY GAME.
O-HO-HO

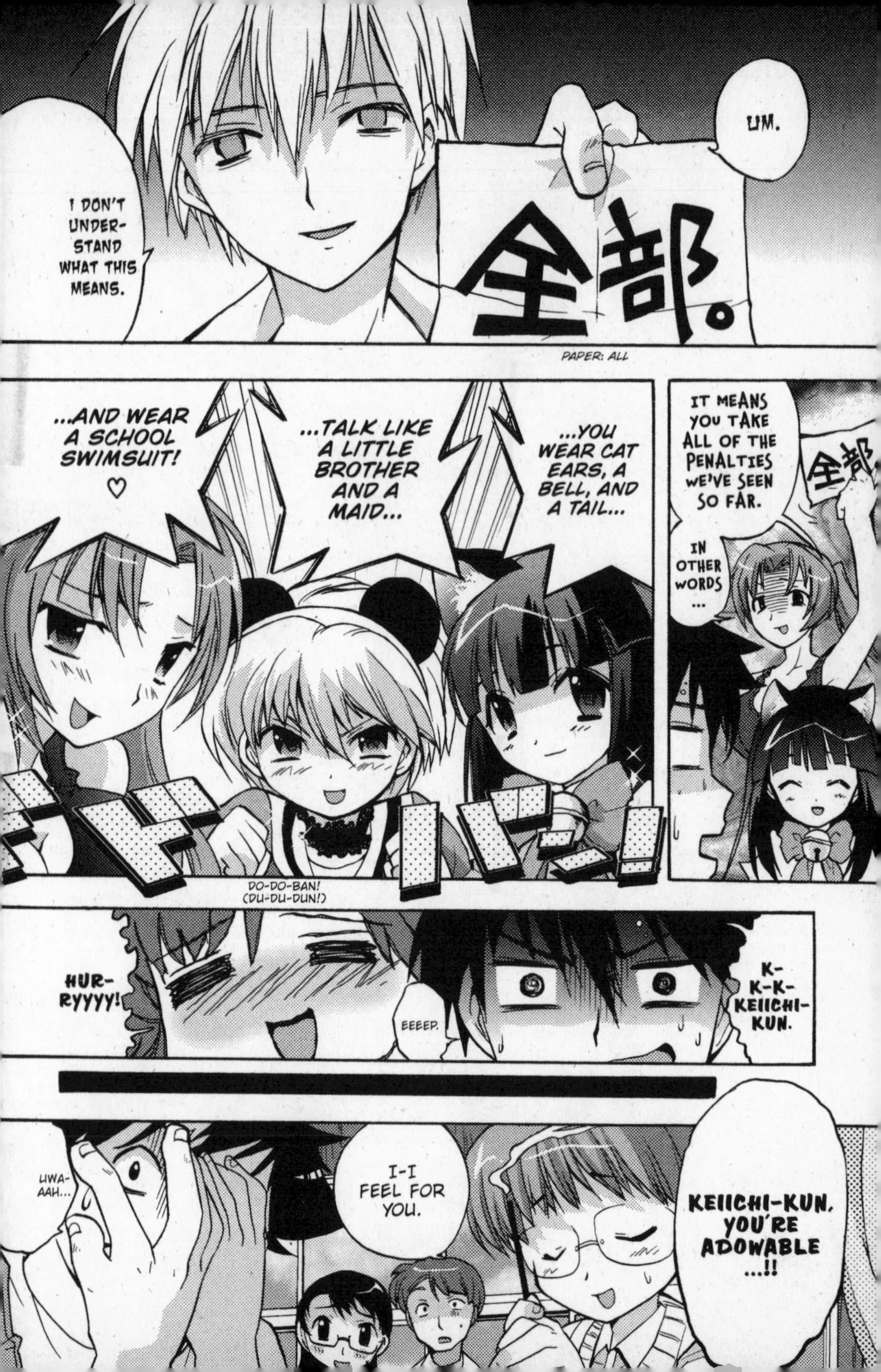
UM.
I DON'T UNDER-STAND WHAT THIS MEANS.
全部。
PAPER: ALL
IT MEANS YOU TAKE ALL OF THE PENALTIES WE'VE SEEN SO FAR.
全部
IN OTHER WORDS...
...YOU WEAR CAT EARS, A BELL, AND A TAIL...
...TALK LIKE A LITTLE BROTHER AND A MAID...
...AND WEAR A SCHOOL SWIMSUIT! ♡
DO-DO-BAN! (DU-DU-DUN!)
K-K-K-KEIICHI-KUN.
EEEEP.
HUR-RYYYY!
KEIICHI-KUN, YOU'RE ADOWABLE ...!!
I-I FEEL FOR YOU.
UWA-AAH...

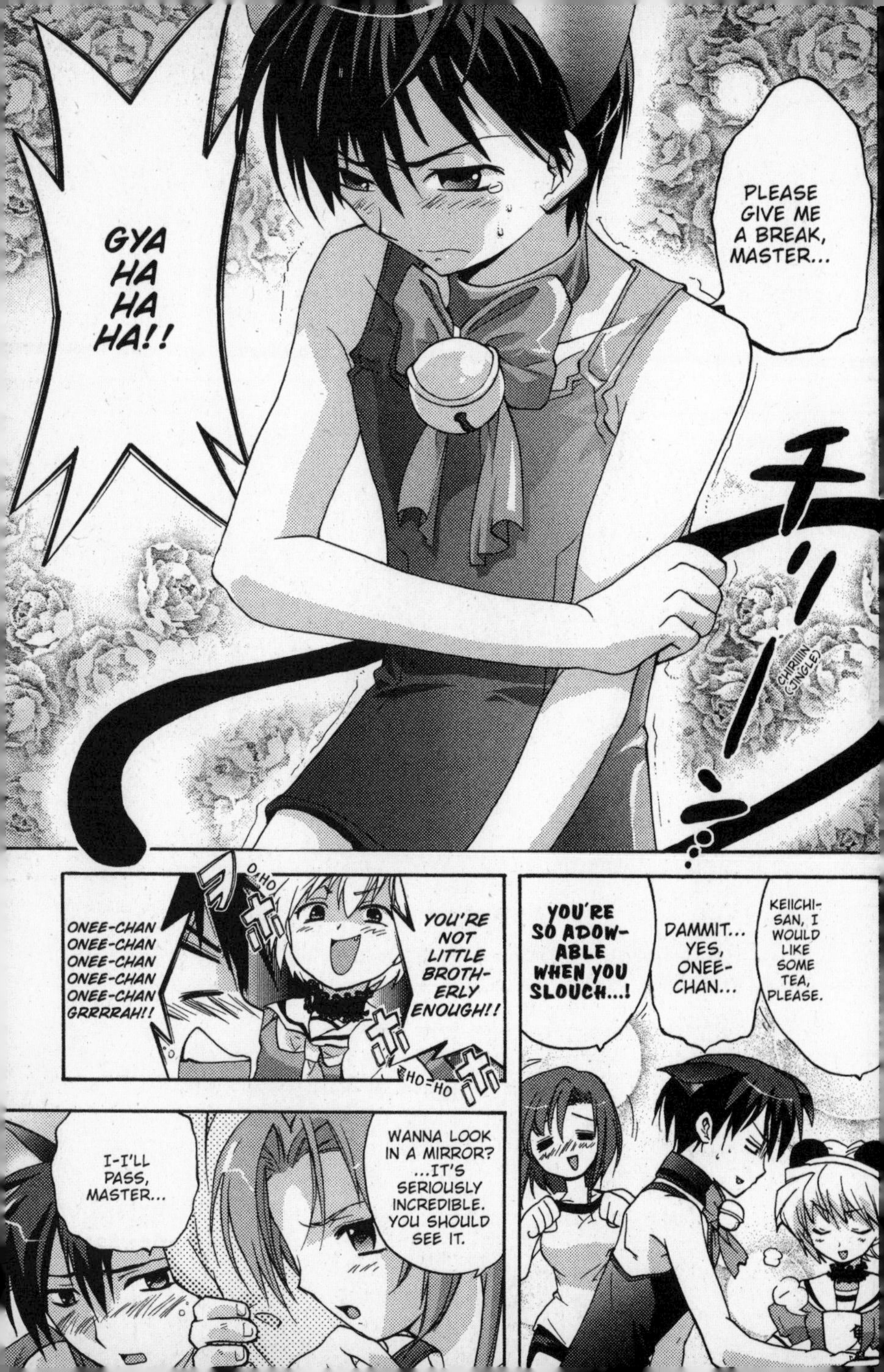
PLEASE GIVE ME A BREAK, MASTER...
CHIRIIIN (JINGLE)
GYA HA HA HA!!
KEIICHI-SAN, I WOULD LIKE SOME TEA, PLEASE.
DAMMIT... YES, ONEE-CHAN...
YOU'RE SO ADOW-ABLE WHEN YOU SLOUCH...!
O-HO
YOU'RE NOT LITTLE BROTH-ERLY ENOUGH!!
ONEE-CHAN ONEE-CHAN ONEE-CHAN ONEE-CHAN ONEE-CHAN GRRRRAH!!
HO-HO
WANNA LOOK IN A MIRROR? ...IT'S SERIOUSLY INCREDIBLE. YOU SHOULD SEE IT.
I-I'LL PASS, MASTER...

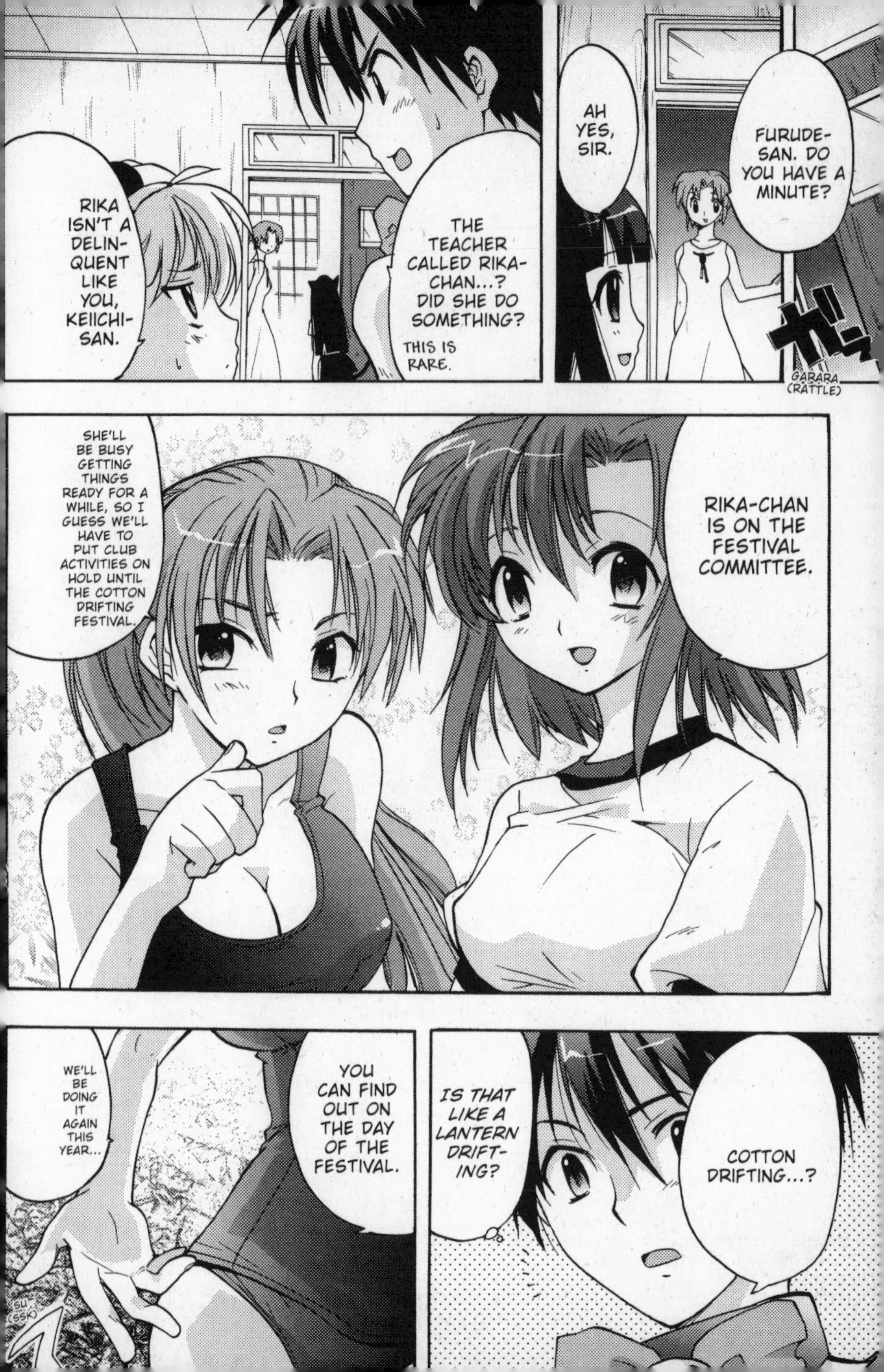
FURUDE-SAN. DO YOU HAVE A MINUTE?
GARARA (RATTLE)
AH YES, SIR.
THE TEACHER CALLED RIKA-CHAN...? DID SHE DO SOMETHING?
THIS IS RARE.
RIKA ISN'T A DELINQUENT LIKE YOU, KEIICHI-SAN.
RIKA-CHAN IS ON THE FESTIVAL COMMITTEE.
SHE'LL BE BUSY GETTING THINGS READY FOR A WHILE, SO I GUESS WE'LL HAVE TO PUT CLUB ACTIVITIES ON HOLD UNTIL THE COTTON DRIFTING FESTIVAL.
COTTON DRIFTING...?
IS THAT LIKE A LANTERN DRIFTING?
YOU CAN FIND OUT ON THE DAY OF THE FESTIVAL.
WE'LL BE DOING IT AGAIN THIS YEAR...
SU (SSK)

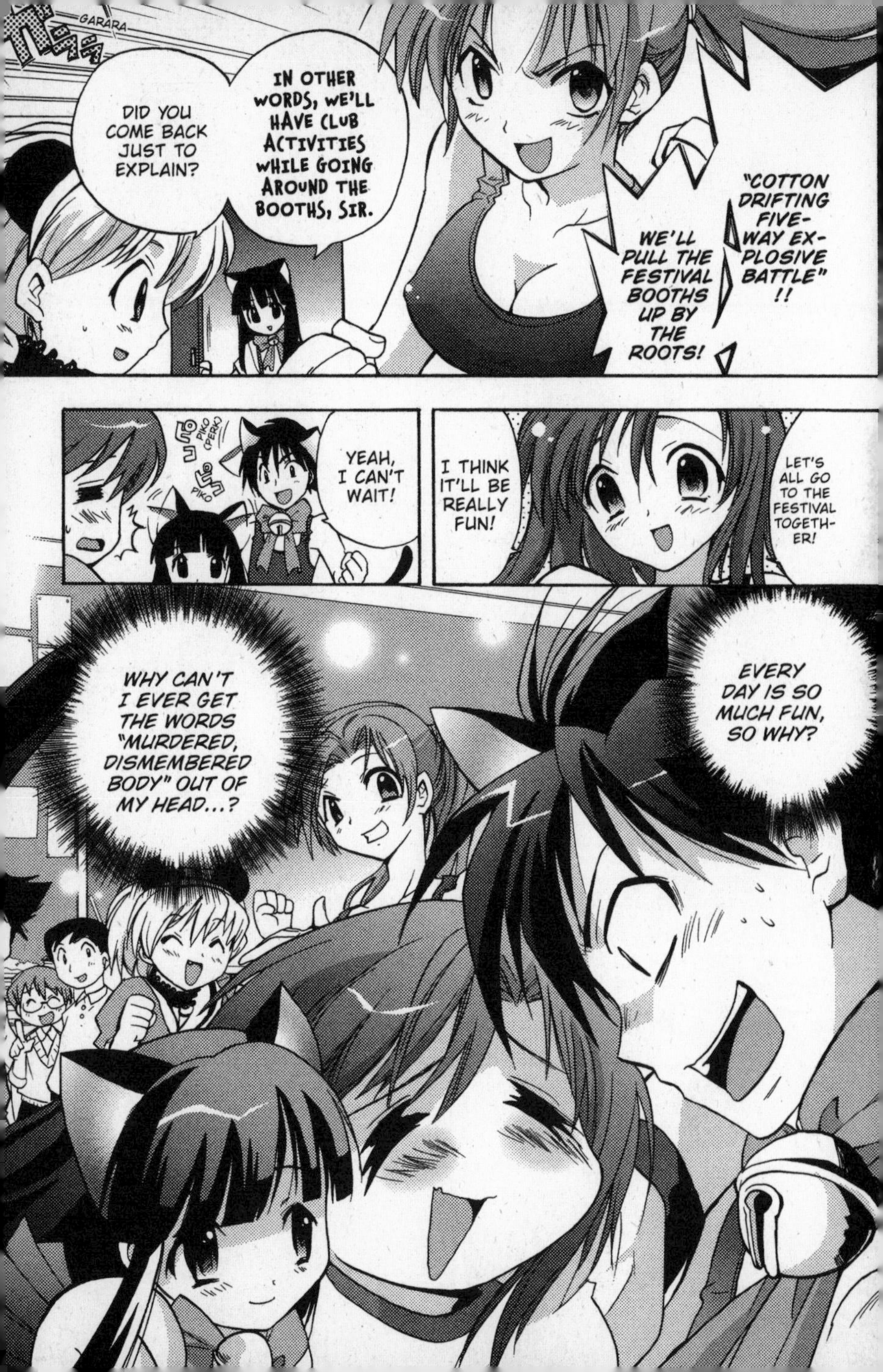
"COTTON DRIFTING FIVE-WAY EXPLOSIVE BATTLE" !!
WE'LL PULL THE FESTIVAL BOOTHS UP BY THE ROOTS!
IN OTHER WORDS, WE'LL HAVE CLUB ACTIVITIES WHILE GOING AROUND THE BOOTHS, SIR.
DID YOU COME BACK JUST TO EXPLAIN?
GARARA
LET'S ALL GO TO THE FESTIVAL TOGETH-ER!
I THINK IT'LL BE REALLY FUN!
YEAH, I CAN'T WAIT!
PIKO (PERK)
PIKO
EVERY DAY IS SO MUCH FUN, SO WHY?
WHY CAN'T I EVER GET THE WORDS "MURDERED, DISMEMBERED BODY" OUT OF MY HEAD...?

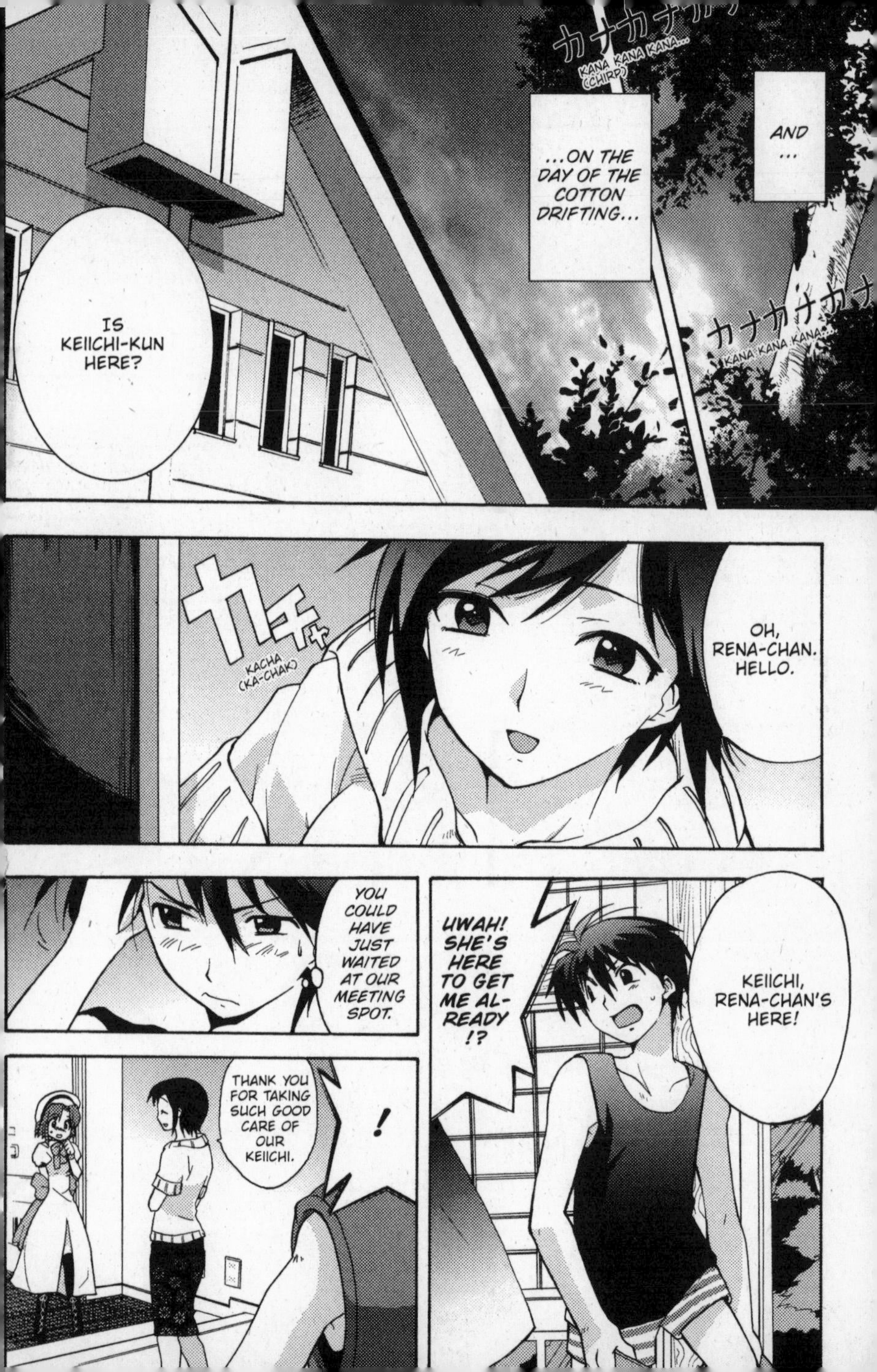

カナカナカナ
KANA KANA KANA... (CHIRP)
AND ...
...ON THE DAY OF THE COTTON DRIFTING...
カナカナカナ
KANA KANA KANA...
IS KEIICHI-KUN HERE?
カチャ
KACHA (KA-CHAK)
OH, RENA-CHAN. HELLO.
KEIICHI, RENA-CHAN'S HERE!
UWAH! SHE'S HERE TO GET ME AL-READY!?
YOU COULD HAVE JUST WAITED AT OUR MEETING SPOT.
THANK YOU FOR TAKING SUCH GOOD CARE OF OUR KEIICHI.
!

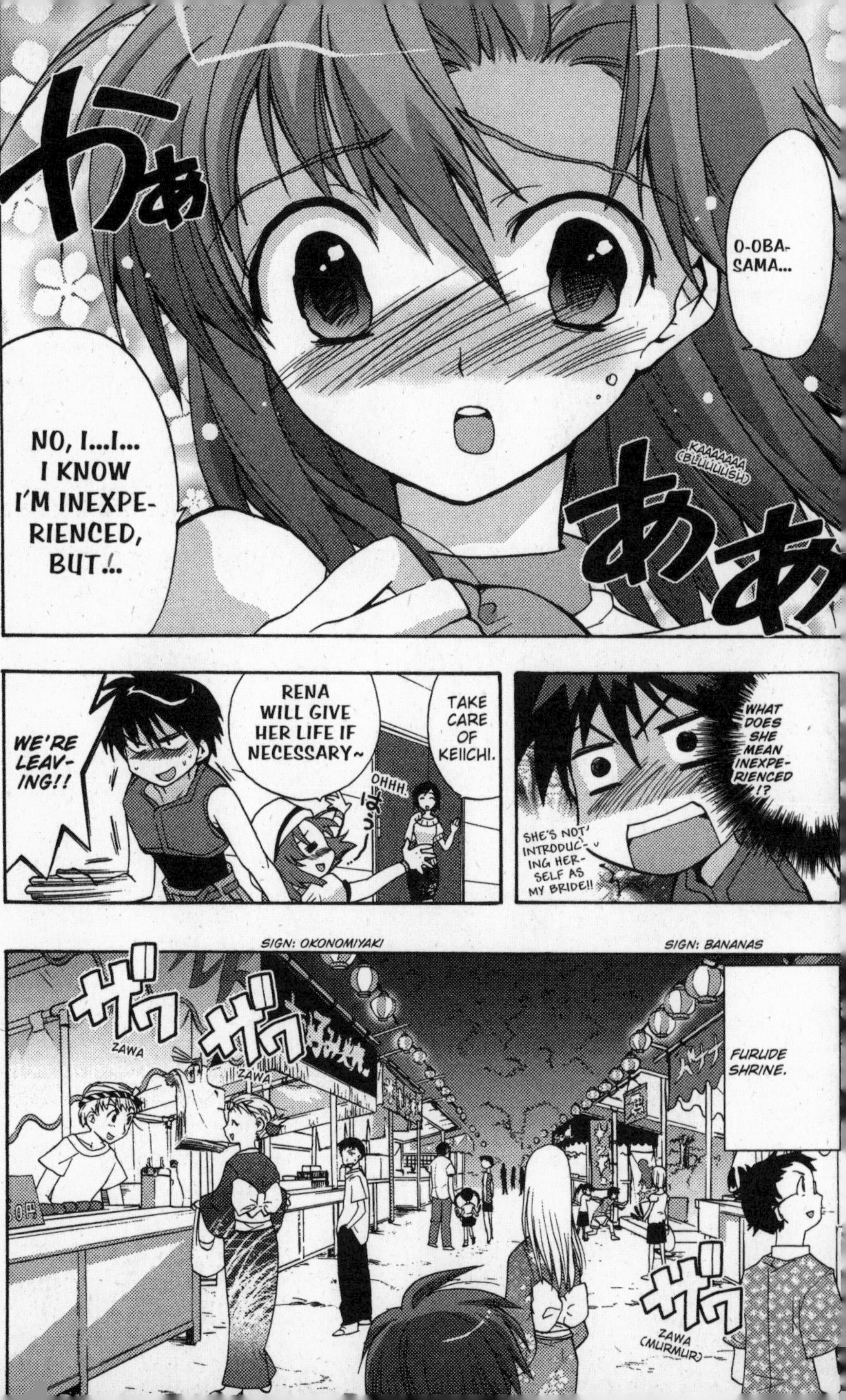
O-OBA-SAMA...
KAAAAAAA (BLUUUUSH)
NO, I...I... I KNOW I'M INEXPERIENCED, BUT...
WHAT DOES SHE MEAN INEXPERIENCED!?
SHE'S NOT INTRODUCING HERSELF AS MY BRIDE!!
TAKE CARE OF KEIICHI.
OHHH.
RENA WILL GIVE HER LIFE IF NECESSARY~
WE'RE LEAVING!!
SIGN: BANANAS
SIGN: OKONOMIYAKI
FURUDE SHRINE.
ZAWA (MURMUR)
ZAWA
ZAWA

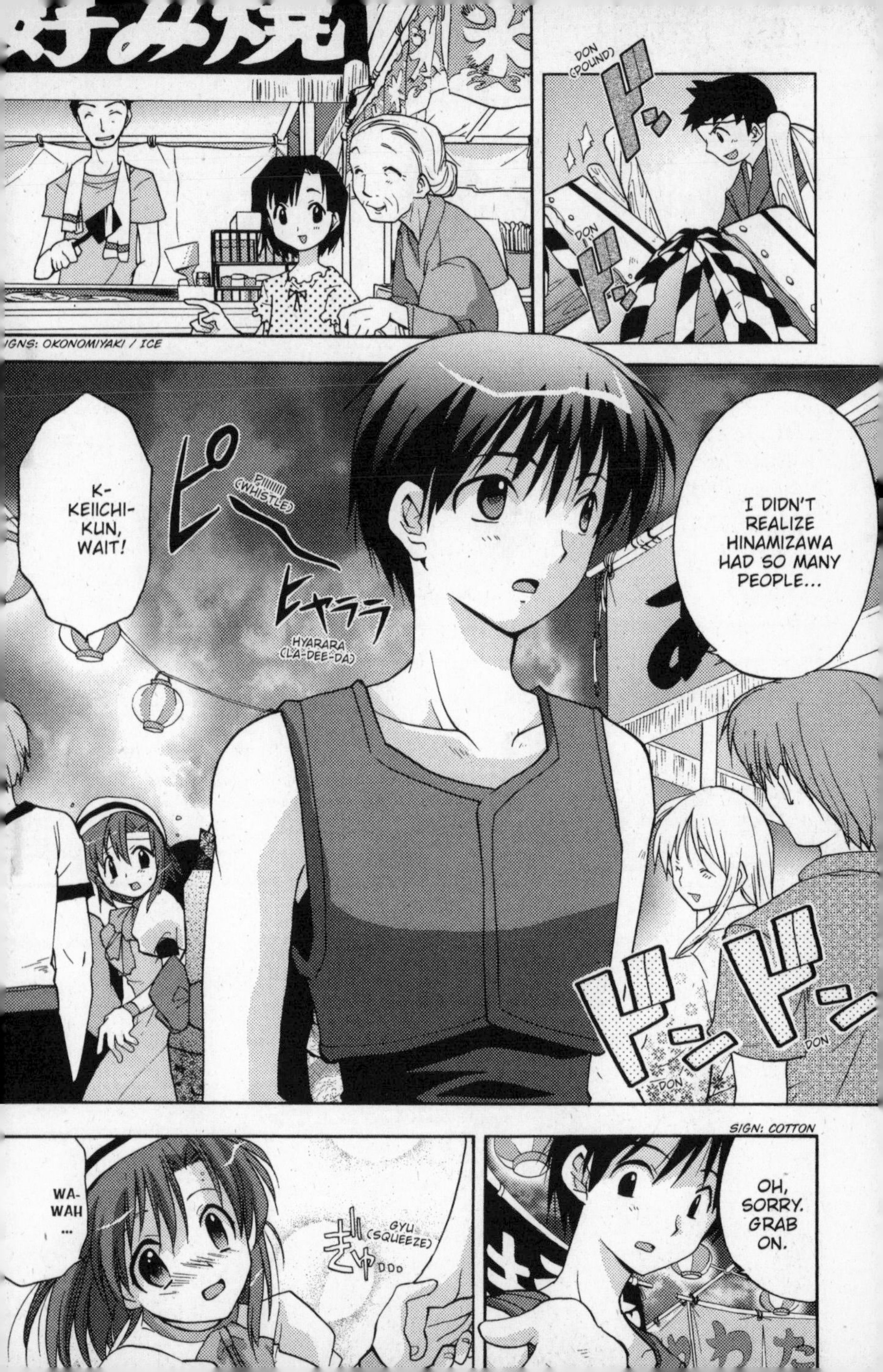
DON (POUND)
DON
IGNS: OKONOMIYAKI / ICE
I DIDN'T REALIZE HINAMIZAWA HAD SO MANY PEOPLE...
PIIIIIII (WHISTLE)
HYARARA (LA-DEE-DA)
K-KEIICHI-KUN, WAIT!
DON
DON
SIGN: COTTON
OH, SORRY. GRAB ON.
GYU (SQUEEZE)
WA-WAH...

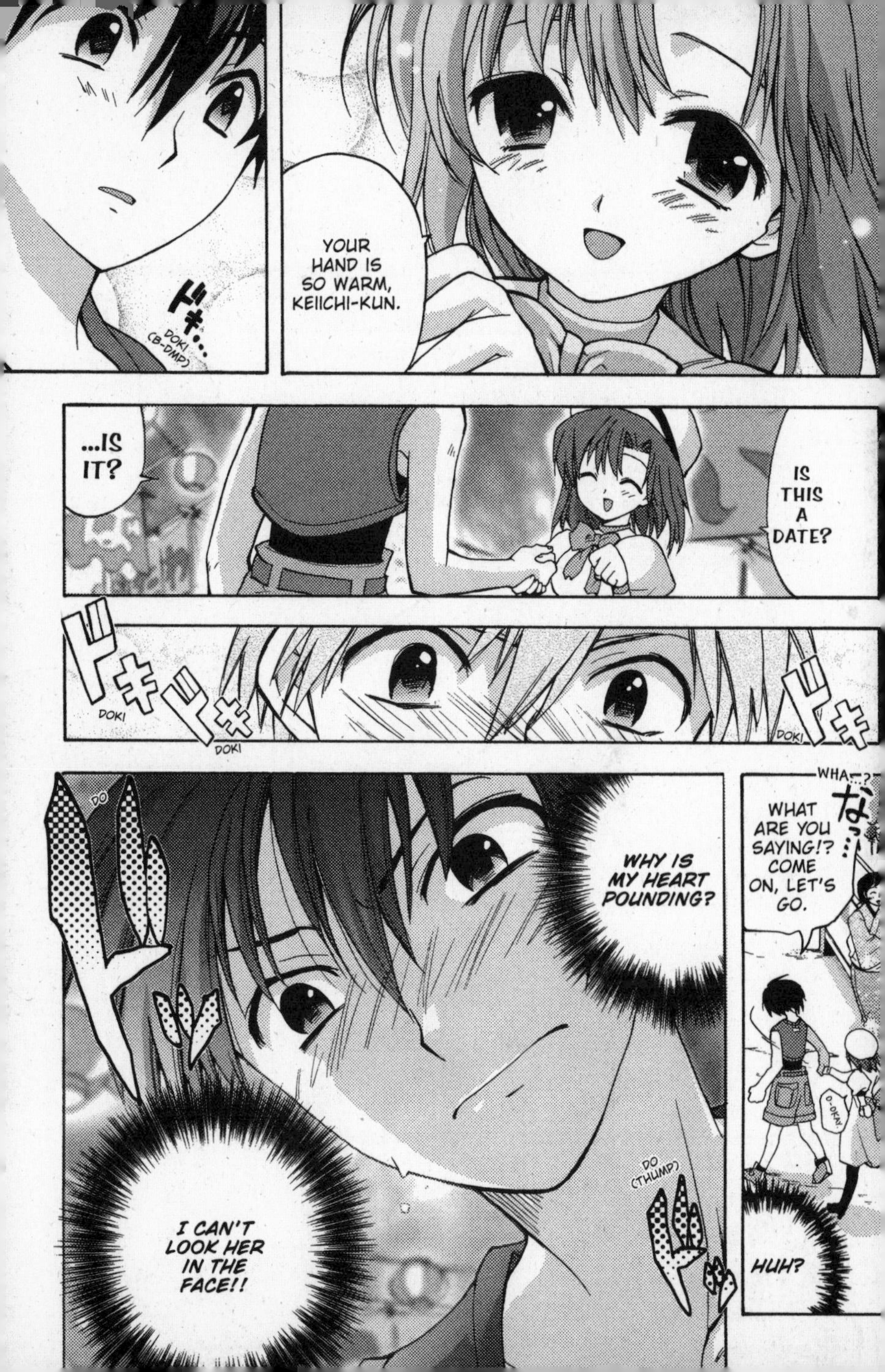
YOUR HAND IS SO WARM, KEIICHI-KUN.
ドキ…
DOKI (B-DMP)
IS THIS A DATE?
...IS IT?
ドキ
DOKI
ドキ
DOKI
ドキ
DOKI
なっ…
WHA...?
WHAT ARE YOU SAYING!? COME ON, LET'S GO.
O-OKAY.
HUH?
WHY IS MY HEART POUNDING?
DO (THUMP)
I CAN'T LOOK HER IN THE FACE!!
DO

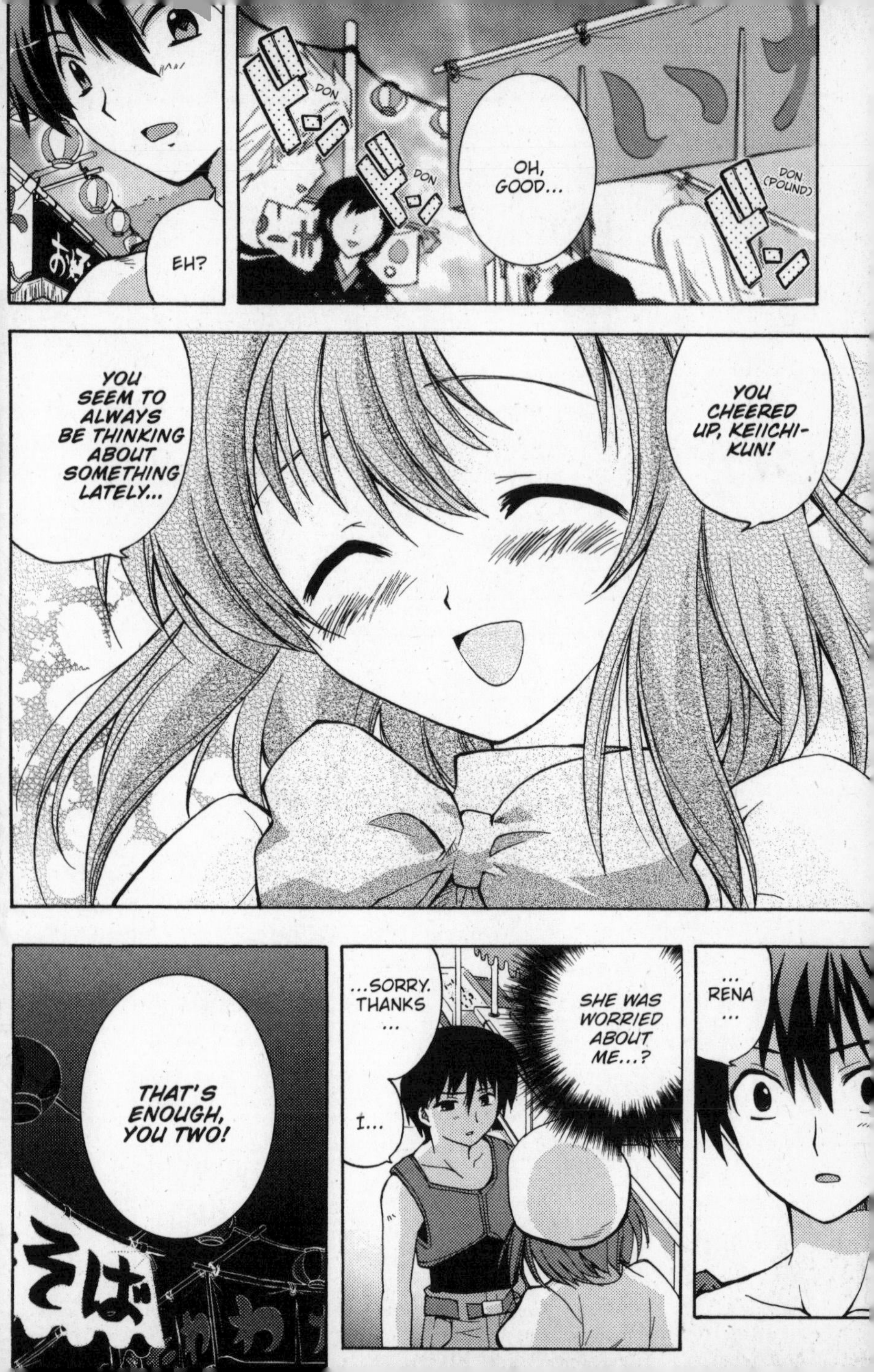
DON (POUND)
OH, GOOD...
DON
DON
EH?
YOU CHEERED UP, KEIICHI-KUN!
YOU SEEM TO ALWAYS BE THINKING ABOUT SOMETHING LATELY...
... RENA ...
SHE WAS WORRIED ABOUT ME...?
...SORRY. THANKS ...
I...
THAT'S ENOUGH, YOU TWO!

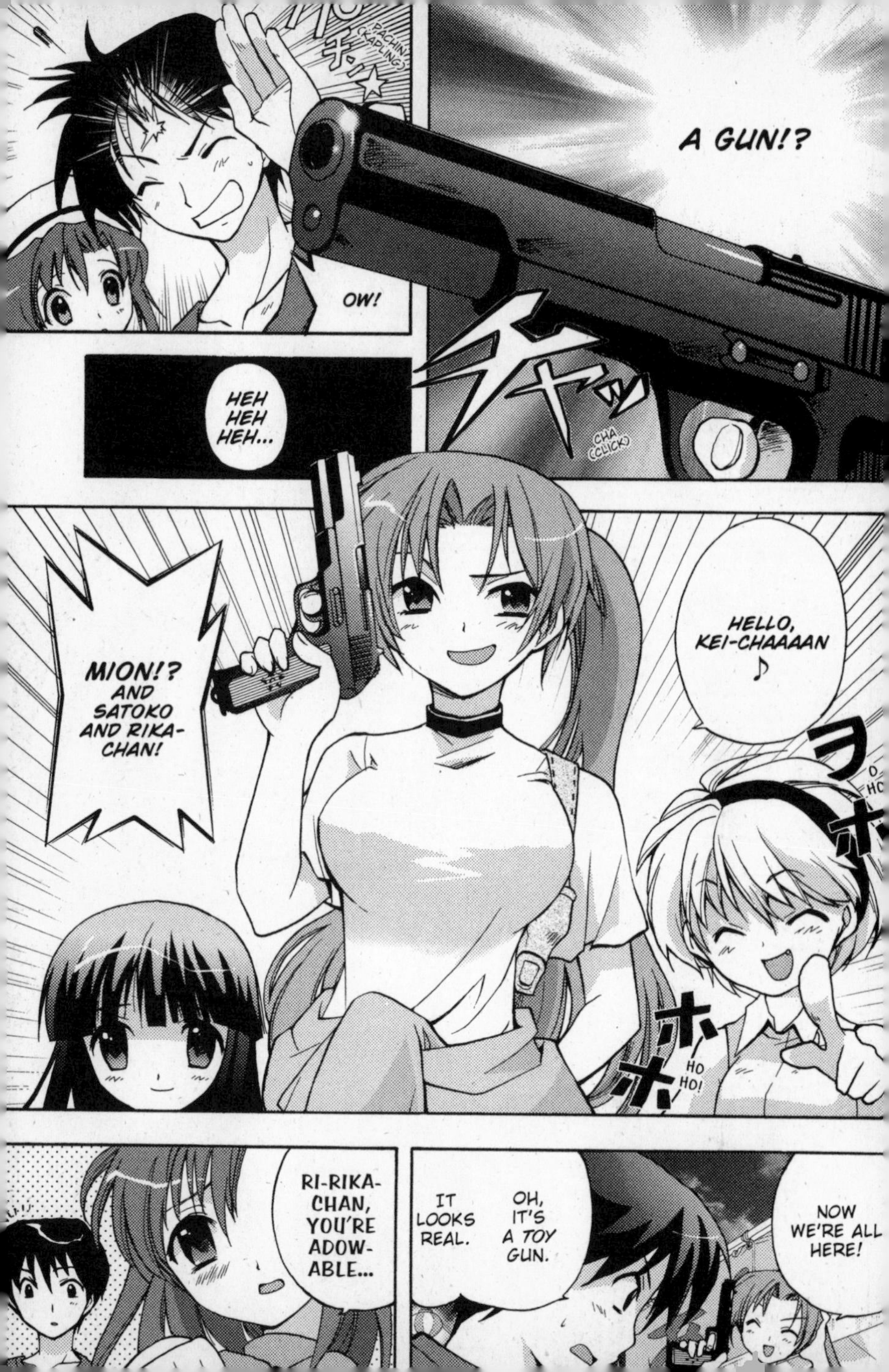
A GUN!?
CHA (CLICK)
PACHIN (KAPLING)
OW!
HEH HEH HEH...
HELLO, KEI-CHAAAAN ♪
HO HO!
MION!? AND SATOKO AND RIKA-CHAN!
NOW WE'RE ALL HERE!
OH, IT'S A *TOY* GUN.
IT LOOKS REAL.
RI-RIKA-CHAN, YOU'RE ADOWABLE...

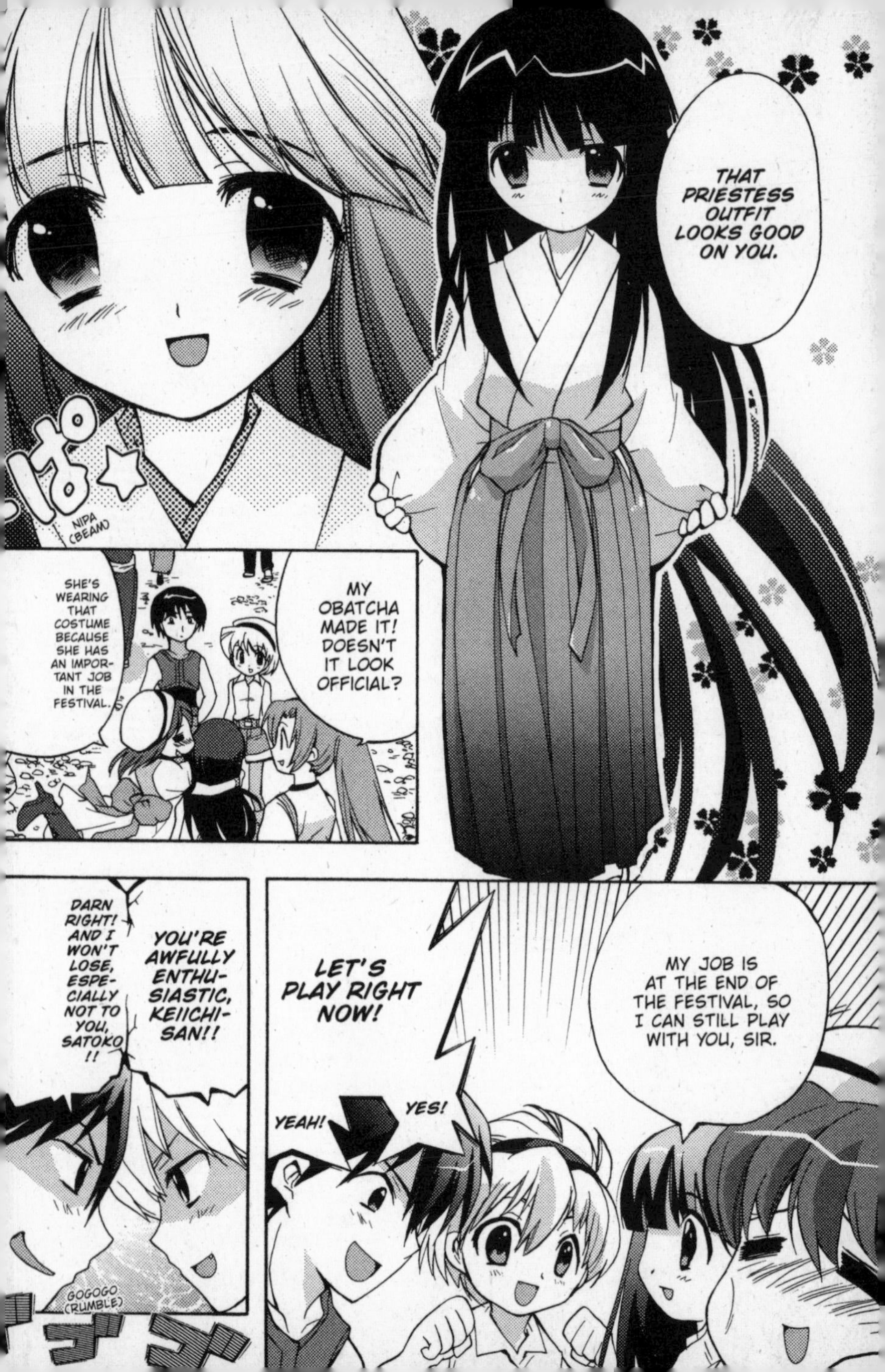
THAT PRIESTESS OUTFIT LOOKS GOOD ON YOU.
にぱ☆
NIPA (BEAM)
MY OBATCHA MADE IT! DOESN'T IT LOOK OFFICIAL?
SHE'S WEARING THAT COSTUME BECAUSE SHE HAS AN IMPORTANT JOB IN THE FESTIVAL.
MY JOB IS AT THE END OF THE FESTIVAL, SO I CAN STILL PLAY WITH YOU, SIR.
LET'S PLAY RIGHT NOW!
YES!
YEAH!
YOU'RE AWFULLY ENTHUSIASTIC, KEIICHI-SAN!!
DARN RIGHT! AND I WON'T LOSE, ESPECIALLY NOT TO YOU, SATOKO!!
GOGOGO (RUMBLE)

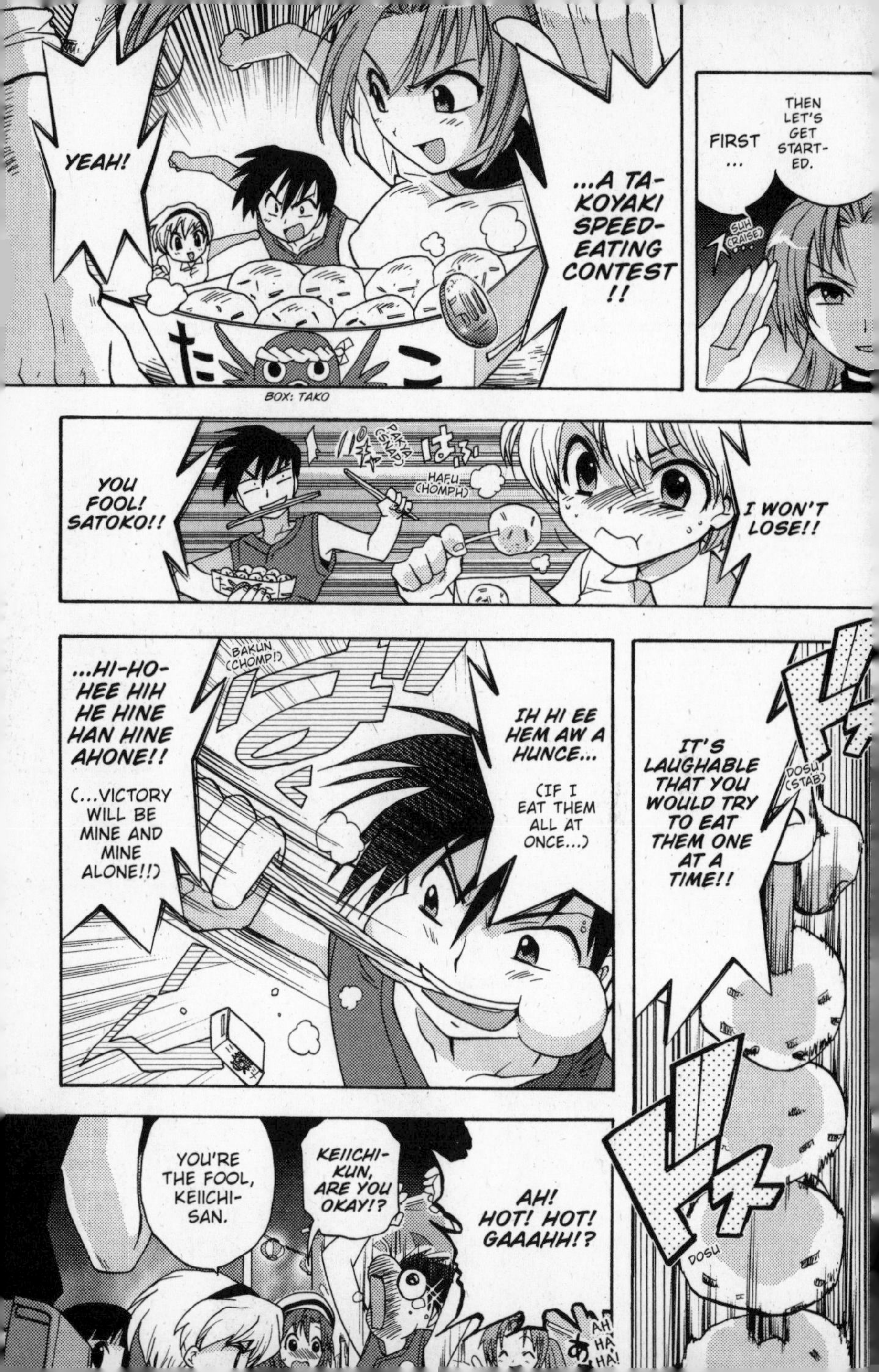
FIRST ...
THEN LET'S GET START-ED.
SUH (RAISE)
...A TA-KOYAKI SPEED-EATING CONTEST!!
YEAH!
BOX: TAKO
I WON'T LOSE!!
HAFU (HOMPH)
PAKIA (SNAP)
YOU FOOL! SATOKO!!
DOSU (STAB)
IT'S LAUGHABLE THAT YOU WOULD TRY TO EAT THEM ONE AT A TIME!!
DOSU
IH HI EE HEM AW A HUNCE...
(IF I EAT THEM ALL AT ONCE...)
BAKUN (CHOMP!)
...HI-HO-HEE HIH HE HINE HAN HINE AHONE!!
(...VICTORY WILL BE MINE AND MINE ALONE!!)
AH! HOT! HOT! GAAAHH!?
KEIICHI-KUN, ARE YOU OKAY!?
YOU'RE THE FOOL, KEIICHI-SAN.
AH HA HA!

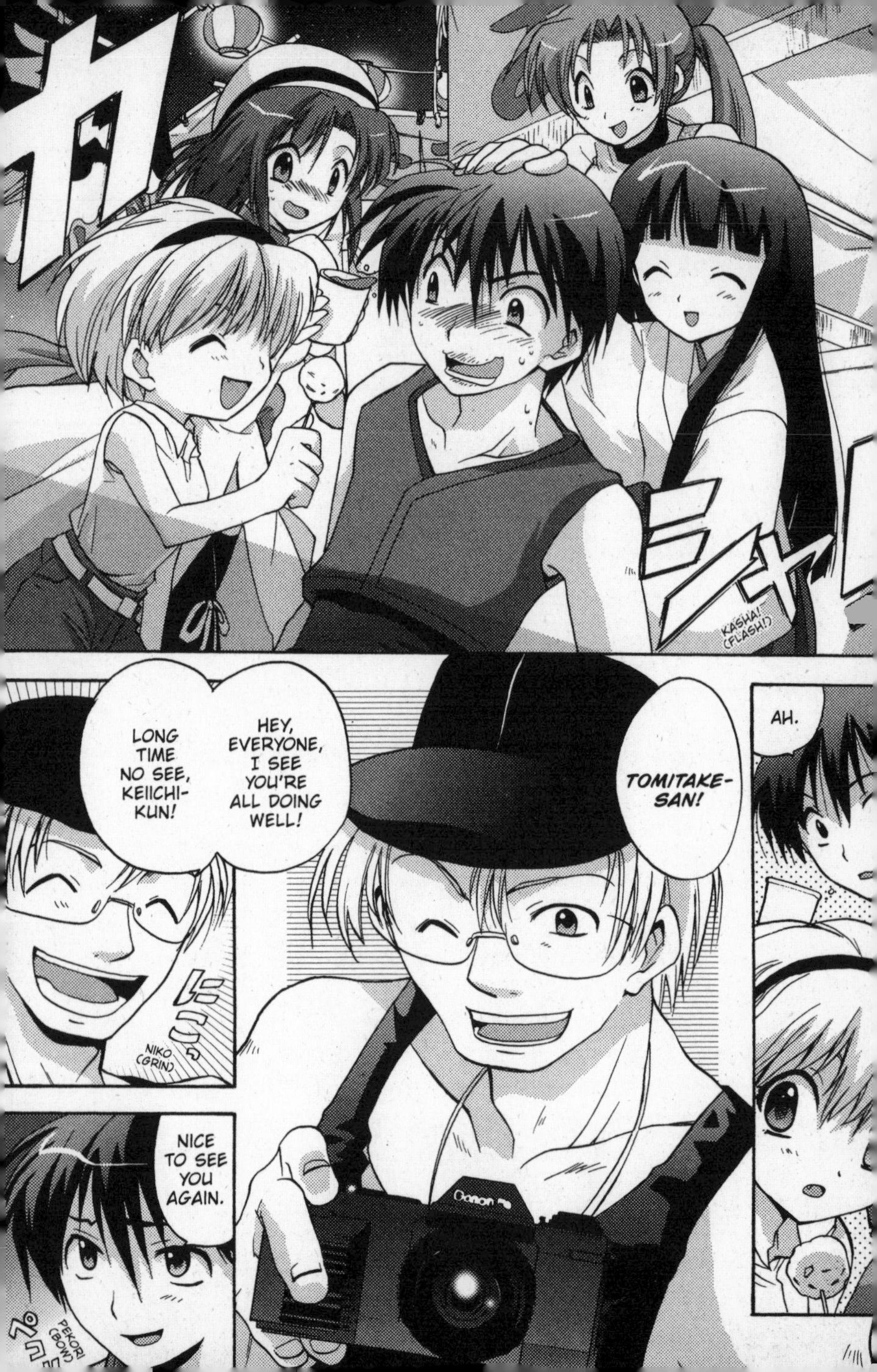
KASHA! (FLASH!)
AH.
TOMITAKE-SAN!
HEY, EVERYONE, I SEE YOU'RE ALL DOING WELL!
LONG TIME NO SEE, KEIICHI-KUN!
NIKO (GRIN)
NICE TO SEE YOU AGAIN.
PEKORI (BOW)

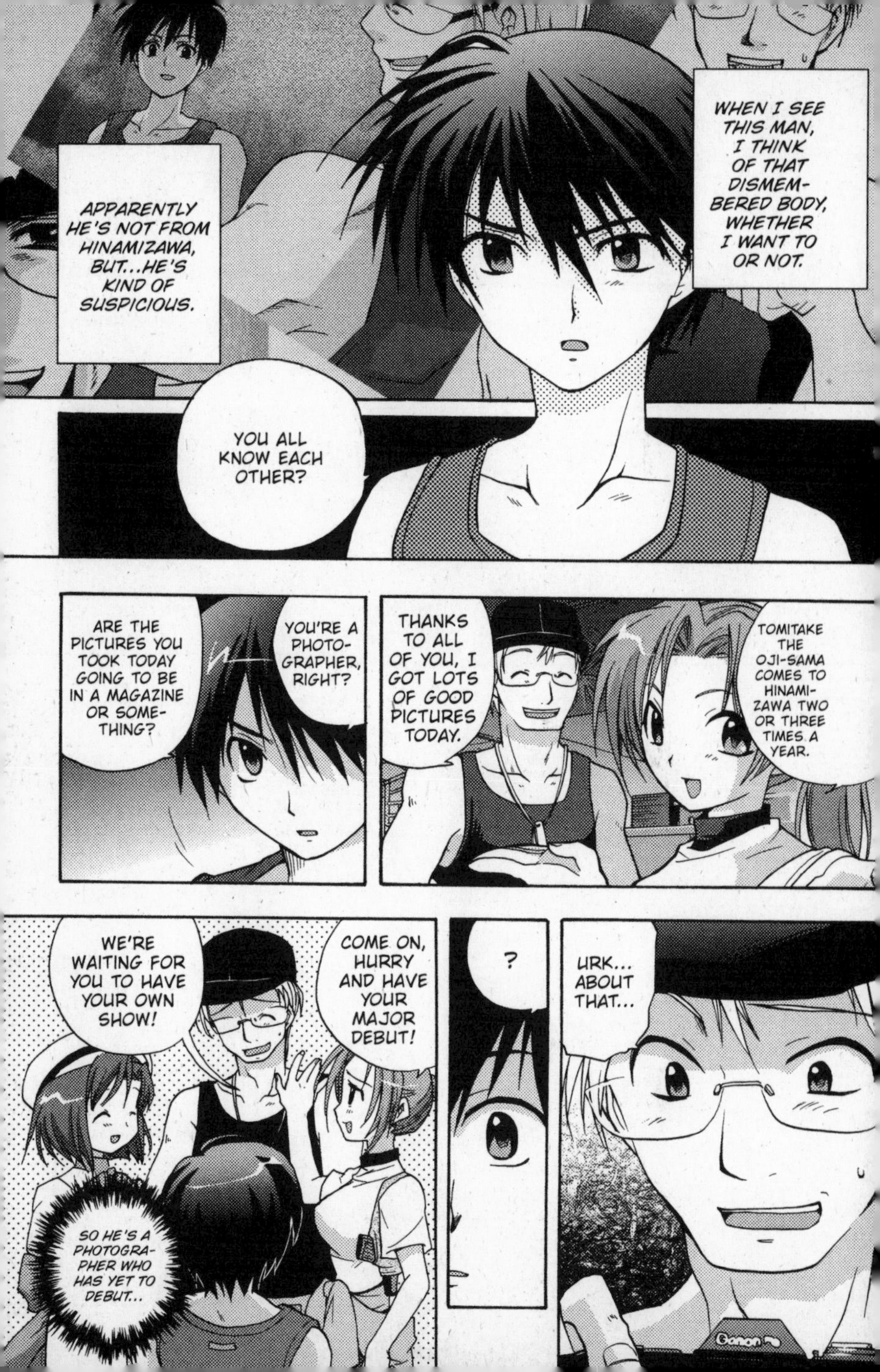
WHEN I SEE THIS MAN, I THINK OF THAT DISMEMBERED BODY, WHETHER I WANT TO OR NOT.
APPARENTLY HE'S NOT FROM HINAMIZAWA, BUT...HE'S KIND OF SUSPICIOUS.
YOU ALL KNOW EACH OTHER?
TOMITAKE THE OJI-SAMA COMES TO HINAMIZAWA TWO OR THREE TIMES A YEAR.
THANKS TO ALL OF YOU, I GOT LOTS OF GOOD PICTURES TODAY.
YOU'RE A PHOTOGRAPHER, RIGHT?
ARE THE PICTURES YOU TOOK TODAY GOING TO BE IN A MAGAZINE OR SOMETHING?
URK... ABOUT THAT...
?
COME ON, HURRY AND HAVE YOUR MAJOR DEBUT!
WE'RE WAITING FOR YOU TO HAVE YOUR OWN SHOW!
SO HE'S A PHOTOGRAPHER WHO HAS YET TO DEBUT...

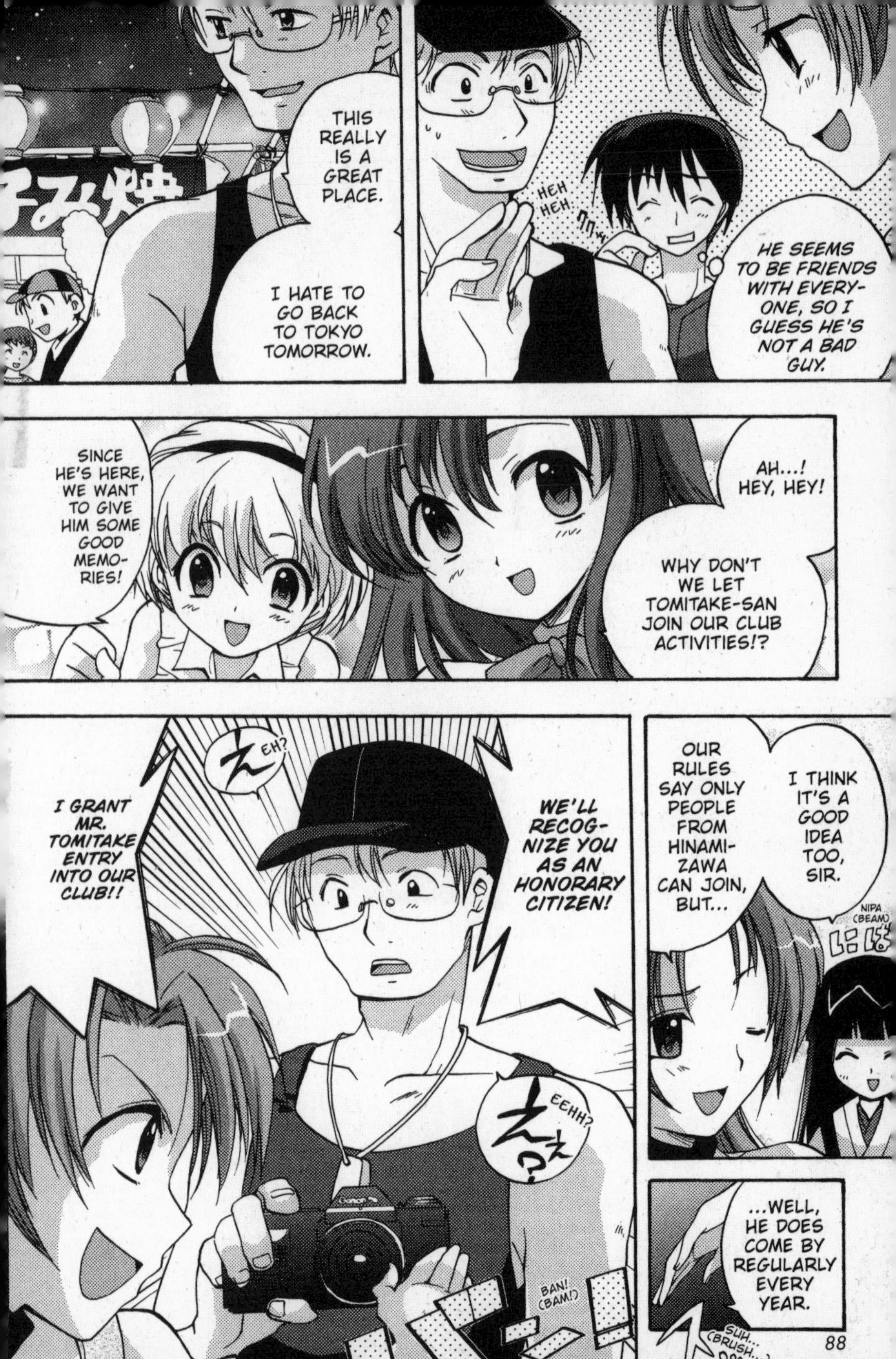
HE SEEMS TO BE FRIENDS WITH EVERY-ONE, SO I GUESS HE'S NOT A BAD GUY.
HEH HEH
THIS REALLY IS A GREAT PLACE.
I HATE TO GO BACK TO TOKYO TOMORROW.
AH...! HEY, HEY!
WHY DON'T WE LET TOMITAKE-SAN JOIN OUR CLUB ACTIVITIES!?
SINCE HE'S HERE, WE WANT TO GIVE HIM SOME GOOD MEMO-RIES!
I THINK IT'S A GOOD IDEA TOO, SIR.
NIPA (BEAM)
OUR RULES SAY ONLY PEOPLE FROM HINAMI-ZAWA CAN JOIN, BUT...
...WELL, HE DOES COME BY REGULARLY EVERY YEAR.
SUH... (BRUSH...)
WE'LL RECOG-NIZE YOU AS AN HONORARY CITIZEN!
EH?
I GRANT MR. TOMITAKE ENTRY INTO OUR CLUB!!
EEHH?
BAN! (BAM!)

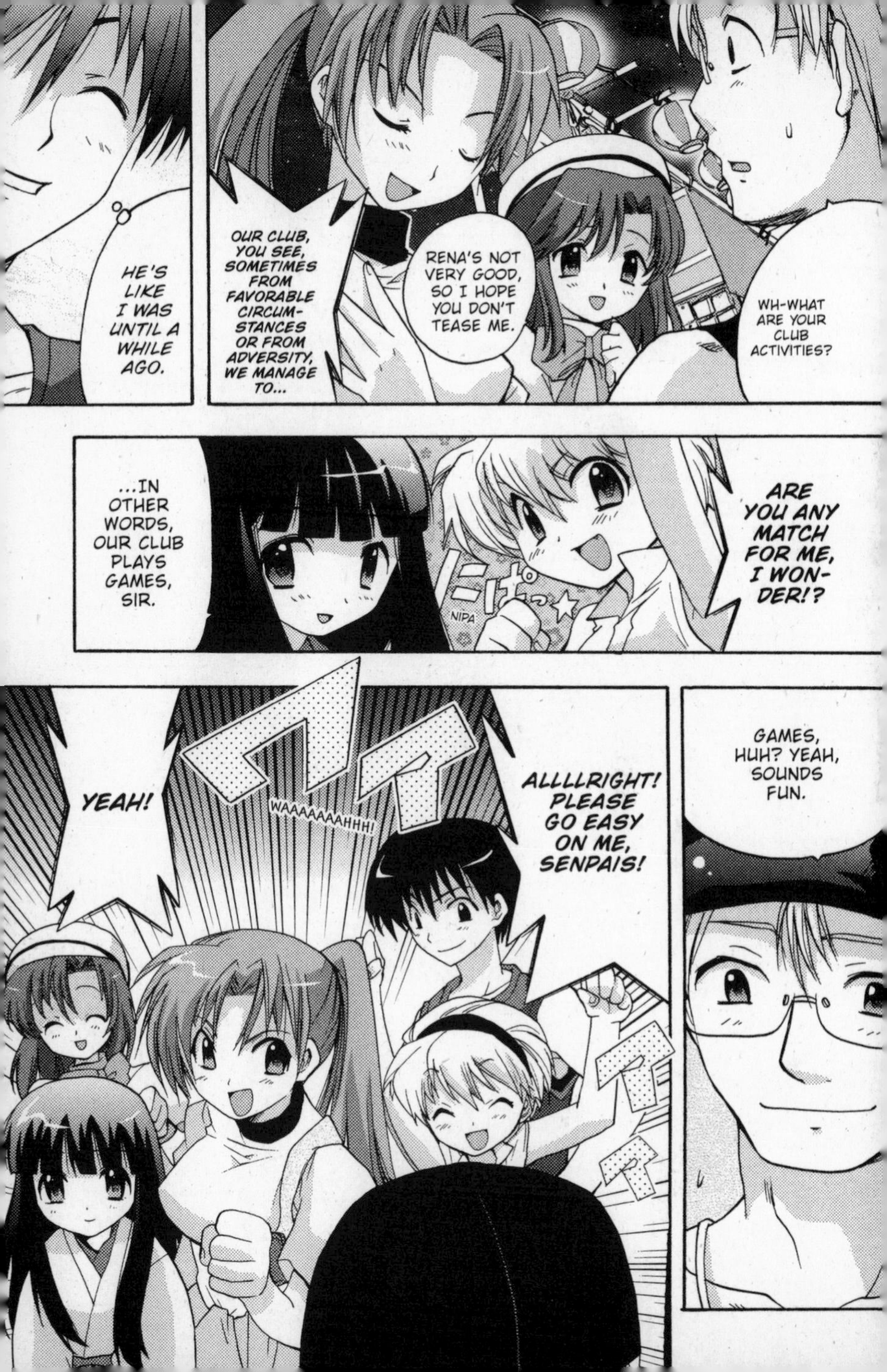
WH-WHAT ARE YOUR CLUB ACTIVITIES?
RENA'S NOT VERY GOOD, SO I HOPE YOU DON'T TEASE ME.
OUR CLUB, YOU SEE, SOMETIMES FROM FAVORABLE CIRCUM-STANCES OR FROM ADVERSITY, WE MANAGE TO...
HE'S LIKE I WAS UNTIL A WHILE AGO.
ARE YOU ANY MATCH FOR ME, I WONDER!?
NIPA
...IN OTHER WORDS, OUR CLUB PLAYS GAMES, SIR.
GAMES, HUH? YEAH, SOUNDS FUN.
ALLLLRIGHT! PLEASE GO EASY ON ME, SENPAIS!
WAAAAAAAAHHH!
YEAH!

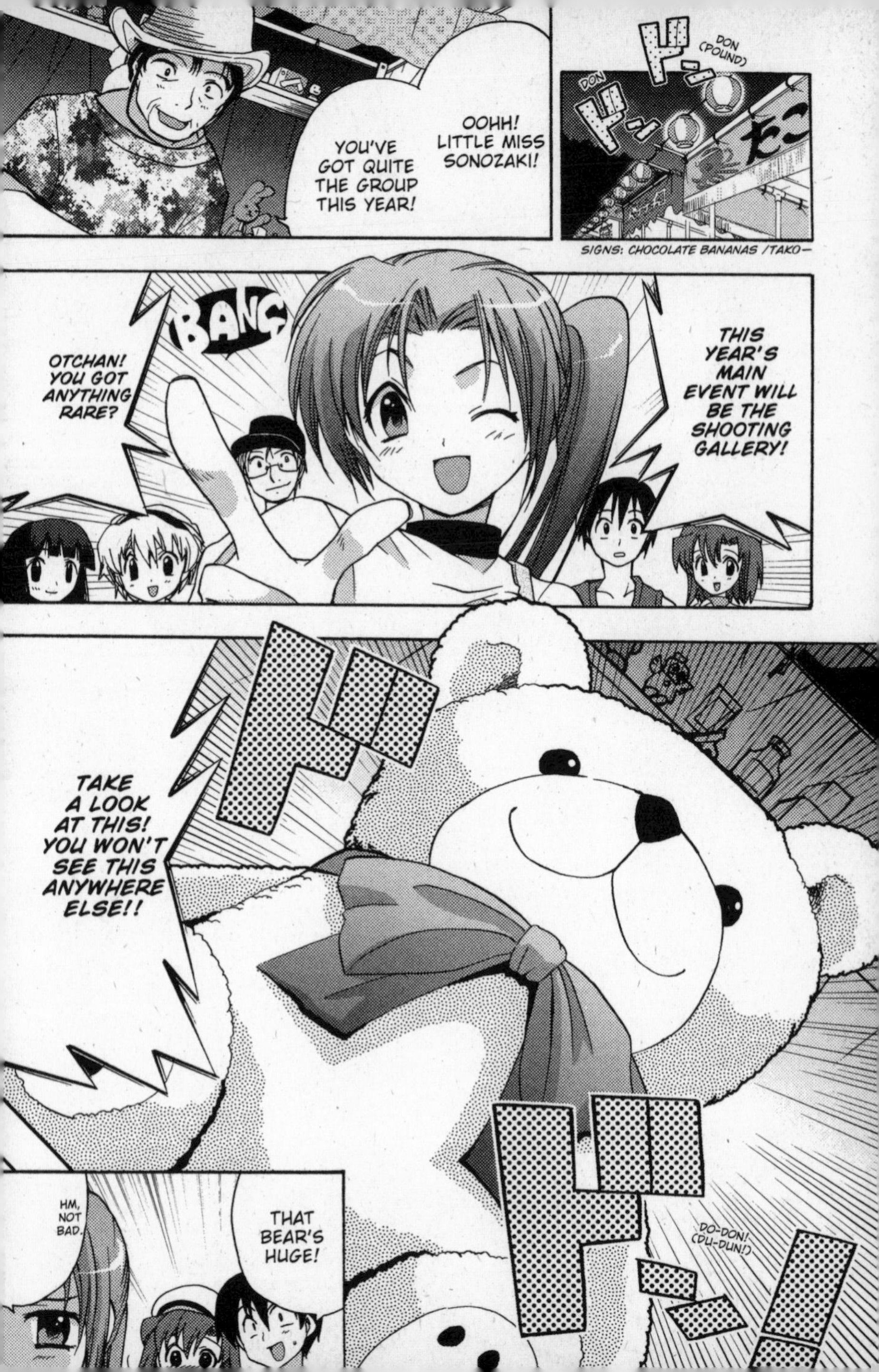
DON (POUND)
DON
SIGNS: CHOCOLATE BANANAS /TAKO—
OOHH! LITTLE MISS SONOZAKI!
YOU'VE GOT QUITE THE GROUP THIS YEAR!
THIS YEAR'S MAIN EVENT WILL BE THE SHOOTING GALLERY!
BANG
OTCHAN! YOU GOT ANYTHING RARE?
TAKE A LOOK AT THIS! YOU WON'T SEE THIS ANYWHERE ELSE!!
DO-DON! (DU-DUN!)
THAT BEAR'S HUGE!
HM, NOT BAD.

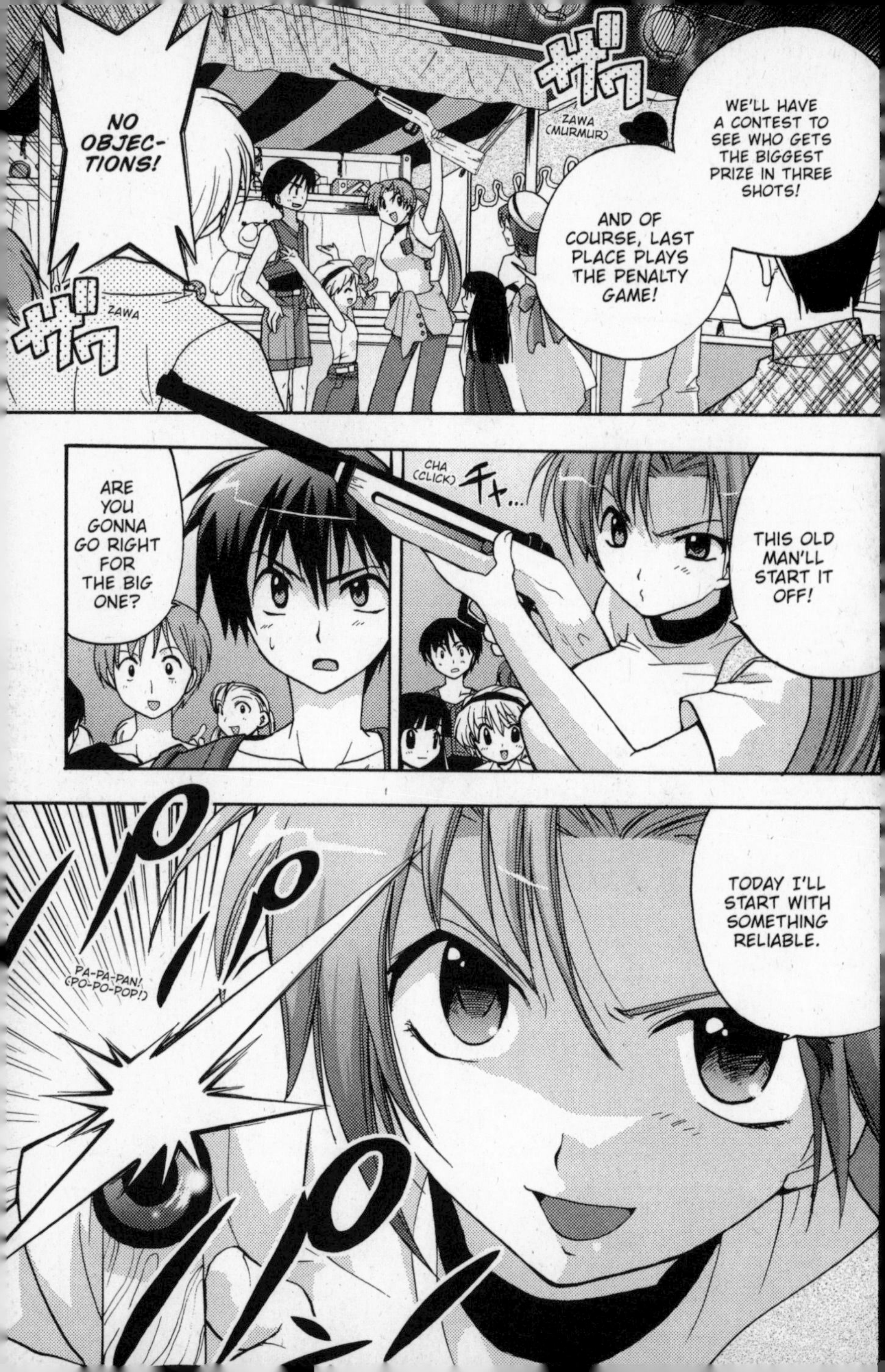
WE'LL HAVE A CONTEST TO SEE WHO GETS THE BIGGEST PRIZE IN THREE SHOTS!
AND OF COURSE, LAST PLACE PLAYS THE PENALTY GAME!
ザワ
ZAWA (MURMUR)
NO OBJECTIONS!
ザワ
ZAWA
THIS OLD MAN'LL START IT OFF!
CHA (CLICK)
チャ...
ARE YOU GONNA GO RIGHT FOR THE BIG ONE?
TODAY I'LL START WITH SOMETHING RELIABLE.
PA-PA-PAN! (PO-PO-POP!)

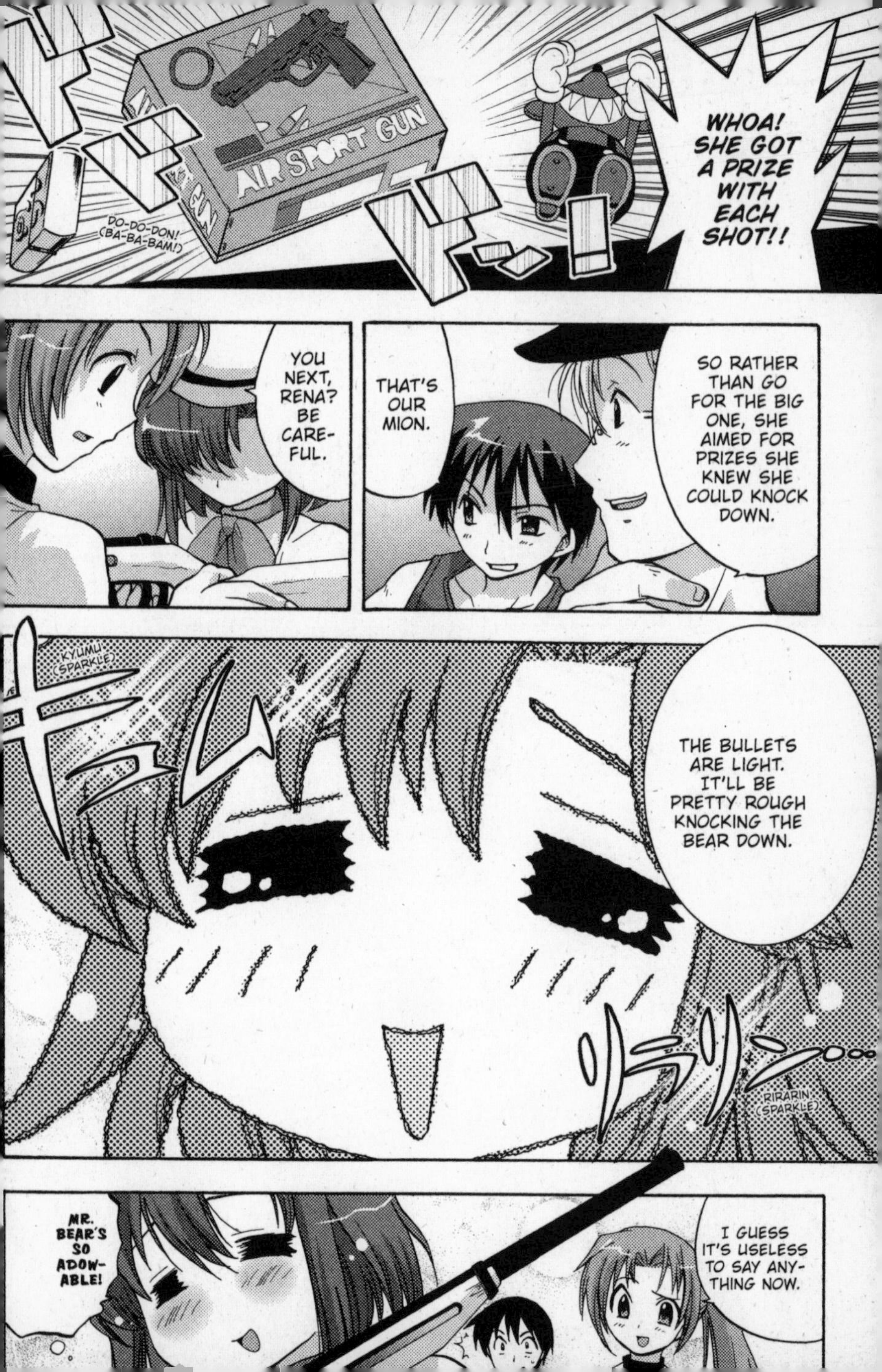
WHOA! SHE GOT A PRIZE WITH EACH SHOT!!
AIR SPORT GUN
DO-DO-DON! (BA-BA-BAM!)
SO RATHER THAN GO FOR THE BIG ONE, SHE AIMED FOR PRIZES SHE KNEW SHE COULD KNOCK DOWN.
THAT'S OUR MION.
YOU NEXT, RENA? BE CARE-FUL.
THE BULLETS ARE LIGHT. IT'LL BE PRETTY ROUGH KNOCKING THE BEAR DOWN.
KYUMU (SPARKLE)
RIRARIN (SPARKLE)
I GUESS IT'S USELESS TO SAY ANY-THING NOW.
MR. BEAR'S SO ADOWABLE!

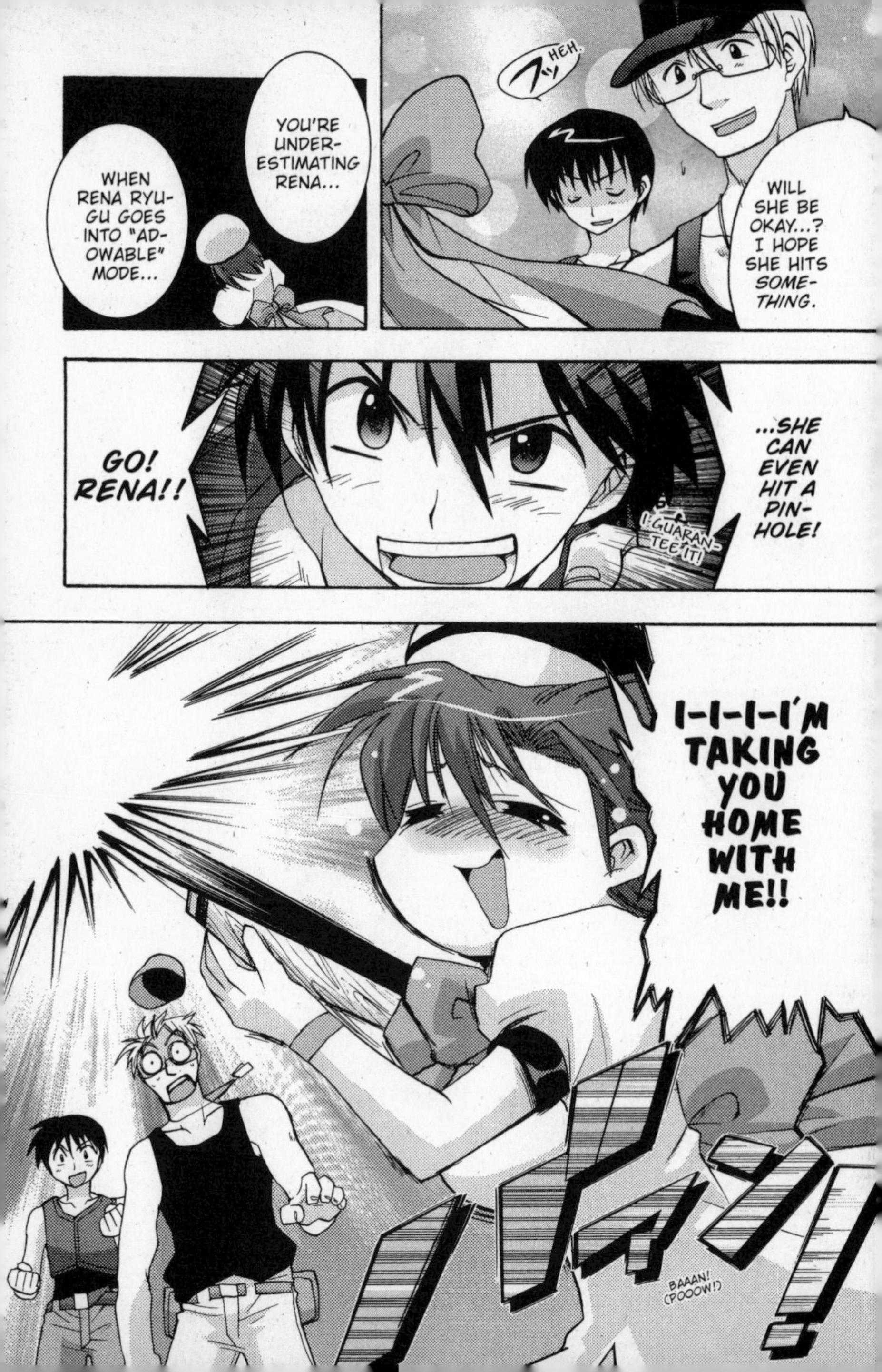
WILL SHE BE OKAY...? I HOPE SHE HITS SOME-THING.
HEH.
YOU'RE UNDER-ESTIMATING RENA...
WHEN RENA RYU-GU GOES INTO "AD-OWABLE" MODE...
...SHE CAN EVEN HIT A PIN-HOLE!
I GUARAN-TEE IT!
GO! RENA!!
I-I-I-I'M TAKING YOU HOME WITH ME!!
BAAAN! (POOOW!)

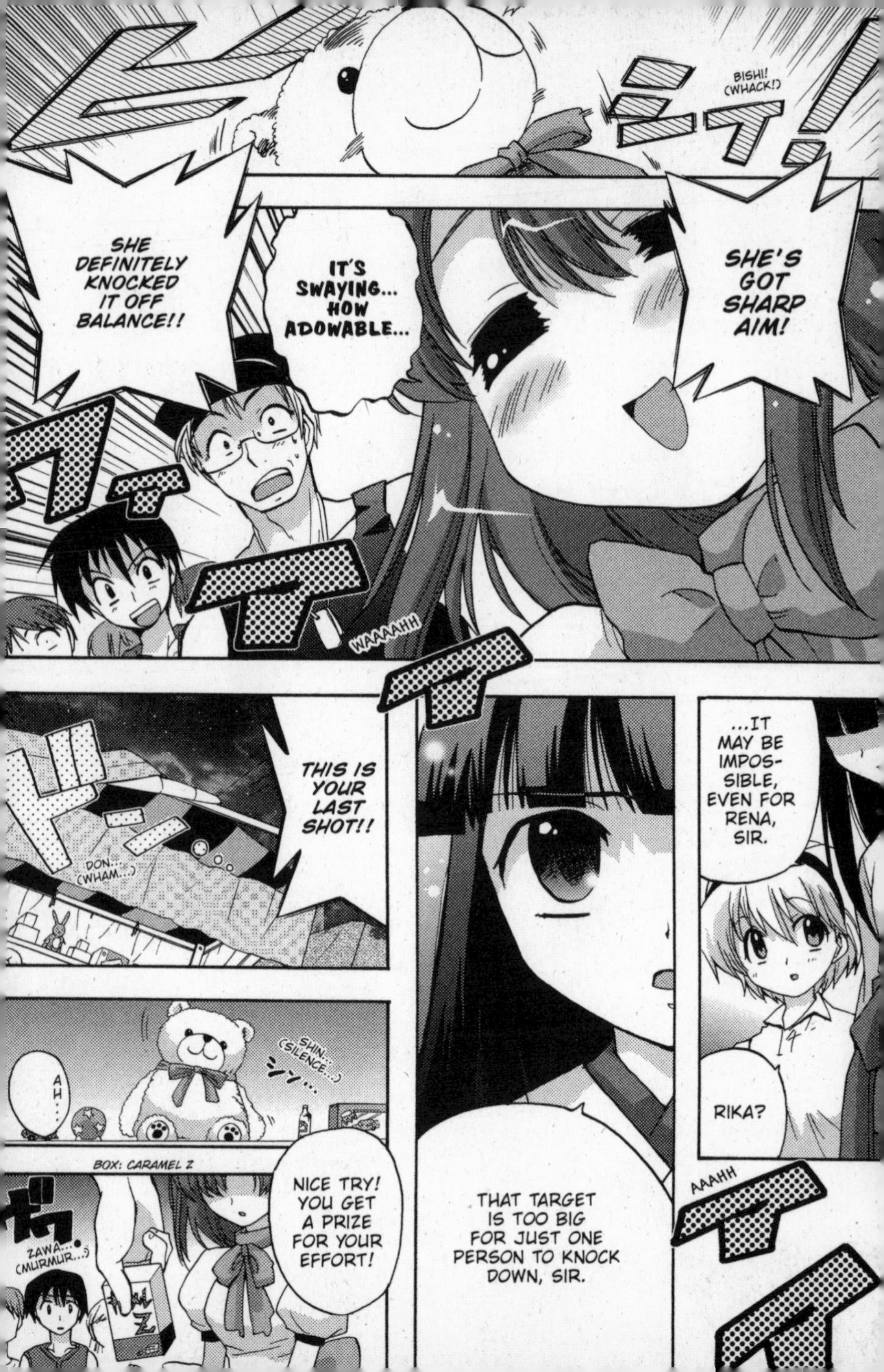
BISHI! (WHACK!)
SHE'S GOT SHARP AIM!
IT'S SWAYING... HOW ADOWABLE...
SHE DEFINITELY KNOCKED IT OFF BALANCE!!
WAAAAHH
...IT MAY BE IMPOSSIBLE, EVEN FOR RENA, SIR.
RIKA?
AAAHH
THAT TARGET IS TOO BIG FOR JUST ONE PERSON TO KNOCK DOWN, SIR.
THIS IS YOUR LAST SHOT!!
DON... (WHAM...)
SHIN... (SILENCE...)
AH...
BOX: CARAMEL Z
NICE TRY! YOU GET A PRIZE FOR YOUR EFFORT!
ZAWA... (MURMUR...)

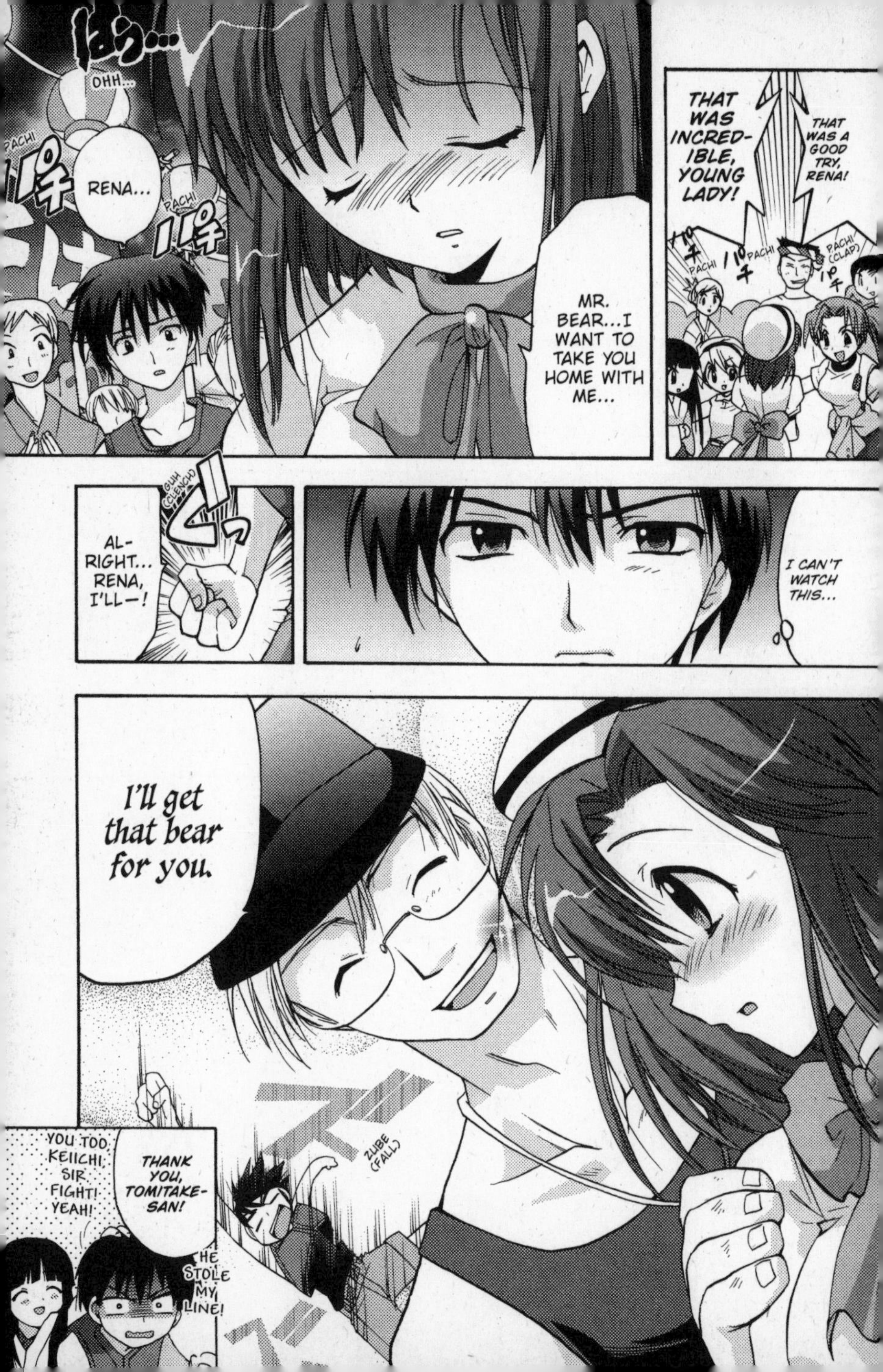
THAT WAS INCREDIBLE, YOUNG LADY!
THAT WAS A GOOD TRY, RENA!
PACHI (CLAP)
PACHI
PACHI
OHH...
PACHI
RENA...
PACHI
MR. BEAR...I WANT TO TAKE YOU HOME WITH ME...
I CAN'T WATCH THIS...
GUH (CLENCH)
AL-RIGHT... RENA, I'LL—!
I'll get that bear for you.
THANK YOU, TOMITAKE-SAN!
ZUBE (FALL)
YOU TOO KEIICHI SIR FIGHT! YEAH!
HE STOLE MY LINE!

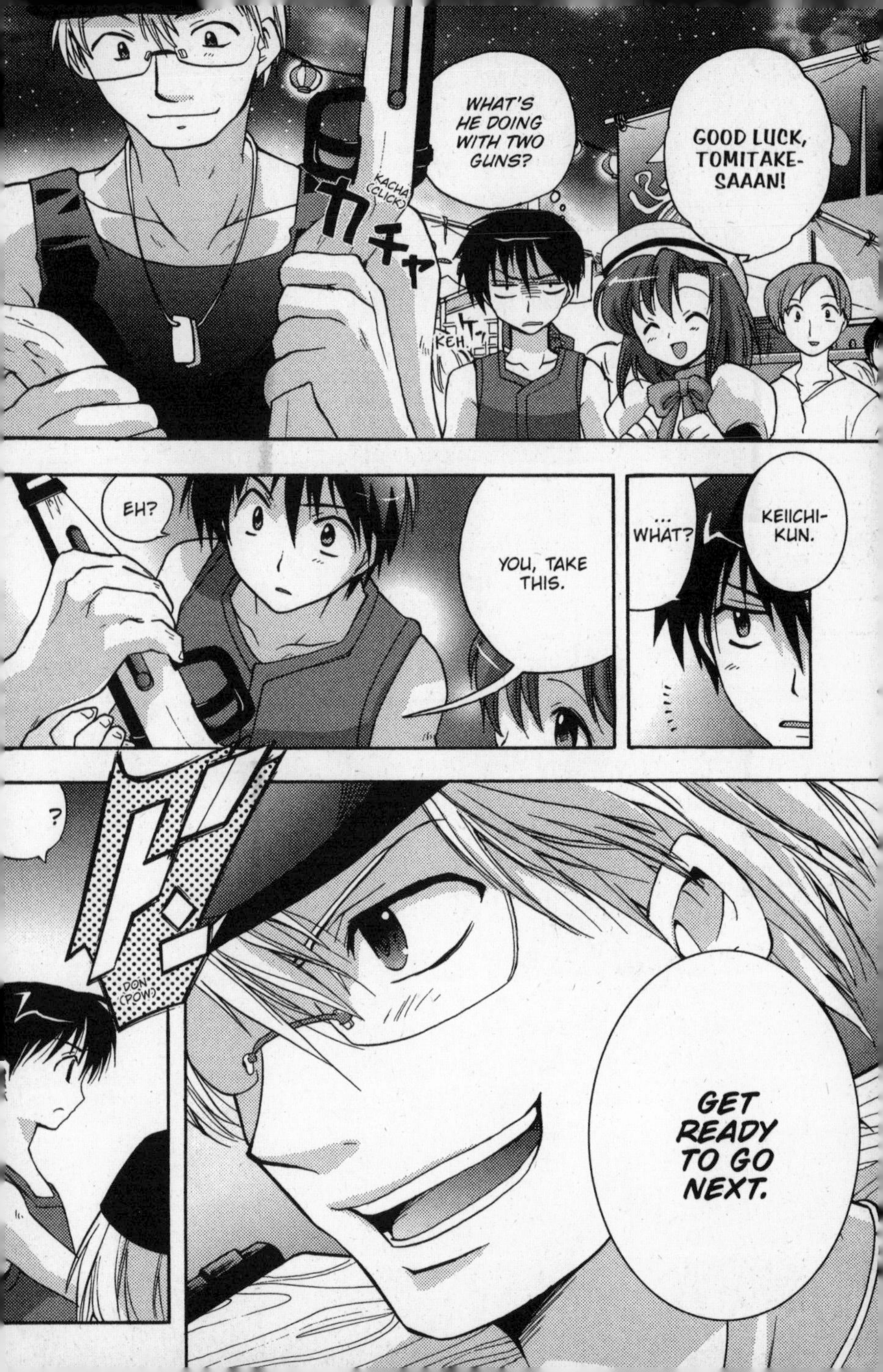
GOOD LUCK, TOMITAKE-SAAAN!
WHAT'S HE DOING WITH TWO GUNS?
KACHA (CLICK)
KEH.
KEIICHI-KUN.
... WHAT?
YOU, TAKE THIS.
EH?
GET READY TO GO NEXT.
DON (POW)
?

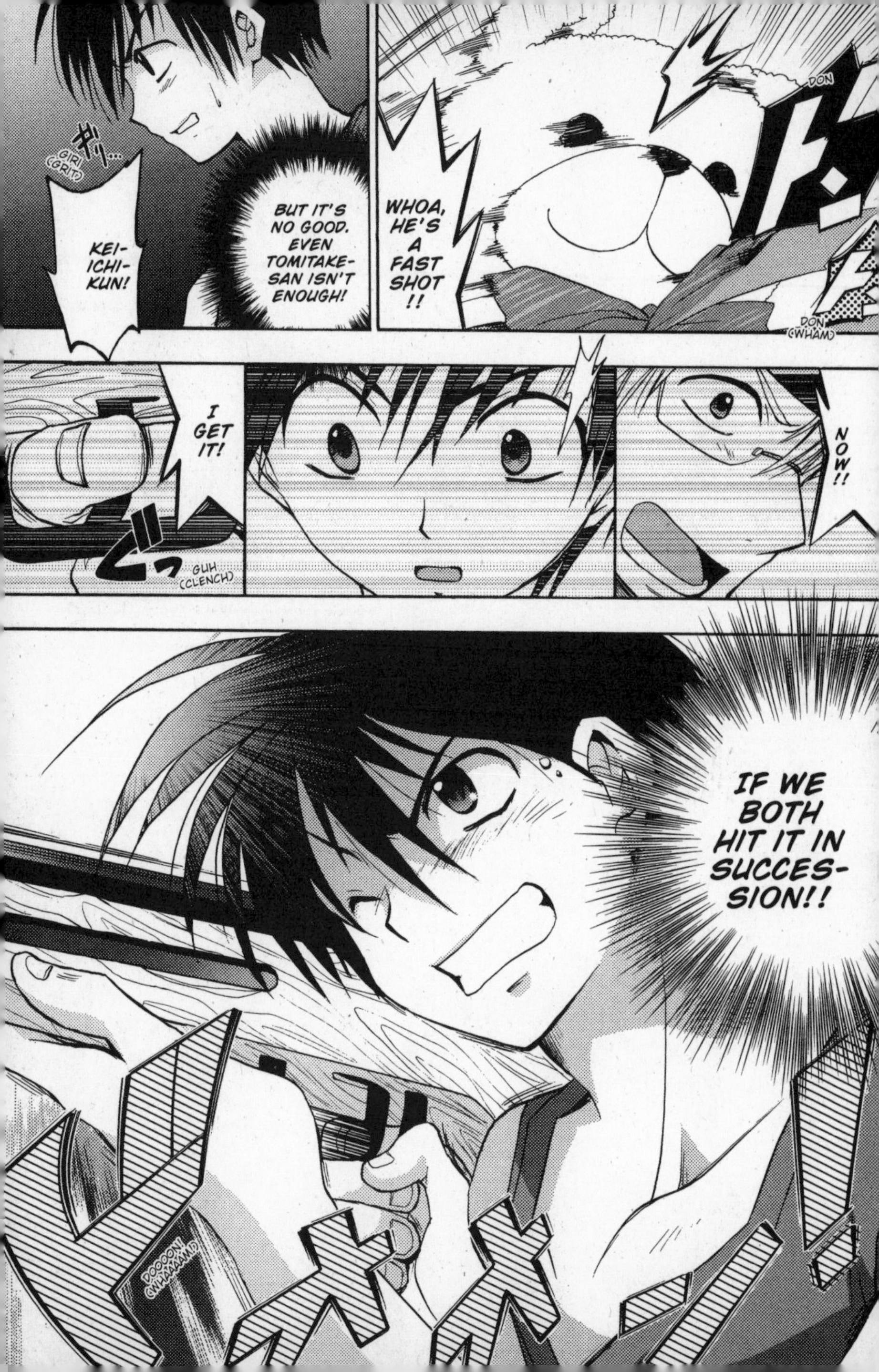
DON
WHOA, HE'S A FAST SHOT!!
DON (WHAM)
BUT IT'S NO GOOD. EVEN TOMITAKE-SAN ISN'T ENOUGH!
GIRI (GRIT)
KEI-ICHI-KUN!
NOW!!
I GET IT!
GUH (CLENCH)
IF WE BOTH HIT IT IN SUCCESSION!!
DOOOON! (WHAAAAM!)

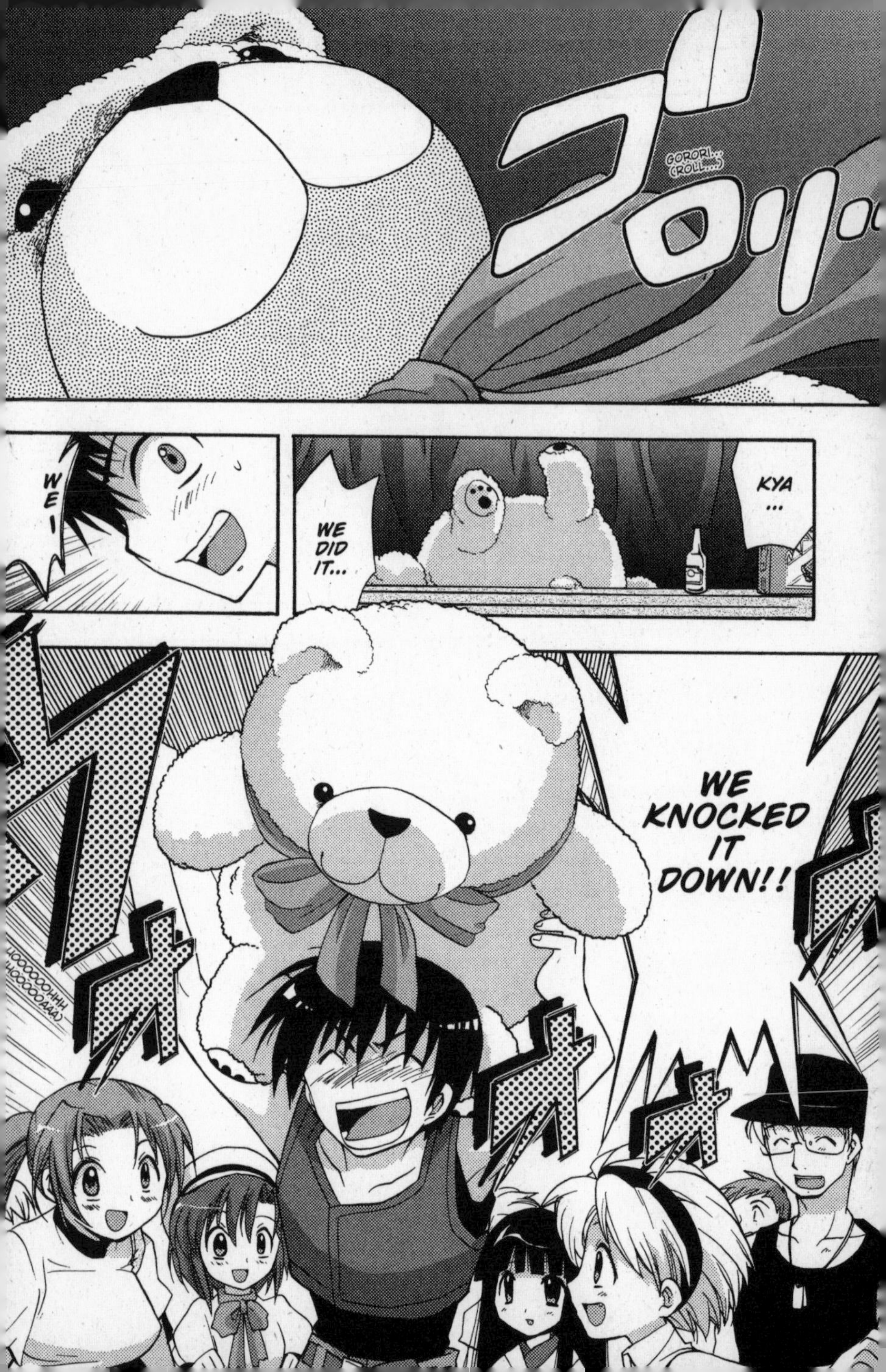
GORORI... (ROLL...)
KYA...
WE DID IT...
WE-I
WE KNOCKED IT DOWN!!
(OOOOOOOHHH
OOOOOOAAA)

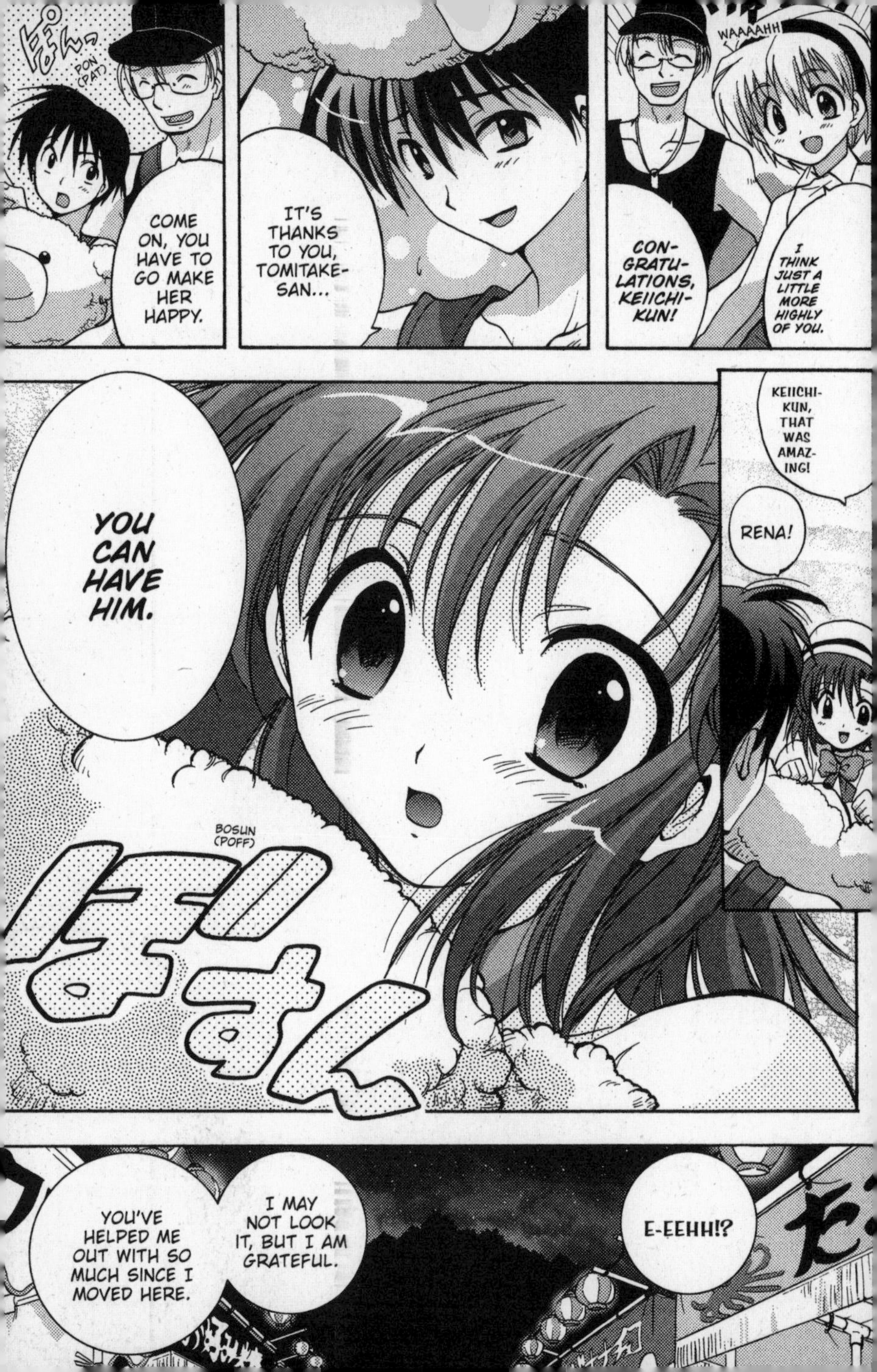
WAAAAHH
I THINK JUST A LITTLE MORE HIGHLY OF YOU.
CONGRATULATIONS, KEIICHI-KUN!
IT'S THANKS TO YOU, TOMITAKE-SAN...
ぽんっ
PON (PAT)
COME ON, YOU HAVE TO GO MAKE HER HAPPY.
KEIICHI-KUN, THAT WAS AMAZING!
RENA!
YOU CAN HAVE HIM.
BOSUN (POFF)
ぼすん
E-EEHH!?
I MAY NOT LOOK IT, BUT I AM GRATEFUL.
YOU'VE HELPED ME OUT WITH SO MUCH SINCE I MOVED HERE.

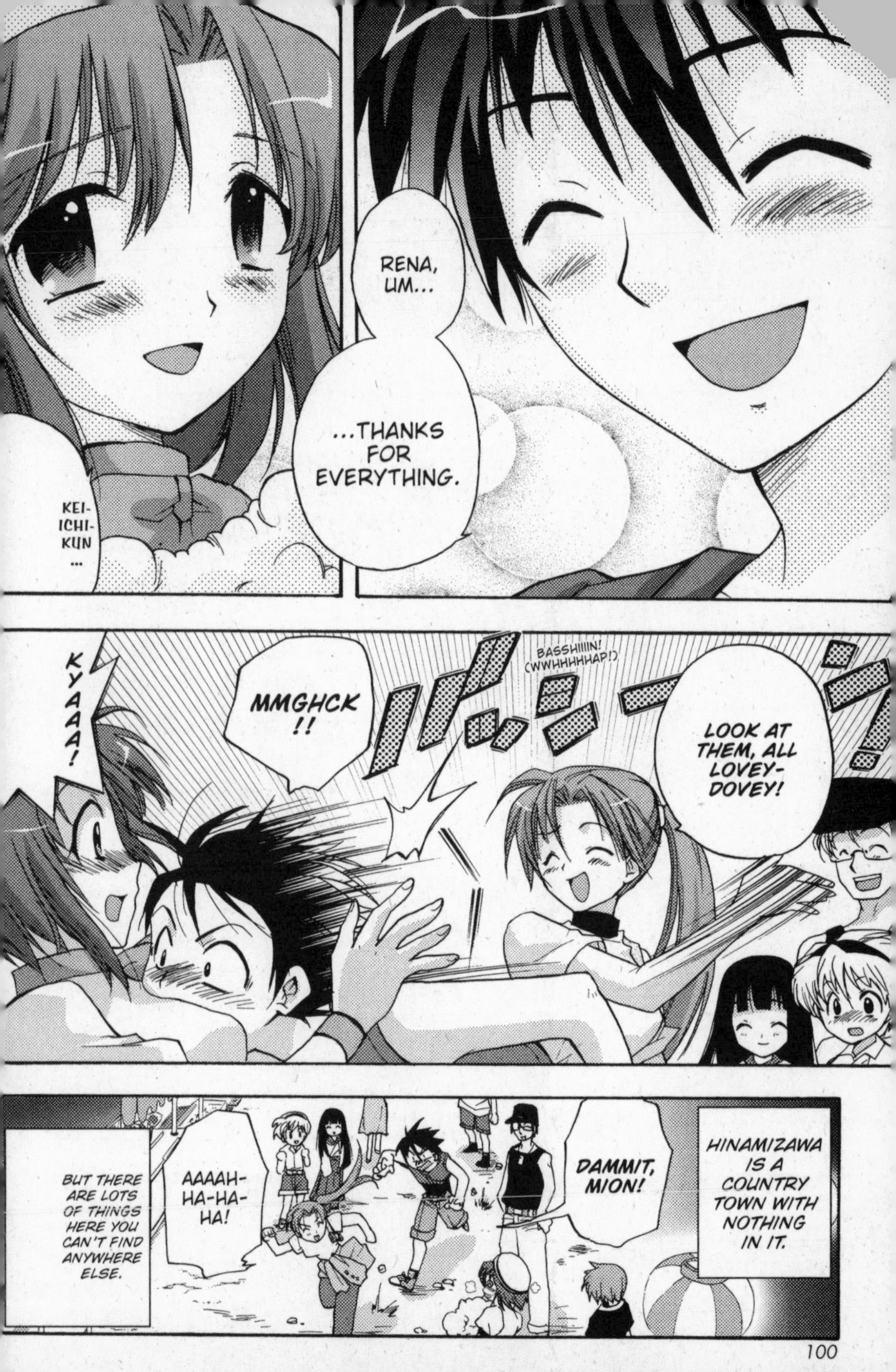
RENA, UM...
...THANKS FOR EVERYTHING.
KEI-ICHI-KUN...
LOOK AT THEM, ALL LOVEY-DOVEY!
BASSHIIIIN! (WWHHHHHHAP!)
MMGHCK!!
KYAAAA!
HINAMIZAWA IS A COUNTRY TOWN WITH NOTHING IN IT.
DAMMIT, MION!
AAAAH-HA-HA-HA!
BUT THERE ARE LOTS OF THINGS HERE YOU CAN'T FIND ANYWHERE ELSE.

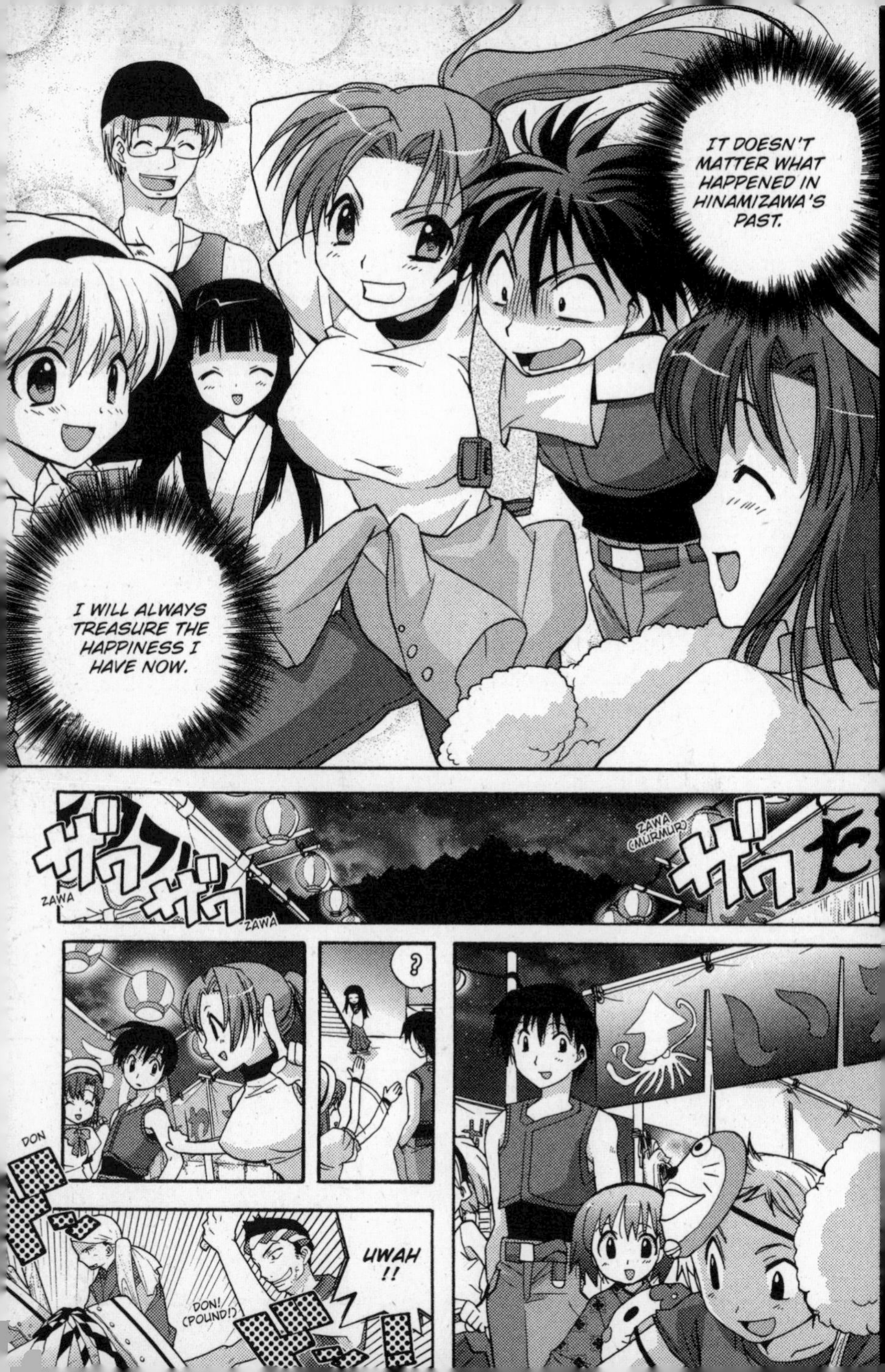

IT DOESN'T MATTER WHAT HAPPENED IN HINAMIZAWA'S PAST.
I WILL ALWAYS TREASURE THE HAPPINESS I HAVE NOW.
ZAWA (MURMUR)
ZAWA
ZAWA
?
DON
UWAH !!
DON! (POUND!)

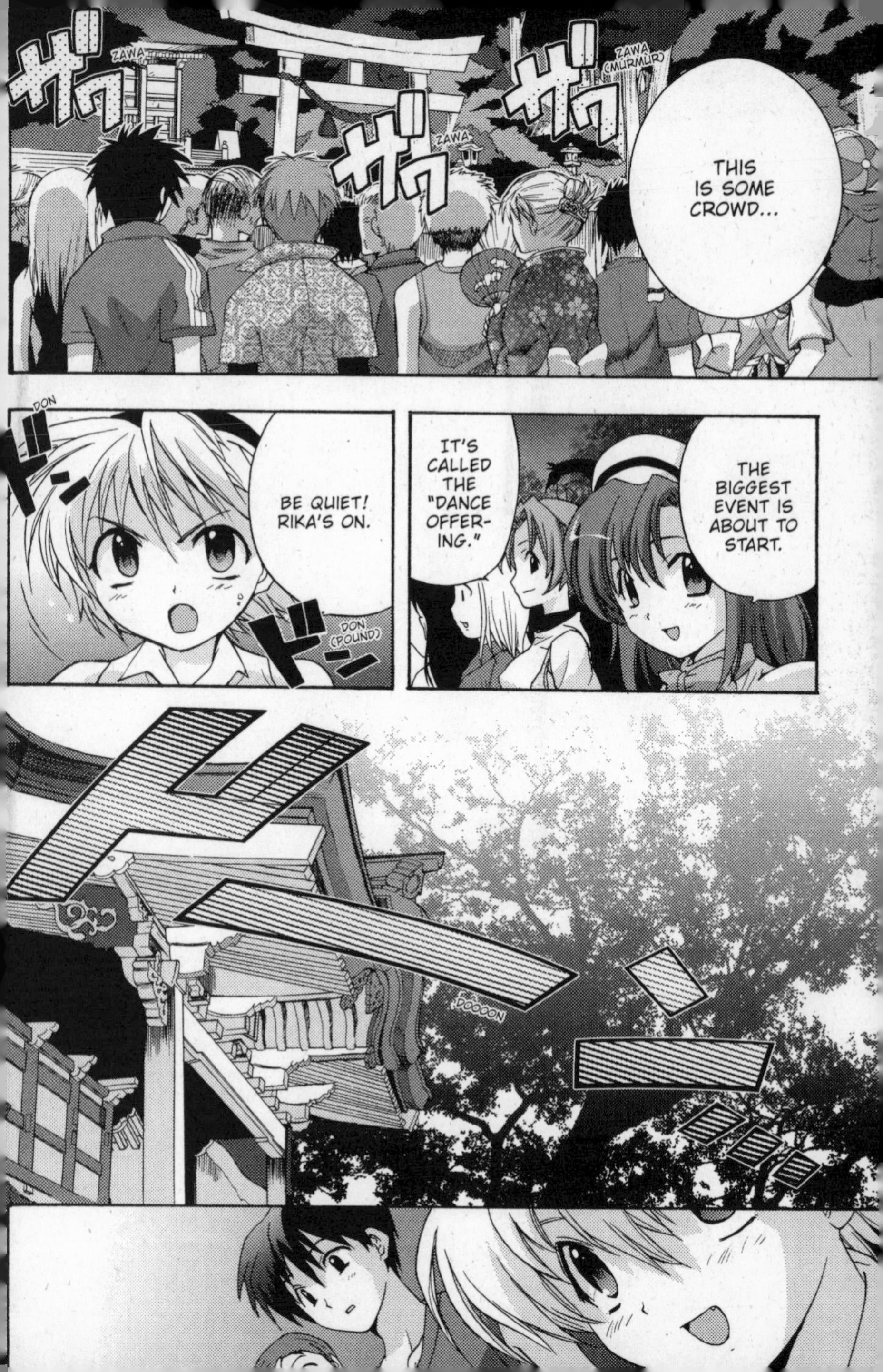
ZAWA (MURMUR)
THIS IS SOME CROWD...
ZAWA
ZAWA
THE BIGGEST EVENT IS ABOUT TO START.
IT'S CALLED THE "DANCE OFFERING."
DON
BE QUIET! RIKA'S ON.
DON (POUND)
DOOOON

ポぅ…
POU...
(GLOW...)

SO RIKA-CHAN'S JOB WAS TO BE THE PRIESTESS IN THE CEREMONY...

カシャ
KASHA
(FLASH)

A HOE AND... IS THAT A FUTON? WHAT A WEIRD CEREMONY.

わっしょい
WASSHOI
(HEAVE-HO)

カシャ
KASHA

ドン
DON
(POUND)

わっしょい
WASSHOI

ドン
DON

わっしょい
WASSHOI

ドン
DON

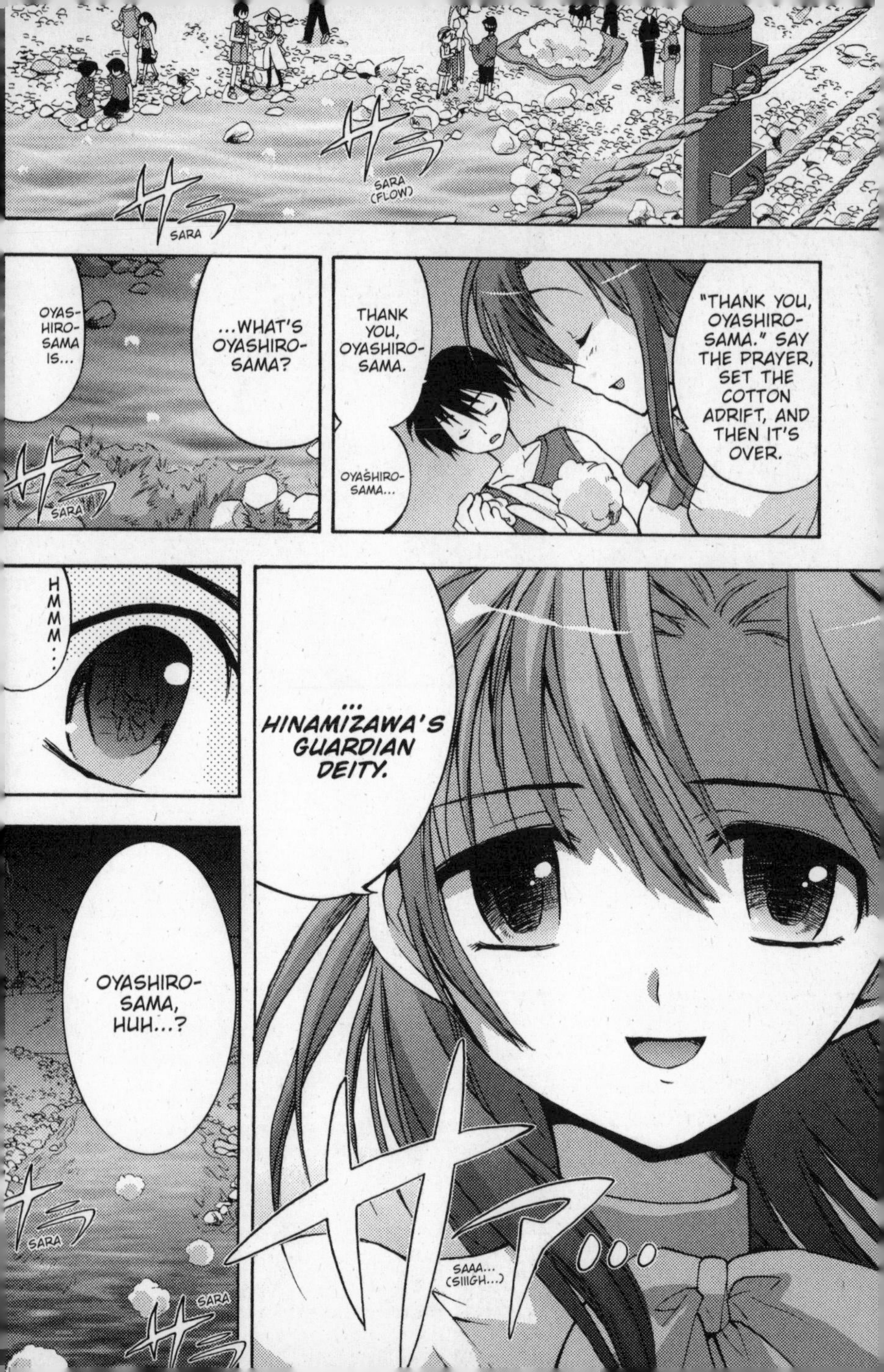
SARA (FLOW)
SARA
"THANK YOU, OYASHIRO-SAMA." SAY THE PRAYER, SET THE COTTON ADRIFT, AND THEN IT'S OVER.
THANK YOU, OYASHIRO-SAMA.
OYASHIRO-SAMA...
...WHAT'S OYASHIRO-SAMA?
OYASHIRO-SAMA IS...
SARA
...HINAMIZAWA'S GUARDIAN DEITY.
SAAA... (SIIIGH...)
HMMM...
OYASHIRO-SAMA, HUH...?
SARA
SARA

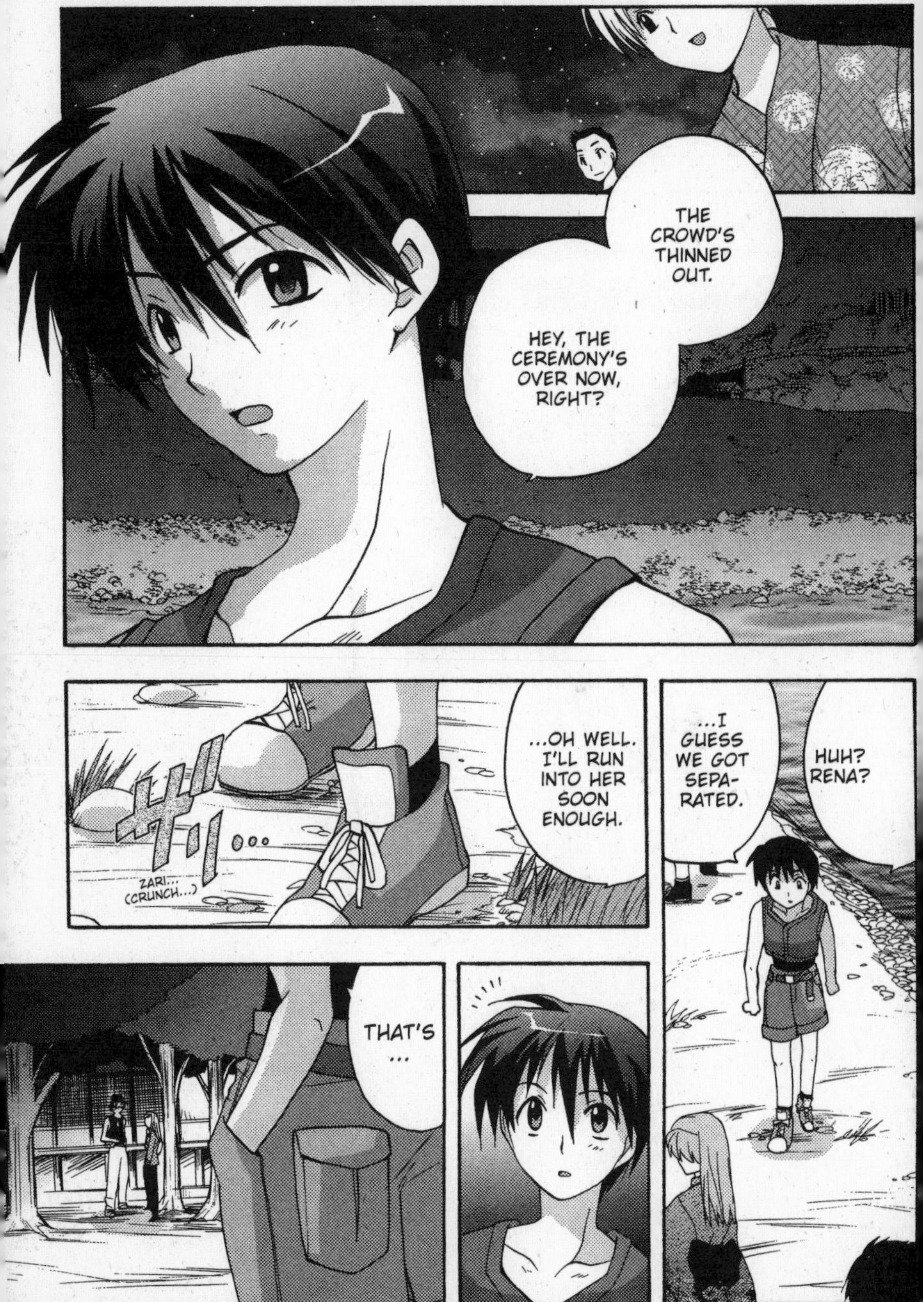
THE CROWD'S THINNED OUT.
HEY, THE CEREMONY'S OVER NOW, RIGHT?
HUH? RENA?
...I GUESS WE GOT SEPA-RATED.
...OH WELL. I'LL RUN INTO HER SOON ENOUGH.
ZARI... (CRUNCH...)
THAT'S ...

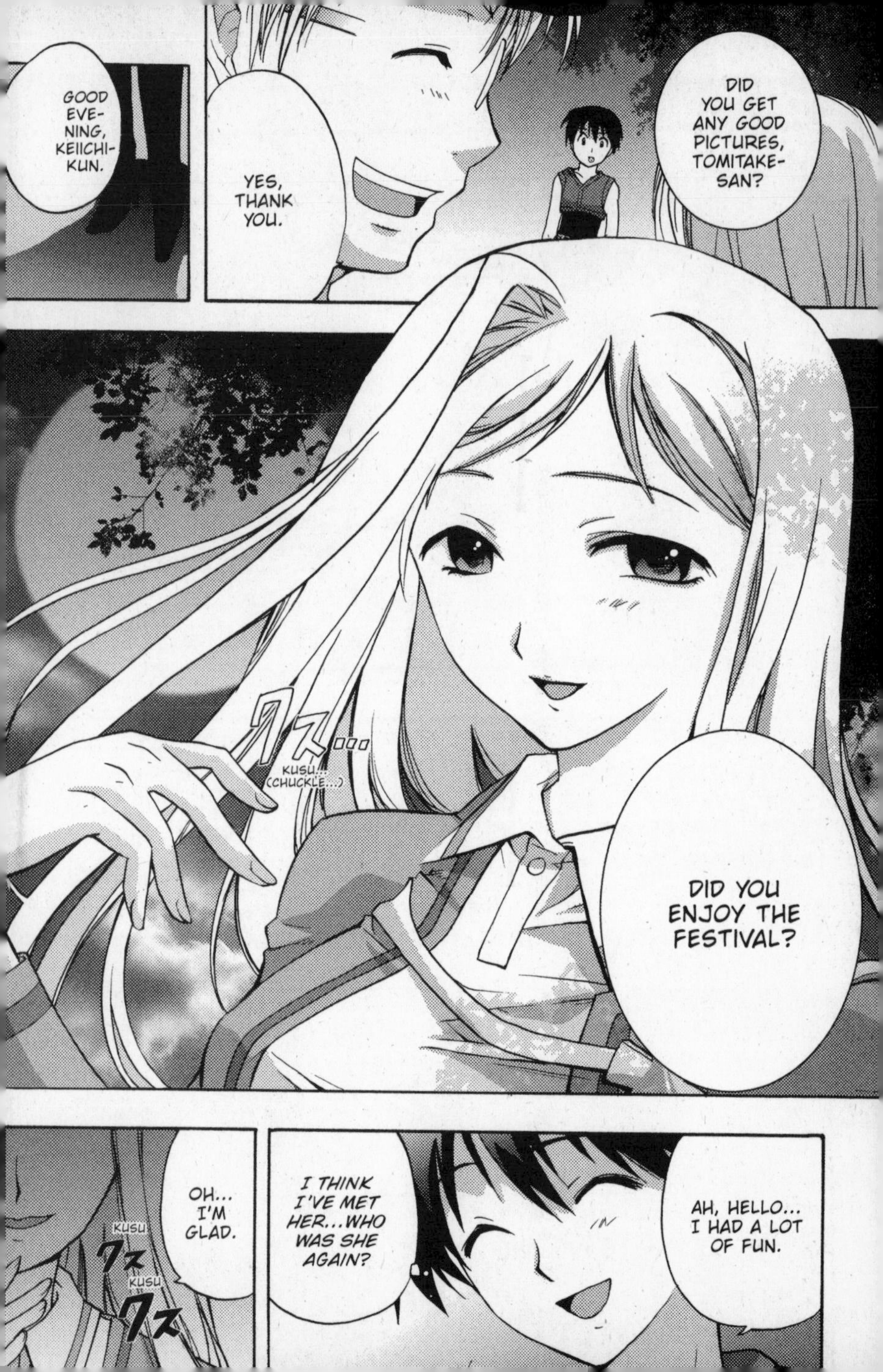
DID YOU GET ANY GOOD PICTURES, TOMITAKE-SAN?
YES, THANK YOU.
GOOD EVE-NING, KEIICHI-KUN.
DID YOU ENJOY THE FESTIVAL?
クス…
KUSU... (CHUCKLE...)
AH, HELLO... I HAD A LOT OF FUN.
I THINK I'VE MET HER...WHO WAS SHE AGAIN?
OH... I'M GLAD.
クス
KUSU
クス
KUSU

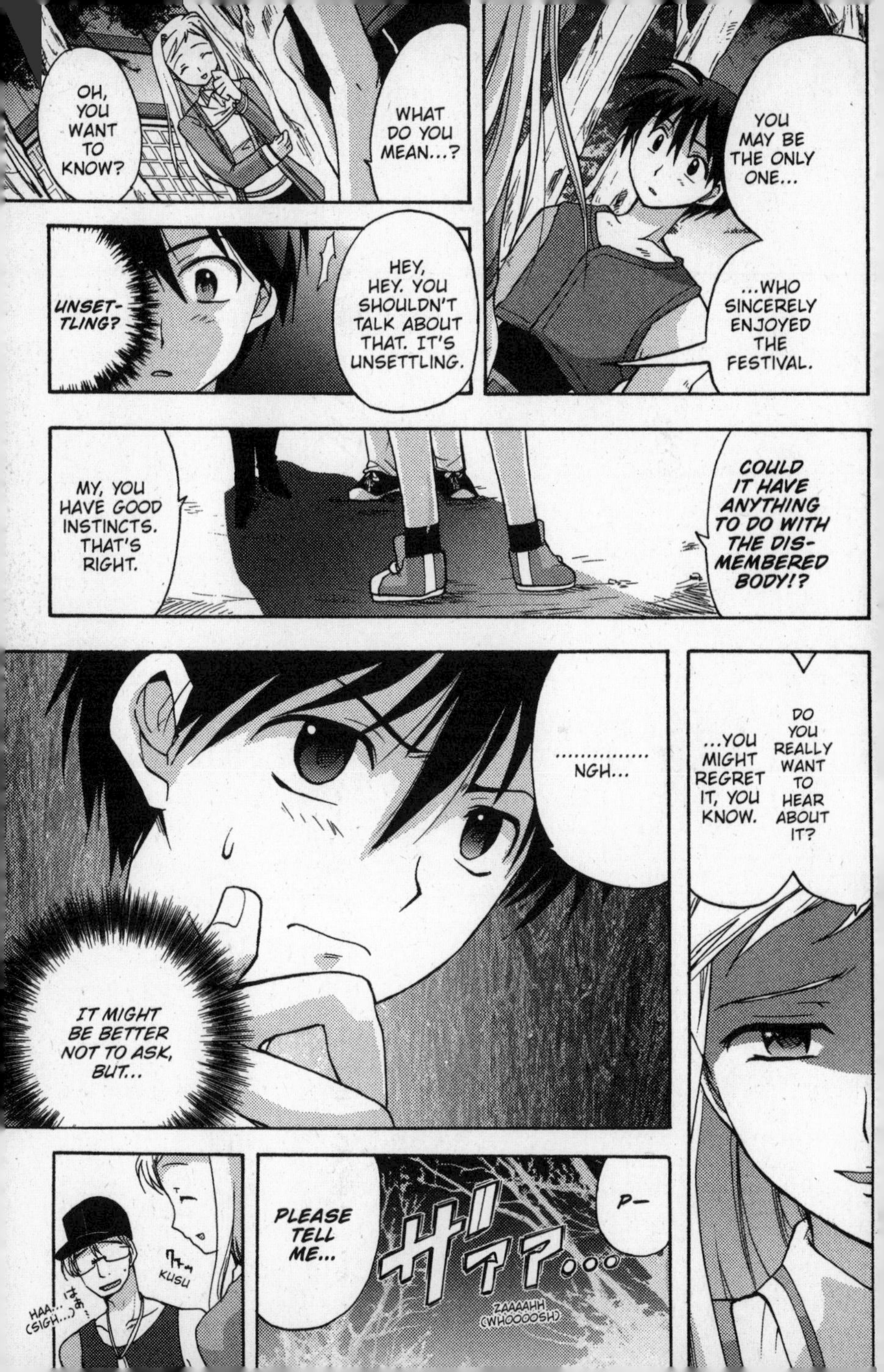
YOU MAY BE THE ONLY ONE...
...WHO SINCERELY ENJOYED THE FESTIVAL.
WHAT DO YOU MEAN...?
OH, YOU WANT TO KNOW?
HEY, HEY. YOU SHOULDN'T TALK ABOUT THAT. IT'S UNSETTLING.
UNSET-TLING?
COULD IT HAVE ANYTHING TO DO WITH THE DIS-MEMBERED BODY!?
MY, YOU HAVE GOOD INSTINCTS. THAT'S RIGHT.
DO YOU REALLY WANT TO HEAR ABOUT IT?
...YOU MIGHT REGRET IT, YOU KNOW.
...............NGH...
IT MIGHT BE BETTER NOT TO ASK, BUT...
P—
PLEASE TELL ME...
ZAAAAHH (WHOOOOSH)
KUSU
HAA... (SIGH...)

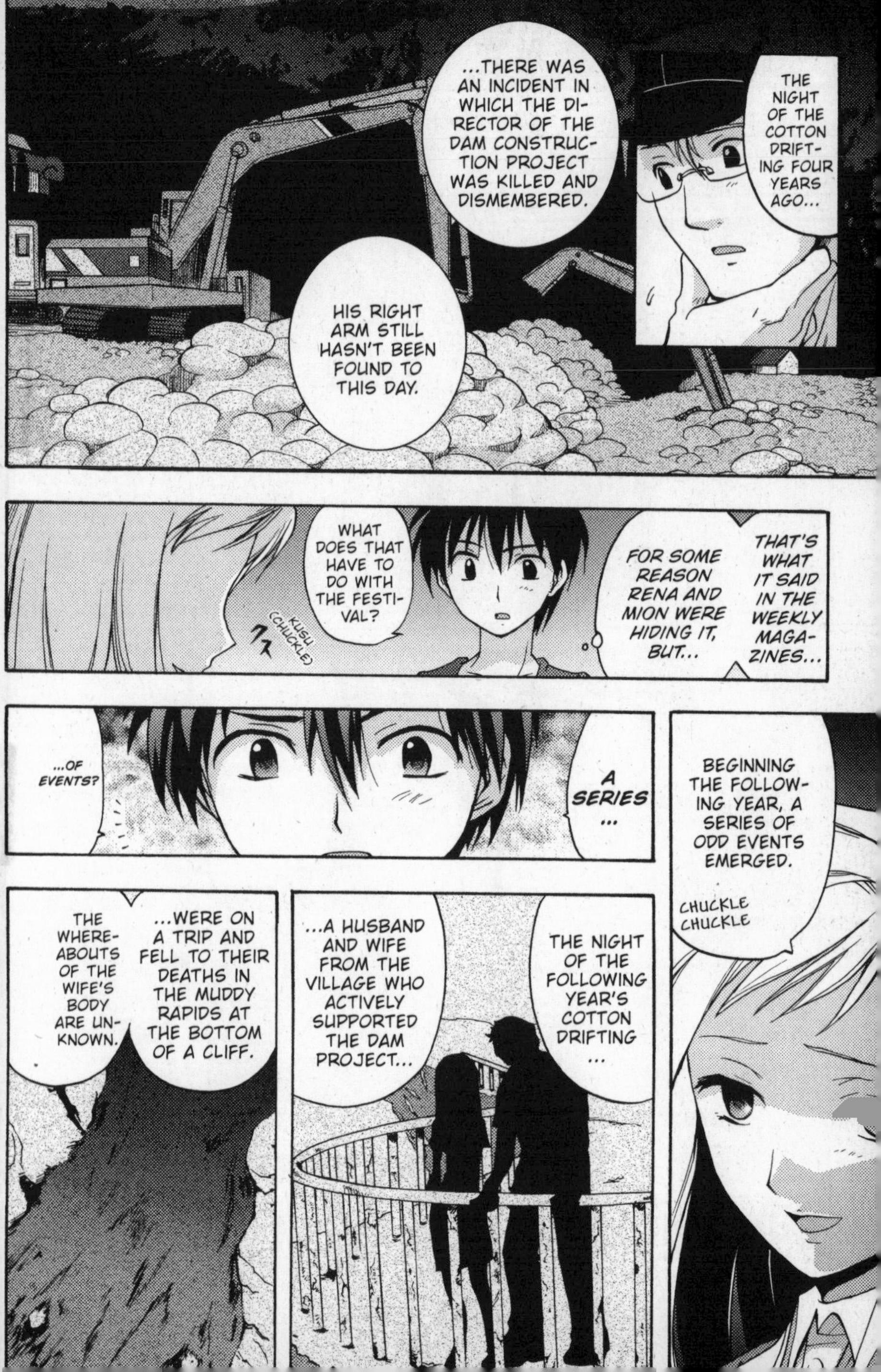
THE NIGHT OF THE COTTON DRIFTING FOUR YEARS AGO...
...THERE WAS AN INCIDENT IN WHICH THE DIRECTOR OF THE DAM CONSTRUCTION PROJECT WAS KILLED AND DISMEMBERED.
HIS RIGHT ARM STILL HASN'T BEEN FOUND TO THIS DAY.
THAT'S WHAT IT SAID IN THE WEEKLY MAGAZINES...
FOR SOME REASON RENA AND MION WERE HIDING IT, BUT...
WHAT DOES THAT HAVE TO DO WITH THE FESTIVAL?
KUSU (CHUCKLE)
BEGINNING THE FOLLOWING YEAR, A SERIES OF ODD EVENTS EMERGED.
CHUCKLE CHUCKLE
A SERIES...
...OF EVENTS?
THE NIGHT OF THE FOLLOWING YEAR'S COTTON DRIFTING...
...A HUSBAND AND WIFE FROM THE VILLAGE WHO ACTIVELY SUPPORTED THE DAM PROJECT...
...WERE ON A TRIP AND FELL TO THEIR DEATHS IN THE MUDDY RAPIDS AT THE BOTTOM OF A CLIFF.
THE WHEREABOUTS OF THE WIFE'S BODY ARE UNKNOWN.

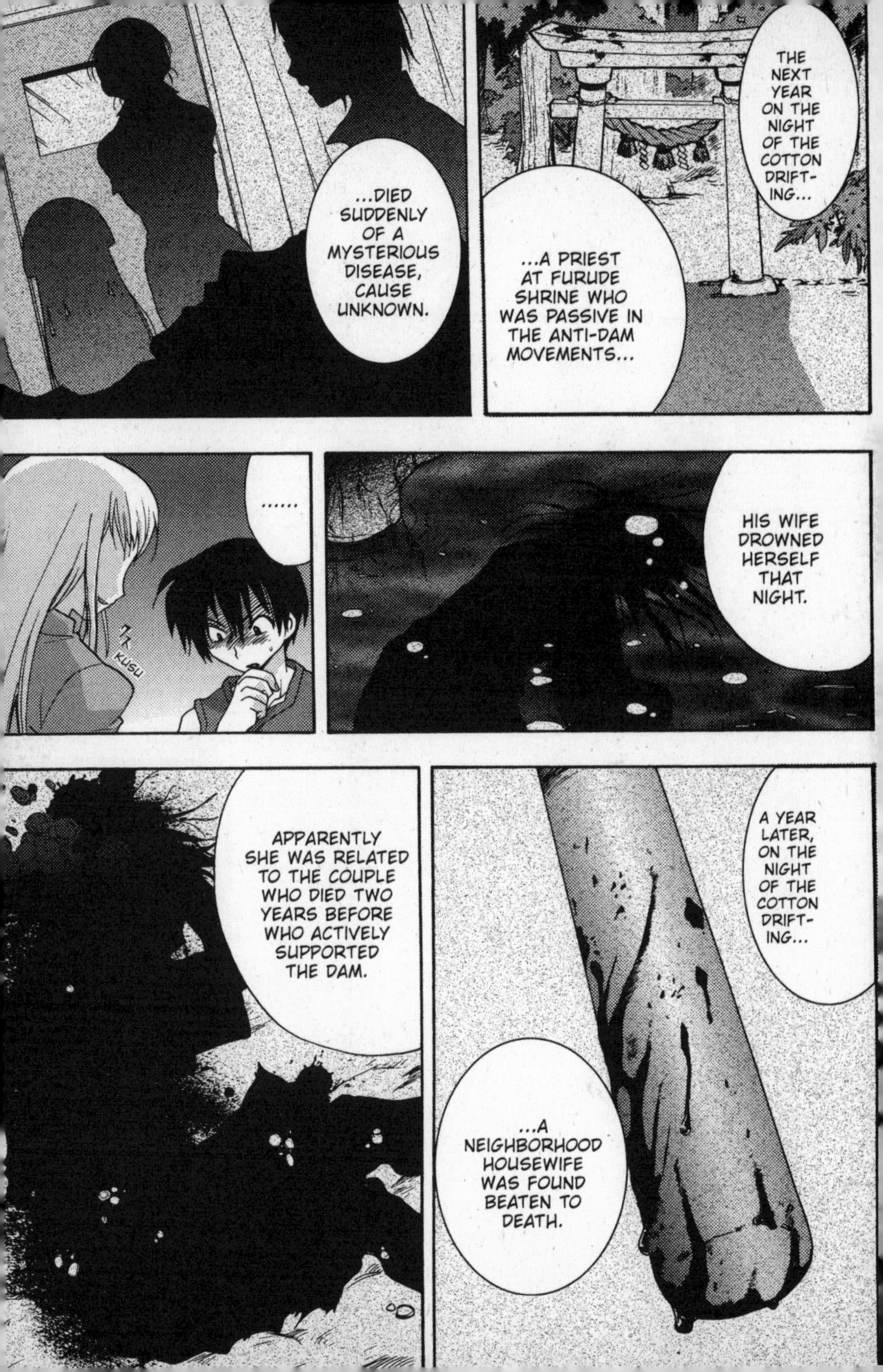
THE NEXT YEAR ON THE NIGHT OF THE COTTON DRIFTING...
...A PRIEST AT FURUDE SHRINE WHO WAS PASSIVE IN THE ANTI-DAM MOVEMENTS...
...DIED SUDDENLY OF A MYSTERIOUS DISEASE, CAUSE UNKNOWN.
HIS WIFE DROWNED HERSELF THAT NIGHT.
......
KUSU
A YEAR LATER, ON THE NIGHT OF THE COTTON DRIFTING...
...A NEIGHBORHOOD HOUSEWIFE WAS FOUND BEATEN TO DEATH.
APPARENTLY SHE WAS RELATED TO THE COUPLE WHO DIED TWO YEARS BEFORE WHO ACTIVELY SUPPORTED THE DAM.

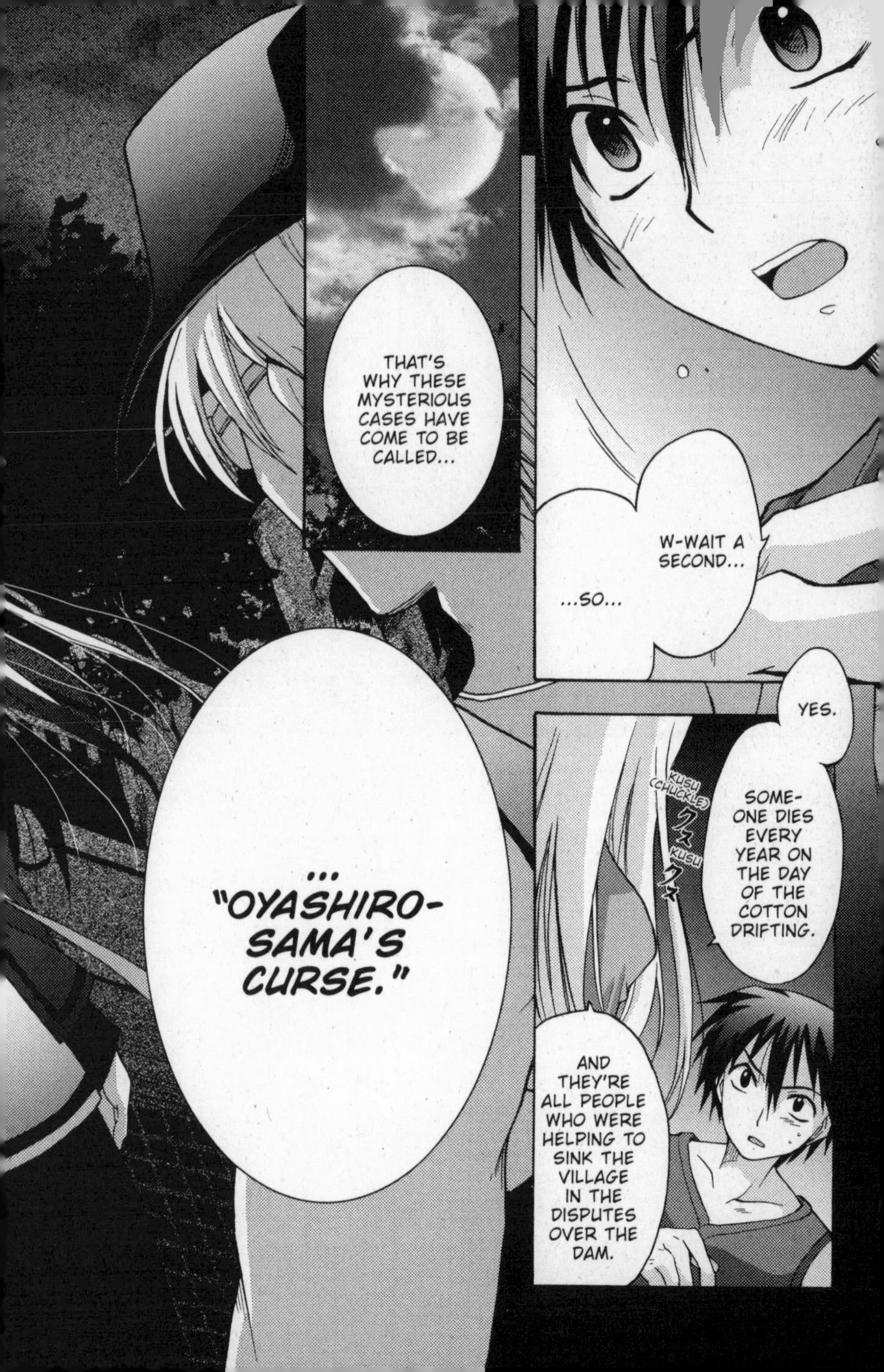
W-WAIT A SECOND...
...SO...
YES.
KUSU (CHUCKLE)
KUSU
SOME-ONE DIES EVERY YEAR ON THE DAY OF THE COTTON DRIFTING.
AND THEY'RE ALL PEOPLE WHO WERE HELPING TO SINK THE VILLAGE IN THE DISPUTES OVER THE DAM.
THAT'S WHY THESE MYSTERIOUS CASES HAVE COME TO BE CALLED...
... "OYASHIRO-SAMA'S CURSE."

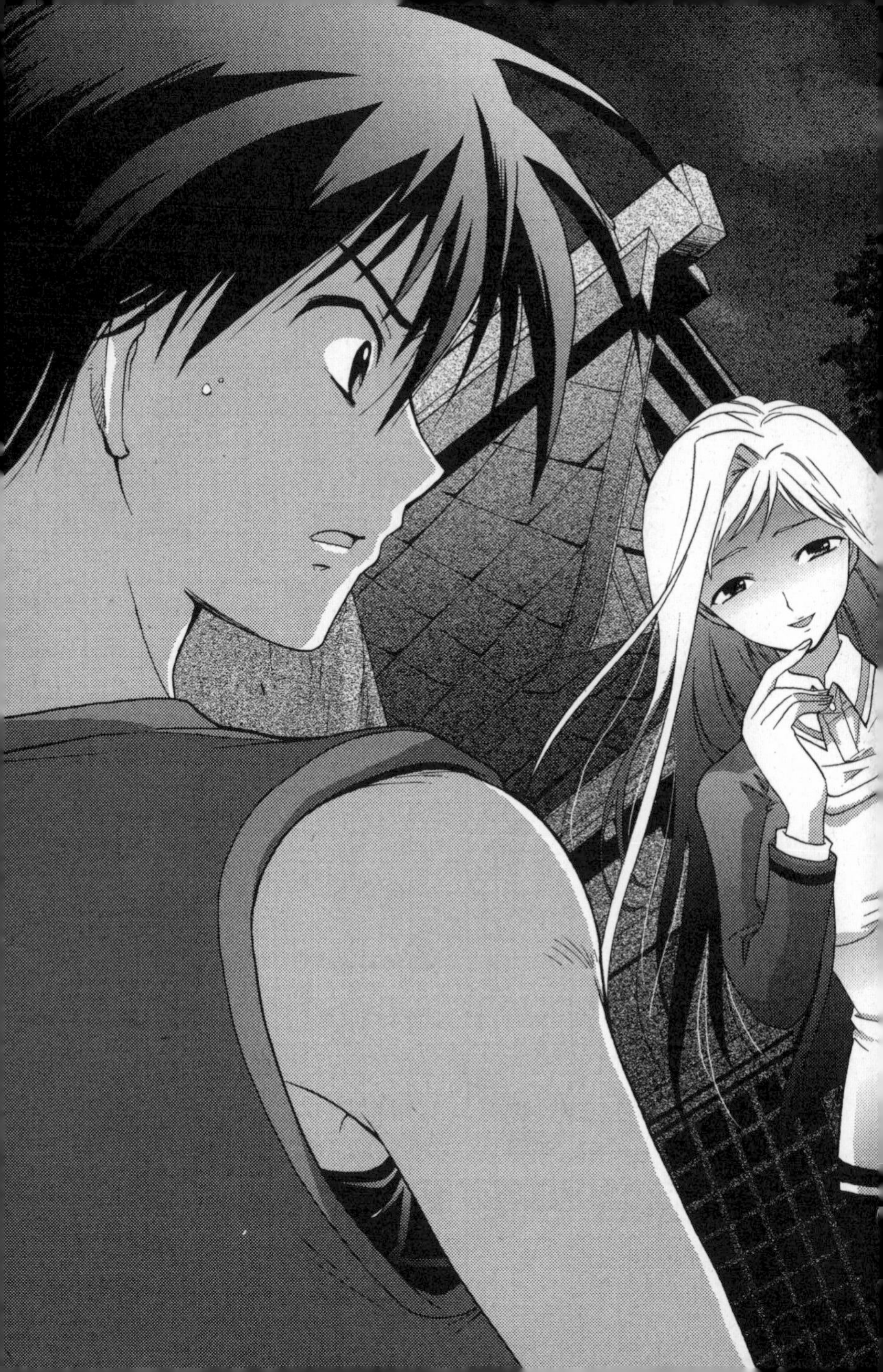

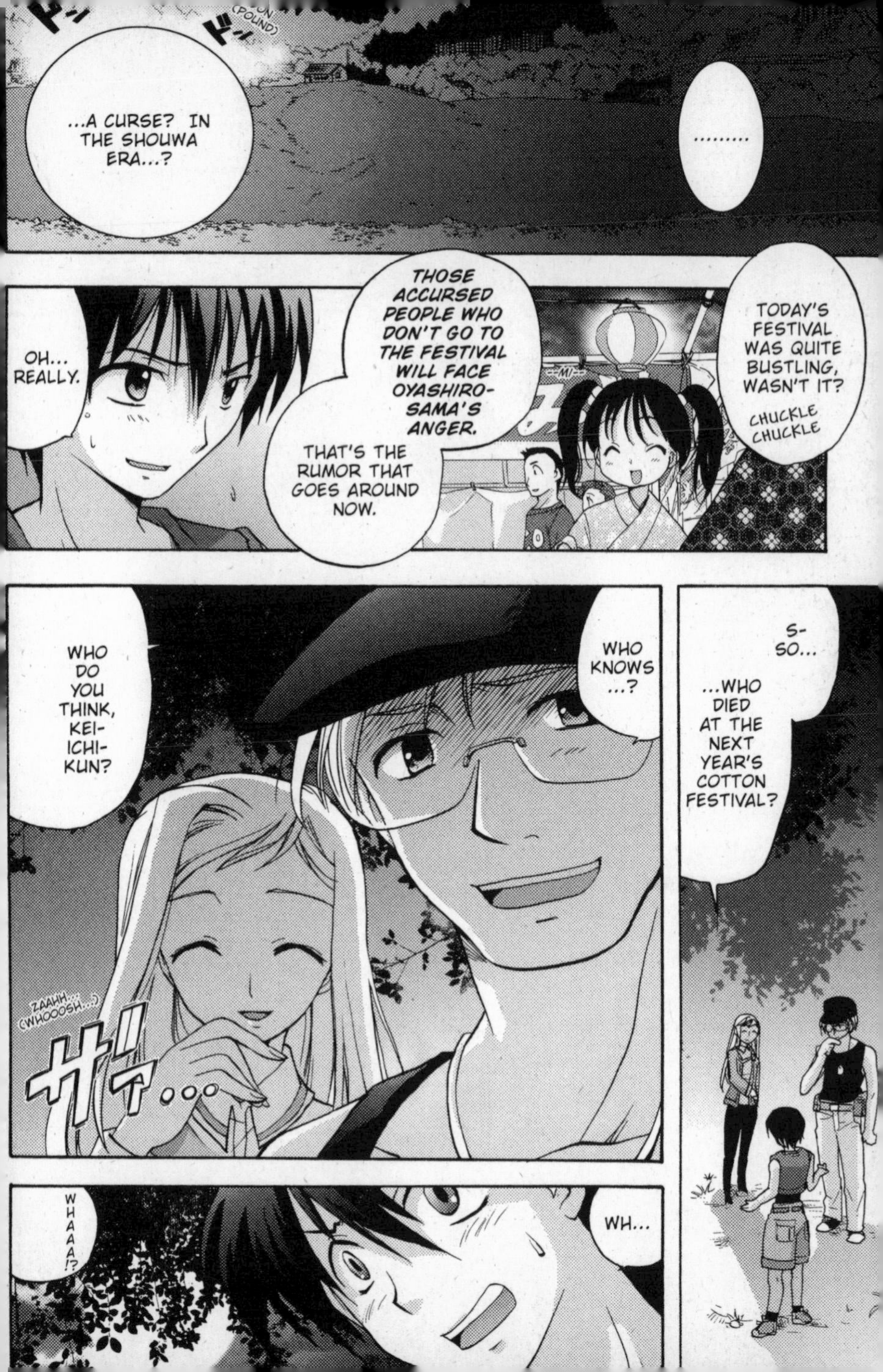
ドッ
ドッ
(POUND)
....
...A CURSE? IN THE SHOUWA ERA...?
TODAY'S FESTIVAL WAS QUITE BUSTLING, WASN'T IT?
CHUCKLE CHUCKLE
~MI~
THOSE ACCURSED PEOPLE WHO DON'T GO TO THE FESTIVAL WILL FACE OYASHIRO-SAMA'S ANGER.
THAT'S THE RUMOR THAT GOES AROUND NOW.
OH... REALLY.
S-SO...
...WHO DIED AT THE NEXT YEAR'S COTTON FESTIVAL?
WHO KNOWS...?
WHO DO YOU THINK, KEI-ICHI-KUN?
ZAAHH... (WHOOOSH...)
ザァ...
WH...
WHAAAA!?

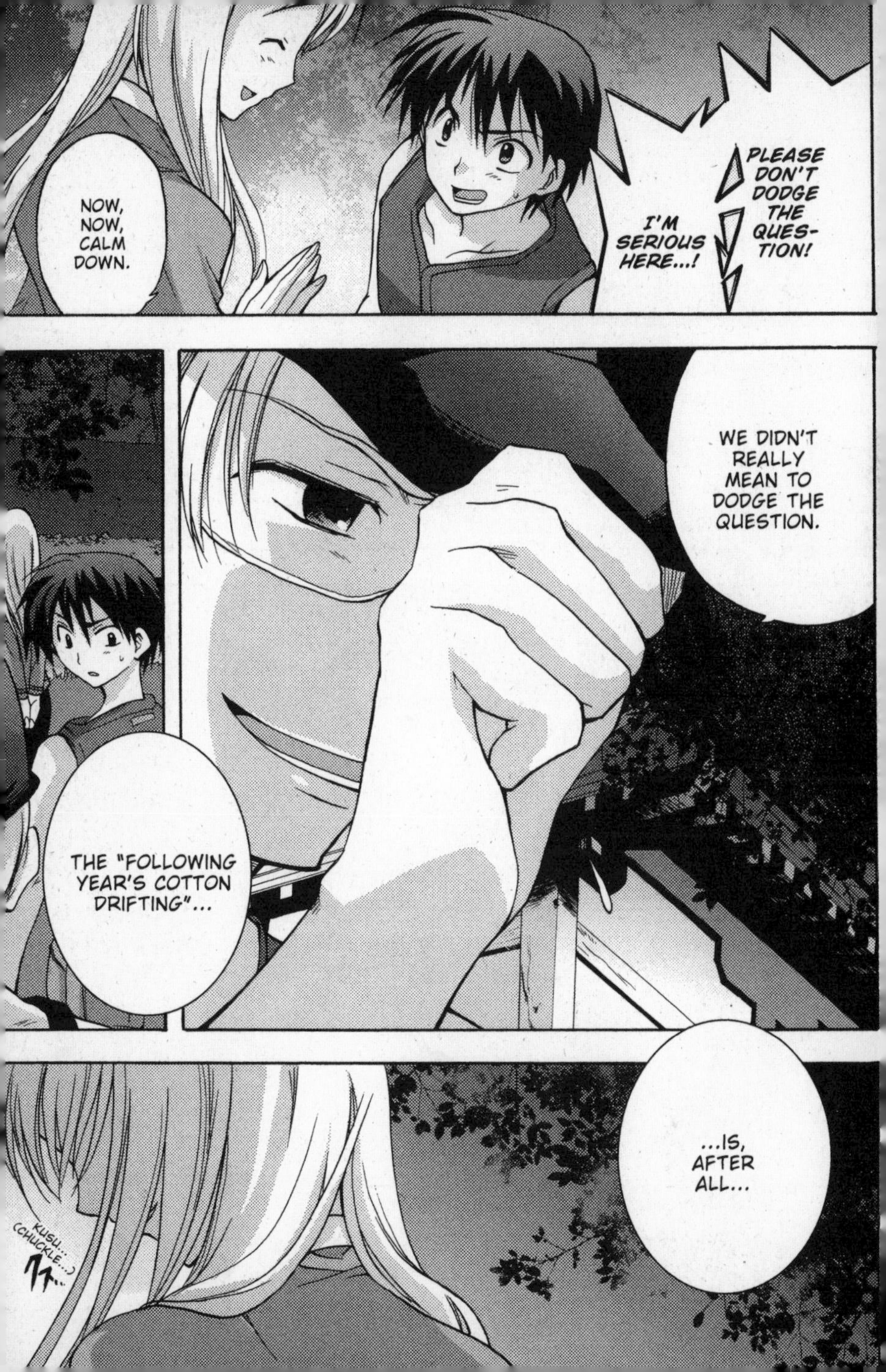
PLEASE DON'T DODGE THE QUES-TION!
I'M SERIOUS HERE...!
NOW, NOW, CALM DOWN.
WE DIDN'T REALLY MEAN TO DODGE THE QUESTION.
THE "FOLLOWING YEAR'S COTTON DRIFTING"...
...IS, AFTER ALL...
KUSU... (CHUCKLE...)

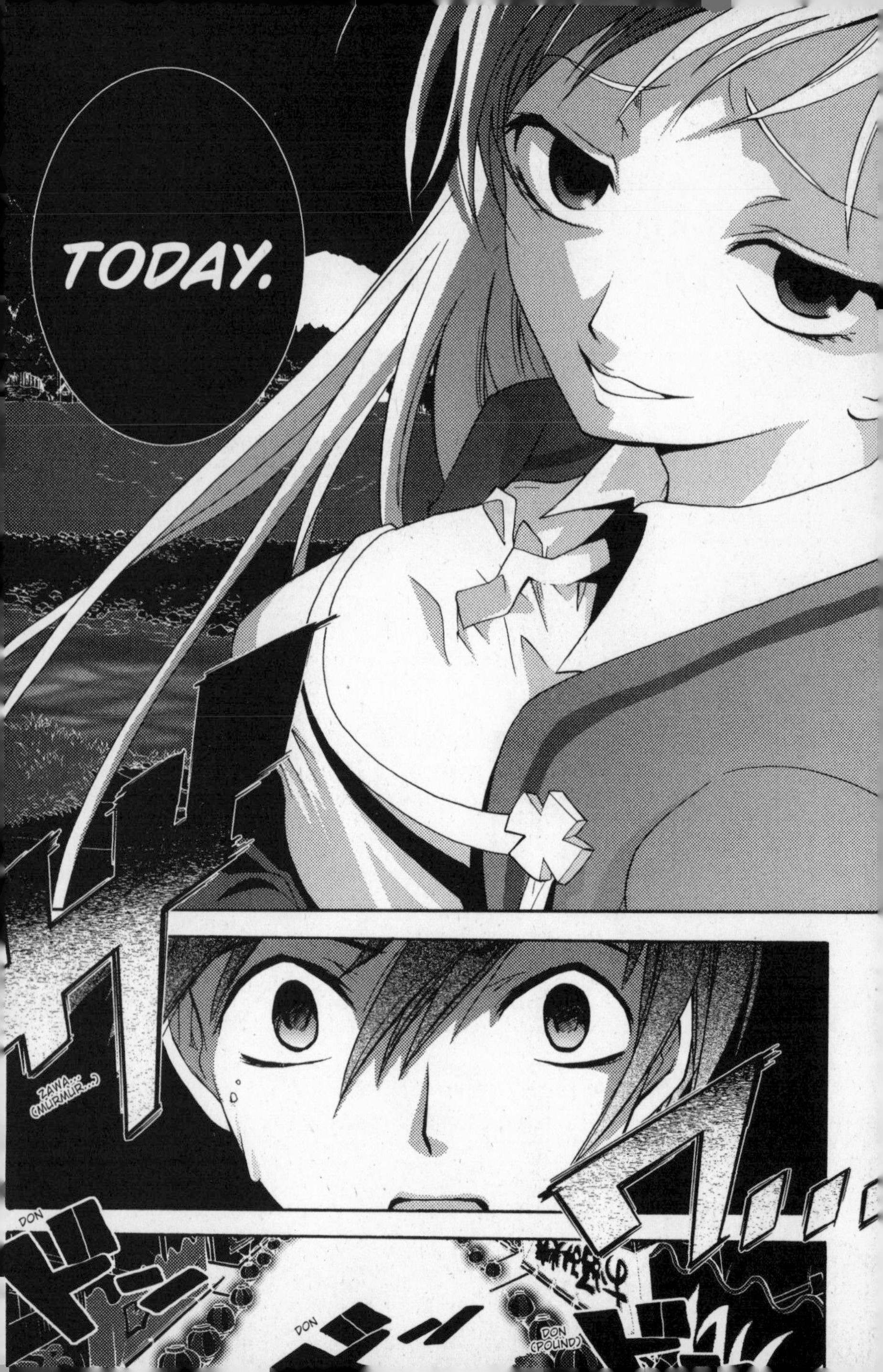
TODAY.
ZAWA... (MURMUR...)
DON (POUND)
DON
DON

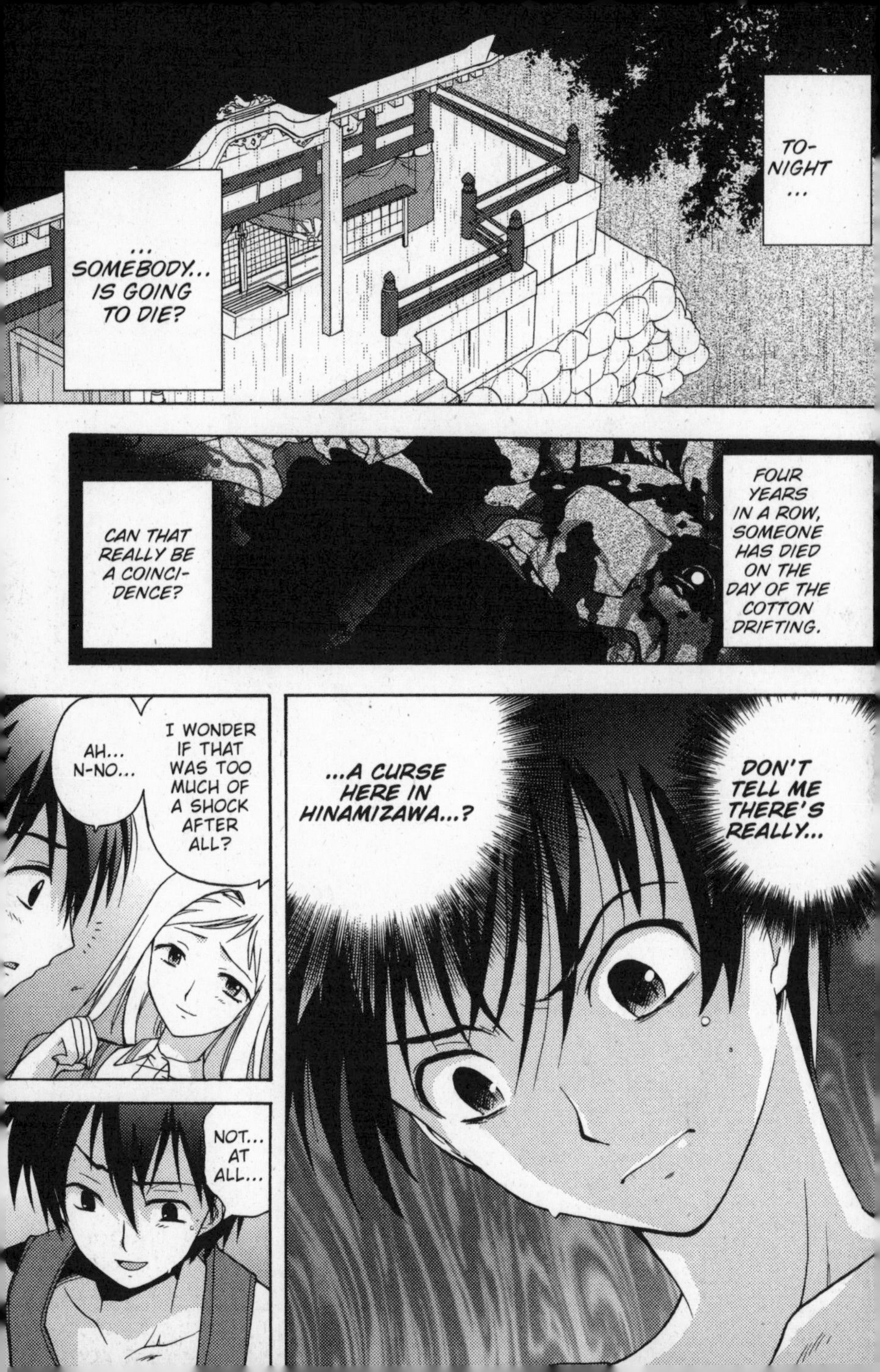
TO-NIGHT...
...SOMEBODY... IS GOING TO DIE?
FOUR YEARS IN A ROW, SOMEONE HAS DIED ON THE DAY OF THE COTTON DRIFTING.
CAN THAT REALLY BE A COINCIDENCE?
DON'T TELL ME THERE'S REALLY...
...A CURSE HERE IN HINAMIZAWA...?
I WONDER IF THAT WAS TOO MUCH OF A SHOCK AFTER ALL?
AH... N-NO...
NOT... AT ALL...

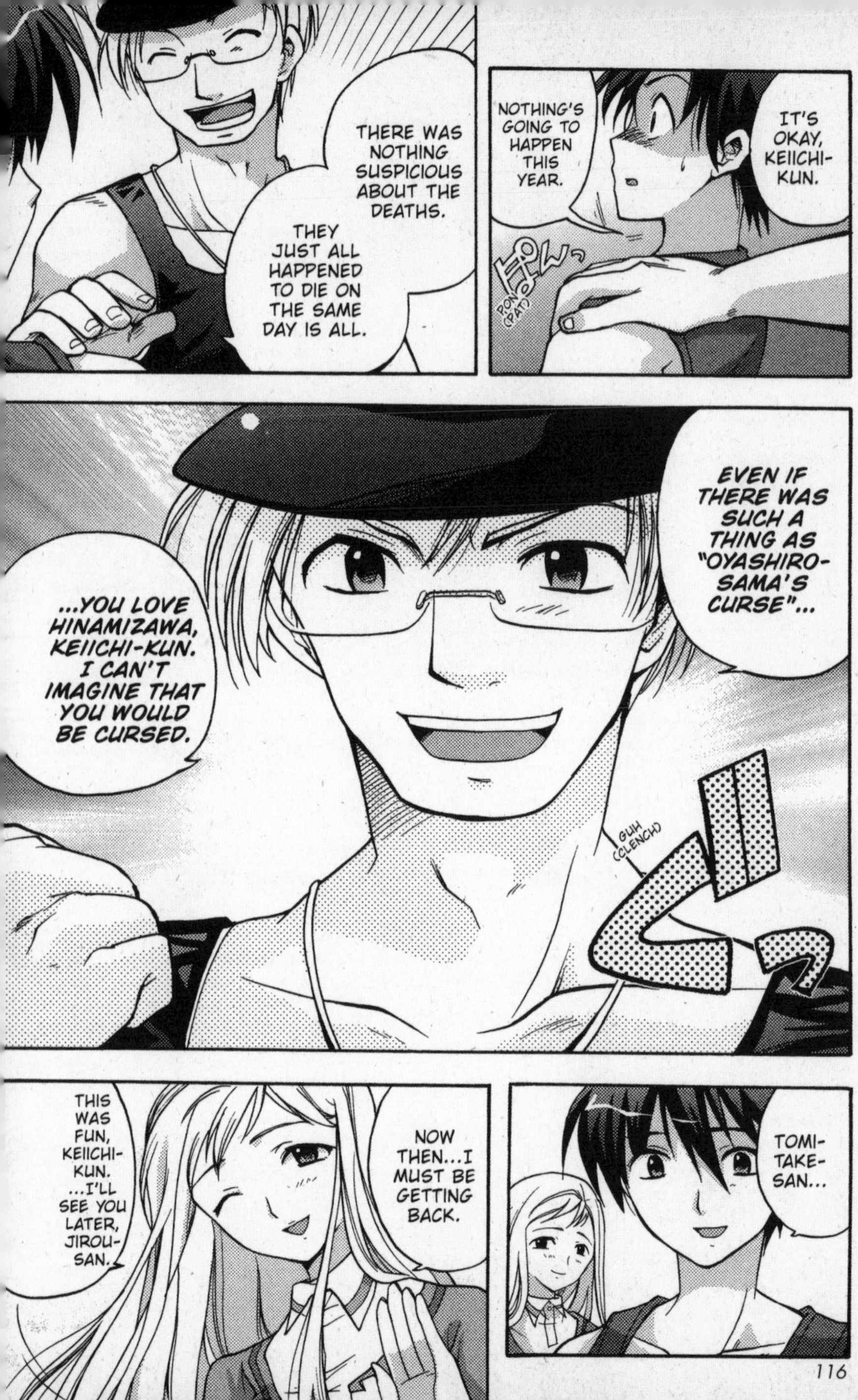
IT'S OKAY, KEIICHI-KUN.
NOTHING'S GOING TO HAPPEN THIS YEAR.
PON (PAT)
THERE WAS NOTHING SUSPICIOUS ABOUT THE DEATHS.
THEY JUST ALL HAPPENED TO DIE ON THE SAME DAY IS ALL.
EVEN IF THERE WAS SUCH A THING AS "OYASHIRO-SAMA'S CURSE"...
...YOU LOVE HINAMIZAWA, KEIICHI-KUN. I CAN'T IMAGINE THAT YOU WOULD BE CURSED.
GUH (CLENCH)
TOMI-TAKE-SAN...
NOW THEN...I MUST BE GETTING BACK.
THIS WAS FUN, KEIICHI-KUN. ...I'LL SEE YOU LATER, JIROU-SAN.

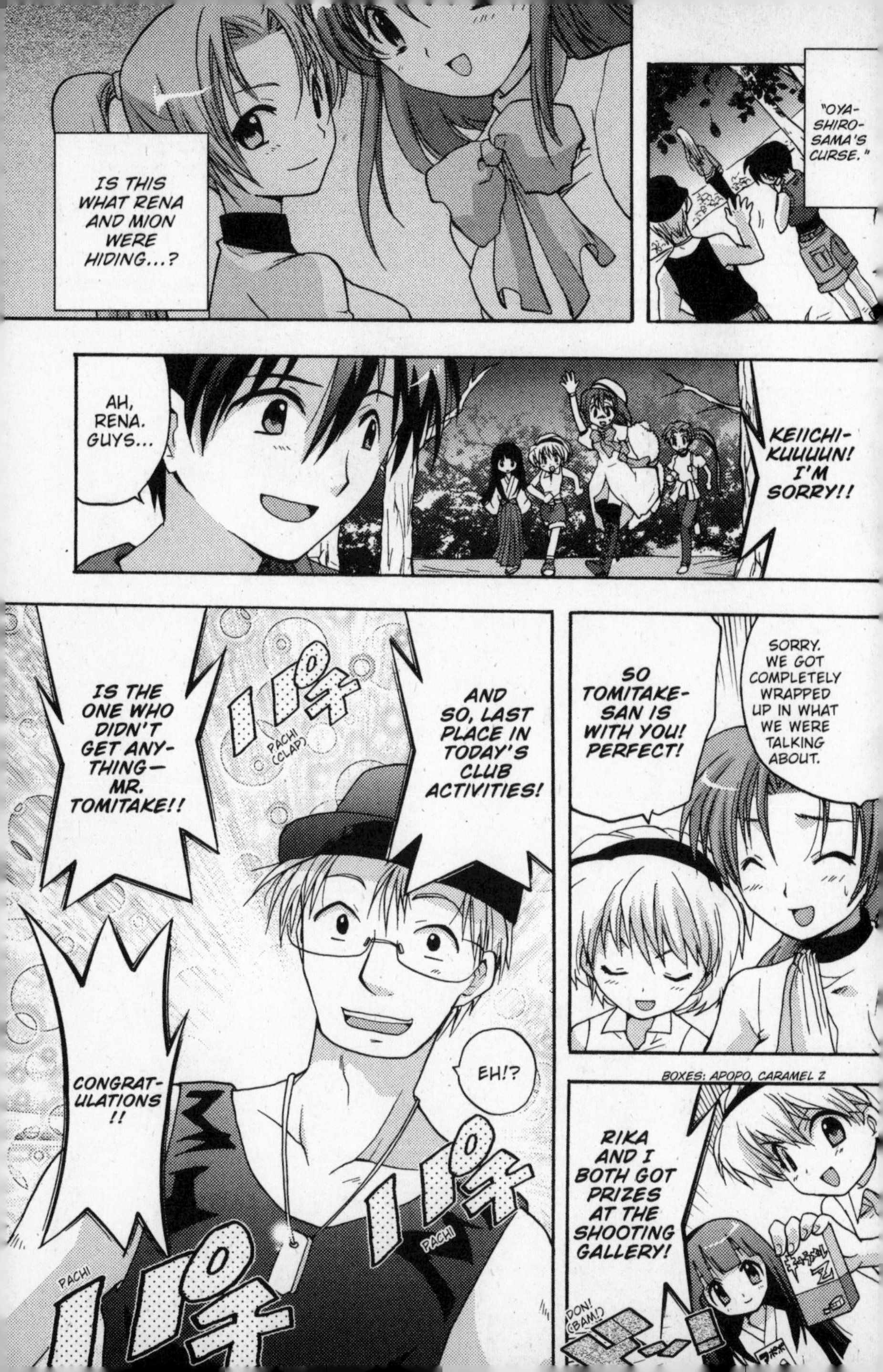
"OYA-SHIRO-SAMA'S CURSE."
IS THIS WHAT RENA AND MION WERE HIDING...?
KEIICHI-KUUUUN! I'M SORRY!!
AH, RENA. GUYS...
SORRY. WE GOT COMPLETELY WRAPPED UP IN WHAT WE WERE TALKING ABOUT.
SO TOMITAKE-SAN IS WITH YOU! PERFECT!
BOXES: APOPO, CARAMEL Z
RIKA AND I BOTH GOT PRIZES AT THE SHOOTING GALLERY!
DON! (BAM!)
AND SO, LAST PLACE IN TODAY'S CLUB ACTIVITIES!
PACHI (CLAP)
IS THE ONE WHO DIDN'T GET ANYTHING—MR. TOMITAKE!!
EH!?
CONGRATULATIONS!!
PACHI
PACHI

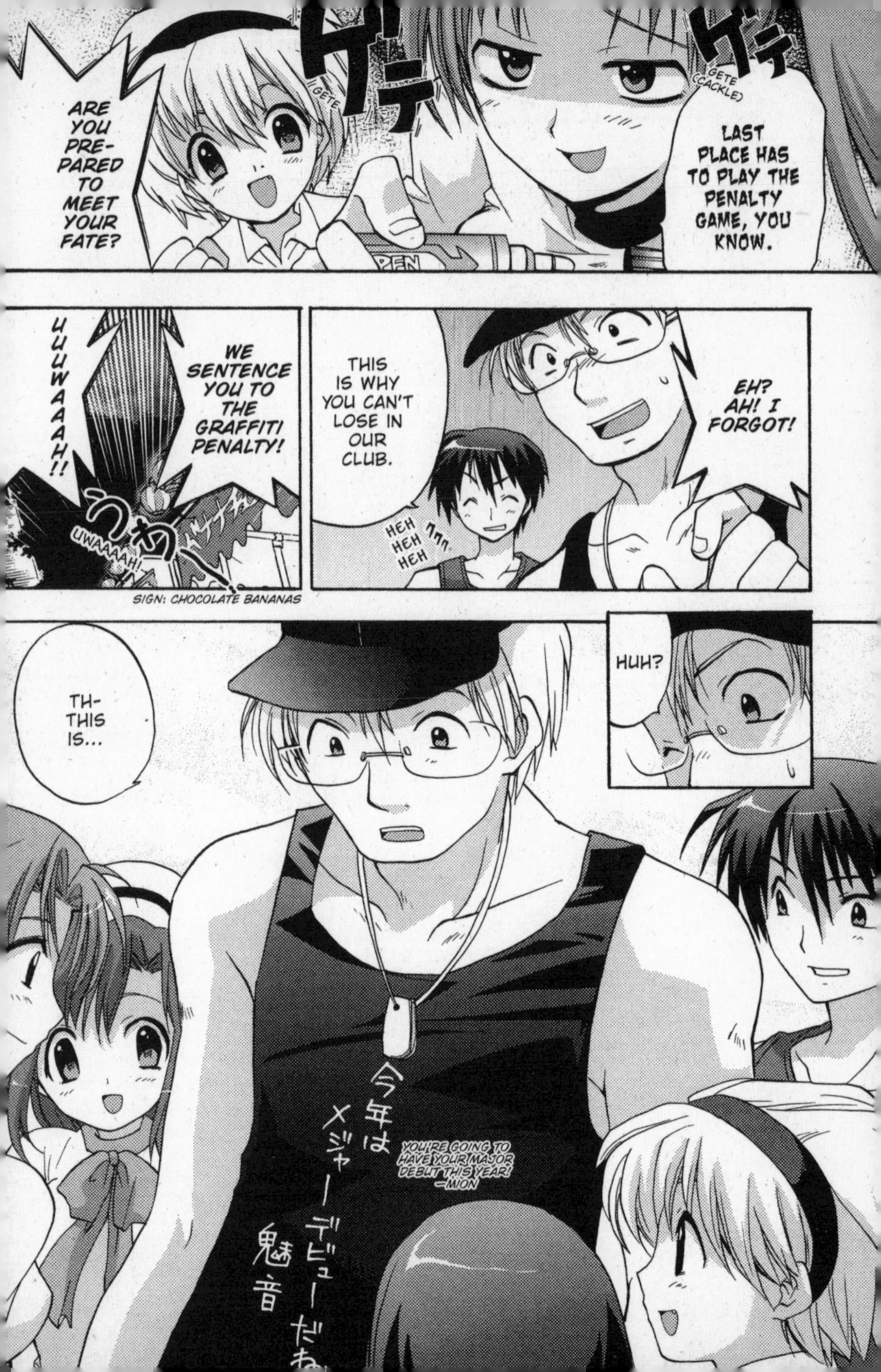
ゲテ
GETE (CACKLE)
LAST PLACE HAS TO PLAY THE PENALTY GAME, YOU KNOW.
ゲテ
GETE
ARE YOU PREPARED TO MEET YOUR FATE?
EH? AH! I FORGOT!
THIS IS WHY YOU CAN'T LOSE IN OUR CLUB.
HEH HEH HEH
WE SENTENCE YOU TO THE GRAFFITI PENALTY!
UUUWAAAAH!!
うわ
UWAAAAH!
SIGN: CHOCOLATE BANANAS
HUH?
TH-THIS IS...
今年はメジャーデビューだね
魅音
YOU'RE GOING TO HAVE YOUR MAJOR DEBUT THIS YEAR! —MION

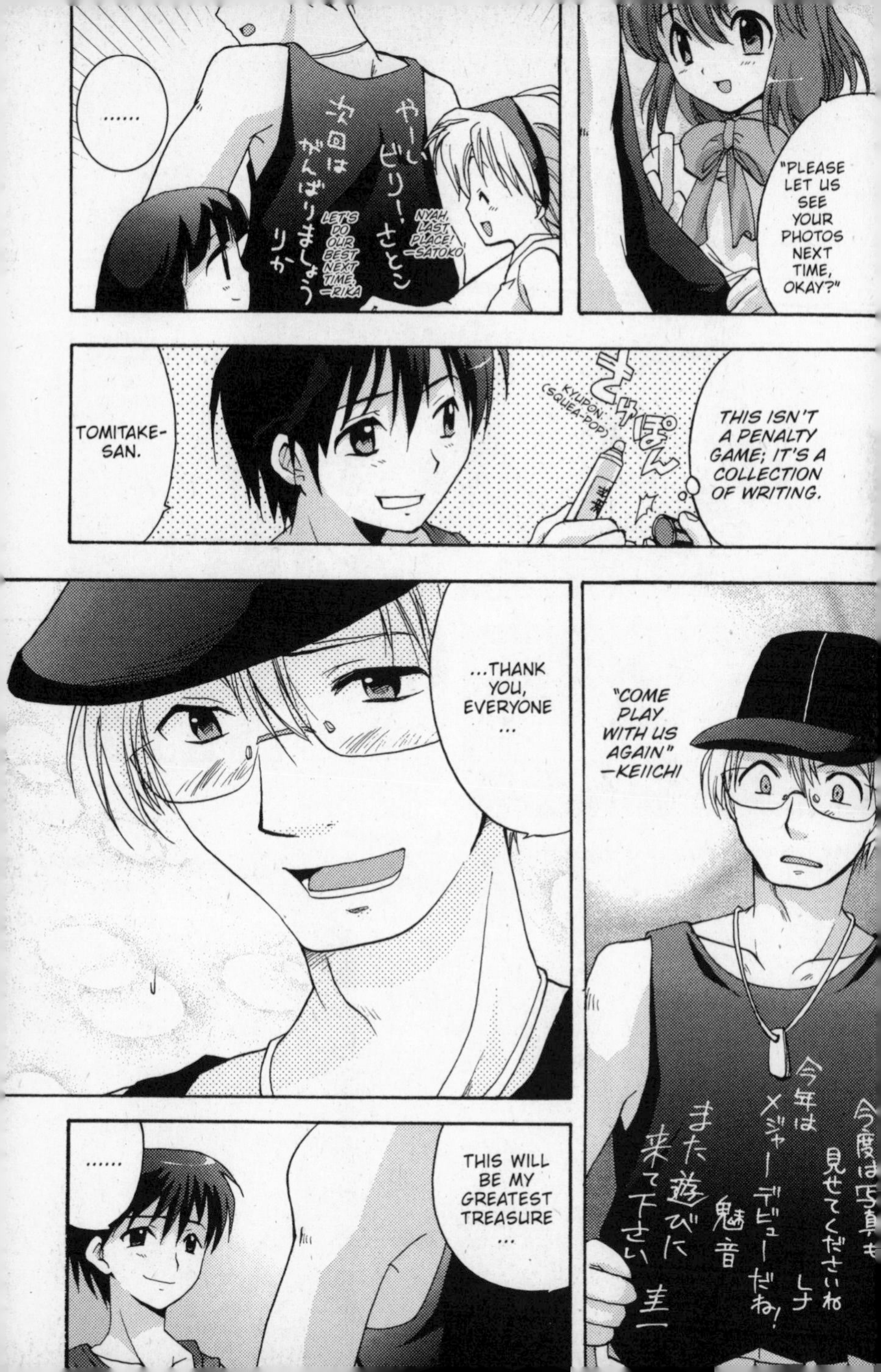
"PLEASE LET US SEE YOUR PHOTOS NEXT TIME, OKAY?"
......
やーいビリー! さとこ
NYAH, LAST PLACE! —SATOKO
次回はがんばりましょう りか
LET'S DO OUR BEST NEXT TIME, —RIKA
THIS ISN'T A PENALTY GAME; IT'S A COLLECTION OF WRITING.
きゅぽん
KYUPON (SQUEA-POP)
TOMITAKE-SAN.
今度は写真も見せてくださいね レナ
今年はメジャーデビューだね! 魅音
また遊びに来て下さい 圭一
"COME PLAY WITH US AGAIN" —KEIICHI
...THANK YOU, EVERYONE ...
THIS WILL BE MY GREATEST TREASURE ...
......

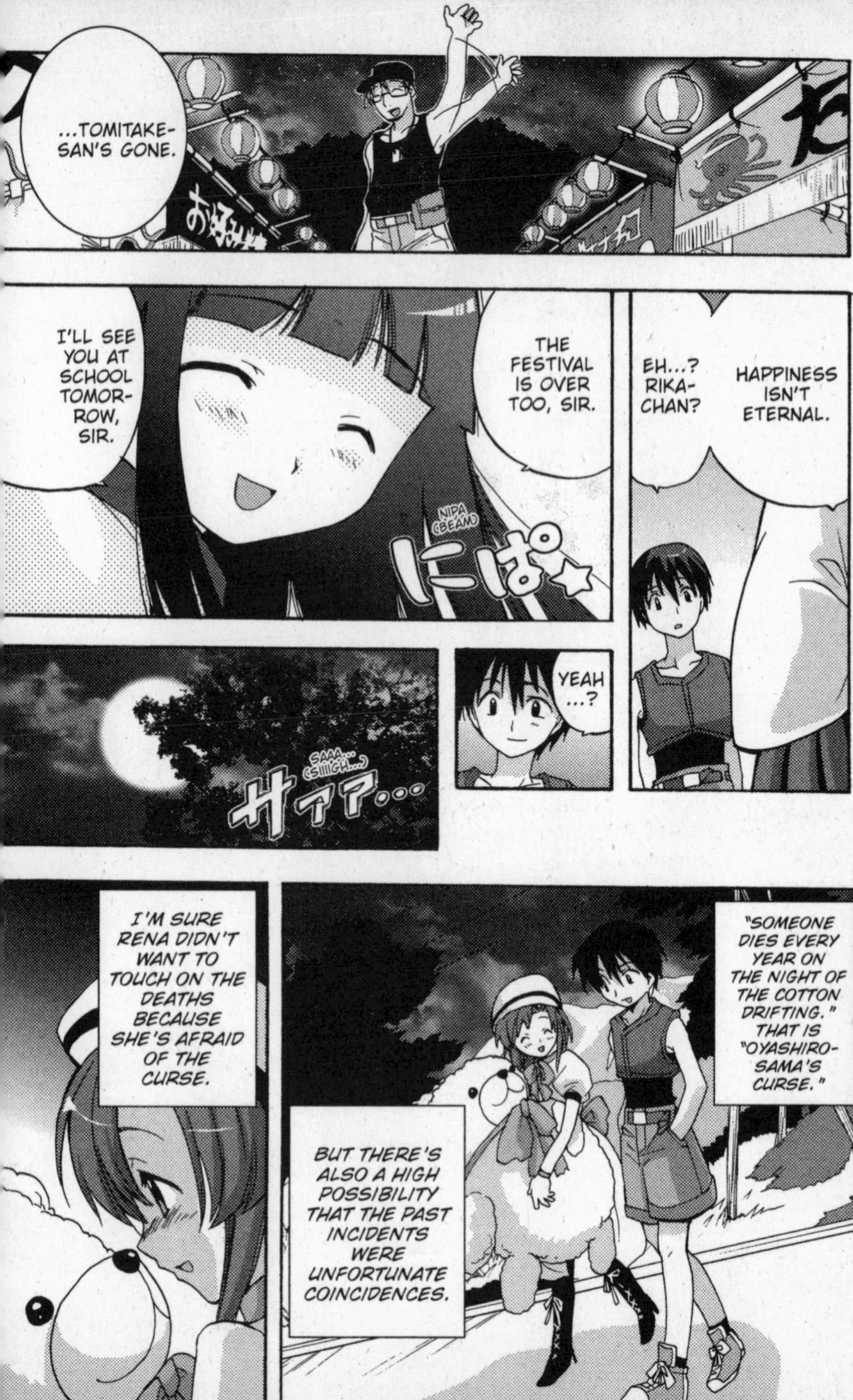
...TOMITAKE-SAN'S GONE.
HAPPINESS ISN'T ETERNAL.
EH...? RIKA-CHAN?
THE FESTIVAL IS OVER TOO, SIR.
I'LL SEE YOU AT SCHOOL TOMORROW, SIR.
NIPA (BEAM)
にぱ☆
YEAH ...?
SAAA... (SIIIGH...)
サァア...
"SOMEONE DIES EVERY YEAR ON THE NIGHT OF THE COTTON DRIFTING." THAT IS "OYASHIRO-SAMA'S CURSE."
BUT THERE'S ALSO A HIGH POSSIBILITY THAT THE PAST INCIDENTS WERE UNFORTUNATE COINCIDENCES.
I'M SURE RENA DIDN'T WANT TO TOUCH ON THE DEATHS BECAUSE SHE'S AFRAID OF THE CURSE.

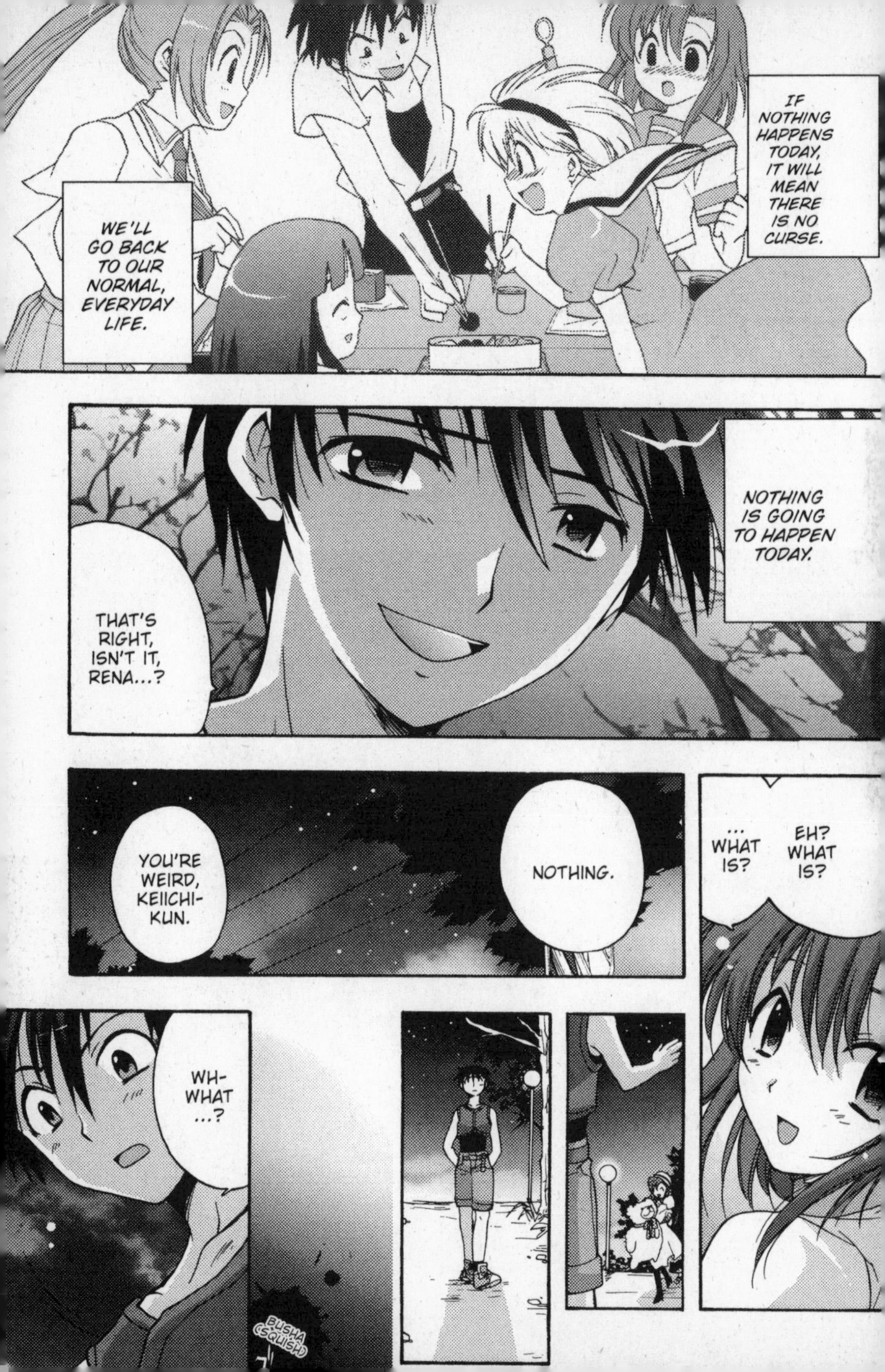
IF NOTHING HAPPENS TODAY, IT WILL MEAN THERE IS NO CURSE.
WE'LL GO BACK TO OUR NORMAL, EVERYDAY LIFE.
NOTHING IS GOING TO HAPPEN TODAY.
THAT'S RIGHT, ISN'T IT, RENA...?
EH? WHAT IS?
... WHAT IS?
NOTHING.
YOU'RE WEIRD, KEIICHI-KUN.
WH-WHAT ...?
BUSHA (SQUISH)

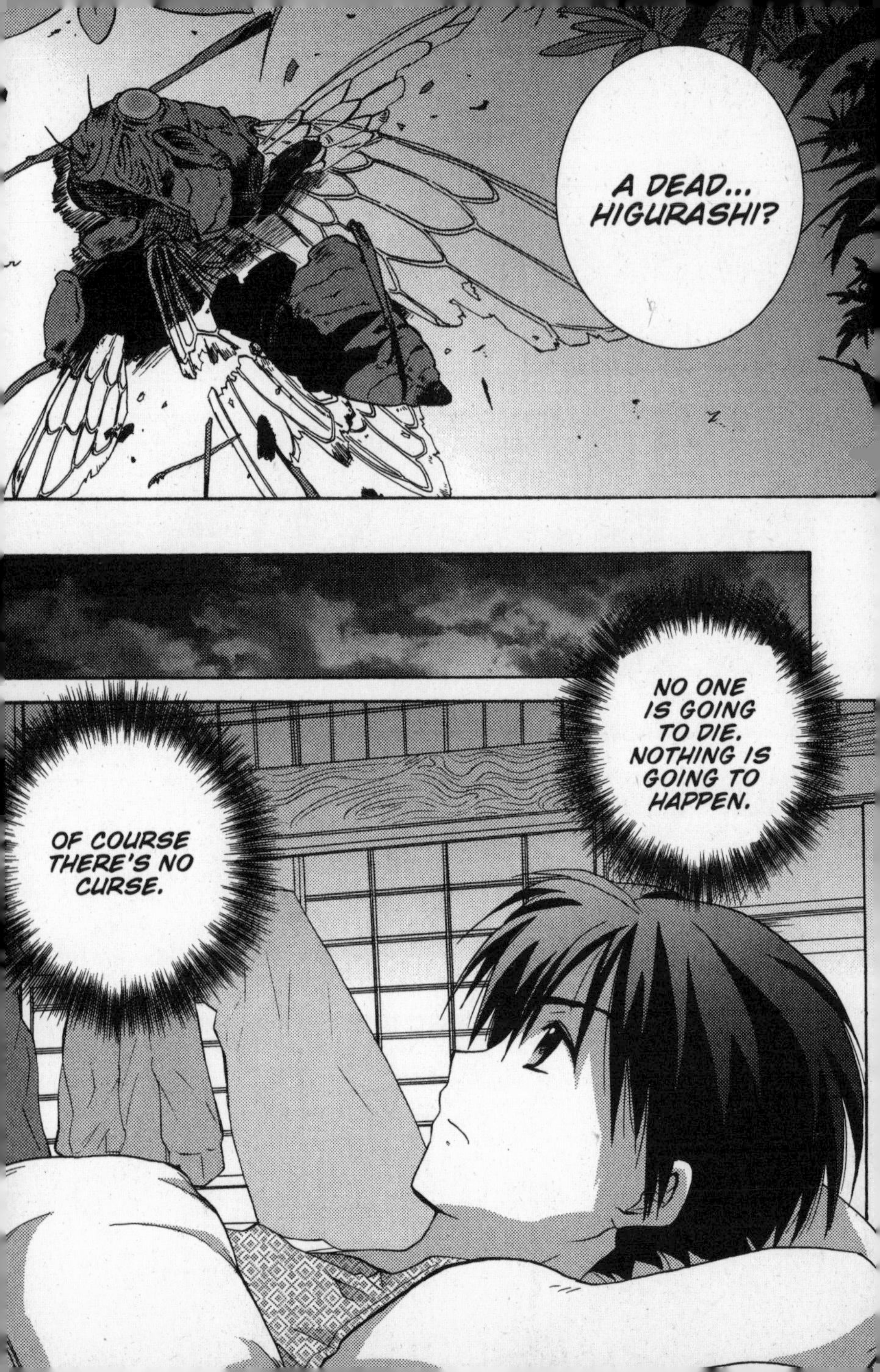
A DEAD... HIGURASHI?
NO ONE IS GOING TO DIE. NOTHING IS GOING TO HAPPEN.
OF COURSE THERE'S NO CURSE.

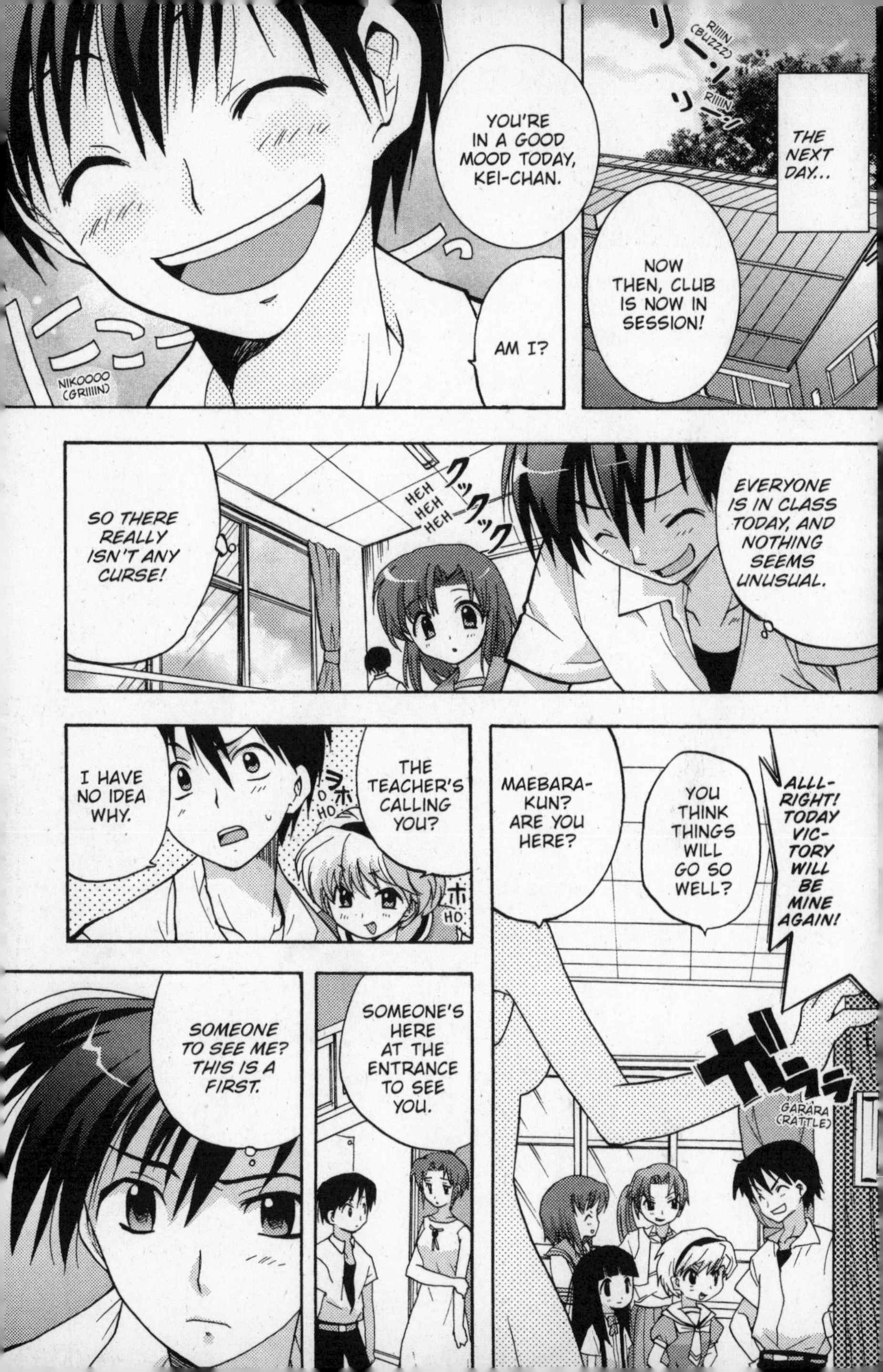
RIIIN (BUZZZ)
RIIIN
THE NEXT DAY...
NOW THEN, CLUB IS NOW IN SESSION!
YOU'RE IN A GOOD MOOD TODAY, KEI-CHAN.
AM I?
NIKOOOO (GRIIIIN)
EVERYONE IS IN CLASS TODAY, AND NOTHING SEEMS UNUSUAL.
HEH HEH HEH
SO THERE REALLY ISN'T ANY CURSE!
ALLL-RIGHT! TODAY VICTORY WILL BE MINE AGAIN!
YOU THINK THINGS WILL GO SO WELL?
MAEBARA-KUN? ARE YOU HERE?
GARARA (RATTLE)
THE TEACHER'S CALLING YOU?
O HO
HO
I HAVE NO IDEA WHY.
SOMEONE'S HERE AT THE ENTRANCE TO SEE YOU.
SOMEONE TO SEE ME? THIS IS A FIRST.

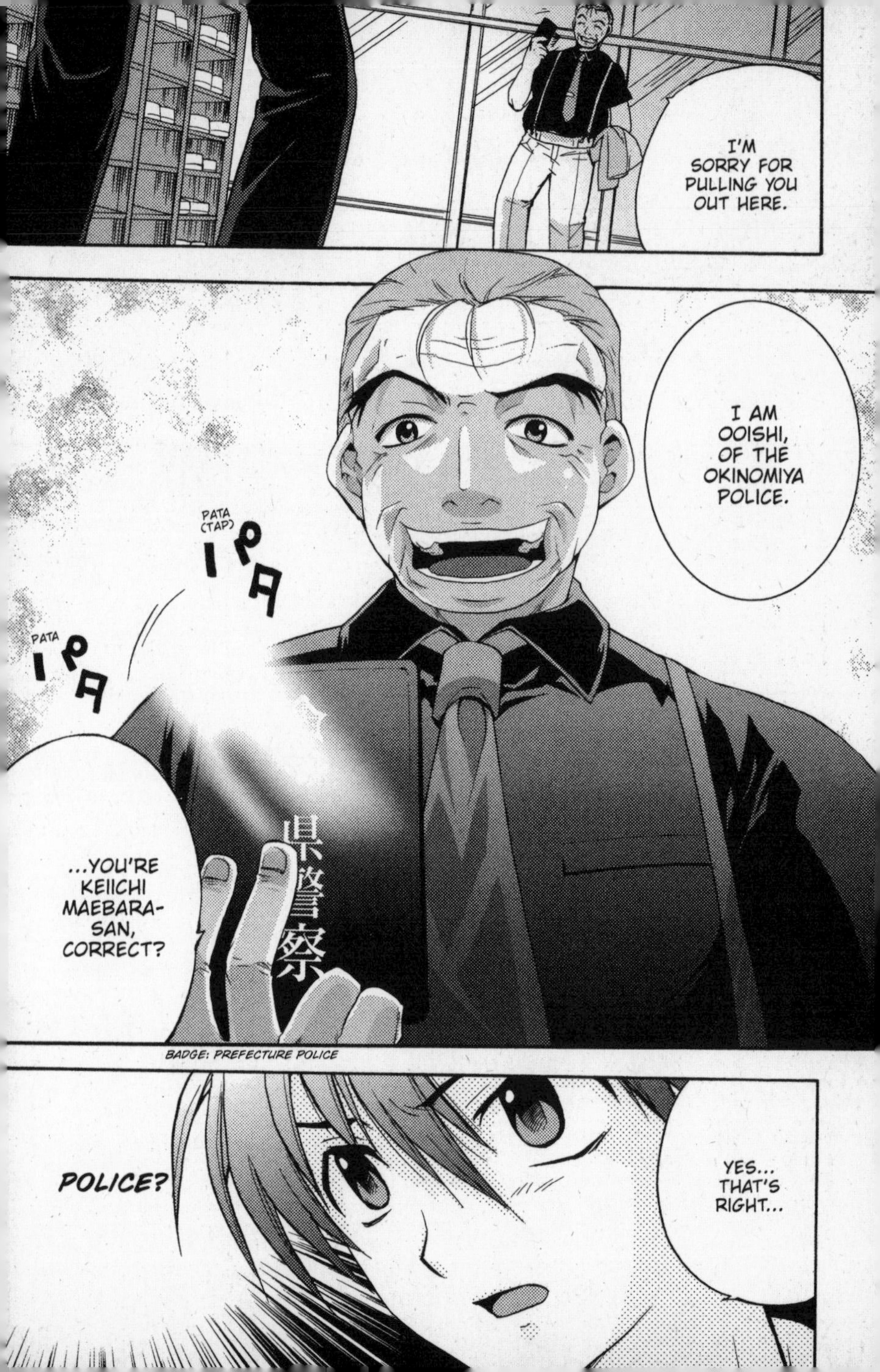
I'M SORRY FOR PULLING YOU OUT HERE.
I AM OOISHI, OF THE OKINOMIYA POLICE.
PATA (TAP)
PATA
県警察
...YOU'RE KEIICHI MAEBARA-SAN, CORRECT?
BADGE: PREFECTURE POLICE
YES... THAT'S RIGHT...
POLICE?

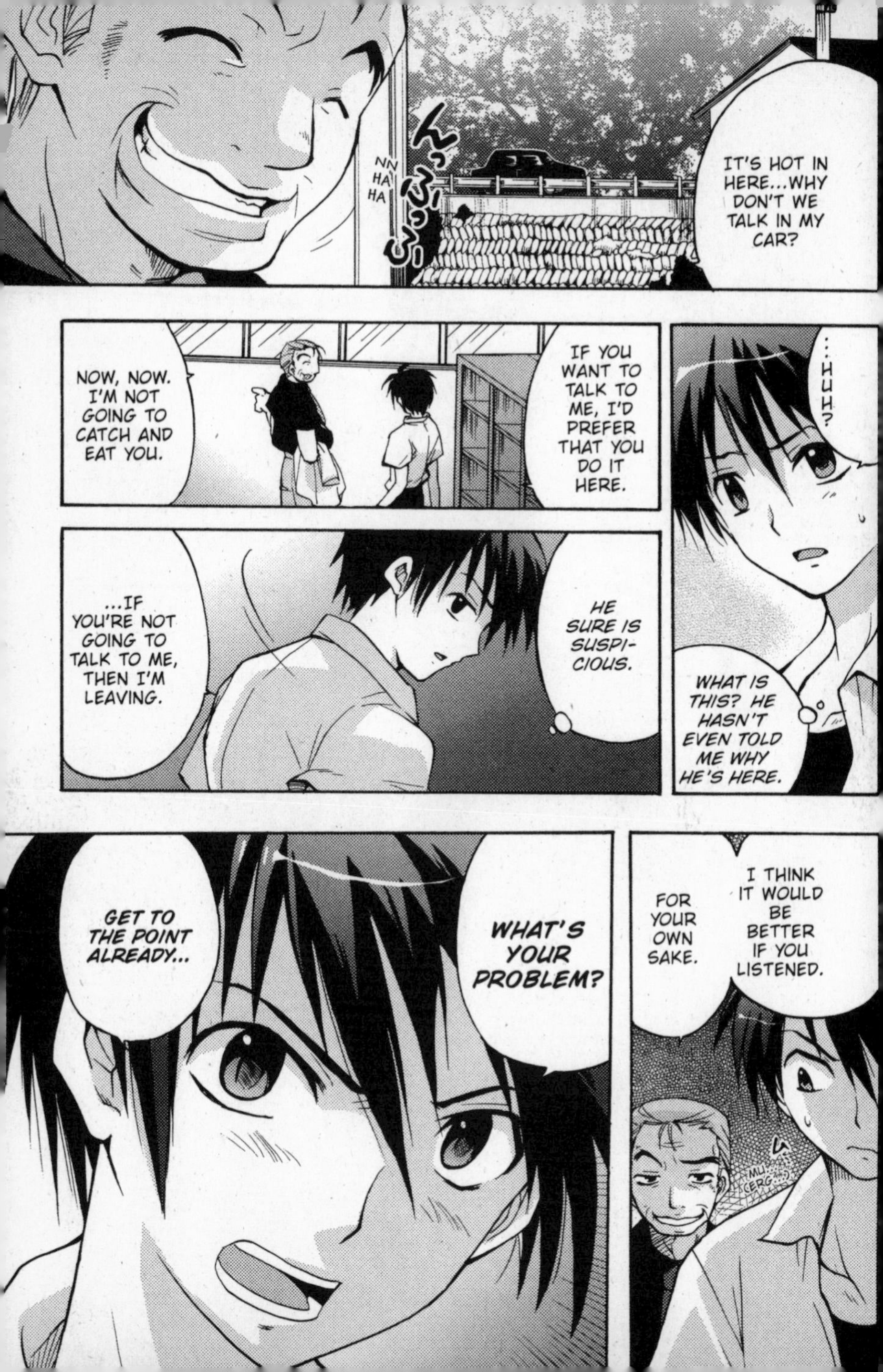
IT'S HOT IN HERE...WHY DON'T WE TALK IN MY CAR?
んっふっふ
NN HA HA
...HUH?
WHAT IS THIS? HE HASN'T EVEN TOLD ME WHY HE'S HERE.
IF YOU WANT TO TALK TO ME, I'D PREFER THAT YOU DO IT HERE.
NOW, NOW. I'M NOT GOING TO CATCH AND EAT YOU.
HE SURE IS SUSPICIOUS.
...IF YOU'RE NOT GOING TO TALK TO ME, THEN I'M LEAVING.
I THINK IT WOULD BE BETTER IF YOU LISTENED.
FOR YOUR OWN SAKE.
む
MU... (ERG...)
WHAT'S YOUR PROBLEM?
GET TO THE POINT ALREADY...

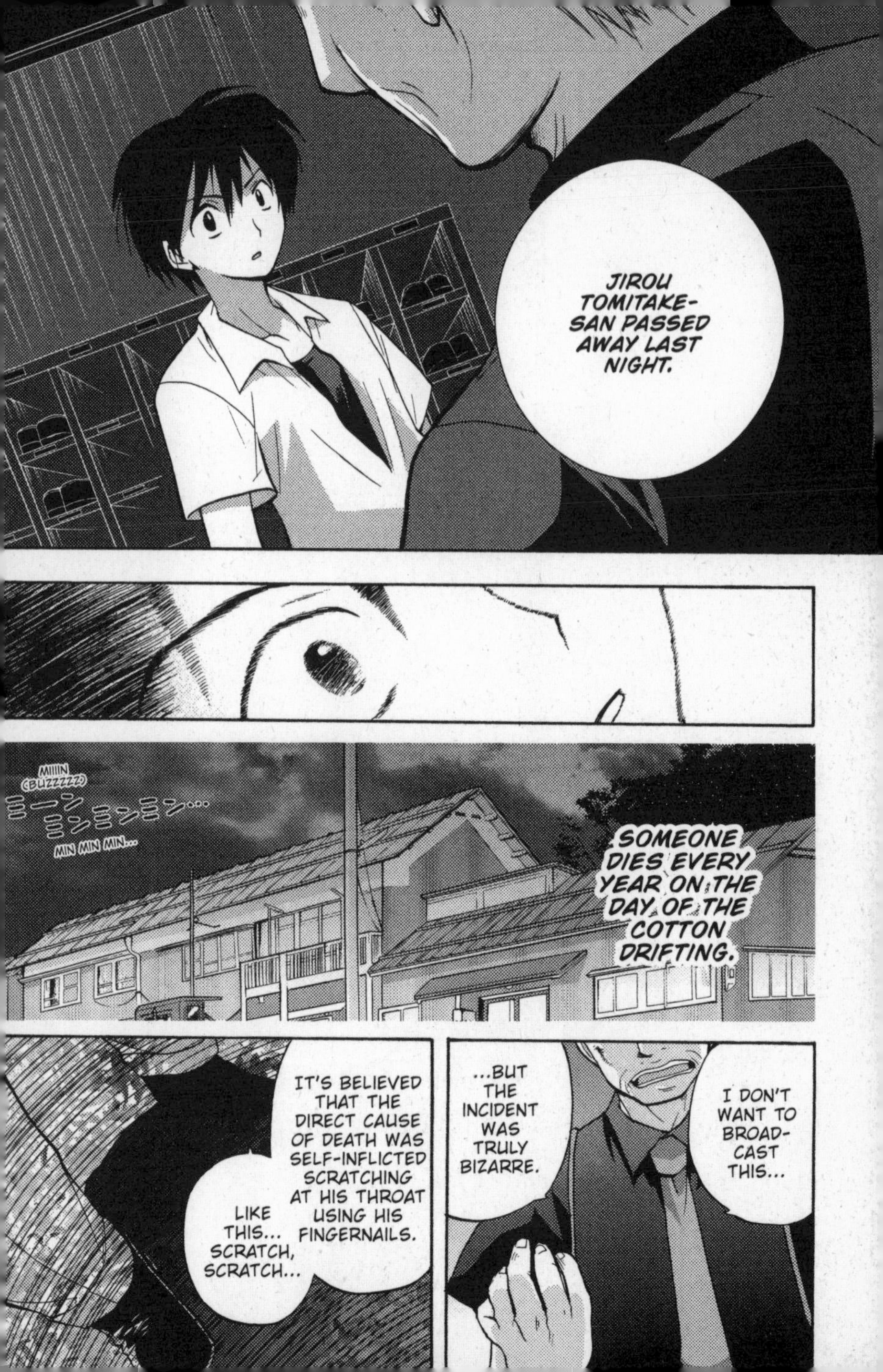
JIROU TOMITAKE-SAN PASSED AWAY LAST NIGHT.
SOMEONE DIES EVERY YEAR ON THE DAY OF THE COTTON DRIFTING.
MIIIN (BUZZZZZ)
ミーン ミンミンミン…
MIN MIN MIN...
I DON'T WANT TO BROAD-CAST THIS...
...BUT THE INCIDENT WAS TRULY BIZARRE.
IT'S BELIEVED THAT THE DIRECT CAUSE OF DEATH WAS SELF-INFLICTED SCRATCHING AT HIS THROAT USING HIS FINGERNAILS.
LIKE THIS... SCRATCH, SCRATCH...

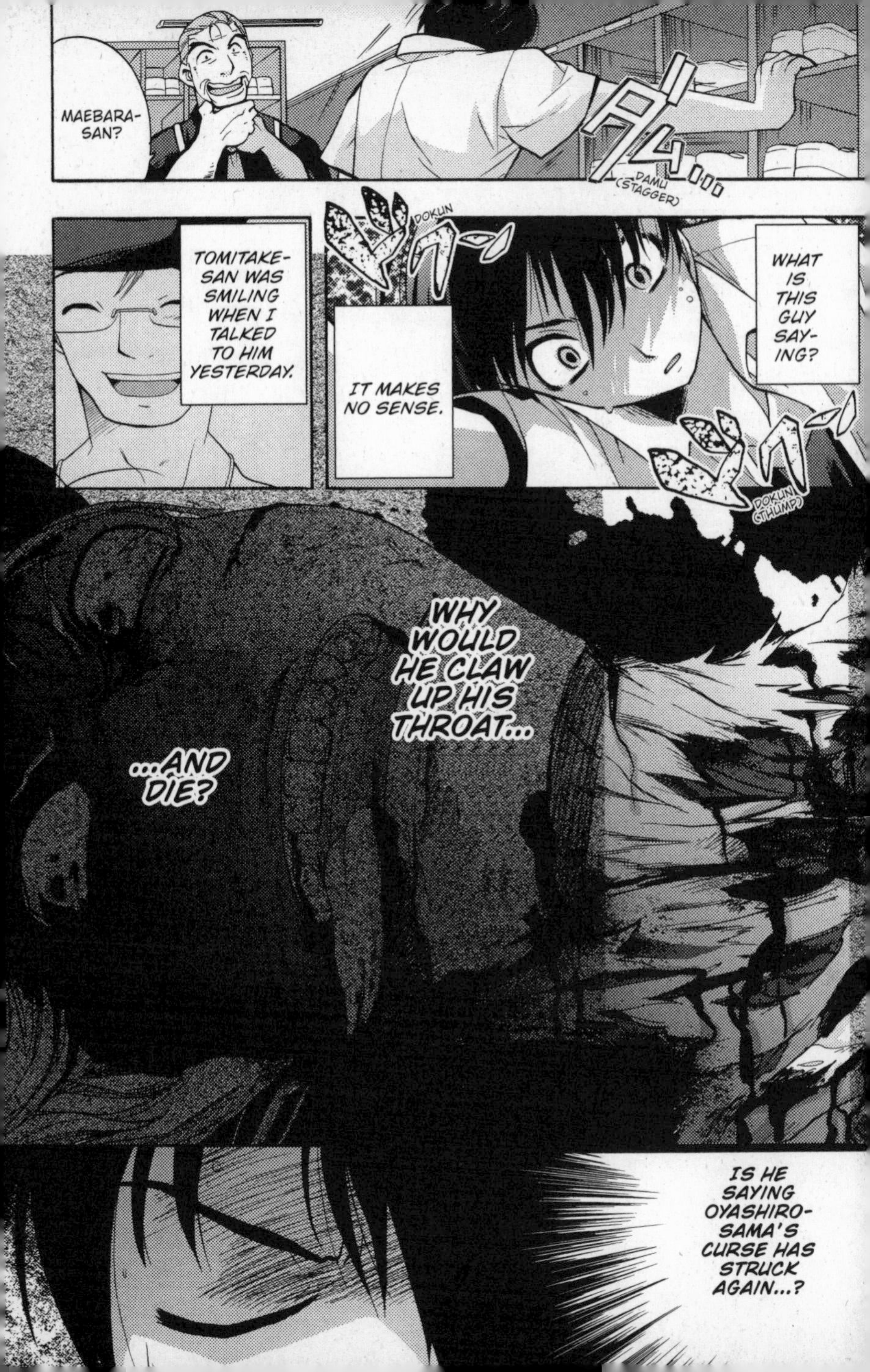
DAMU (STAGGER)
MAEBARA-SAN?
WHAT IS THIS GUY SAYING?
DOKUN
IT MAKES NO SENSE.
DOKUN (THUMP)
TOMITAKE-SAN WAS SMILING WHEN I TALKED TO HIM YESTERDAY.
WHY WOULD HE CLAW UP HIS THROAT...
...AND DIE?
IS HE SAYING OYASHIRO-SAMA'S CURSE HAS STRUCK AGAIN...?

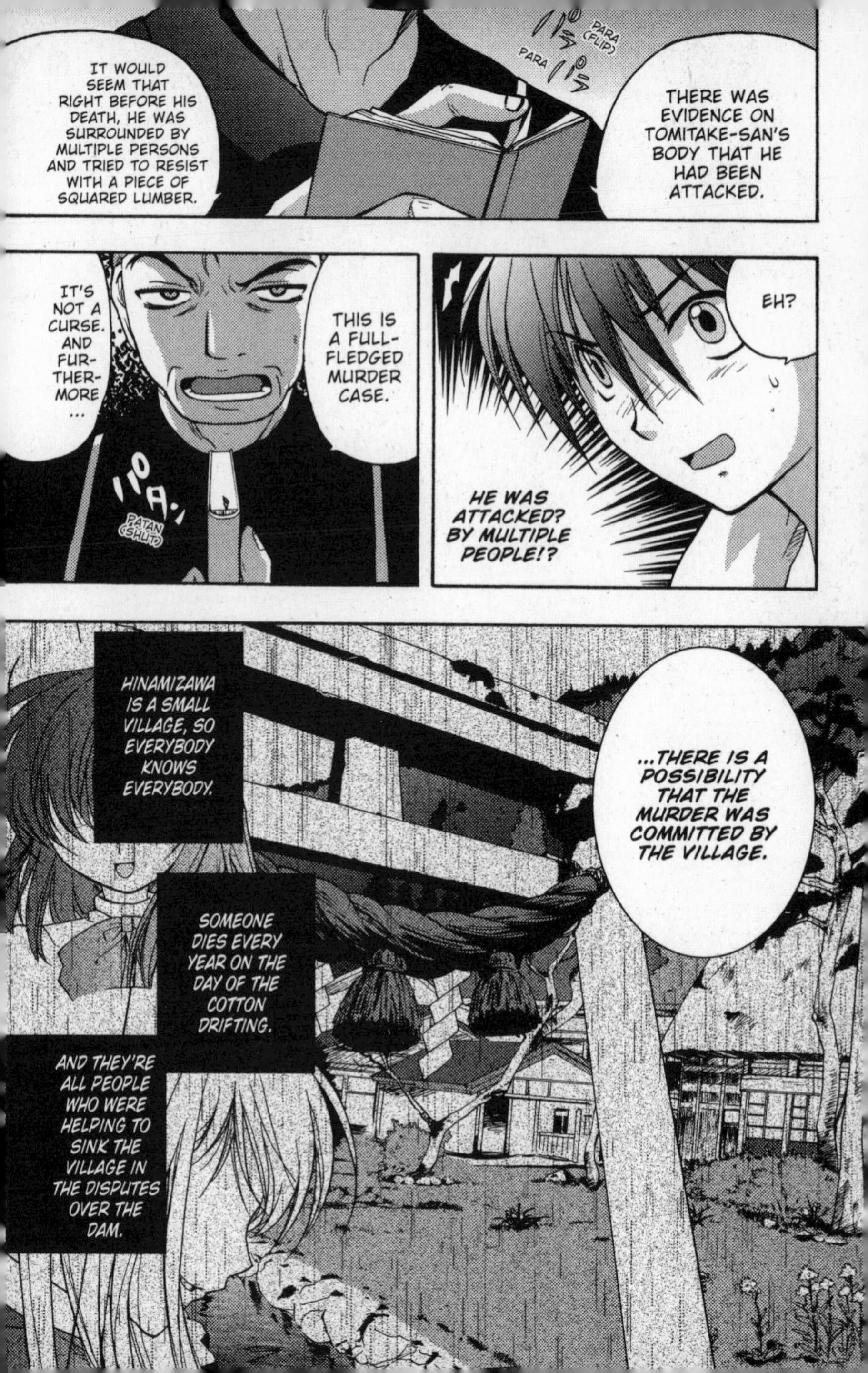
PARA (FLIP)
PARA
THERE WAS EVIDENCE ON TOMITAKE-SAN'S BODY THAT HE HAD BEEN ATTACKED.
IT WOULD SEEM THAT RIGHT BEFORE HIS DEATH, HE WAS SURROUNDED BY MULTIPLE PERSONS AND TRIED TO RESIST WITH A PIECE OF SQUARED LUMBER.
EH?
HE WAS ATTACKED? BY MULTIPLE PEOPLE!?
THIS IS A FULL-FLEDGED MURDER CASE.
IT'S NOT A CURSE. AND FURTHERMORE...
PATAN (SHUT)
...THERE IS A POSSIBILITY THAT THE MURDER WAS COMMITTED BY THE VILLAGE.
HINAMIZAWA IS A SMALL VILLAGE, SO EVERYBODY KNOWS EVERYBODY.
SOMEONE DIES EVERY YEAR ON THE DAY OF THE COTTON DRIFTING.
AND THEY'RE ALL PEOPLE WHO WERE HELPING TO SINK THE VILLAGE IN THE DISPUTES OVER THE DAM.

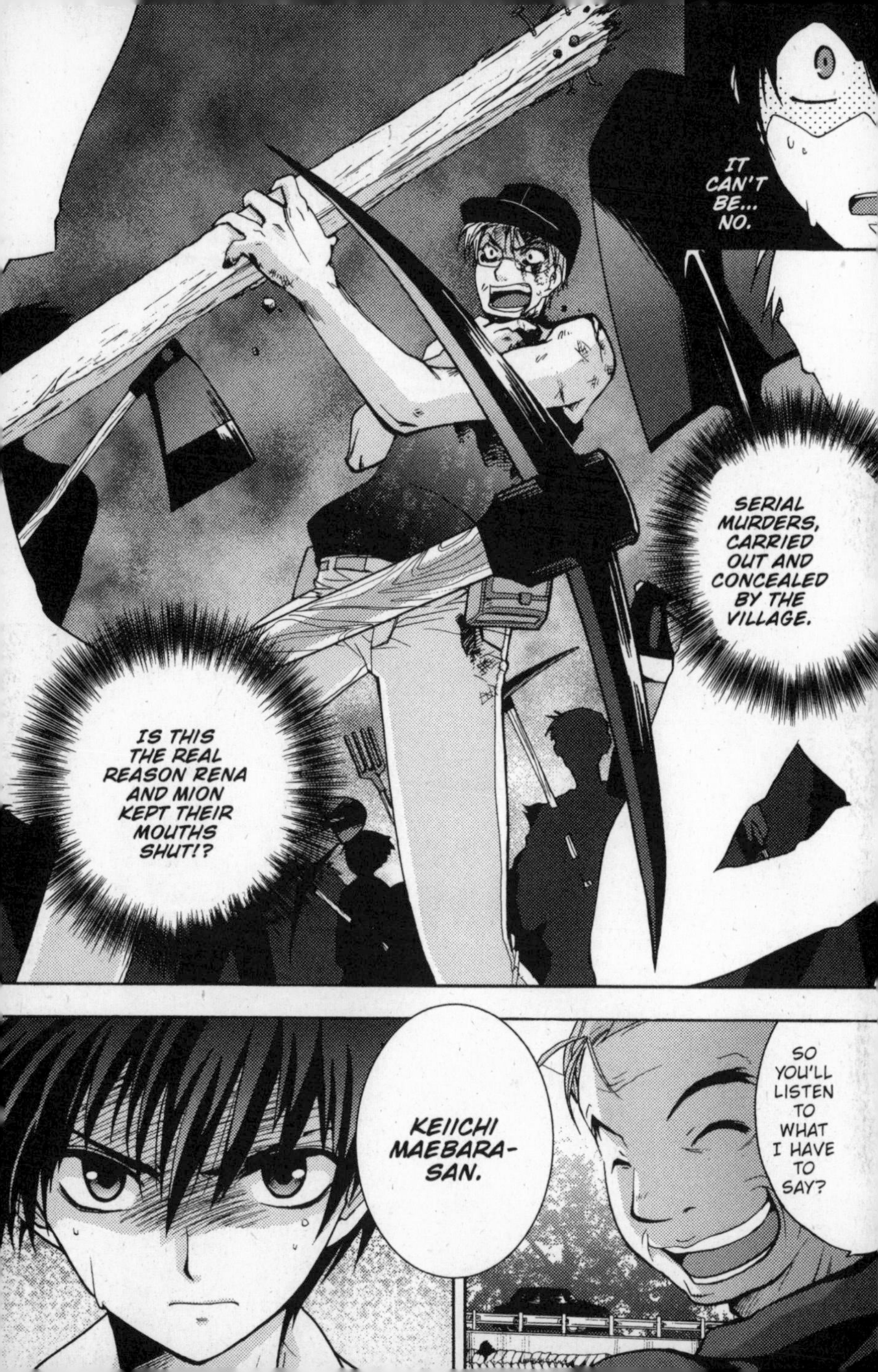
IT CAN'T BE... NO.
SERIAL MURDERS, CARRIED OUT AND CONCEALED BY THE VILLAGE.
IS THIS THE REAL REASON RENA AND MION KEPT THEIR MOUTHS SHUT!?
SO YOU'LL LISTEN TO WHAT I HAVE TO SAY?
KEIICHI MAEBARA-SAN.

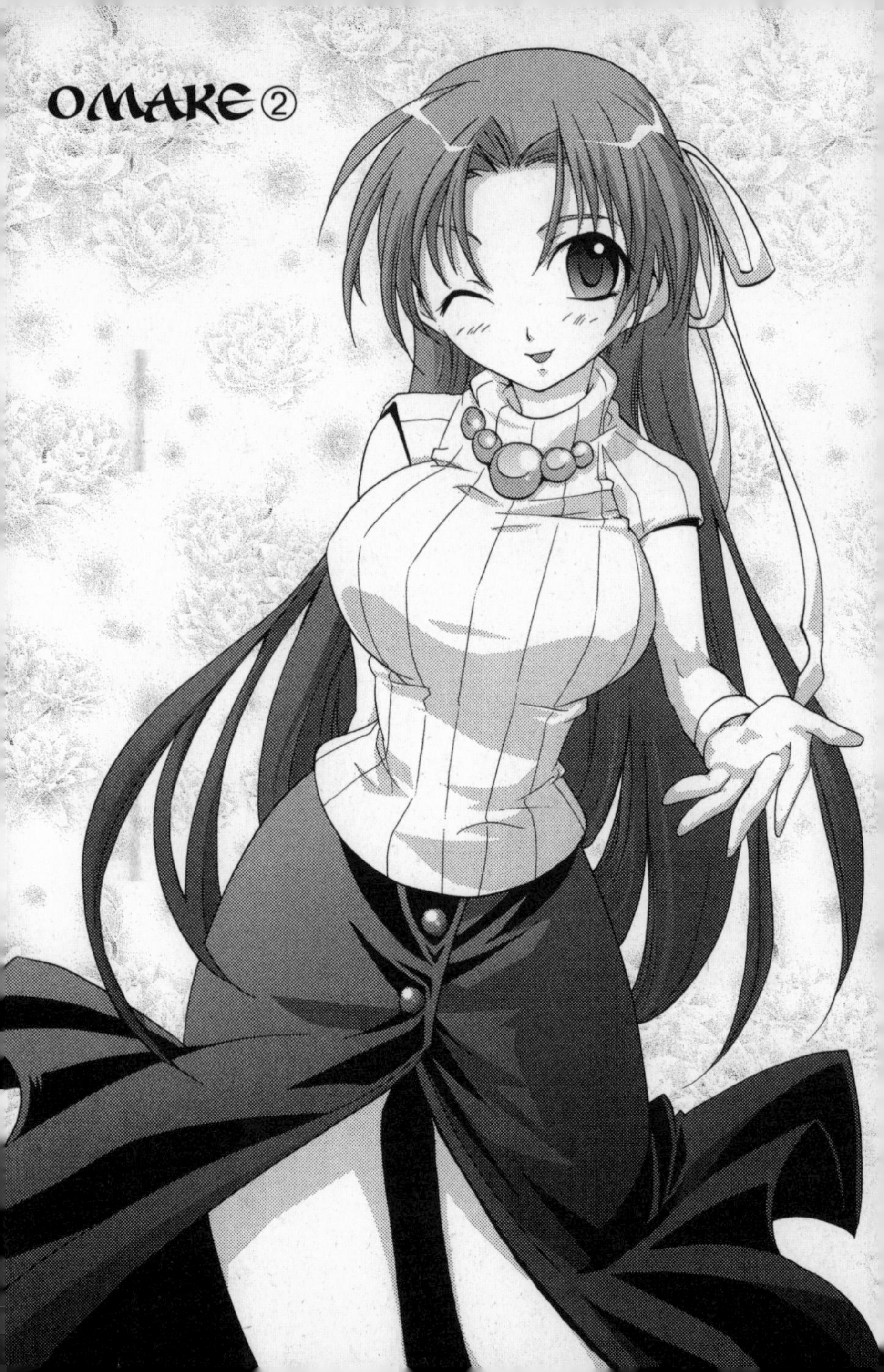
OMAKE ②

BONUS MANGA: "MAID IN HEAVEN"

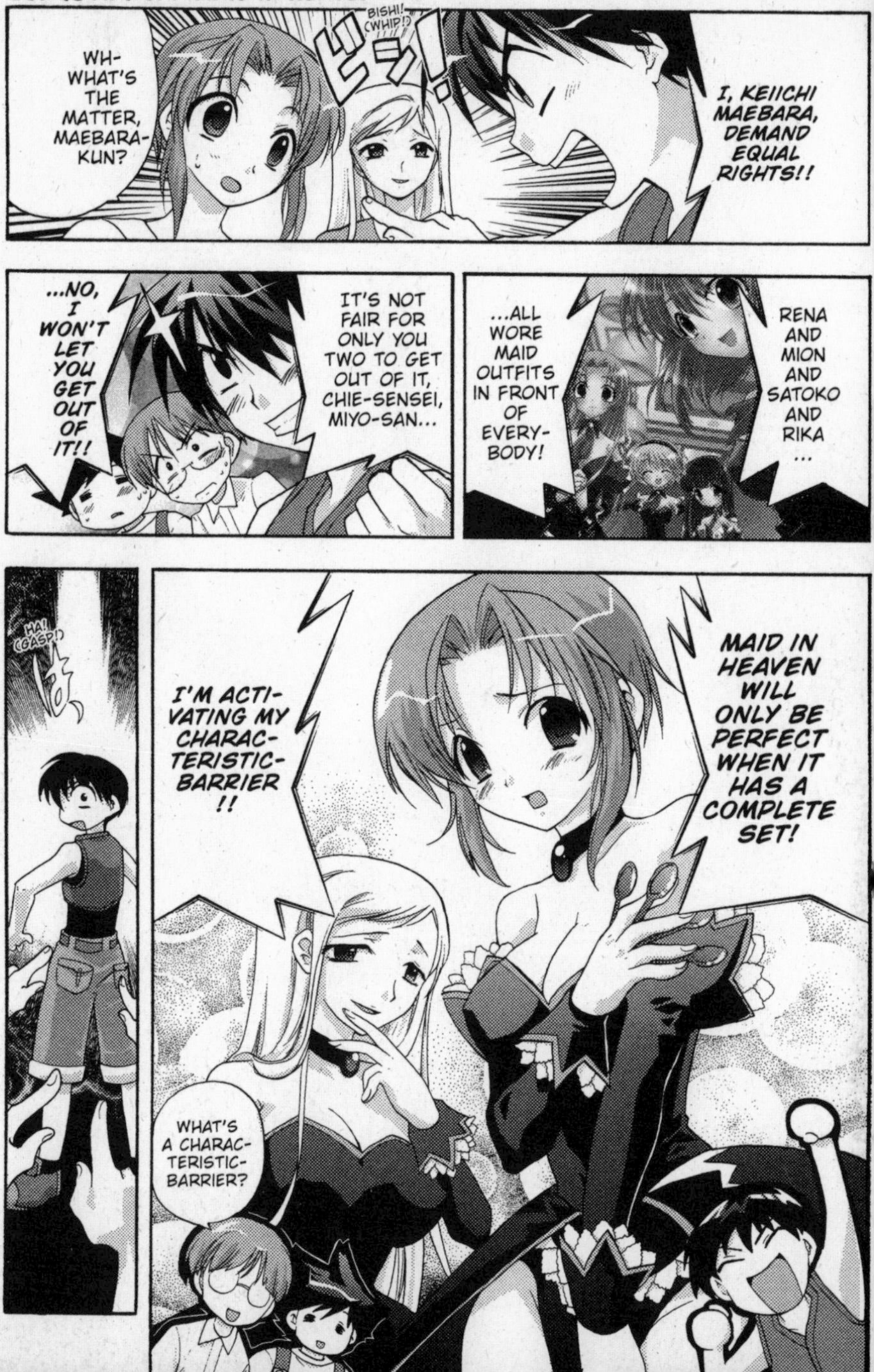
I, KEIICHI MAEBARA, DEMAND EQUAL RIGHTS!!
BISHI! (WHIP!)
WH-WHAT'S THE MATTER, MAEBARA-KUN?
RENA AND MION AND SATOKO AND RIKA ...
...ALL WORE MAID OUTFITS IN FRONT OF EVERY-BODY!
IT'S NOT FAIR FOR ONLY YOU TWO TO GET OUT OF IT, CHIE-SENSEI, MIYO-SAN...
...NO, I WON'T LET YOU GET OUT OF IT!!
MAID IN HEAVEN WILL ONLY BE PERFECT WHEN IT HAS A COMPLETE SET!
I'M ACTI-VATING MY CHARAC-TERISTIC-BARRIER !!
WHAT'S A CHARAC-TERISTIC-BARRIER?
HA! (GASP!)

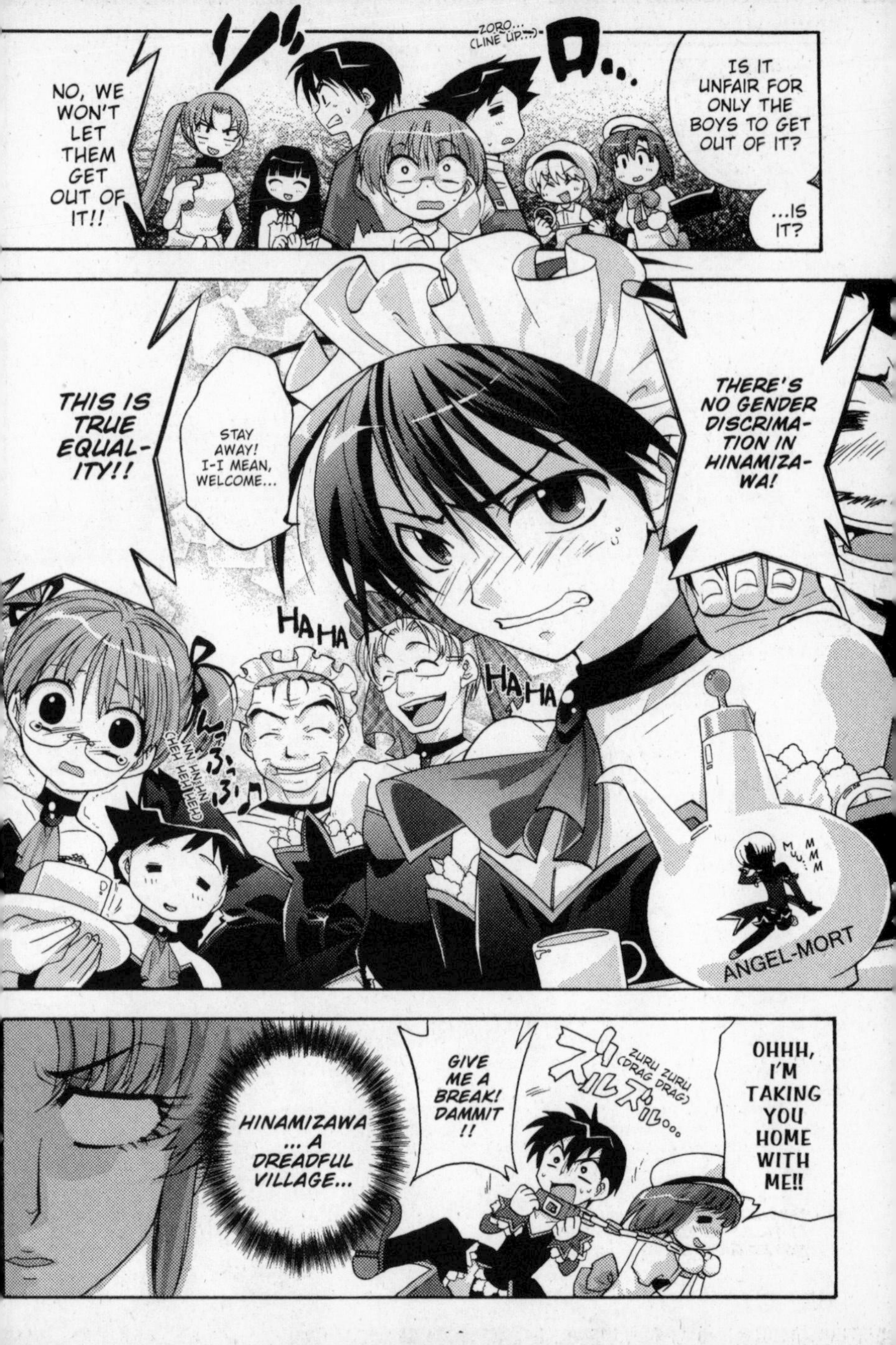
IS IT UNFAIR FOR ONLY THE BOYS TO GET OUT OF IT?
...IS IT?
ZORO... (LINE UP...)
NO, WE WON'T LET THEM GET OUT OF IT!!
THERE'S NO GENDER DISCRIMATION IN HINAMIZAWA!
STAY AWAY! I-I MEAN, WELCOME...
THIS IS TRUE EQUALITY!!
HAHA
HAHA
NN HNHN (HEH HEH HEH)
MUU... MMM
ANGEL-MORT
OHHH, I'M TAKING YOU HOME WITH ME!!
ZURU ZURU (DRAG DRAG)
GIVE ME A BREAK! DAMMIT!!
HINAMIZAWA... A DREADFUL VILLAGE...

THE STRONGEST NOVEL GAME

WHAT IS "HIGURASHI WHEN THEY CRY"!?

"HIGURASHI WHEN THEY CRY" IS A PC VERSION DOUJIN NOVEL GAME THAT WAS PRESENTED AT A DOUJINSHI CONVENTION. BUT IT HAS CROSSED THAT BARRIER AND ENTERED THE WORLD OF COMICS, DRAMA CDS, AND TV ANIME; ITS POPULARITY KNOWS NO BOUNDS. FACE THE SECRETS OF ITS AMAZINGNESS!!

① THE "MYSTERIES" ARE INCREDIBLE!!

WHAT MAKES "HIGURASHI" EPIC IS THAT "YOU DON'T KNOW THE TRUTH JUST FROM READING IT." THE USER NEEDS TO REASON OUT THE TRUTH IN THEIR OWN WAY AS THEY READ.

THE SCENARIOS PREPARED ARE THREE: "ABDUCTED BY DEMONS," "COTTON DRIFTING," "CURSE KILLING" (PLUS THE EXTRA CHAPTER, "KILLING TIME").

THE CHARACTERS THAT APPEAR IN THE THREE SCENARIOS ARE ALMOST THE SAME, BUT DEVELOPMENTS IN EACH ARE VASTLY DIFFERENT. BUT EACH SCENARIO CENTERS AROUND THE SERIES OF MYSTERIOUS INCIDENTS CALLED "OYASHIRO-SAMA'S CURSE."

WHAT IS THE TRUTH OF THESE INCIDENTS? ARE THEY CAUSED BY PEOPLE, A CURSE, OR MERE COINCIDENCE...?

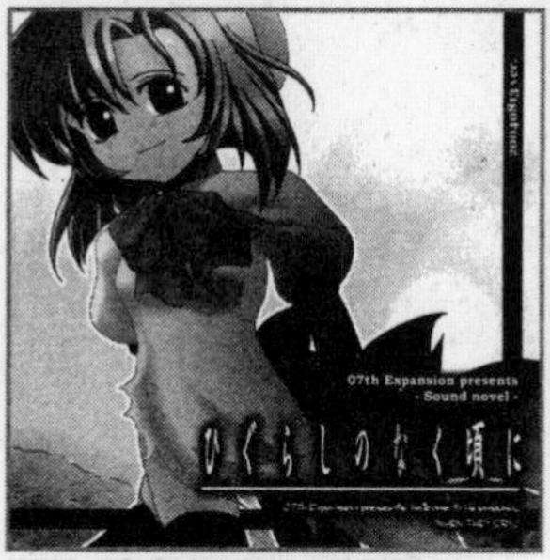
07th Expansion presents
- Sound novel -
ひぐらしのなく頃に

TITLE: HIGURASHI WHEN THEY CRY

FOR RETAILERS AND WAYS TO GET IT, CHECK THE OFFICIAL HOMEPAGE (IN JAPANESE): HTTP://07TH-EXPANSION.NET/. THE NEW "SOLUTION ARCS" ARE BEING PRESENTED IN SUCCESSION TOO!! (CURRENT AS OF DECEMBER, 2005)

TEXT: "THE MYSTERY HAPPENS EVERY YEAR. ...ALWAYS ON THIS NIGHT."

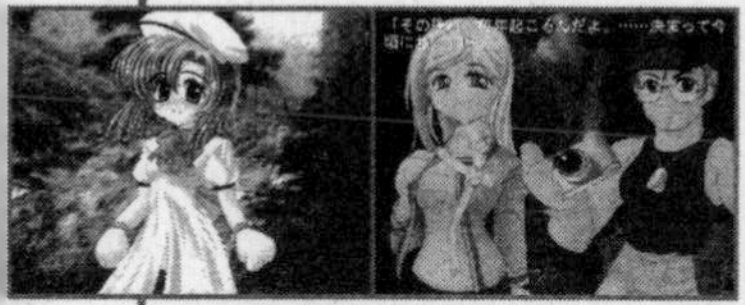

② THE "HORROR" IS INCREDIBLE!!

BASED ON THE CLUES SPREAD THROUGHOUT EACH SCENARIO, A HOT DEBATE HAS DEVELOPED ON THE INTERNET OVER THE TRUTH. THAT'S JUST HOW POWERFULLY ALLURING THE "MYSTERY" IS.

ANOTHER ASPECT OF ITS CHARM IS THE "HORROR." THEIR ENJOYABLE NORMAL LIVES FALL INTO UNBELIEVABLE ABNORMALITY AT THE SLIGHTEST OPPORTUNITY. THE LOVABLE CHARACTERS SUDDENLY BECOME THE MAIN CHARACTERS OF A TRAGEDY. ITS EXQUISITE TEXT AND PRODUCTION WITH ITS TWISTS AND TURNS CREATE A FEAR THAT SENDS CHILLS DOWN YOUR SPINE. THIS HAS GOTTEN MANY USERS HOOKED.

③ THE "CHARACTERS" ARE INCREDIBLE!!

AS IS THEIR CHARM. THE CHARACTERS ASSERT THEIR INDIVIDUALITY IN FULL AND WITHOUT MERCY THEY ENJOY NORMAL LIFE WITH THEIR CLUB ACTIVITIES...

...AND EVEN IN THE ABNORMAL DAYS THAT VISIT THEM LATER. THEY EACH HAVE MANY FANS PASSIONATE ENOUGH TO BUILD FIGURES OF THEM.

④ "RYUKISHI 07" IS INCREDIBLE!!

THE TEXT AND THE PICTURES OF THIS SHOCKING WORK WERE ALL MADE BY ONE PERSON—RYUKISHI 07. IN THE GAME INDUSTRY, WHERE EPIC GAMES MADE BY LARGE TEAMS HAVE BECOME MAINSTREAM, THE TALENT AND PASSION OF THIS ONE PERSON HAVE CREATED A SENSATION.

EVERYTHING ABOUT "HIGURASHI" IS INCREDIBLE. IT TRULY IS THE STRONGEST NOVEL GAME!!

TEXT: "EH?.. WHAT DO YOU MEAN...?.. RENA GAVE A TERRIBLE SCREAM BACK THEN."

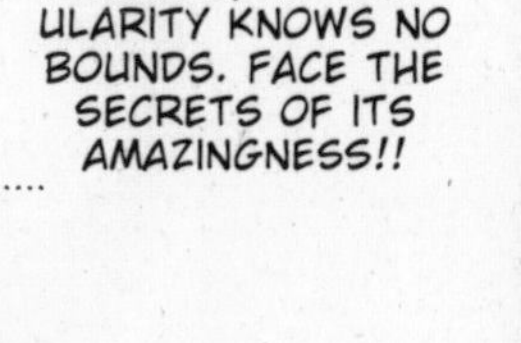

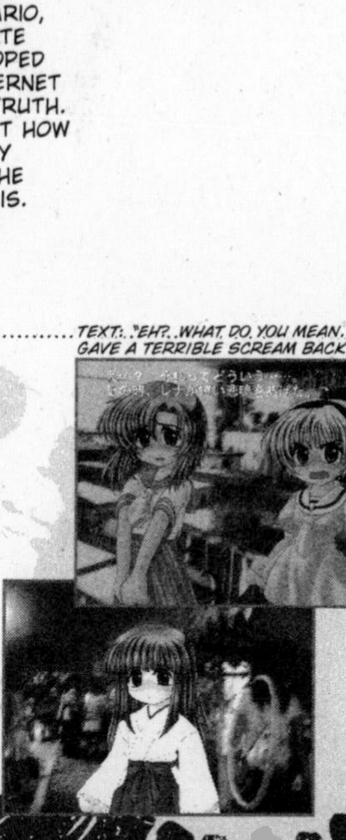

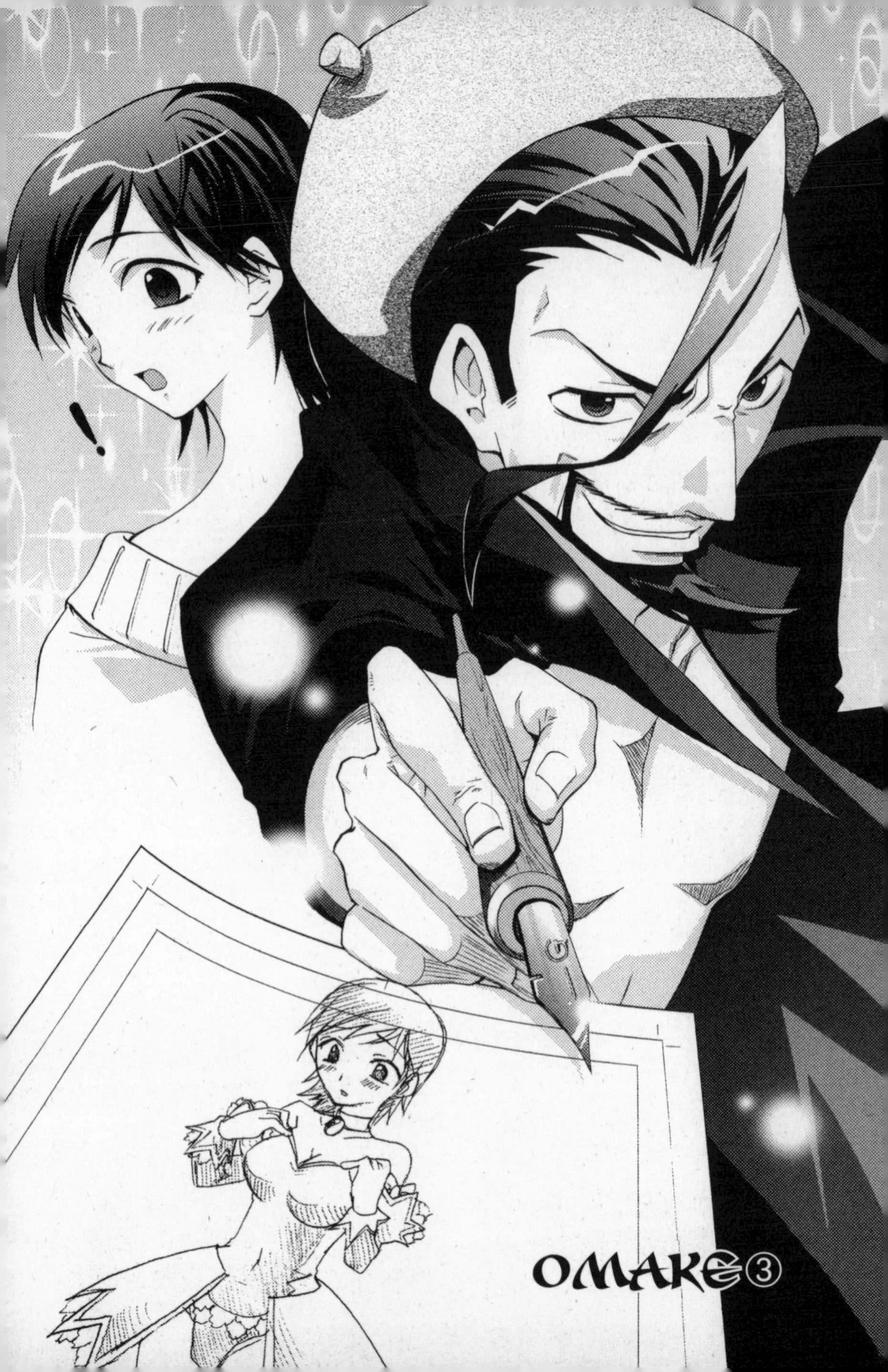
!
OMAKE③

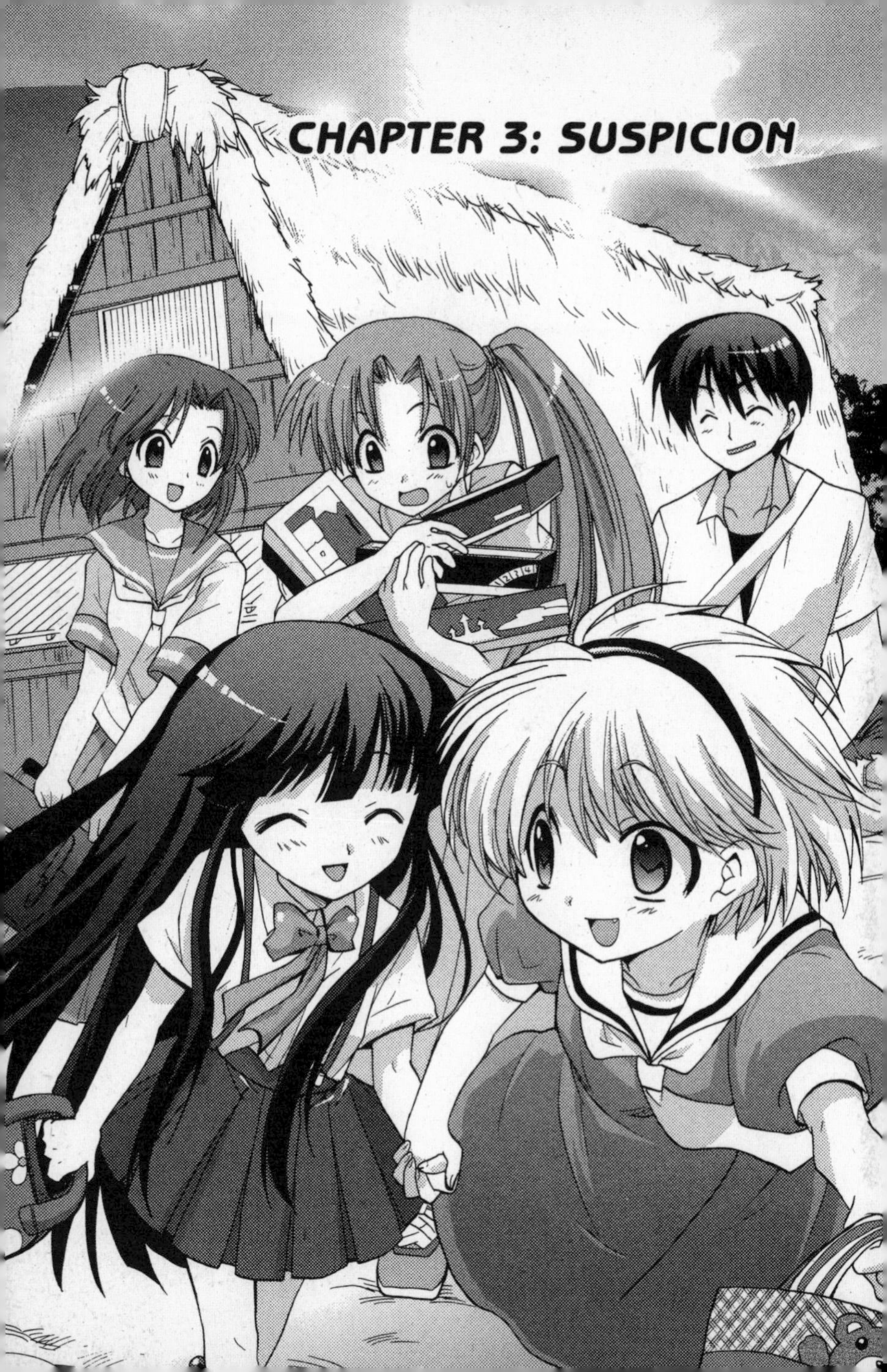
CHAPTER 3: SUSPICION

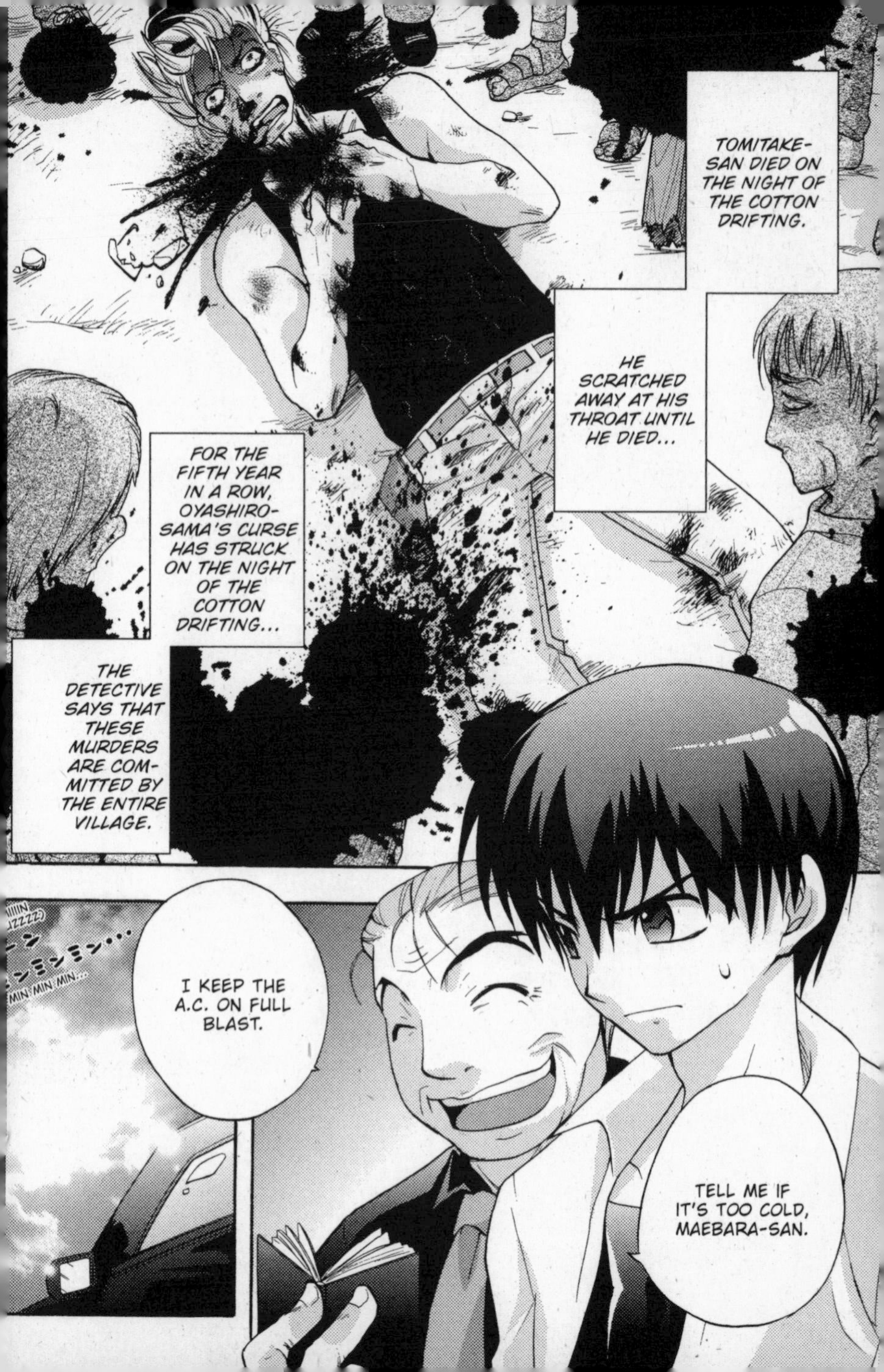
TOMITAKE-SAN DIED ON THE NIGHT OF THE COTTON DRIFTING.
HE SCRATCHED AWAY AT HIS THROAT UNTIL HE DIED...
FOR THE FIFTH YEAR IN A ROW, OYASHIRO-SAMA'S CURSE HAS STRUCK ON THE NIGHT OF THE COTTON DRIFTING...
THE DETECTIVE SAYS THAT THESE MURDERS ARE COM-MITTED BY THE ENTIRE VILLAGE.
I KEEP THE A.C. ON FULL BLAST.
MIN MIN MIN...
TELL ME IF IT'S TOO COLD, MAEBARA-SAN.

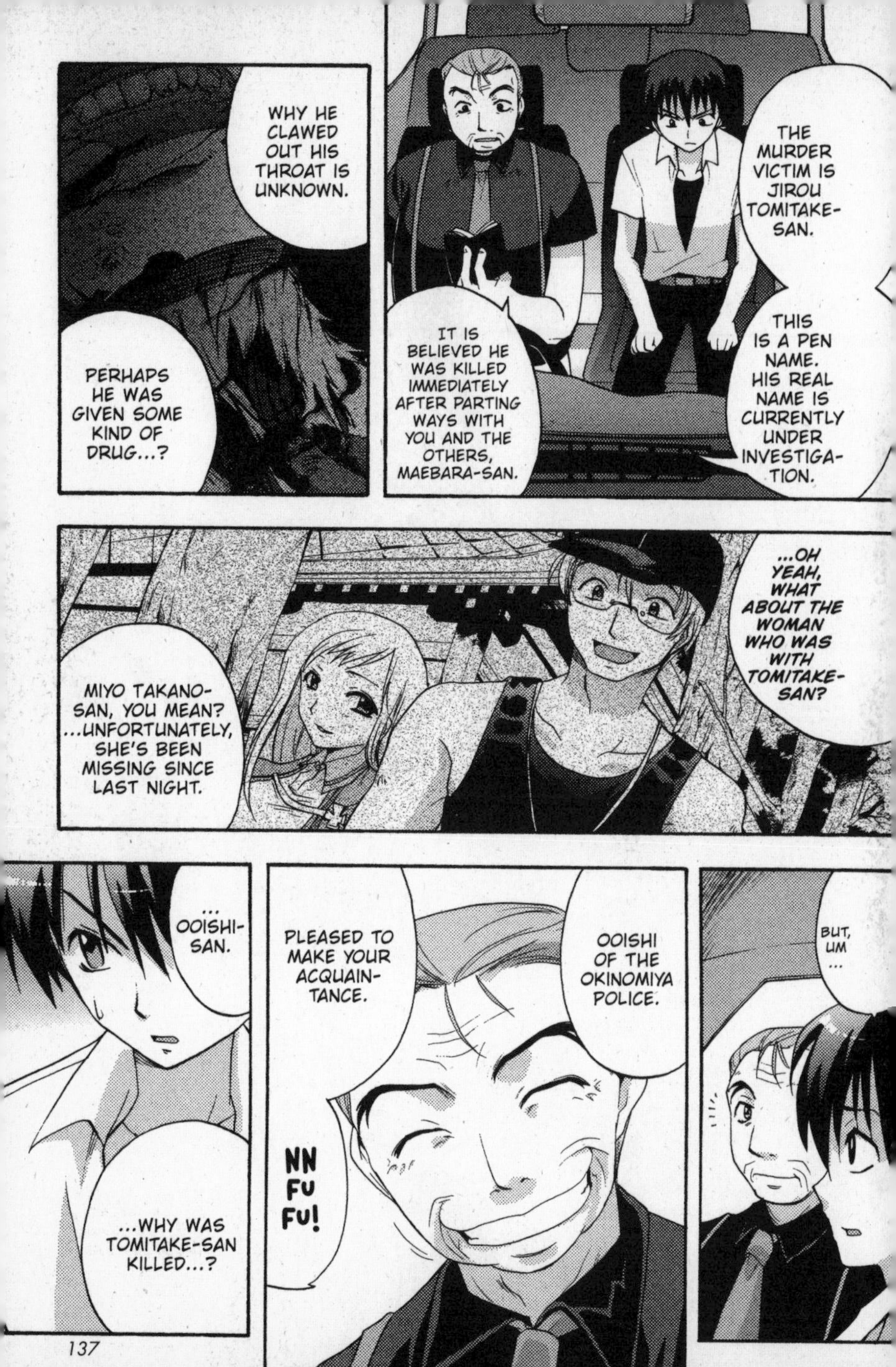
THE MURDER VICTIM IS JIROU TOMITAKE-SAN.
THIS IS A PEN NAME. HIS REAL NAME IS CURRENTLY UNDER INVESTIGATION.
IT IS BELIEVED HE WAS KILLED IMMEDIATELY AFTER PARTING WAYS WITH YOU AND THE OTHERS, MAEBARA-SAN.
WHY HE CLAWED OUT HIS THROAT IS UNKNOWN.
PERHAPS HE WAS GIVEN SOME KIND OF DRUG...?
...OH YEAH, WHAT ABOUT THE WOMAN WHO WAS WITH TOMITAKE-SAN?
MIYO TAKANO-SAN, YOU MEAN? ...UNFORTUNATELY, SHE'S BEEN MISSING SINCE LAST NIGHT.
BUT, UM ...
OOISHI OF THE OKINOMIYA POLICE.
PLEASED TO MAKE YOUR ACQUAINTANCE.
NN FU FU!
... OOISHI-SAN.
...WHY WAS TOMITAKE-SAN KILLED...?

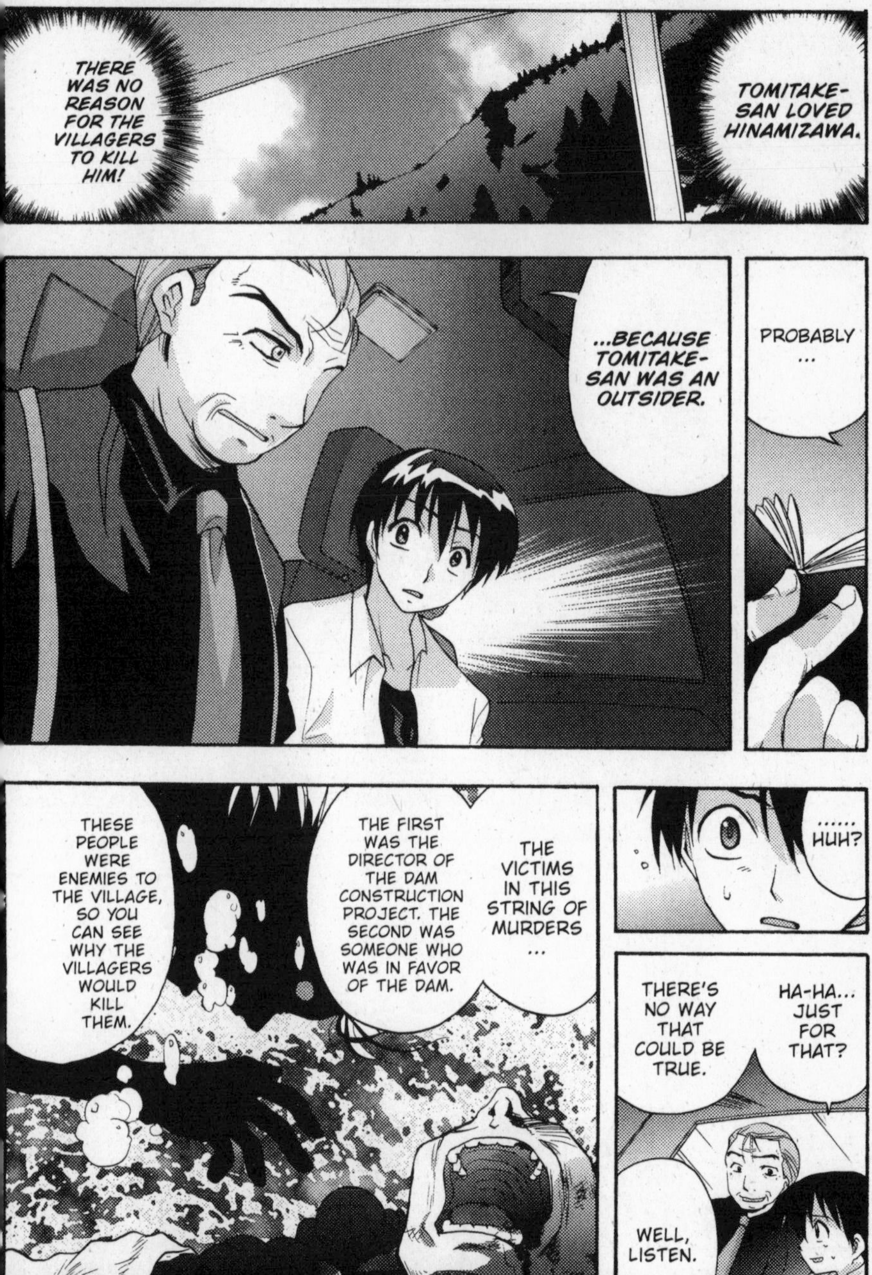
TOMITAKE-SAN LOVED HINAMIZAWA.
THERE WAS NO REASON FOR THE VILLAGERS TO KILL HIM!
PROBABLY ...
...BECAUSE TOMITAKE-SAN WAS AN OUTSIDER.
......HUH?
HA-HA... JUST FOR THAT?
THERE'S NO WAY THAT COULD BE TRUE.
WELL, LISTEN.
THE VICTIMS IN THIS STRING OF MURDERS ...
THE FIRST WAS THE DIRECTOR OF THE DAM CONSTRUCTION PROJECT. THE SECOND WAS SOMEONE WHO WAS IN FAVOR OF THE DAM.
THESE PEOPLE WERE ENEMIES TO THE VILLAGE, SO YOU CAN SEE WHY THE VILLAGERS WOULD KILL THEM.

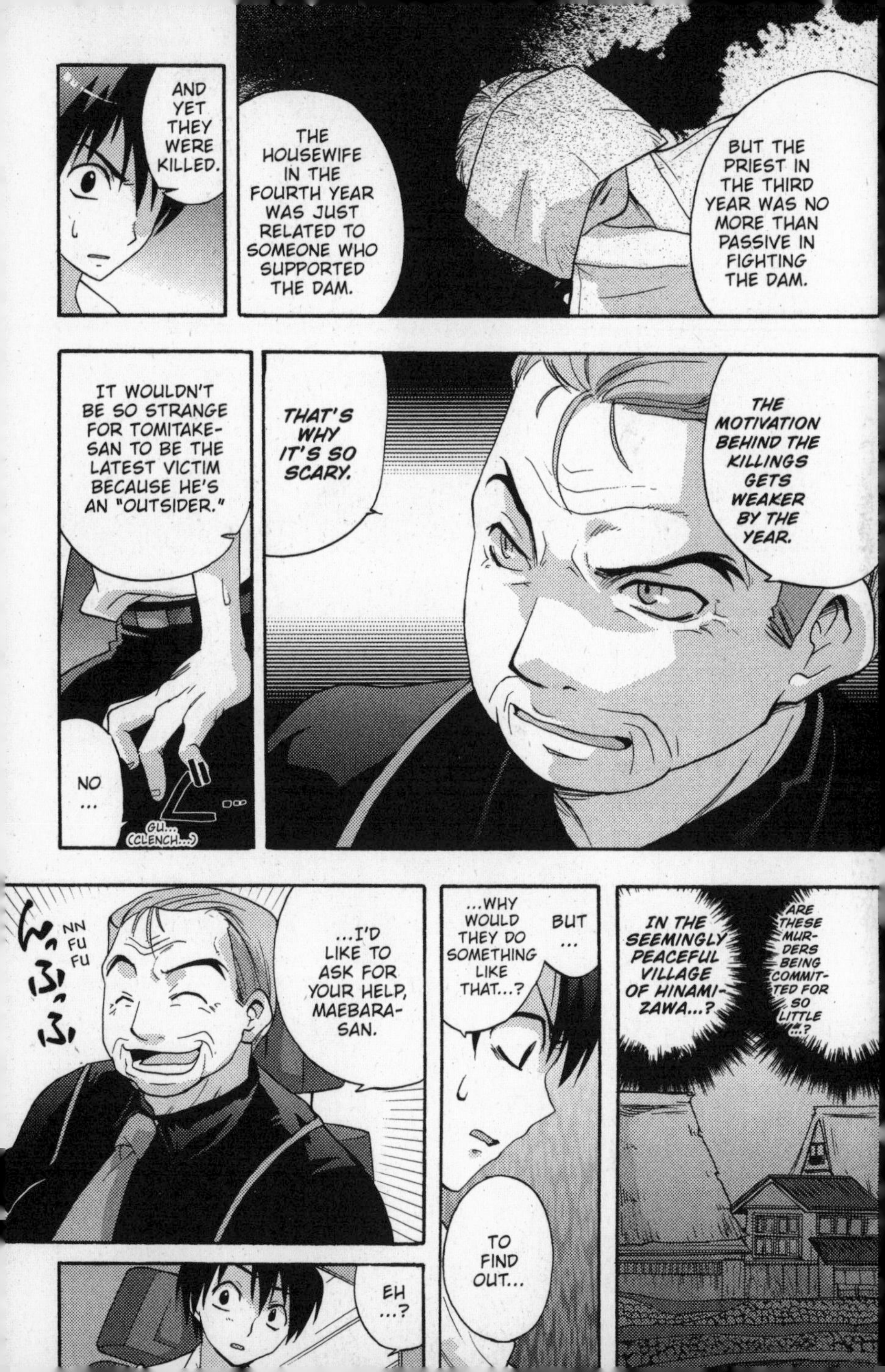
BUT THE PRIEST IN THE THIRD YEAR WAS NO MORE THAN PASSIVE IN FIGHTING THE DAM.
THE HOUSEWIFE IN THE FOURTH YEAR WAS JUST RELATED TO SOMEONE WHO SUPPORTED THE DAM.
AND YET THEY WERE KILLED.
THE MOTIVATION BEHIND THE KILLINGS GETS WEAKER BY THE YEAR.
THAT'S WHY IT'S SO SCARY.
IT WOULDN'T BE SO STRANGE FOR TOMITAKE-SAN TO BE THE LATEST VICTIM BECAUSE HE'S AN "OUTSIDER."
NO ...
GU... (CLENCH...)
ARE THESE MURDERS BEING COMMITTED FOR SO LITTLE...?
IN THE SEEMINGLY PEACEFUL VILLAGE OF HINAMIZAWA...?
BUT ...
...WHY WOULD THEY DO SOMETHING LIKE THAT...?
NN FU FU
...I'D LIKE TO ASK FOR YOUR HELP, MAEBARA-SAN.
TO FIND OUT...
EH ...?

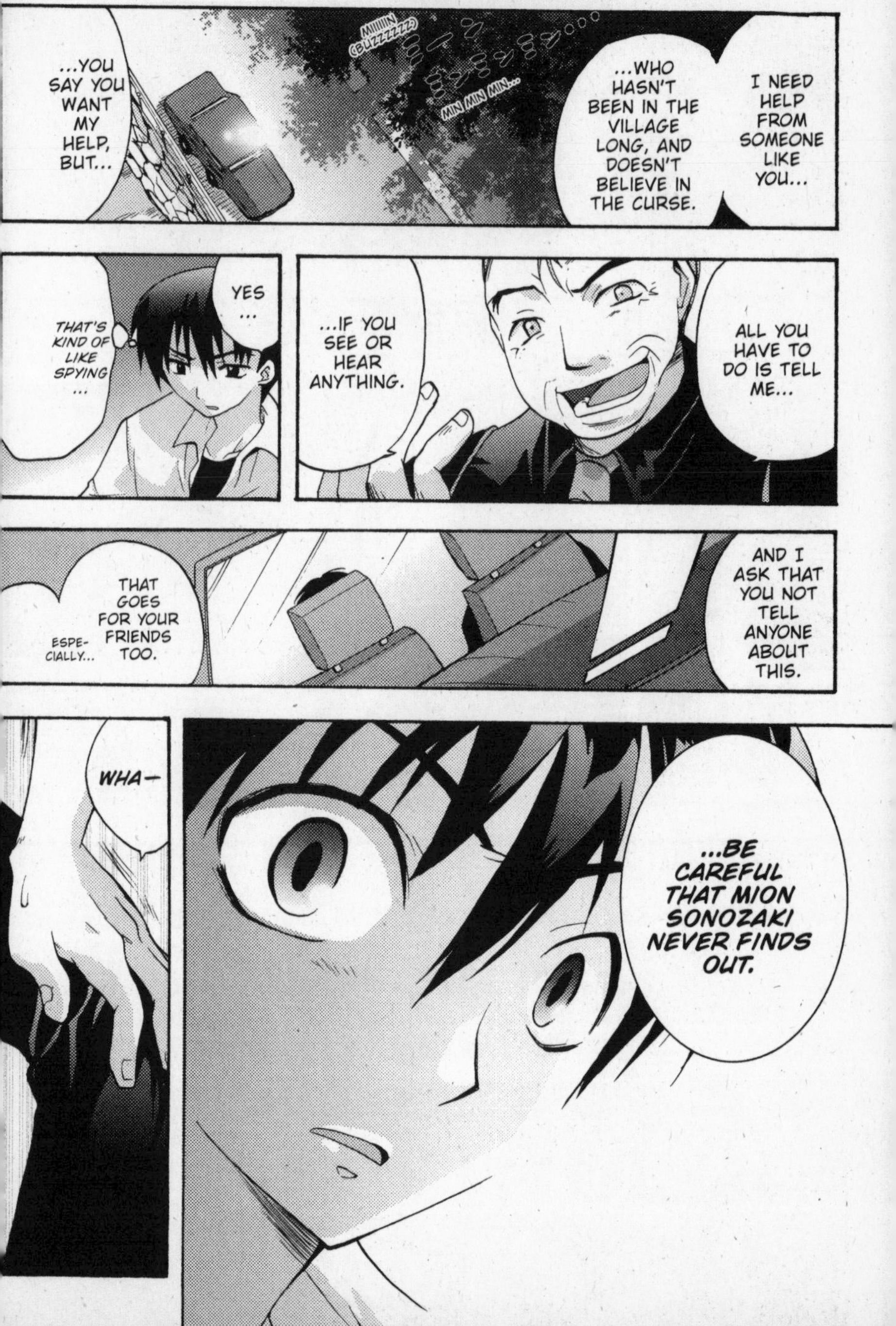
I NEED HELP FROM SOMEONE LIKE YOU...
...WHO HASN'T BEEN IN THE VILLAGE LONG, AND DOESN'T BELIEVE IN THE CURSE.
MIN MIN MIN...
MIIIIIN (BUZZZZZZZ)
...YOU SAY YOU WANT MY HELP, BUT...
ALL YOU HAVE TO DO IS TELL ME...
...IF YOU SEE OR HEAR ANYTHING.
YES...
THAT'S KIND OF LIKE SPYING...
AND I ASK THAT YOU NOT TELL ANYONE ABOUT THIS.
THAT GOES FOR YOUR FRIENDS TOO.
ESPECIALLY...
...BE CAREFUL THAT MION SONOZAKI NEVER FINDS OUT.
WHA-

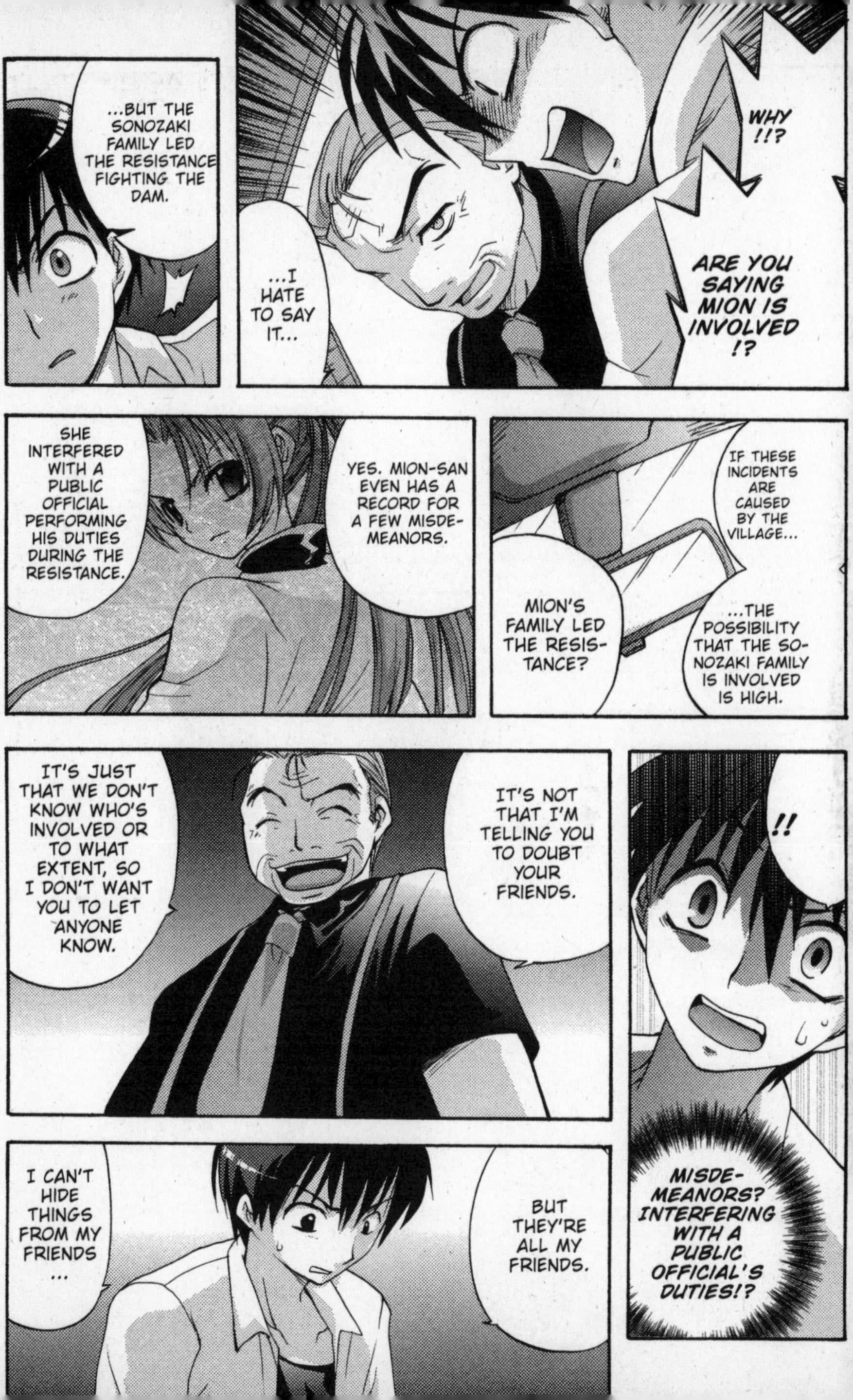
WHY!!?
ARE YOU SAYING MION IS INVOLVED!?
...I HATE TO SAY IT...
...BUT THE SONOZAKI FAMILY LED THE RESISTANCE FIGHTING THE DAM.
IF THESE INCIDENTS ARE CAUSED BY THE VILLAGE...
...THE POSSIBILITY THAT THE SONOZAKI FAMILY IS INVOLVED IS HIGH.
MION'S FAMILY LED THE RESISTANCE?
YES. MION-SAN EVEN HAS A RECORD FOR A FEW MISDEMEANORS.
SHE INTERFERED WITH A PUBLIC OFFICIAL PERFORMING HIS DUTIES DURING THE RESISTANCE.
!!
MISDEMEANORS? INTERFERING WITH A PUBLIC OFFICIAL'S DUTIES!?
IT'S NOT THAT I'M TELLING YOU TO DOUBT YOUR FRIENDS.
IT'S JUST THAT WE DON'T KNOW WHO'S INVOLVED OR TO WHAT EXTENT, SO I DON'T WANT YOU TO LET ANYONE KNOW.
BUT THEY'RE ALL MY FRIENDS.
I CAN'T HIDE THINGS FROM MY FRIENDS...

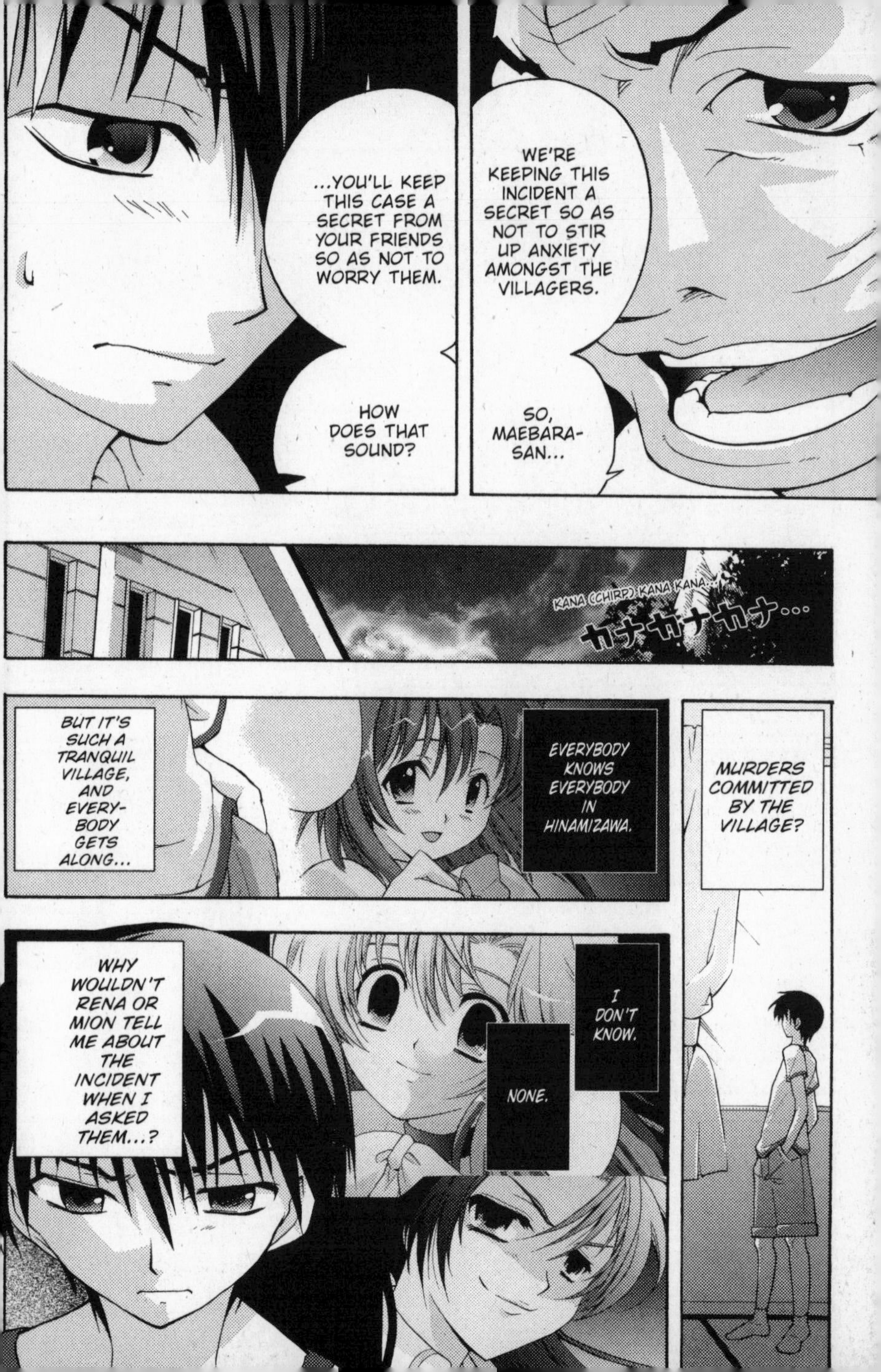
WE'RE KEEPING THIS INCIDENT A SECRET SO AS NOT TO STIR UP ANXIETY AMONGST THE VILLAGERS.
SO, MAEBARA-SAN...
...YOU'LL KEEP THIS CASE A SECRET FROM YOUR FRIENDS SO AS NOT TO WORRY THEM.
HOW DOES THAT SOUND?
KANA (CHIRP) KANA KANA...
カナカナカナ…
MURDERS COMMITTED BY THE VILLAGE?
EVERYBODY KNOWS EVERYBODY IN HINAMIZAWA.
BUT IT'S SUCH A TRANQUIL VILLAGE, AND EVERY-BODY GETS ALONG...
I DON'T KNOW.
NONE.
WHY WOULDN'T RENA OR MION TELL ME ABOUT THE INCIDENT WHEN I ASKED THEM...?

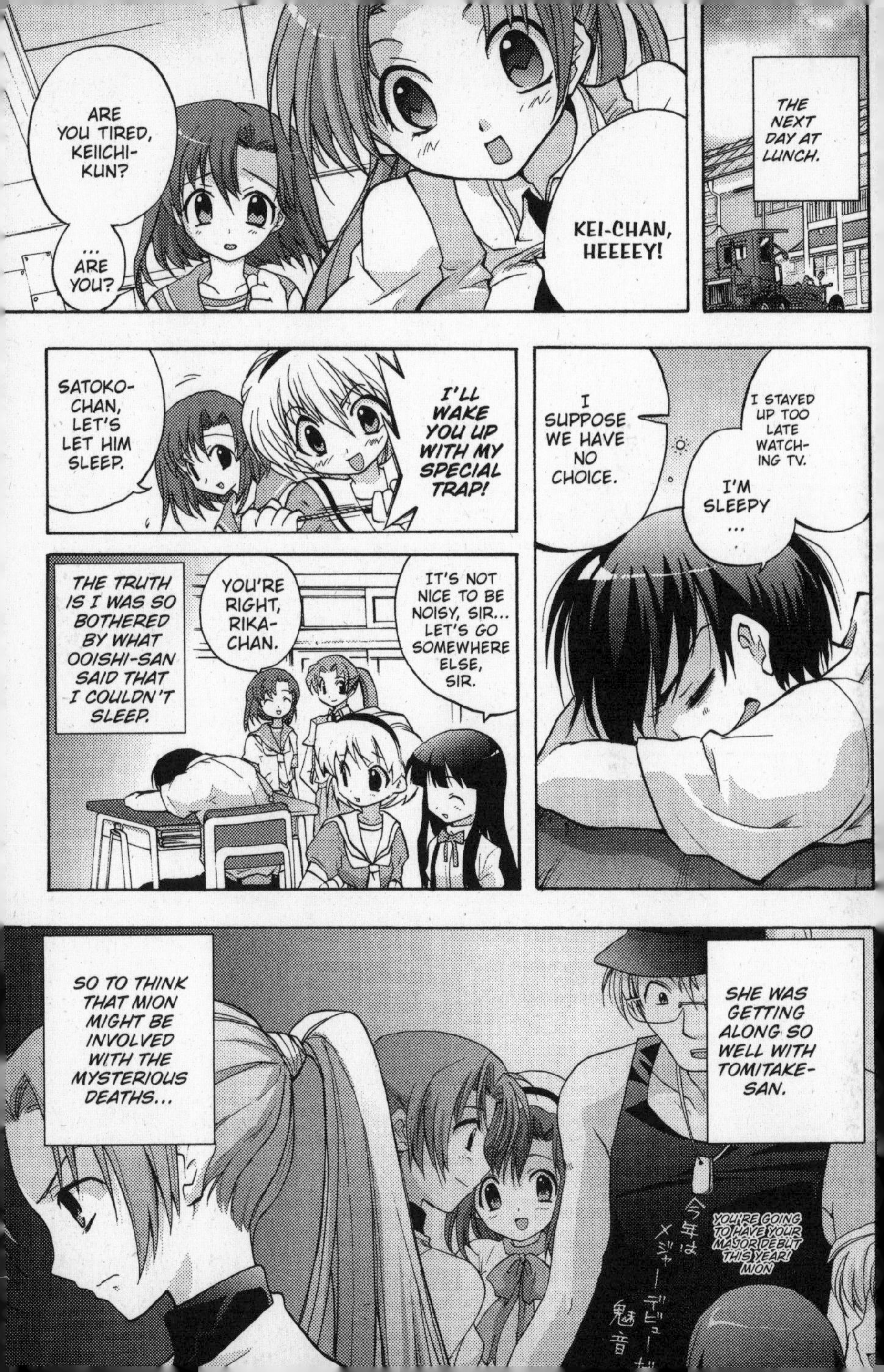
THE NEXT DAY AT LUNCH.
KEI-CHAN, HEEEEY!
ARE YOU TIRED, KEIICHI-KUN?
... ARE YOU?
I STAYED UP TOO LATE WATCHING TV.
I'M SLEEPY ...
I SUPPOSE WE HAVE NO CHOICE.
I'LL WAKE YOU UP WITH MY SPECIAL TRAP!
SATOKO-CHAN, LET'S LET HIM SLEEP.
IT'S NOT NICE TO BE NOISY, SIR... LET'S GO SOMEWHERE ELSE, SIR.
YOU'RE RIGHT, RIKA-CHAN.
THE TRUTH IS I WAS SO BOTHERED BY WHAT OOISHI-SAN SAID THAT I COULDN'T SLEEP.
SHE WAS GETTING ALONG SO WELL WITH TOMITAKE-SAN.
今年はメジャーデビューだ 魅音
YOU'RE GOING TO HAVE YOUR MAJOR DEBUT THIS YEAR! MION
SO TO THINK THAT MION MIGHT BE INVOLVED WITH THE MYSTERIOUS DEATHS...

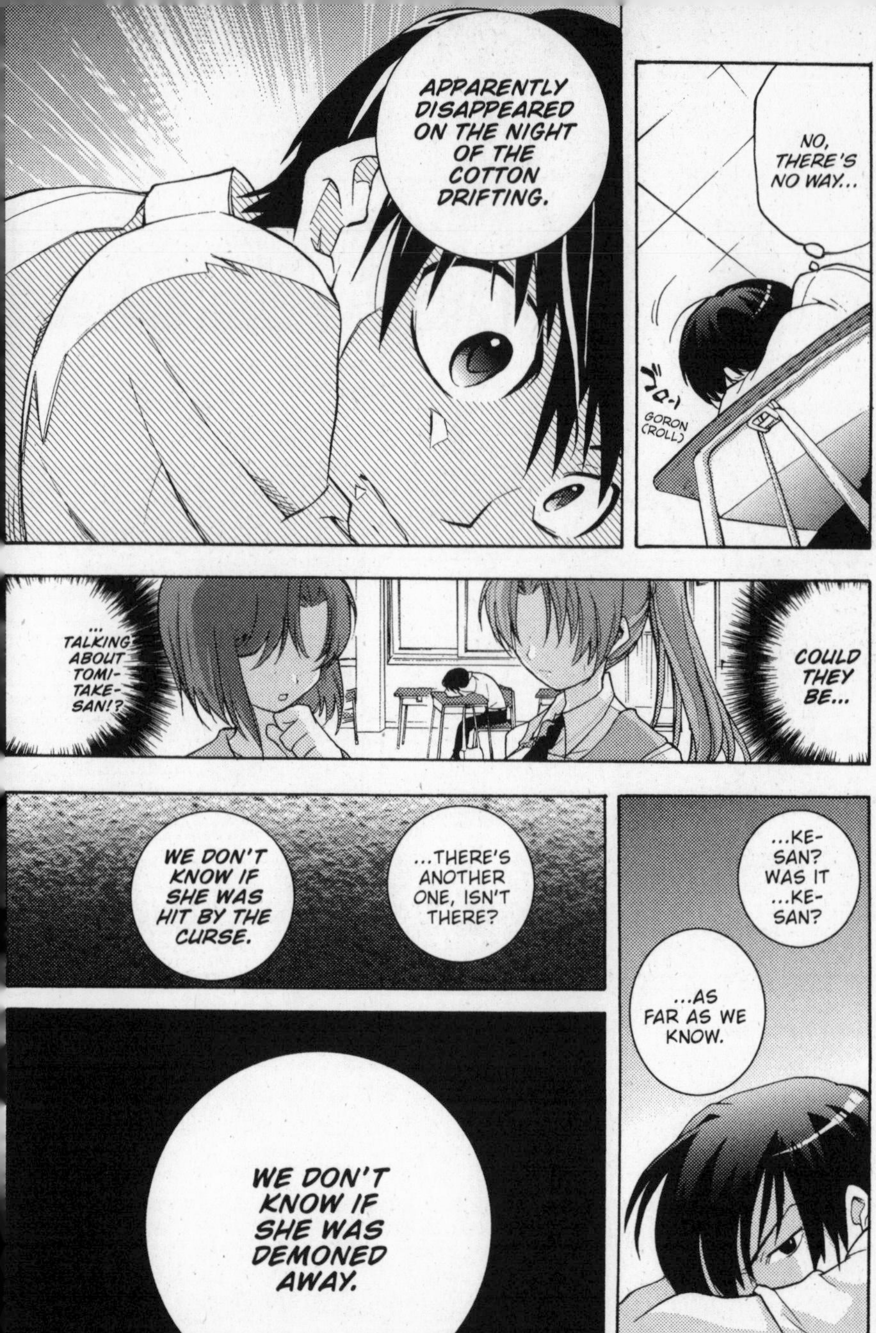
NO, THERE'S NO WAY...
GORON (ROLL)
APPARENTLY DISAPPEARED ON THE NIGHT OF THE COTTON DRIFTING.
COULD THEY BE...
...TALKING ABOUT TOMI-TAKE-SAN!?
...KE-SAN? WAS IT ...KE-SAN?
...AS FAR AS WE KNOW.
...THERE'S ANOTHER ONE, ISN'T THERE?
WE DON'T KNOW IF SHE WAS HIT BY THE CURSE.
WE DON'T KNOW IF SHE WAS DEMONED AWAY.

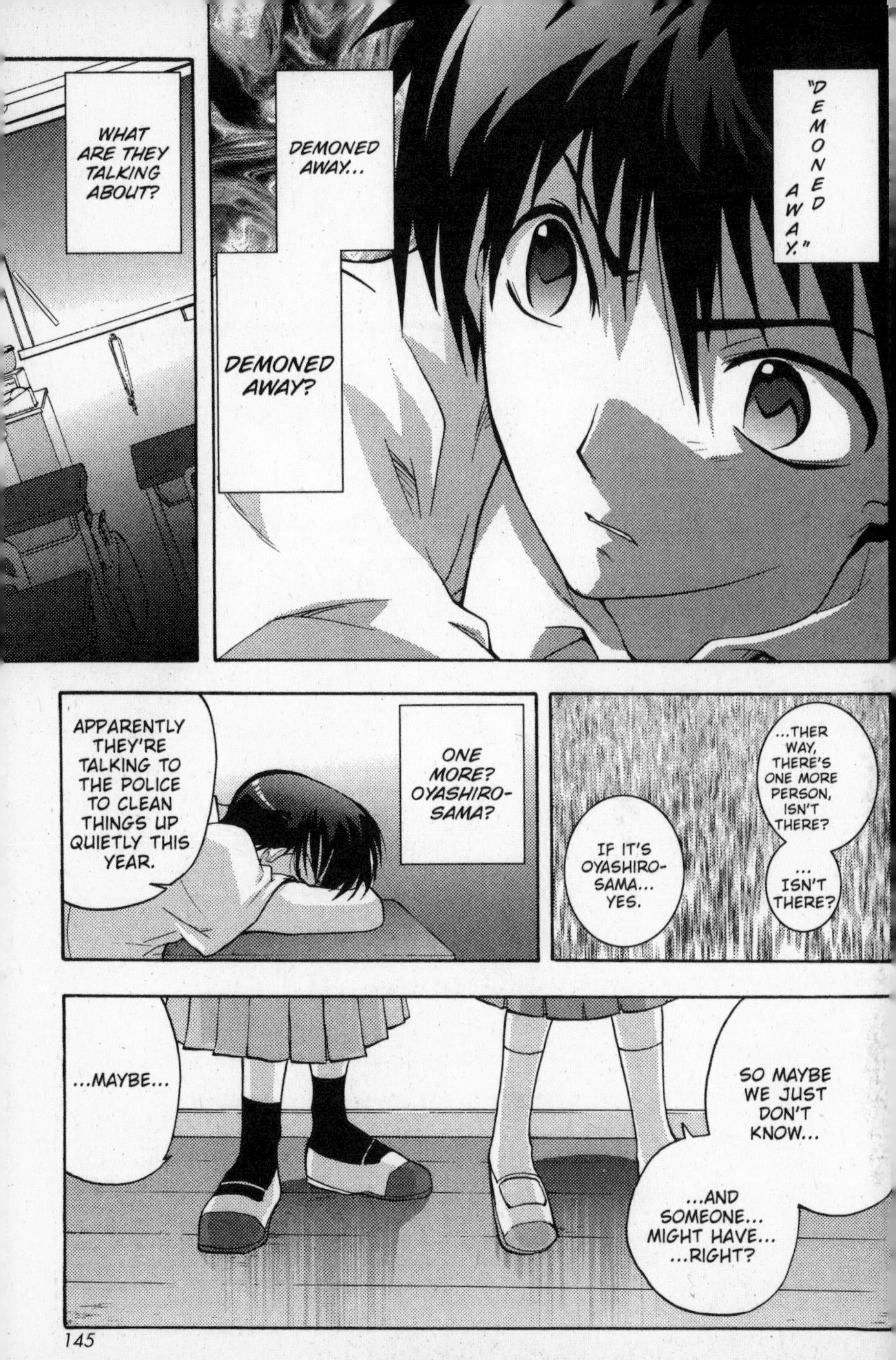
"DEMONED AWAY."
DEMONED AWAY...
DEMONED AWAY?
WHAT ARE THEY TALKING ABOUT?
...THER WAY, THERE'S ONE MORE PERSON, ISN'T THERE?
...ISN'T THERE?
IF IT'S OYASHIRO-SAMA... YES.
ONE MORE? OYASHIRO-SAMA?
APPARENTLY THEY'RE TALKING TO THE POLICE TO CLEAN THINGS UP QUIETLY THIS YEAR.
SO MAYBE WE JUST DON'T KNOW...
...AND SOMEONE... MIGHT HAVE... ...RIGHT?
...MAYBE...

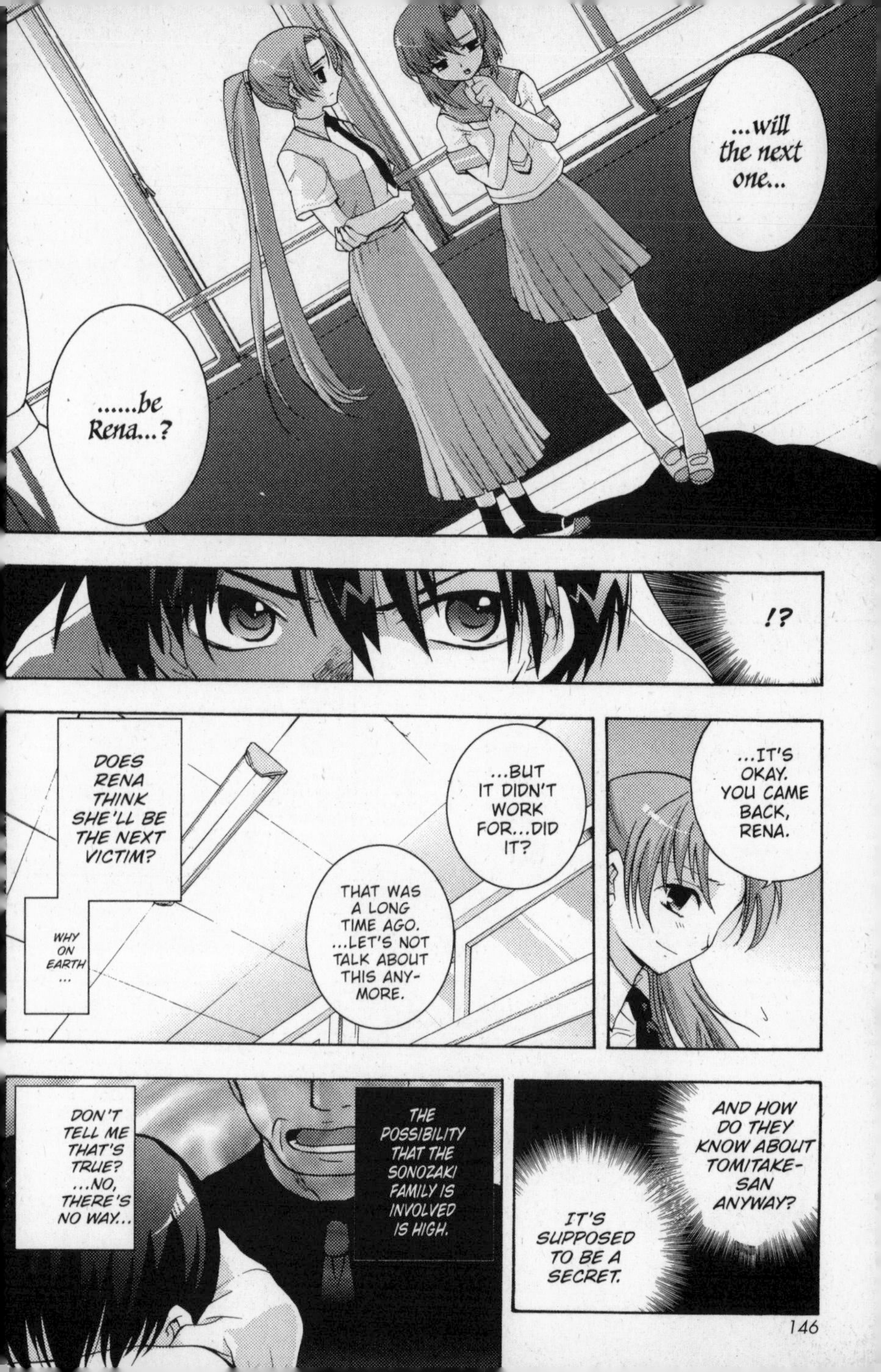
...will the next one...
......be Rena...?
!?
...IT'S OKAY. YOU CAME BACK, RENA.
...BUT IT DIDN'T WORK FOR...DID IT?
THAT WAS A LONG TIME AGO. ...LET'S NOT TALK ABOUT THIS ANY-MORE.
DOES RENA THINK SHE'LL BE THE NEXT VICTIM?
WHY ON EARTH...
AND HOW DO THEY KNOW ABOUT TOMITAKE-SAN ANYWAY?
IT'S SUPPOSED TO BE A SECRET.
THE POSSIBILITY THAT THE SONOZAKI FAMILY IS INVOLVED IS HIGH.
DON'T TELL ME THAT'S TRUE? ...NO, THERE'S NO WAY...

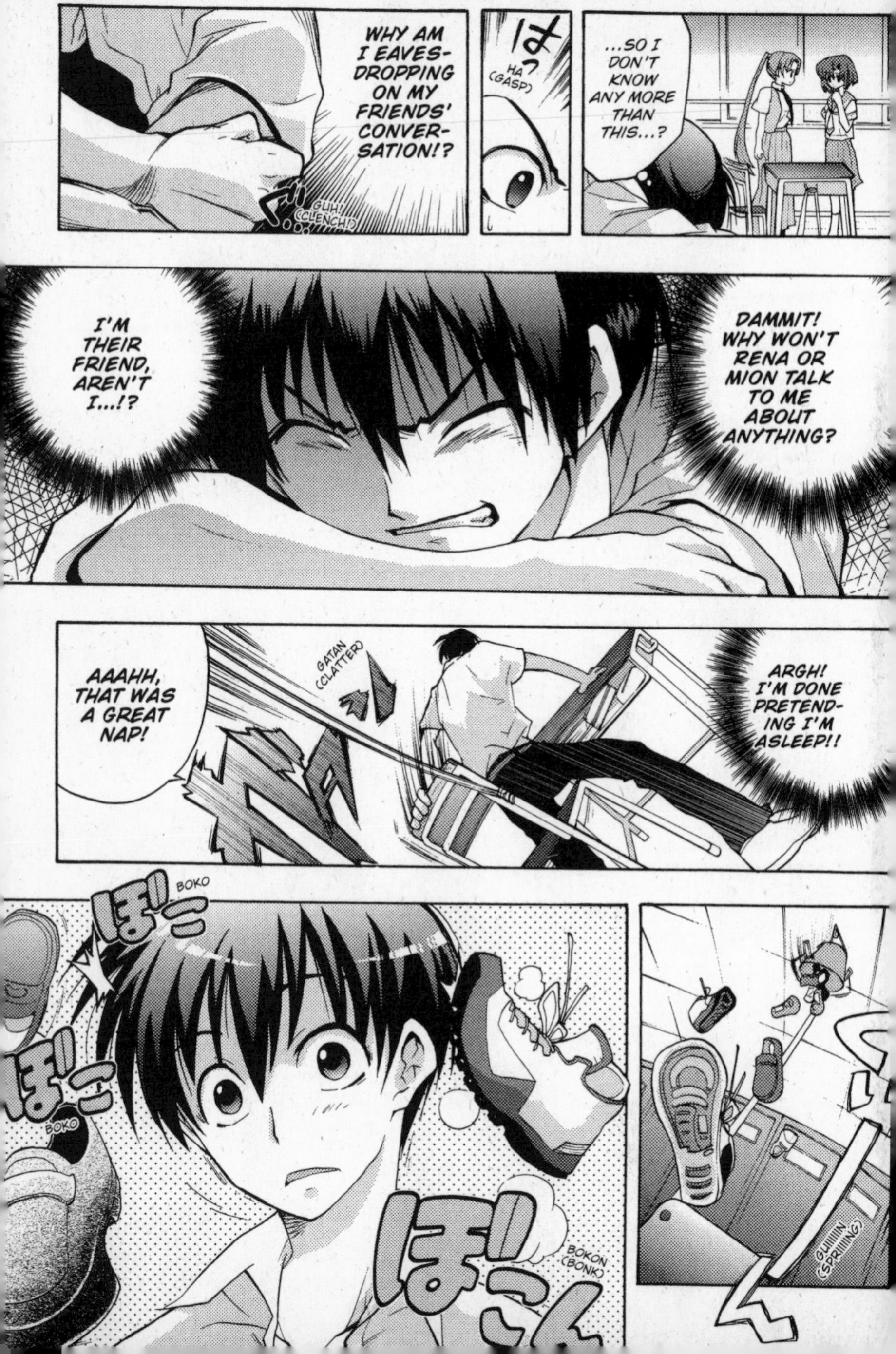
...SO I DON'T KNOW ANY MORE THAN THIS...?
はっ
HA (GASP)
WHY AM I EAVES-DROPPING ON MY FRIENDS' CONVERSATION!?
GUH! (CLENCH!)
DAMMIT! WHY WON'T RENA OR MION TALK TO ME ABOUT ANYTHING?
I'M THEIR FRIEND, AREN'T I...!?
ARGH! I'M DONE PRETENDING I'M ASLEEP!!
GATAN (CLATTER)
AAAHH, THAT WAS A GREAT NAP!
GUIIIIN (SPRIIIING)
ぼこ
BOKO
ぼこ
BOKO
ぼこん
BOKON (BONK)

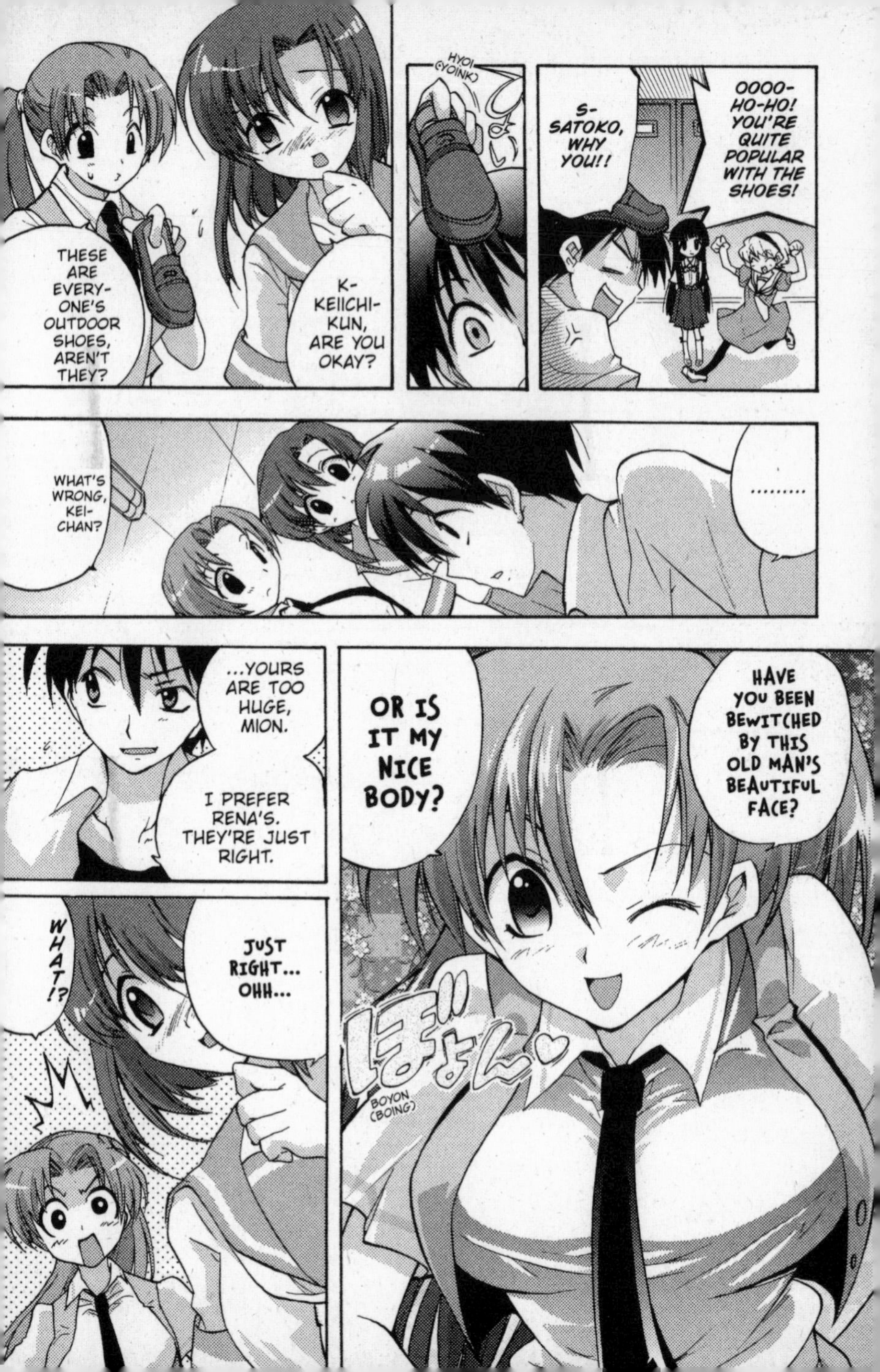
OOOO-HO-HO! YOU'RE QUITE POPULAR WITH THE SHOES!
S-SATOKO, WHY YOU!!
HYOI (YOINK)
K-KEIICHI-KUN, ARE YOU OKAY?
THESE ARE EVERYONE'S OUTDOOR SHOES, AREN'T THEY?
....
WHAT'S WRONG, KEI-CHAN?
HAVE YOU BEEN BEWITCHED BY THIS OLD MAN'S BEAUTIFUL FACE?
OR IS IT MY NICE BODY?
BOYON (BOING)
...YOURS ARE TOO HUGE, MION.
I PREFER RENA'S. THEY'RE JUST RIGHT.
JUST RIGHT... OHH...
WHAT!?

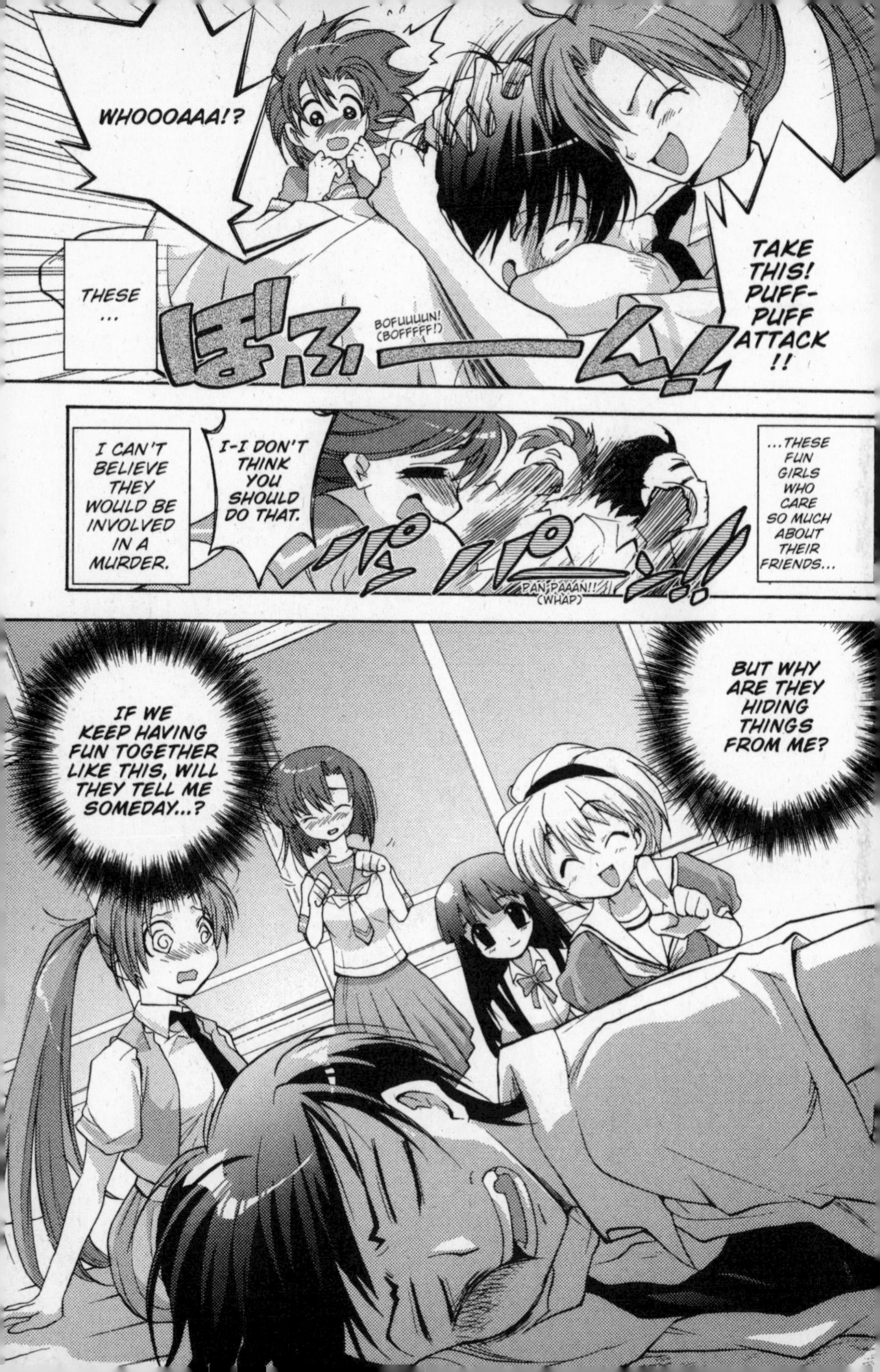
TAKE THIS! PUFF-PUFF ATTACK!!
WHOOOAAA!?
BOFUUUUN! (BOFFFFF!)
THESE...
...THESE FUN GIRLS WHO CARE SO MUCH ABOUT THEIR FRIENDS...
I-I DON'T THINK YOU SHOULD DO THAT.
PAN PAAAN!! (WHAP)
I CAN'T BELIEVE THEY WOULD BE INVOLVED IN A MURDER.
BUT WHY ARE THEY HIDING THINGS FROM ME?
IF WE KEEP HAVING FUN TOGETHER LIKE THIS, WILL THEY TELL ME SOMEDAY...?

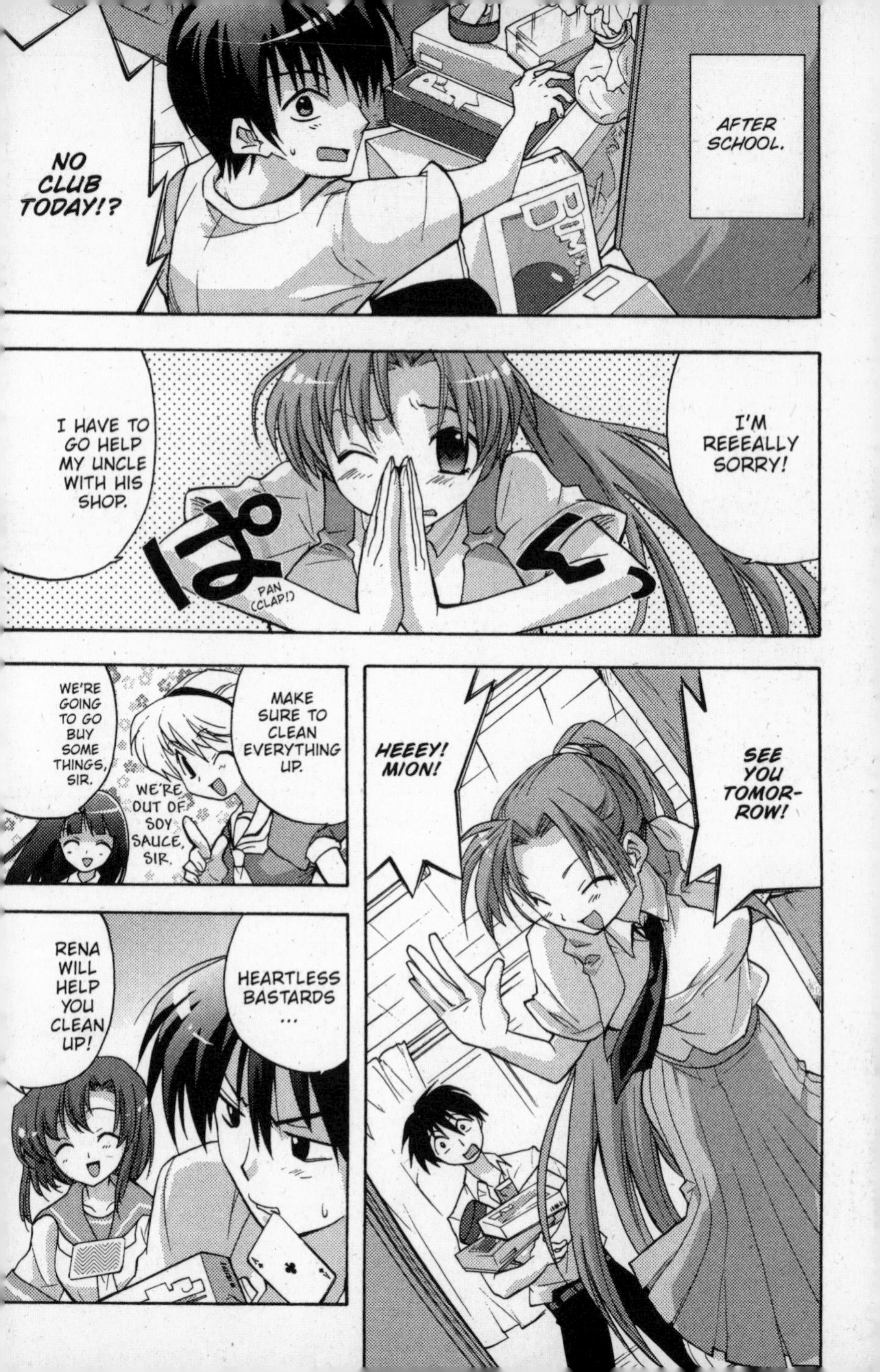
AFTER SCHOOL.
NO CLUB TODAY!?
I'M REEEALLY SORRY!
I HAVE TO GO HELP MY UNCLE WITH HIS SHOP.
PAN (CLAP!)
SEE YOU TOMOR-ROW!
HEEEY! MION!
MAKE SURE TO CLEAN EVERYTHING UP.
WE'RE OUT OF SOY SAUCE, SIR.
WE'RE GOING TO GO BUY SOME THINGS, SIR.
HEARTLESS BASTARDS ...
RENA WILL HELP YOU CLEAN UP!

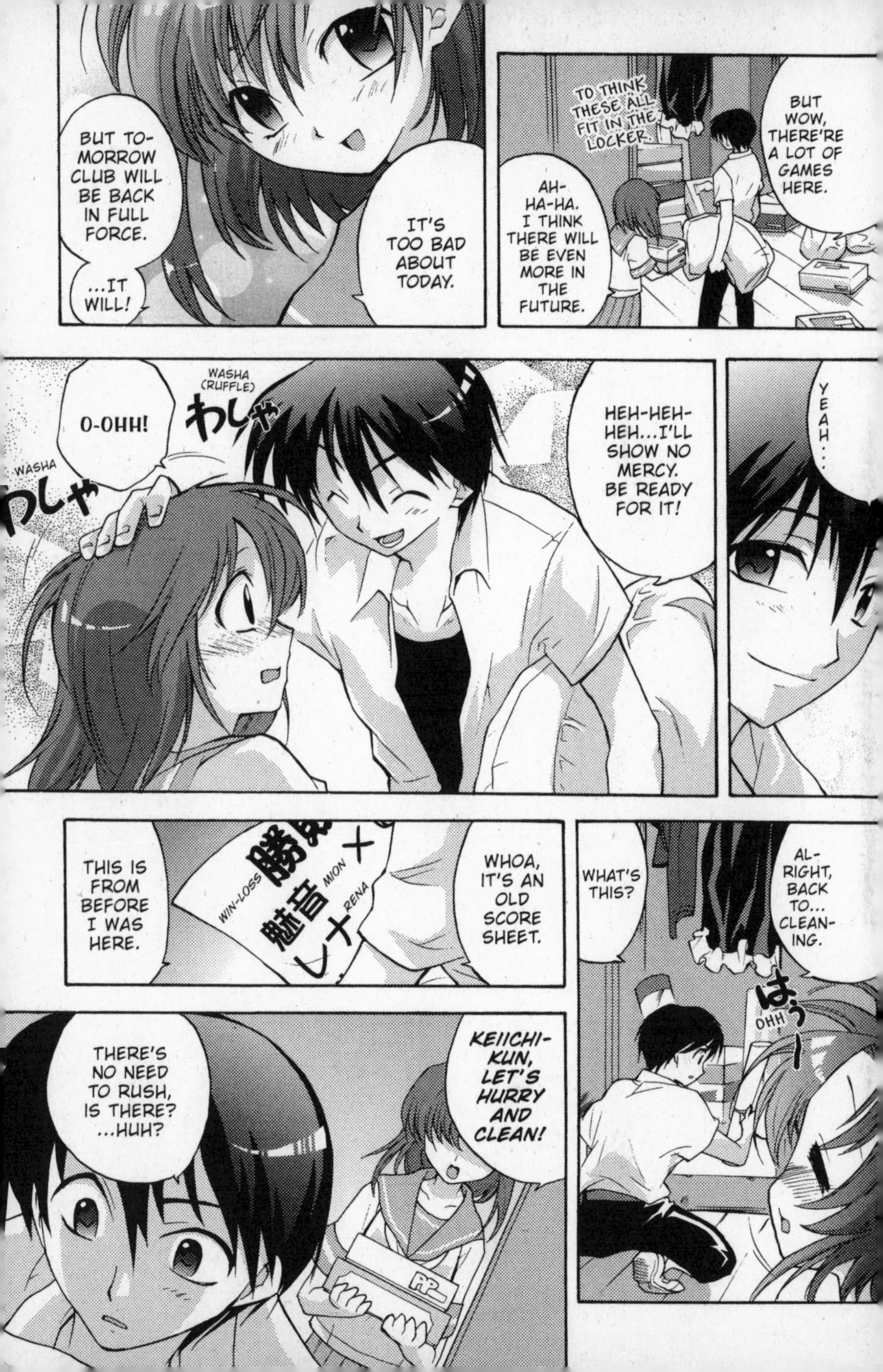
BUT WOW, THERE'RE A LOT OF GAMES HERE.
TO THINK THESE ALL FIT IN THE LOCKER.
AH-HA-HA. I THINK THERE WILL BE EVEN MORE IN THE FUTURE.
IT'S TOO BAD ABOUT TODAY.
BUT TO-MORROW CLUB WILL BE BACK IN FULL FORCE.
...IT WILL!
YEAH...
HEH-HEH-HEH...I'LL SHOW NO MERCY. BE READY FOR IT!
わしゃ
WASHA (RUFFLE)
O-OHH!
わしゃ
WASHA
ALRIGHT, BACK TO... CLEANING.
WHAT'S THIS?
はぅー
OHH
WHOA, IT'S AN OLD SCORE SHEET.
WIN-LOSS
魅音
MION
レナ
RENA
THIS IS FROM BEFORE I WAS HERE.
KEIICHI-KUN, LET'S HURRY AND CLEAN!
THERE'S NO NEED TO RUSH, IS THERE? ...HUH?

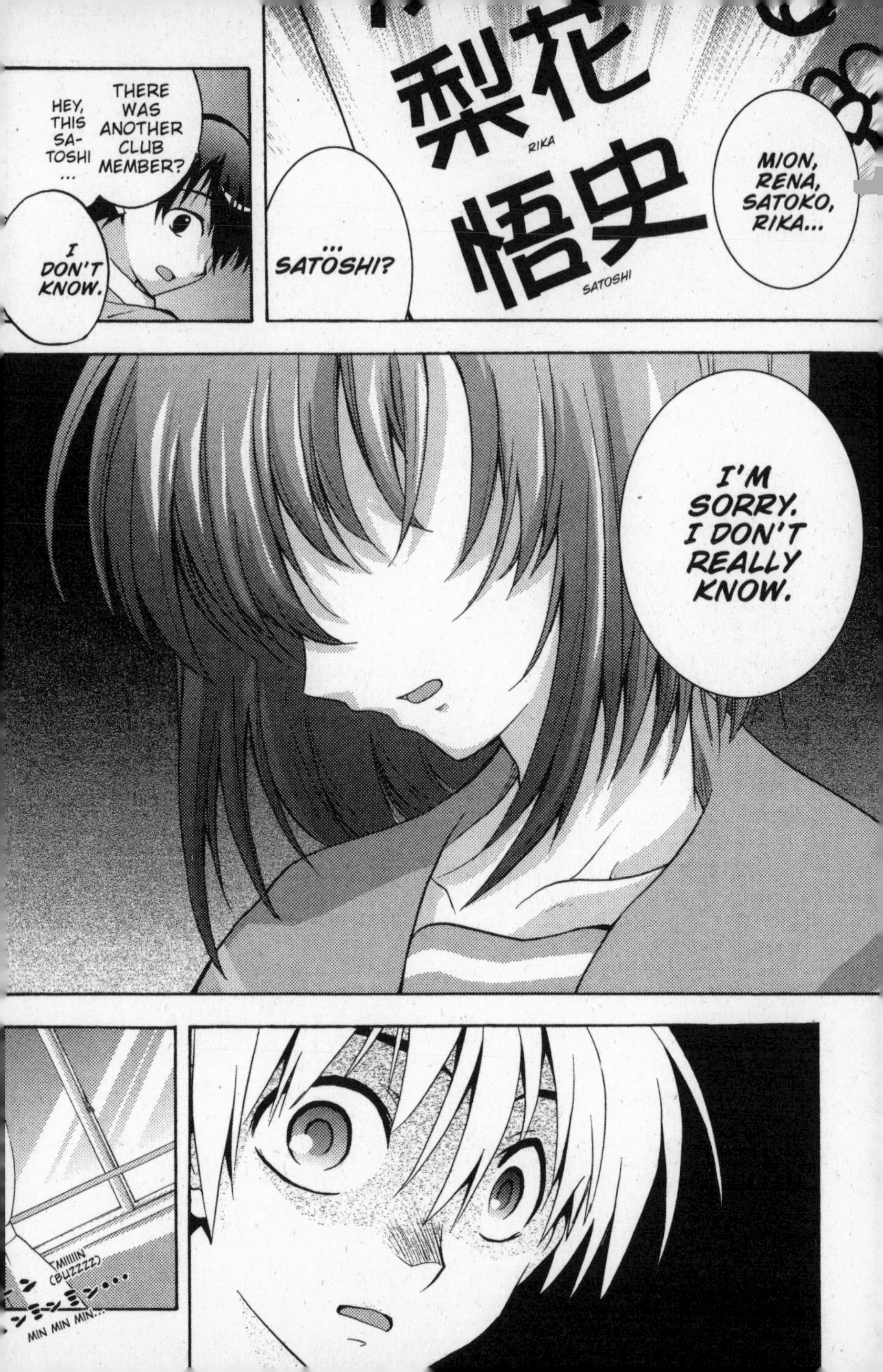
MION, RENA, SATOKO, RIKA...
梨花
RIKA
悟史
SATOSHI
... SATOSHI?
THERE WAS ANOTHER CLUB MEMBER?
HEY, THIS SA-TOSHI ...
I DON'T KNOW.
I'M SORRY. I DON'T REALLY KNOW.
MIIIIIN (BUZZZZZ) ...
MIN MIN MIN...

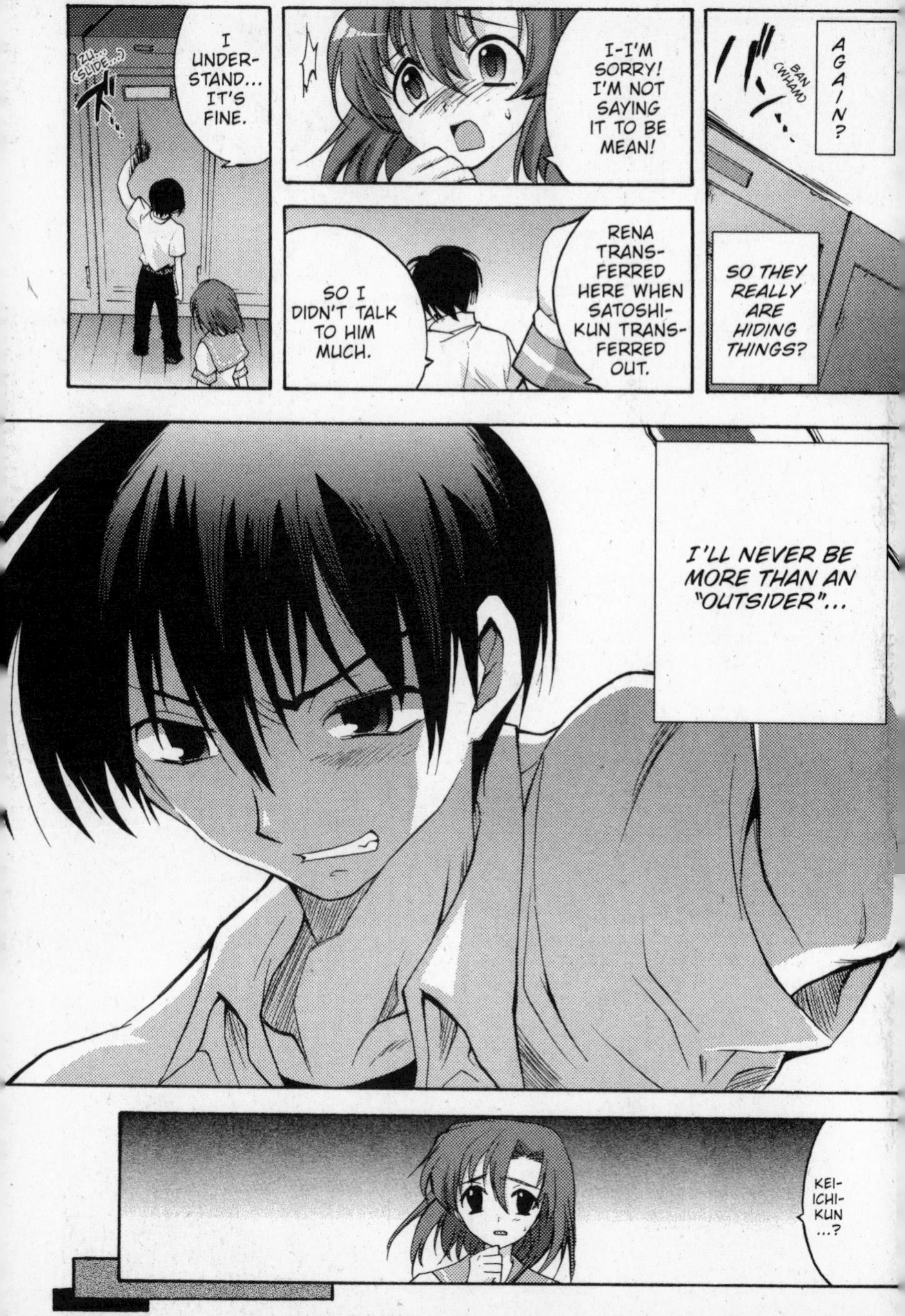
AGAIN?
BAN (WHAM)
SO THEY REALLY ARE HIDING THINGS?
I-I'M SORRY! I'M NOT SAYING IT TO BE MEAN!
RENA TRANSFERRED HERE WHEN SATOSHI-KUN TRANSFERRED OUT.
SO I DIDN'T TALK TO HIM MUCH.
I UNDERSTAND... IT'S FINE.
ZU... (SLIDE...)
I'LL NEVER BE MORE THAN AN "OUTSIDER"...
KEICHI-KUN ...?

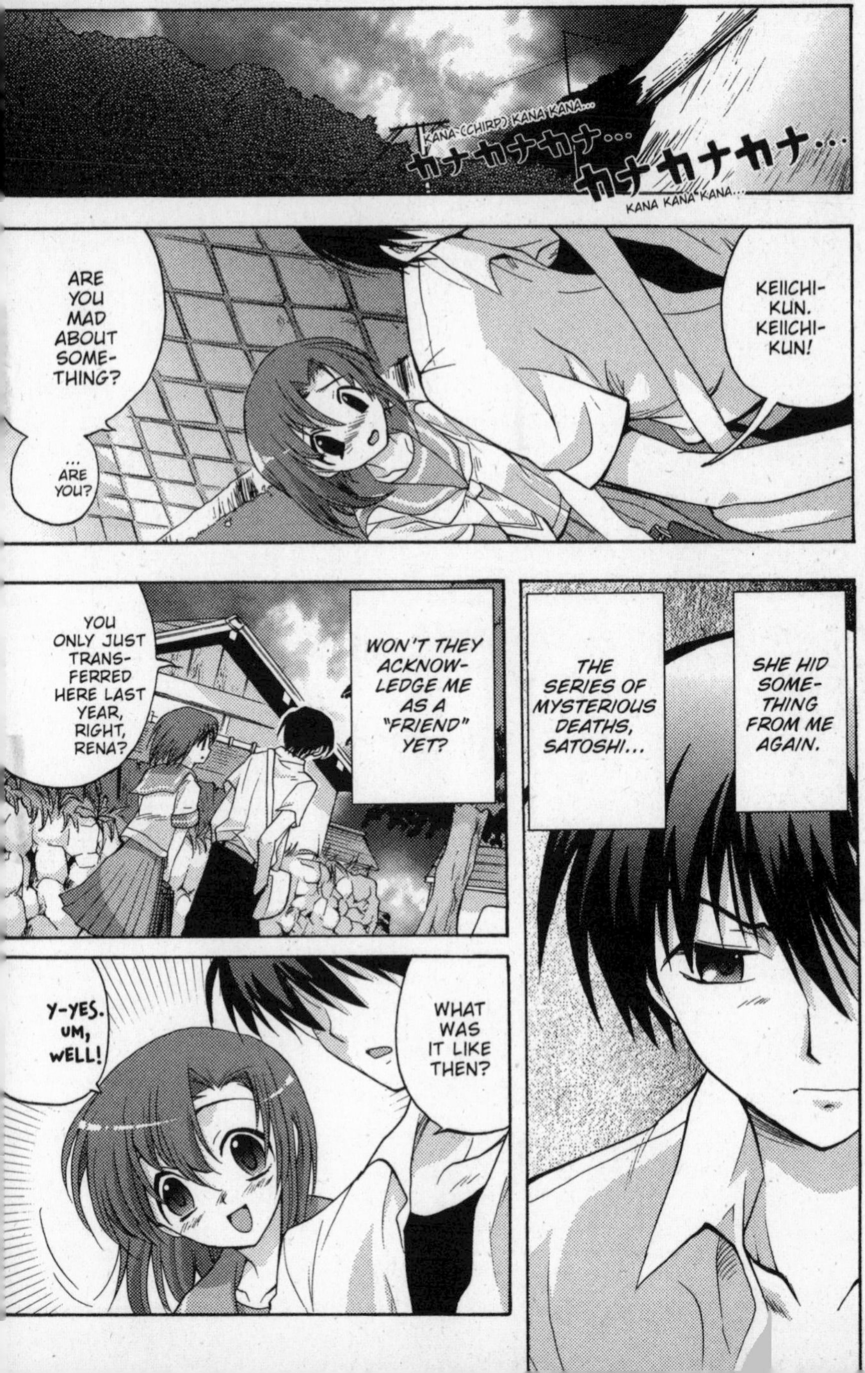
KANA-(CHIRP) KANA KANA...
カナカナカナ...
カナカナカナ...
KANA KANA KANA...
KEIICHI-KUN. KEIICHI-KUN!
ARE YOU MAD ABOUT SOMETHING?
...ARE YOU?
SHE HID SOMETHING FROM ME AGAIN.
THE SERIES OF MYSTERIOUS DEATHS, SATOSHI...
WON'T THEY ACKNOWLEDGE ME AS A "FRIEND" YET?
YOU ONLY JUST TRANSFERRED HERE LAST YEAR, RIGHT, RENA?
WHAT WAS IT LIKE THEN?
Y-YES. UM, WELL!

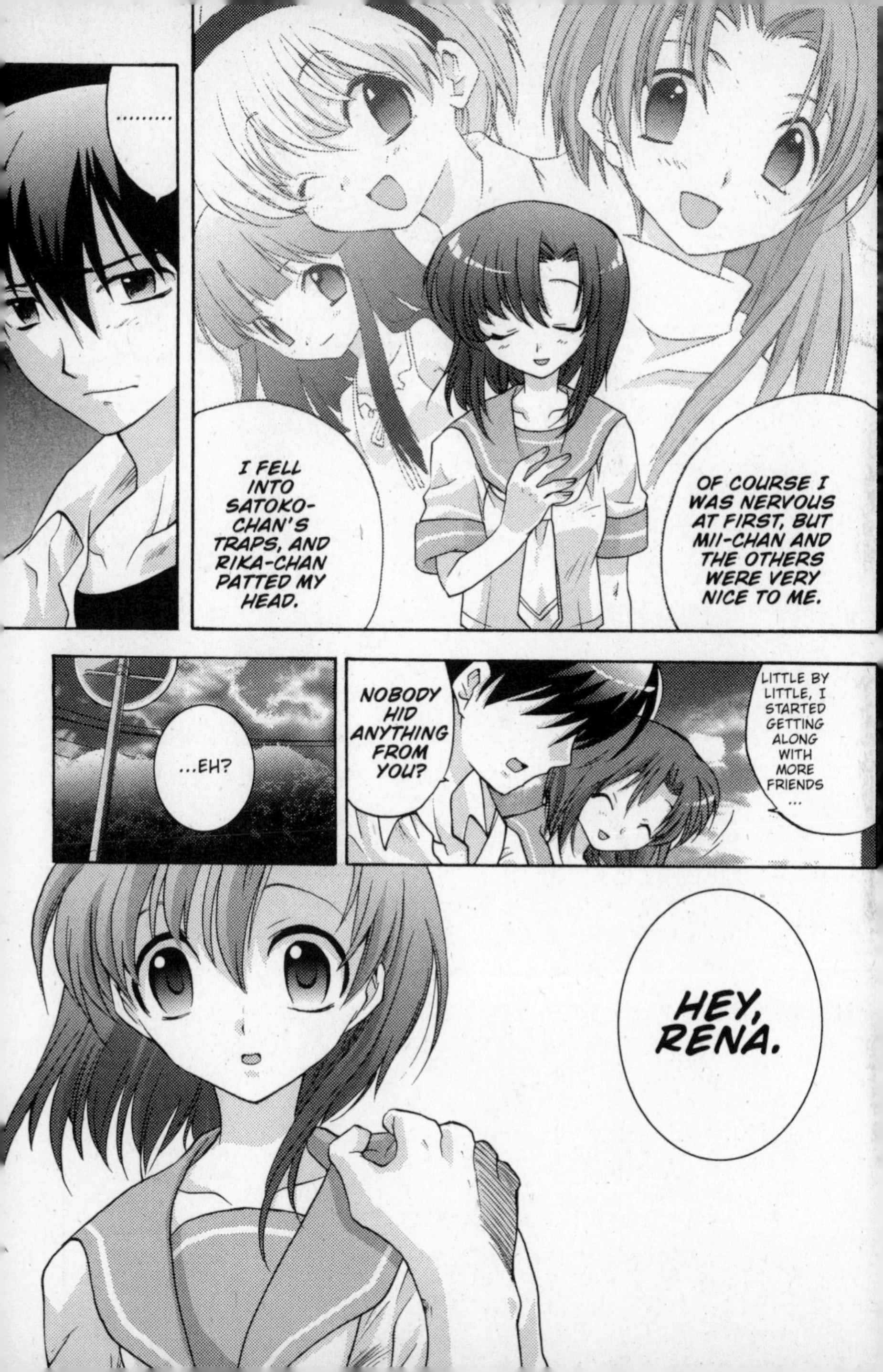
OF COURSE I WAS NERVOUS AT FIRST, BUT MII-CHAN AND THE OTHERS WERE VERY NICE TO ME.
I FELL INTO SATOKO-CHAN'S TRAPS, AND RIKA-CHAN PATTED MY HEAD.
....
LITTLE BY LITTLE, I STARTED GETTING ALONG WITH MORE FRIENDS ...
NOBODY HID ANYTHING FROM YOU?
...EH?
HEY, RENA.

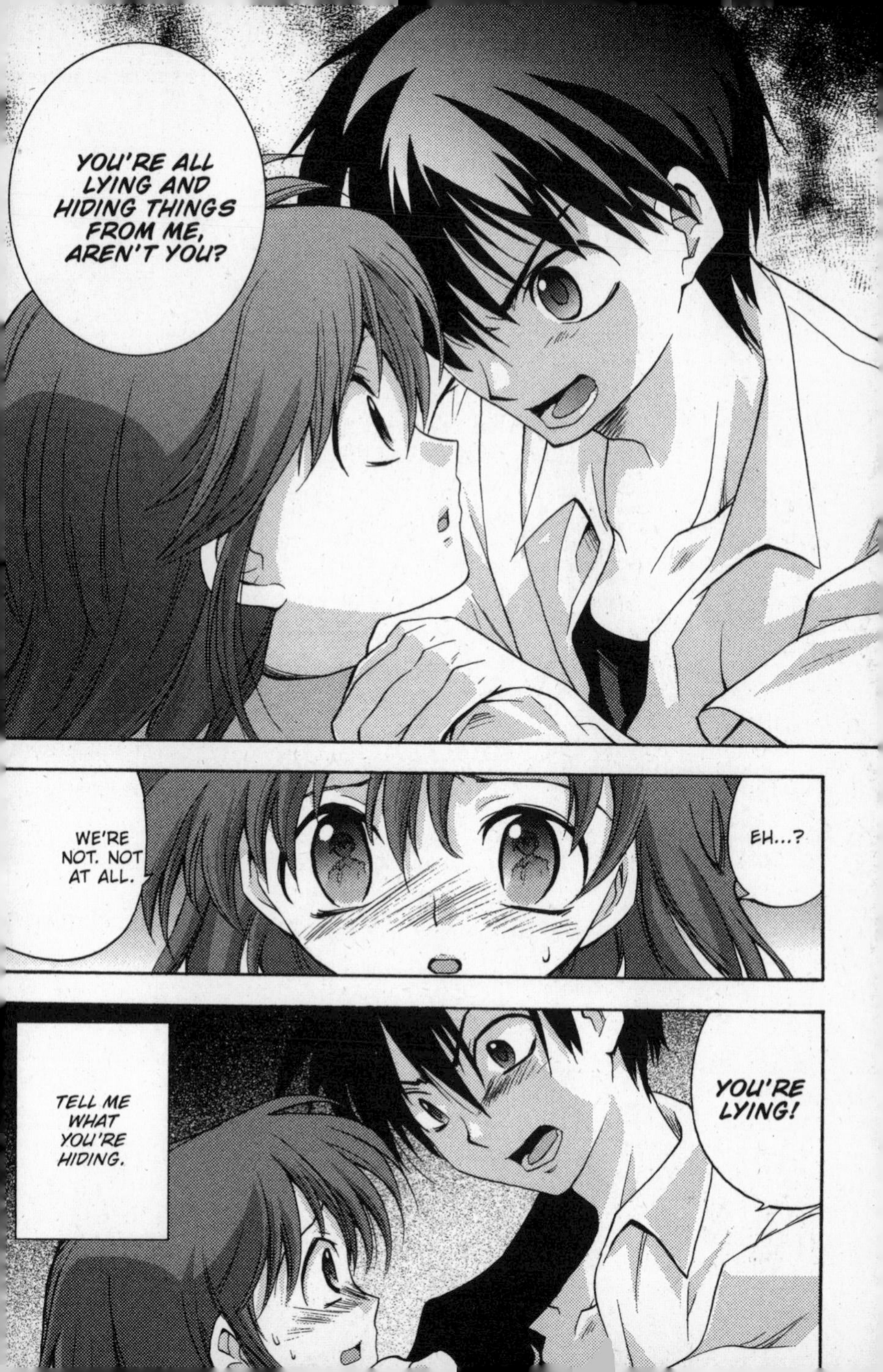
YOU'RE ALL LYING AND HIDING THINGS FROM ME, AREN'T YOU?
EH...?
WE'RE NOT. NOT AT ALL.
YOU'RE LYING!
TELL ME WHAT YOU'RE HIDING.

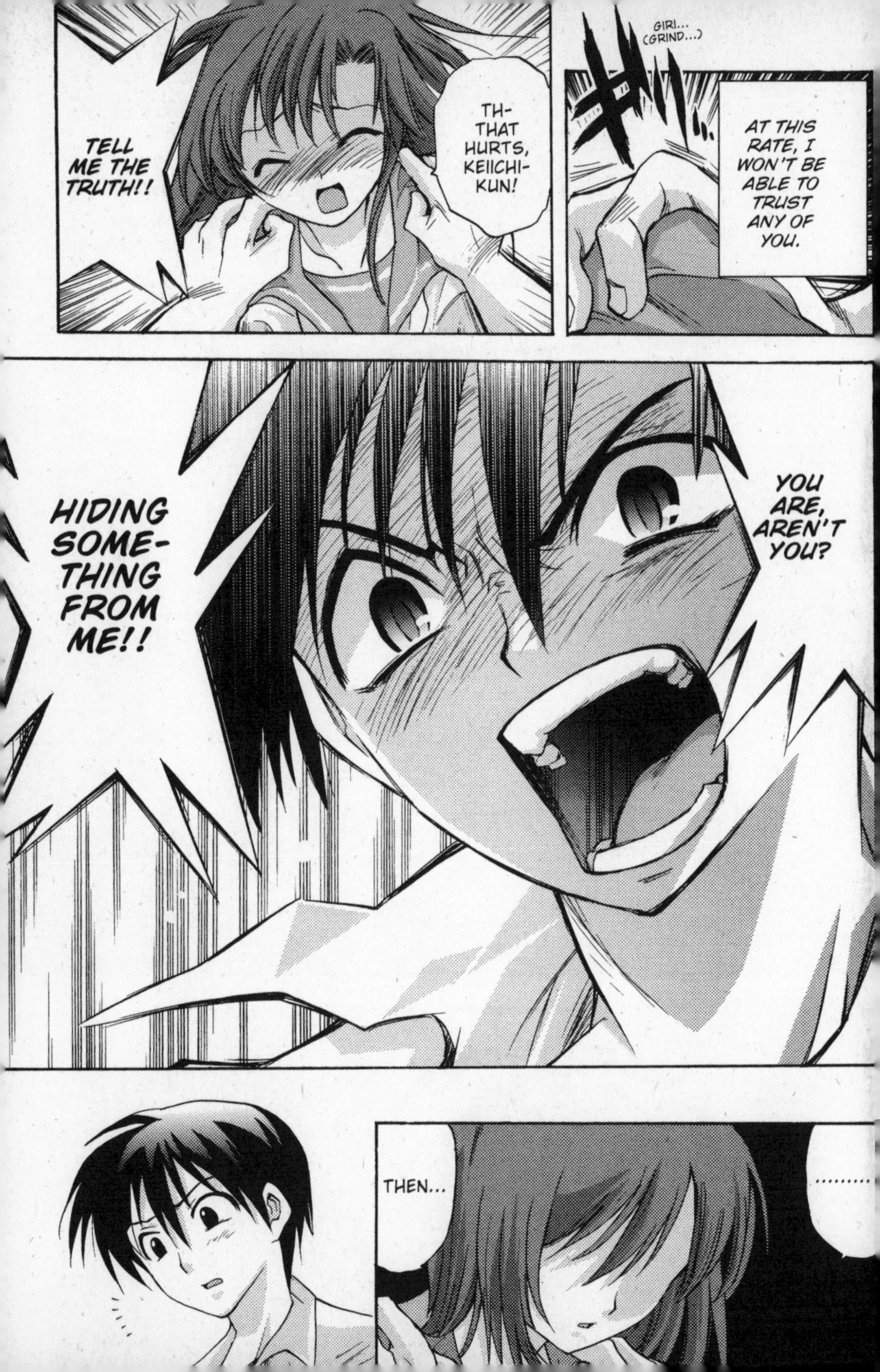
GIRI... (GRIND...)
AT THIS RATE, I WON'T BE ABLE TO TRUST ANY OF YOU.
TH-THAT HURTS, KEIICHI-KUN!
TELL ME THE TRUTH!!
YOU ARE, AREN'T YOU?
HIDING SOMETHING FROM ME!!
....
THEN...

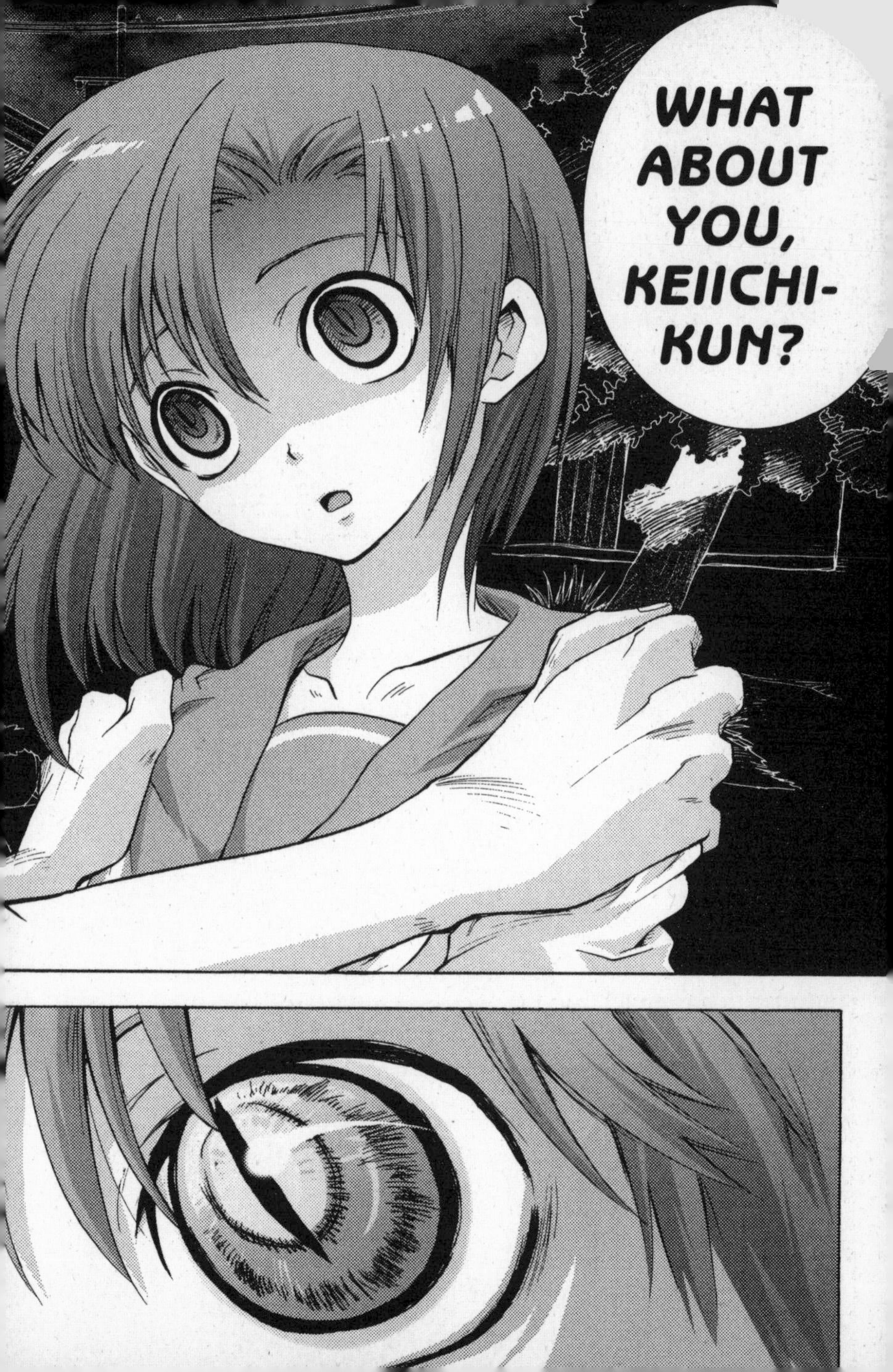
WHAT ABOUT YOU, KEIICHI-KUN?

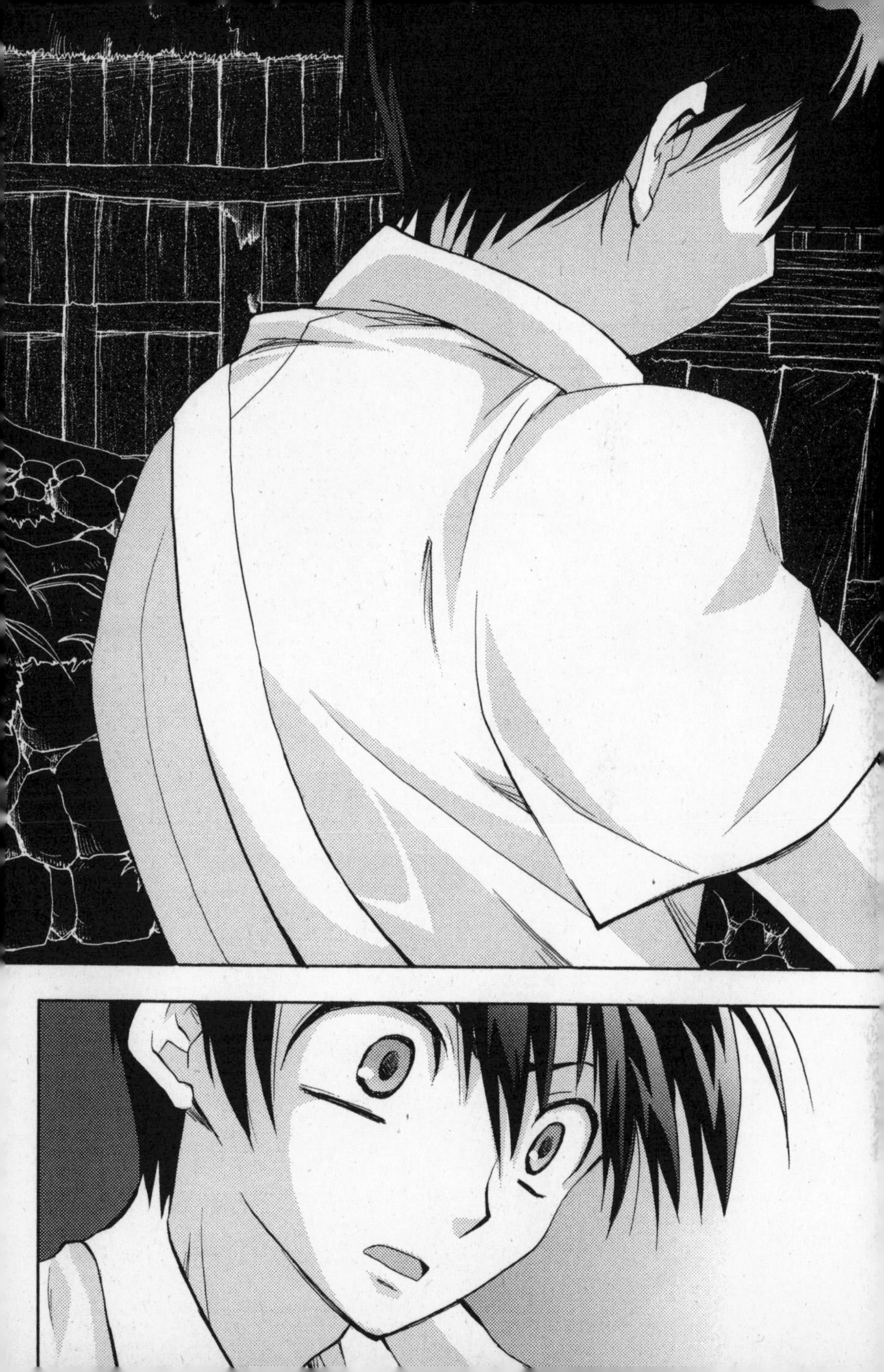

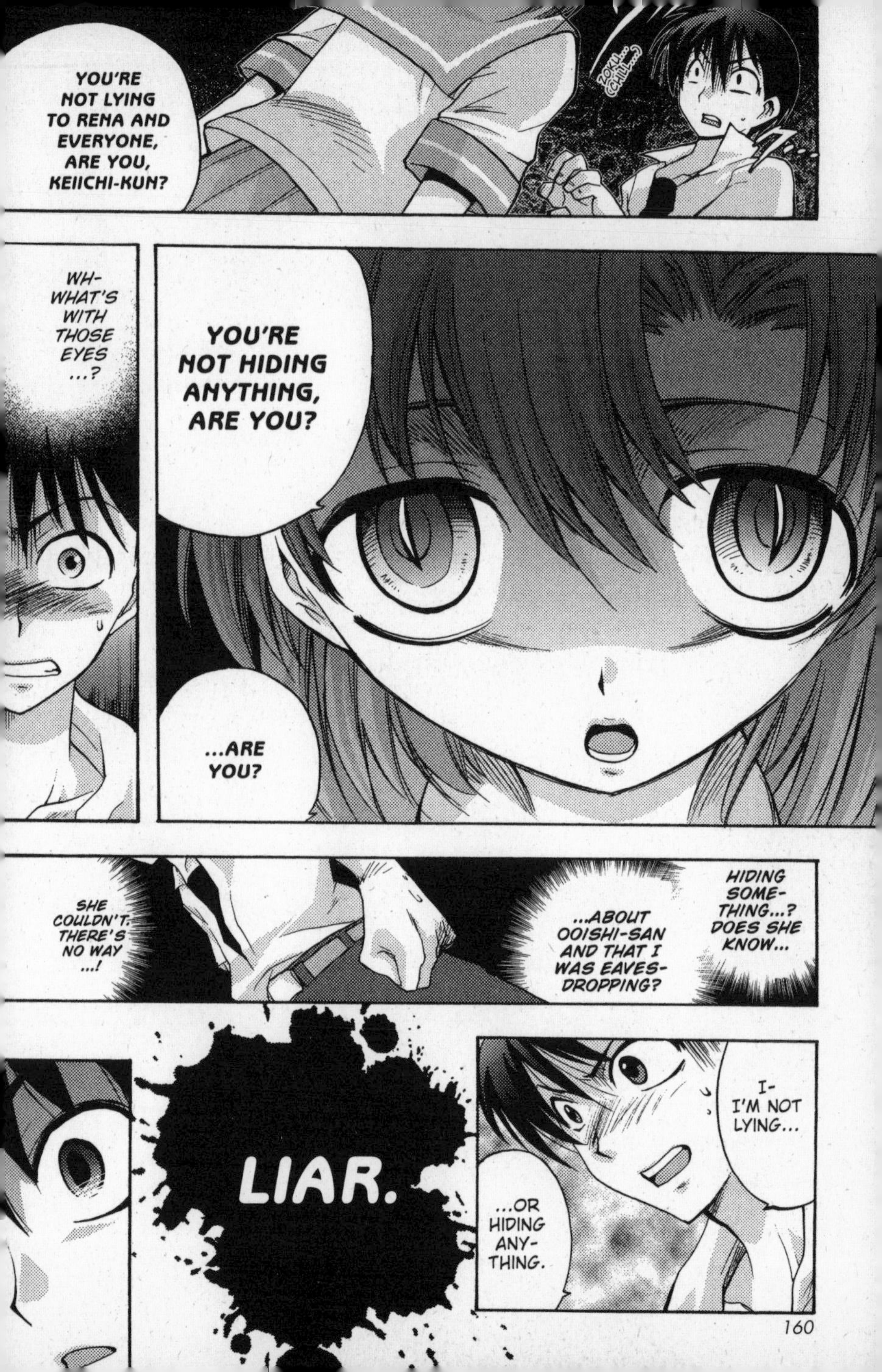
YOU'RE NOT LYING TO RENA AND EVERYONE, ARE YOU, KEIICHI-KUN?
ZOKU... (CHILL...)
YOU'RE NOT HIDING ANYTHING, ARE YOU?
...ARE YOU?
WH- WHAT'S WITH THOSE EYES ...?
HIDING SOME-THING...? DOES SHE KNOW...
...ABOUT OOISHI-SAN AND THAT I WAS EAVES-DROPPING?
SHE COULDN'T. THERE'S NO WAY ...!
I- I'M NOT LYING...
...OR HIDING ANY-THING.
LIAR.

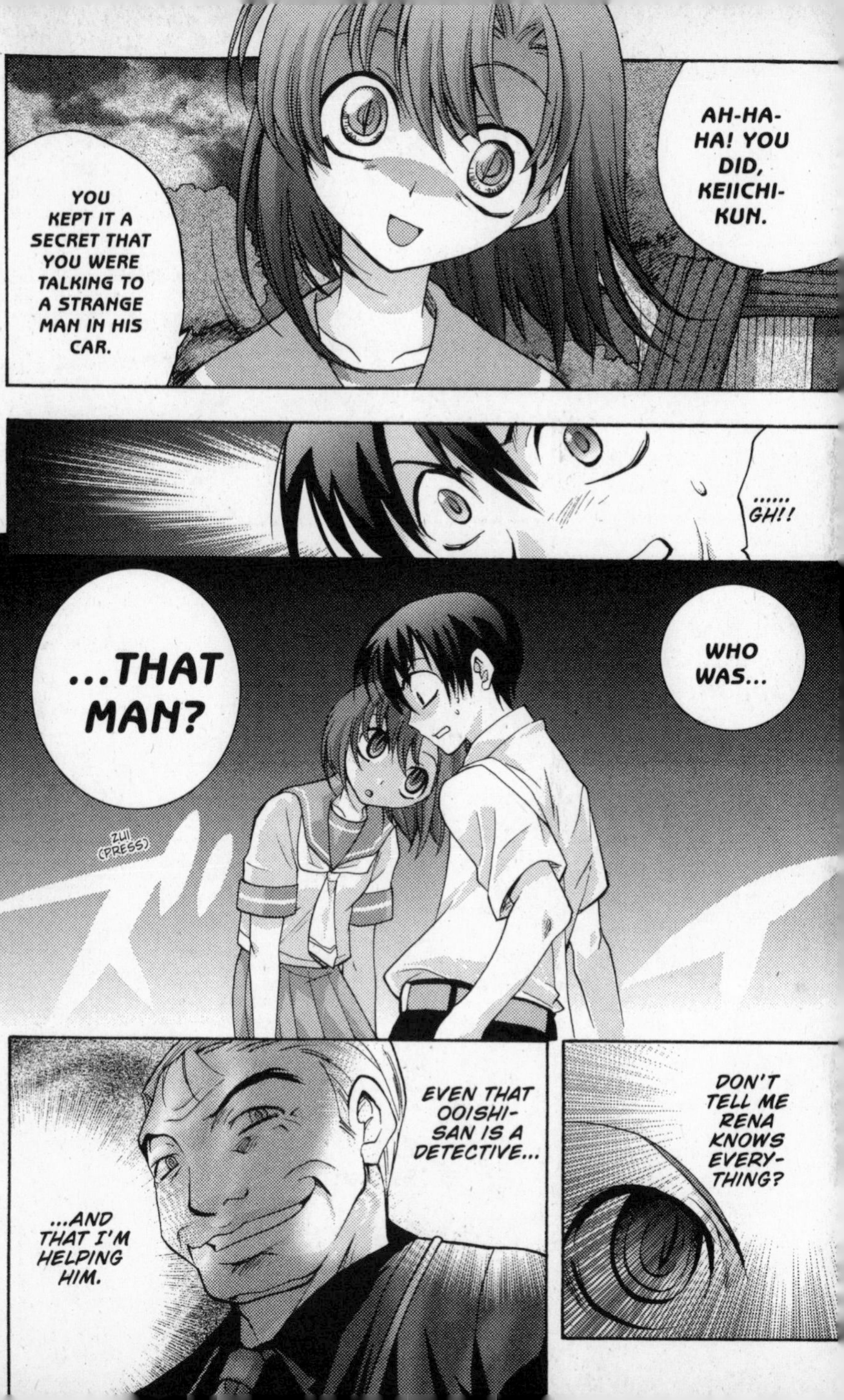
AH-HA-HA! YOU DID, KEIICHI-KUN.
YOU KEPT IT A SECRET THAT YOU WERE TALKING TO A STRANGE MAN IN HIS CAR.
......GH!!
WHO WAS...
...THAT MAN?
ZUI (PRESS)
DON'T TELL ME RENA KNOWS EVERYTHING?
EVEN THAT OOISHI-SAN IS A DETECTIVE...
...AND THAT I'M HELPING HIM.

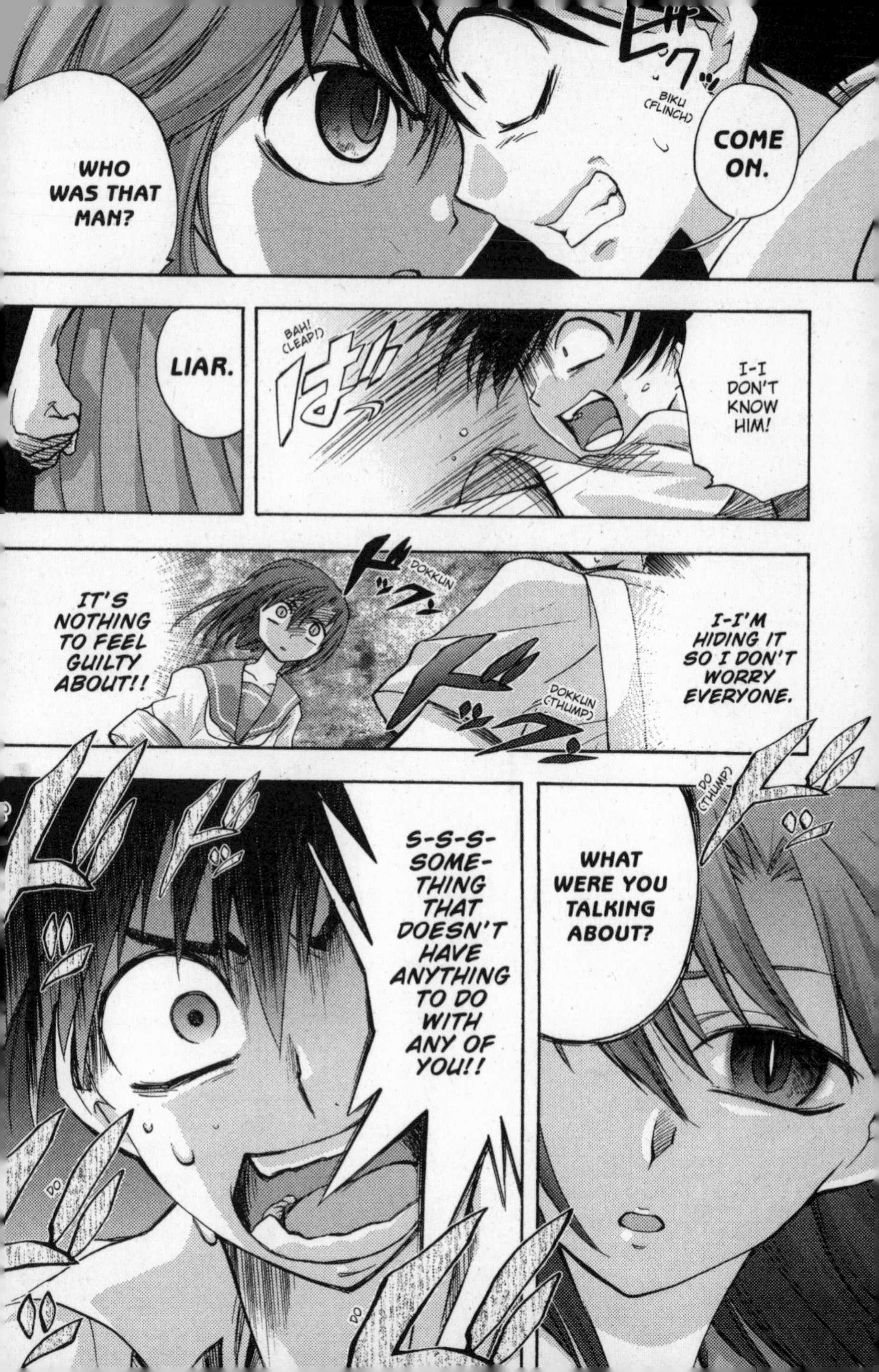
BIKU (FLINCH)
COME ON.
WHO WAS THAT MAN?
BAH! (LEAP!)
I-I DON'T KNOW HIM!
LIAR.
DOKKUN
I-I'M HIDING IT SO I DON'T WORRY EVERYONE.
DOKKUN (THUMP)
IT'S NOTHING TO FEEL GUILTY ABOUT!!
DO (THUMP)
WHAT WERE YOU TALKING ABOUT?
S-S-S-SOMETHING THAT DOESN'T HAVE ANYTHING TO DO WITH ANY OF YOU!!
DO
DO

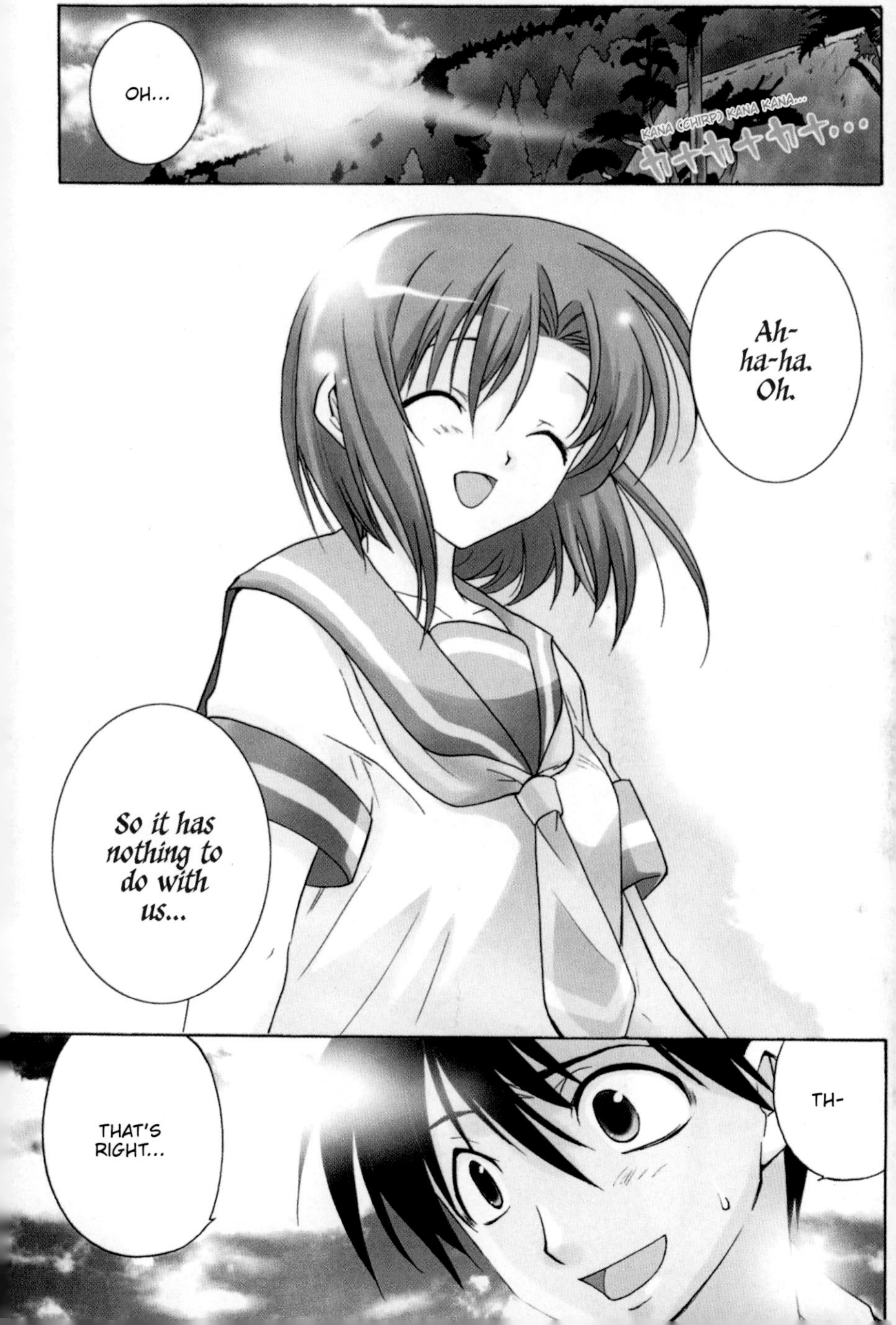
KANA (CHIRP) KANA KANA...
カナカナカナ・・・
OH...
Ah-ha-ha. Oh.
So it has nothing to do with us...
TH-
THAT'S RIGHT...

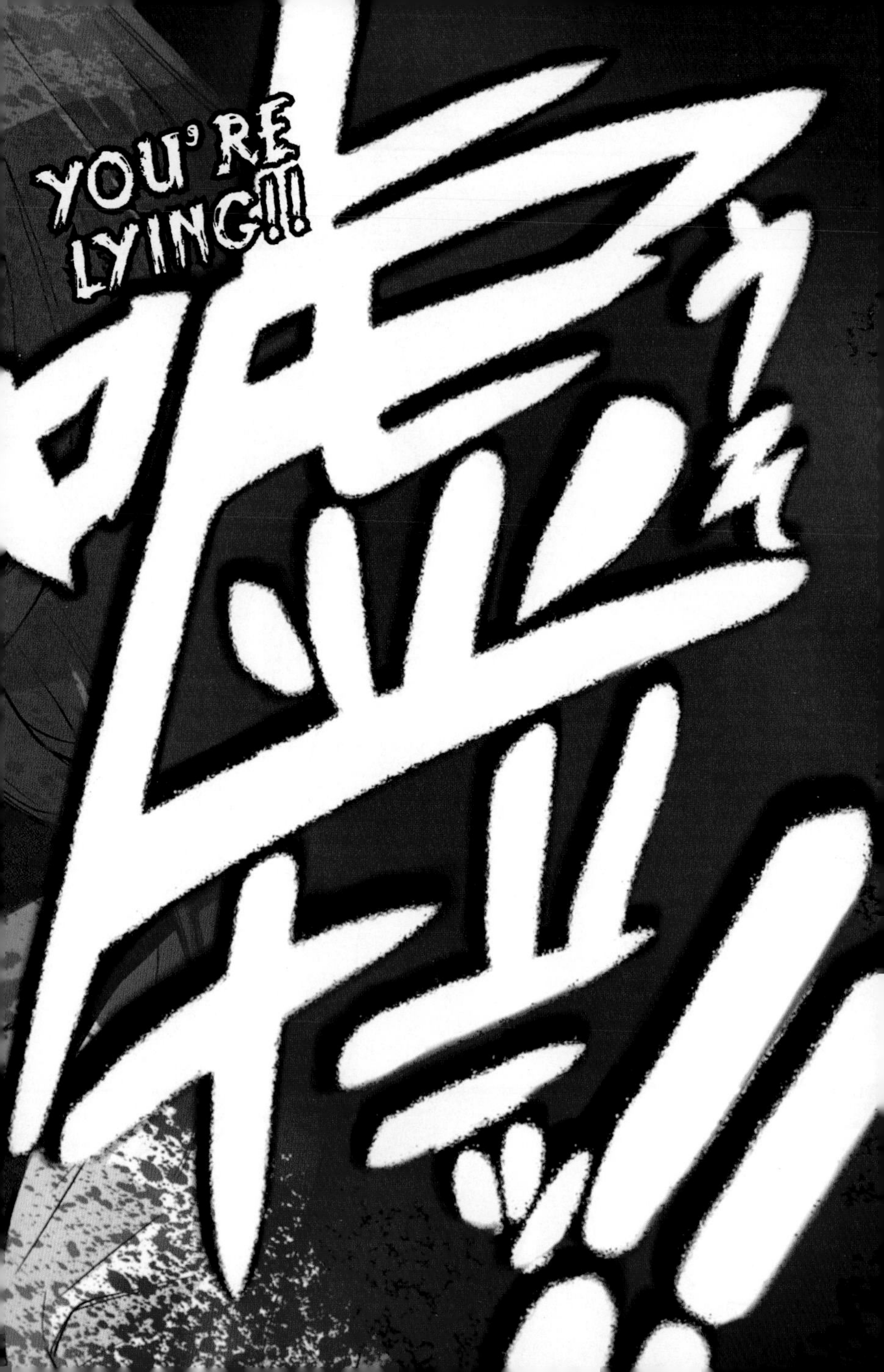
YOU'RE LYING!!

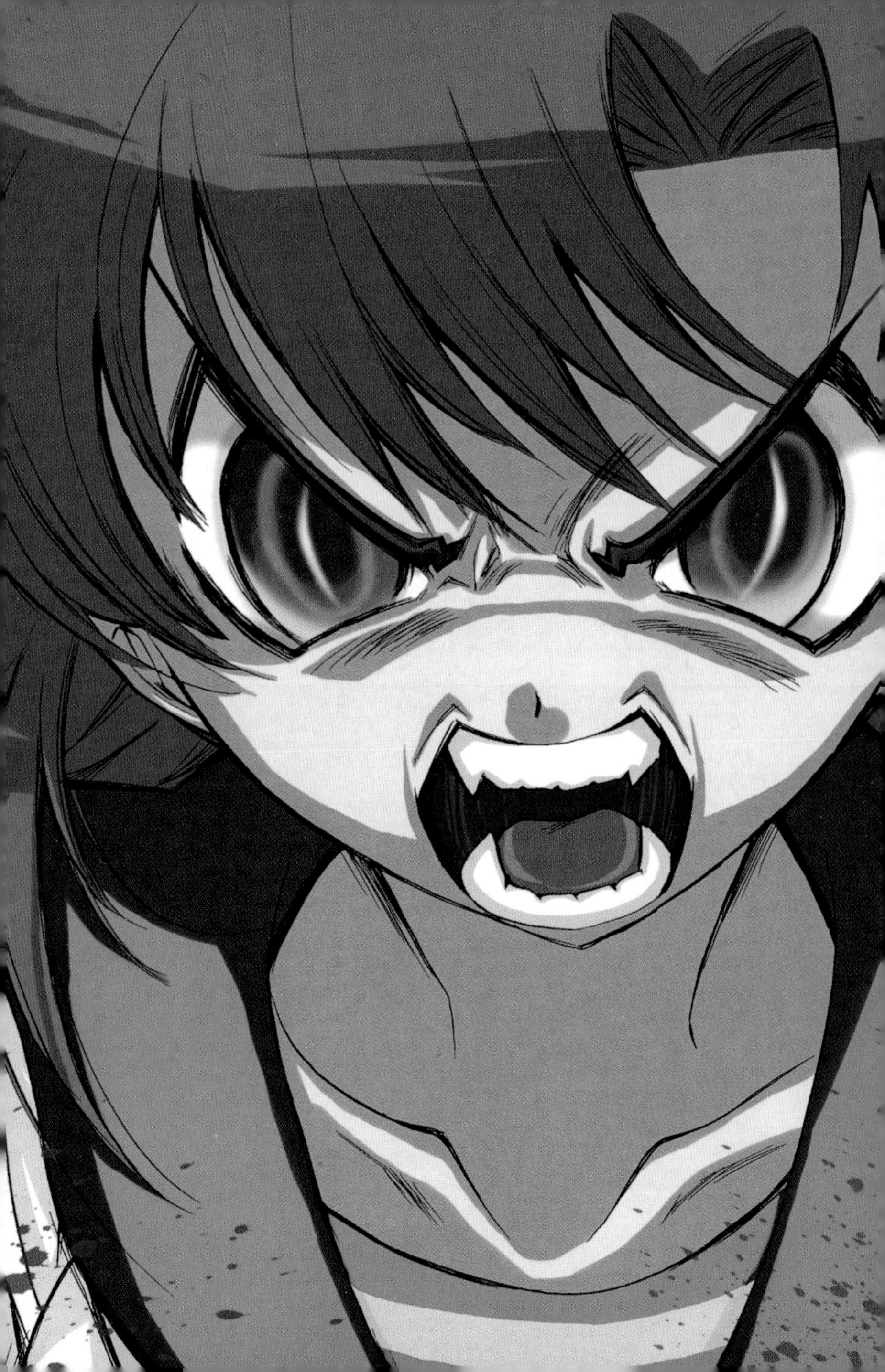

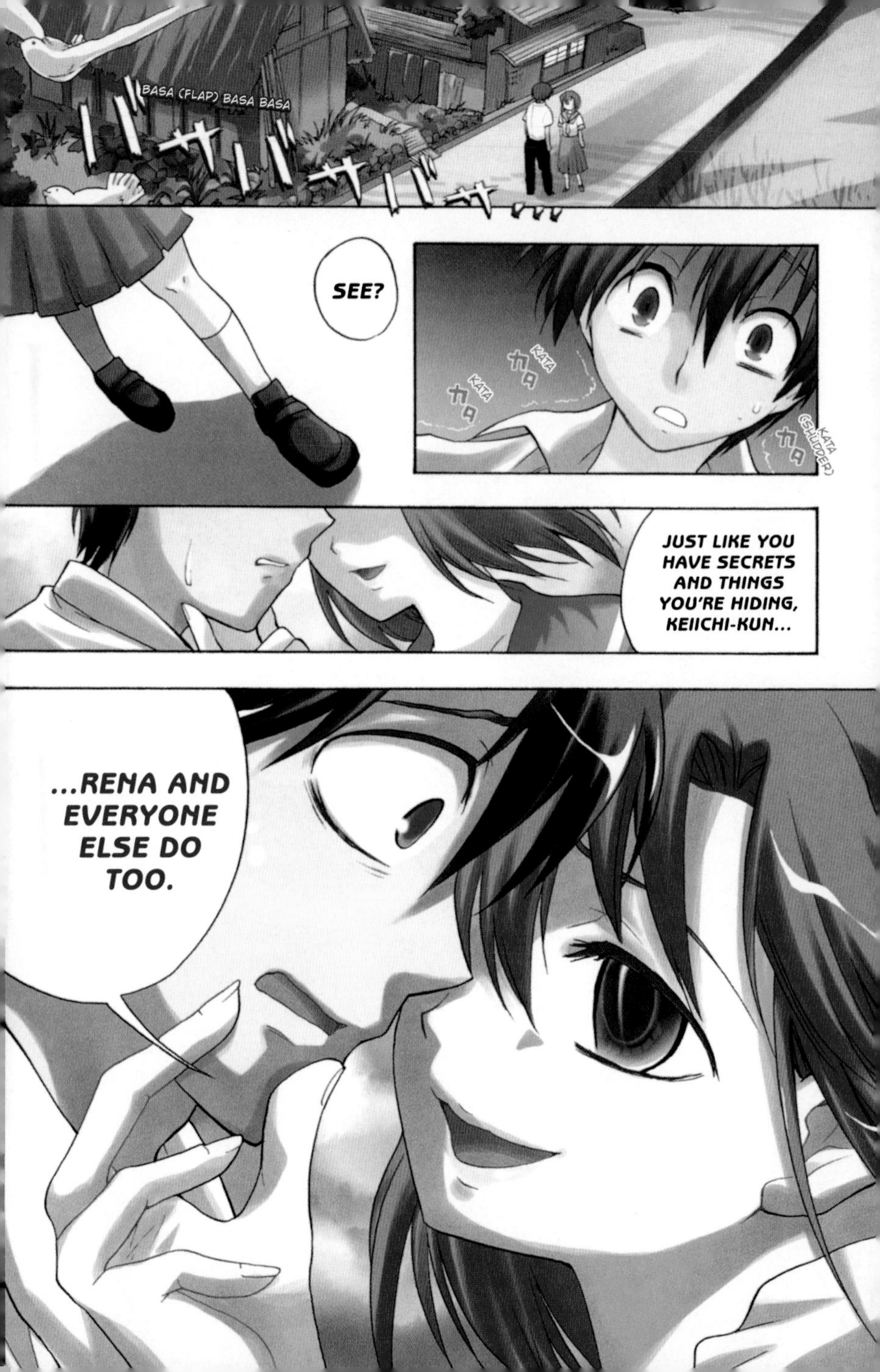
BASA (FLAP) BASA BASA
KATA (SHUDDER)
KATA
KATA
SEE?
JUST LIKE YOU HAVE SECRETS AND THINGS YOU'RE HIDING, KEIICHI-KUN...
...RENA AND EVERYONE ELSE DO TOO.

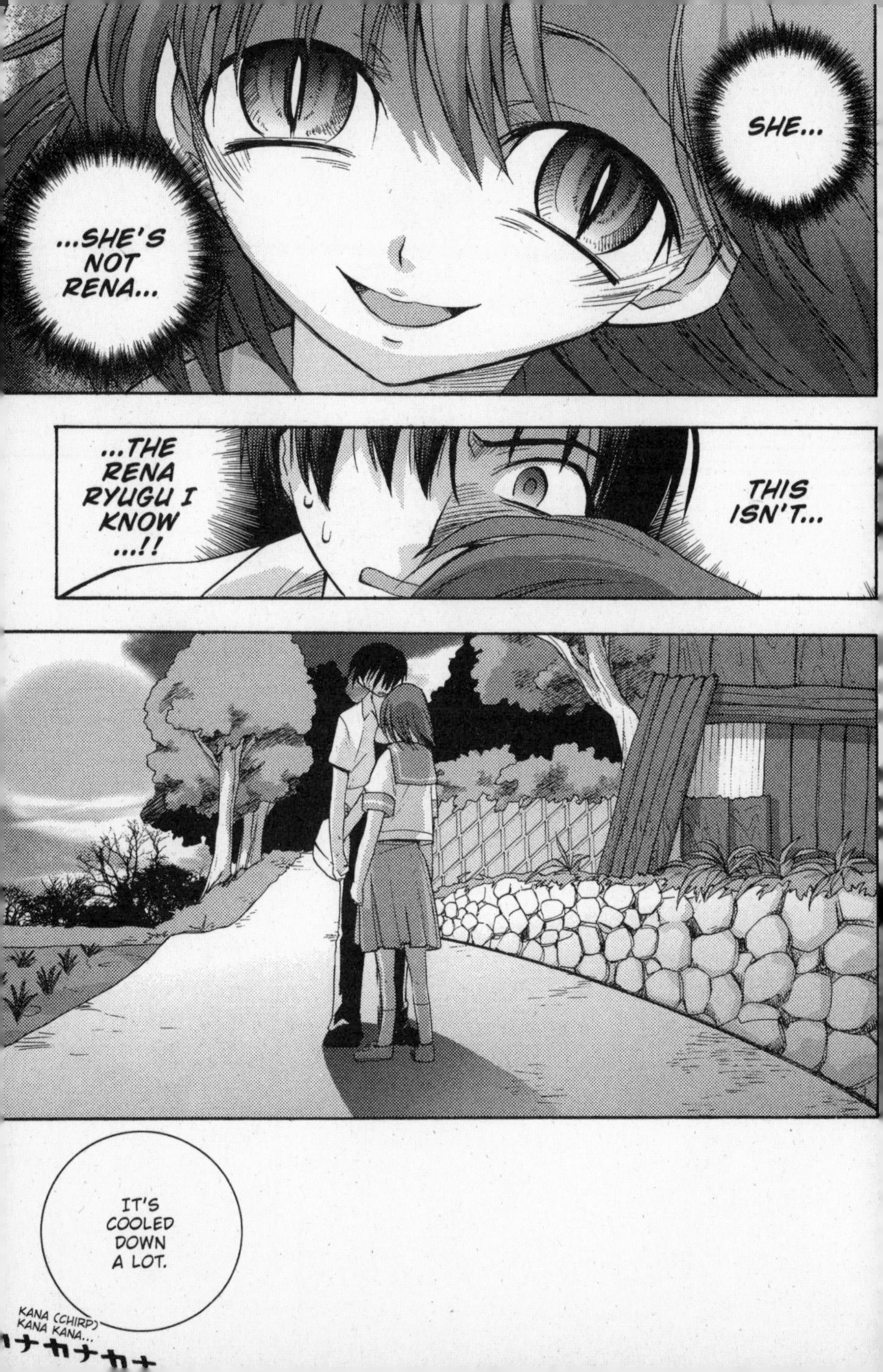
SHE...
...SHE'S NOT RENA...
THIS ISN'T...
...THE RENA RYUGU I KNOW ...!!
IT'S COOLED DOWN A LOT.
KANA (CHIRP) KANA KANA...

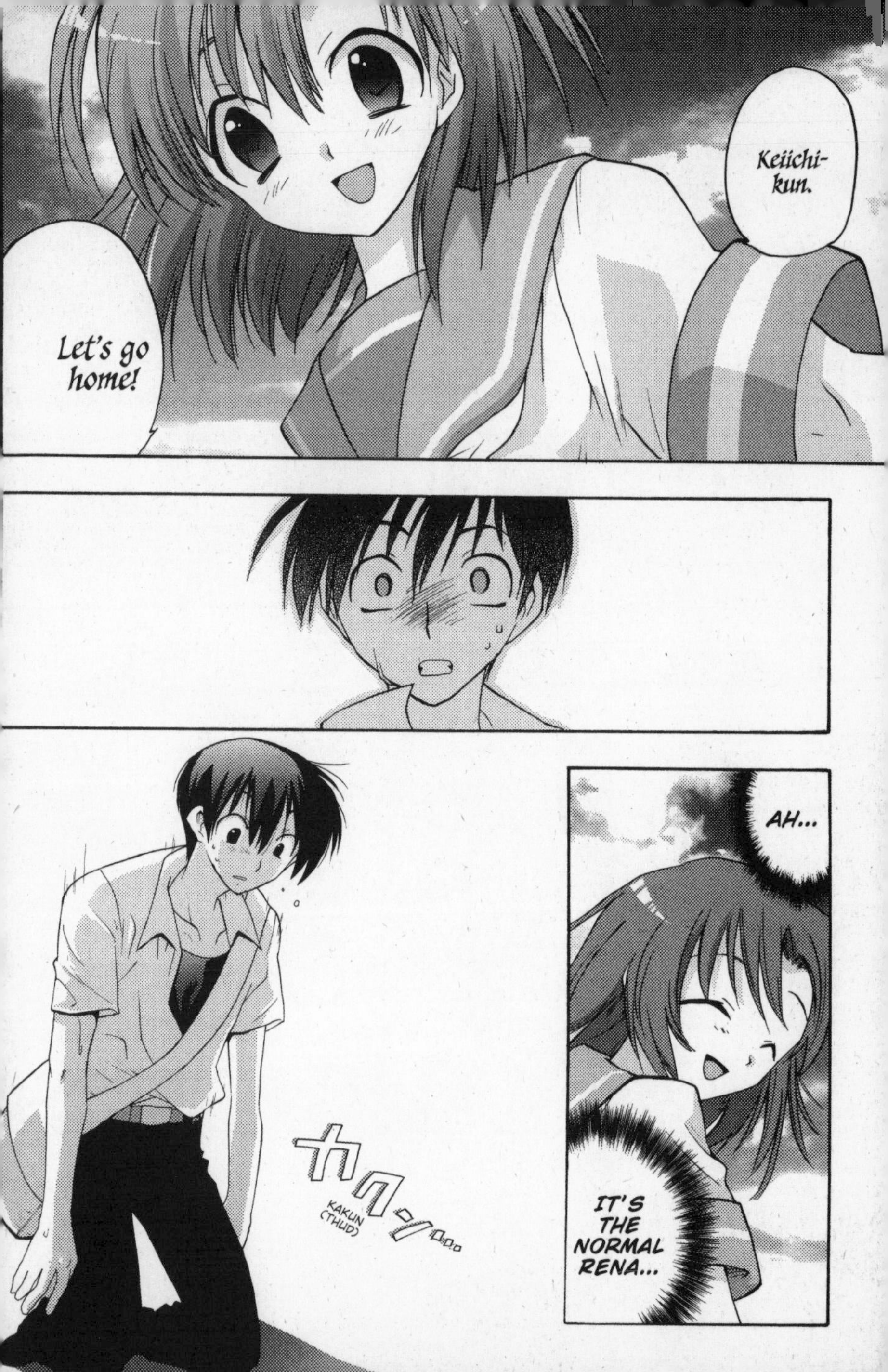
Keiichi-kun.
Let's go home!
AH...
IT'S THE NORMAL RENA...
カクン
KAKUN (THUD)

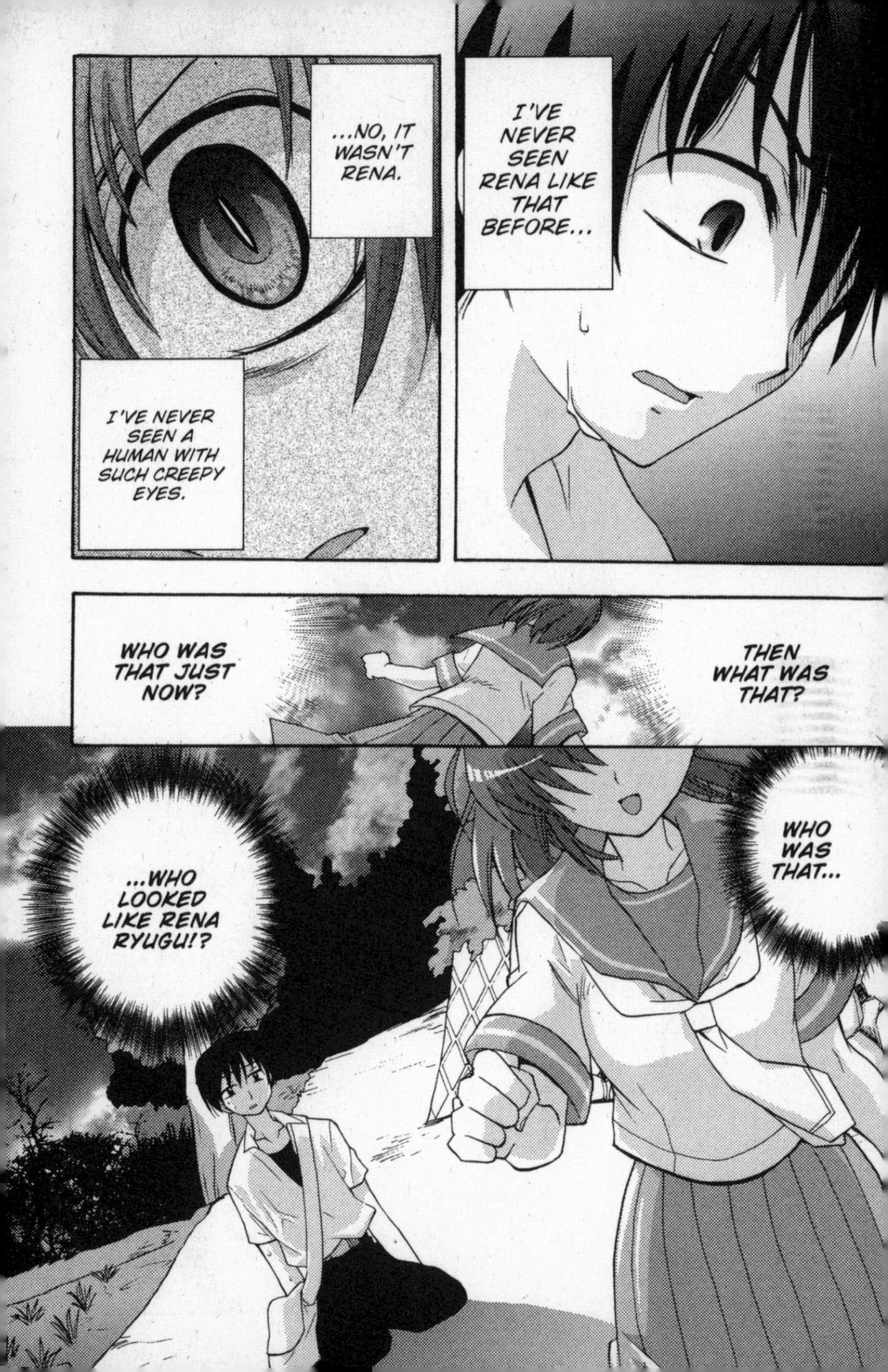
I'VE NEVER SEEN RENA LIKE THAT BEFORE...
...NO, IT WASN'T RENA.
I'VE NEVER SEEN A HUMAN WITH SUCH CREEPY EYES.
THEN WHAT WAS THAT?
WHO WAS THAT JUST NOW?
WHO WAS THAT...
...WHO LOOKED LIKE RENA RYUGU!?

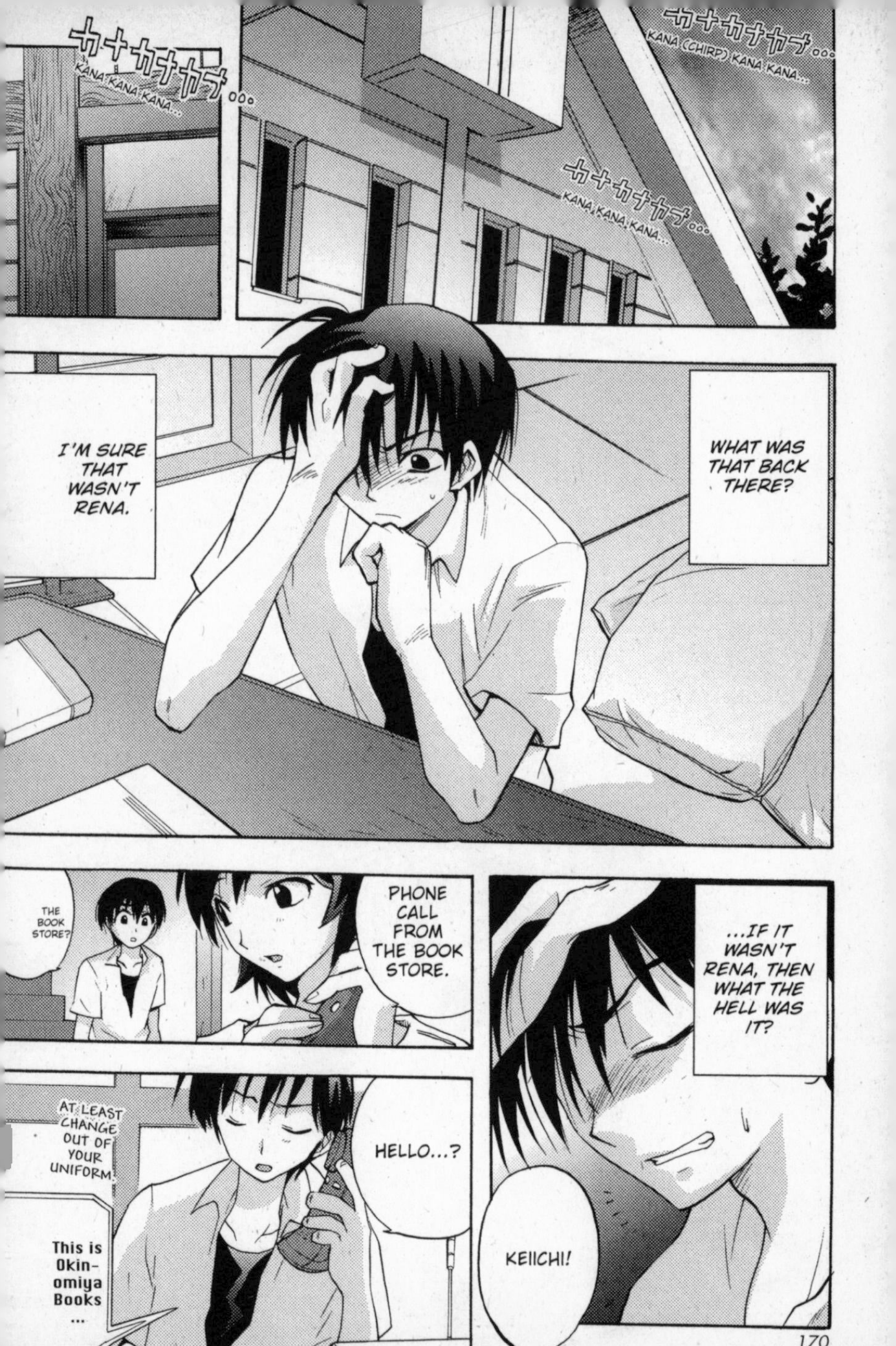
カナカナカナ…
KANA (CHIRP) KANA KANA...
カナカナカナ…
KANA KANA KANA...
カナカナカナ…
KANA KANA KANA...
WHAT WAS THAT BACK THERE?
I'M SURE THAT WASN'T RENA.
...IF IT WASN'T RENA, THEN WHAT THE HELL WAS IT?
KEIICHI!
PHONE CALL FROM THE BOOK STORE.
THE BOOK STORE?
HELLO...?
AT LEAST CHANGE OUT OF YOUR UNIFORM.
This is Okinomiya Books ...

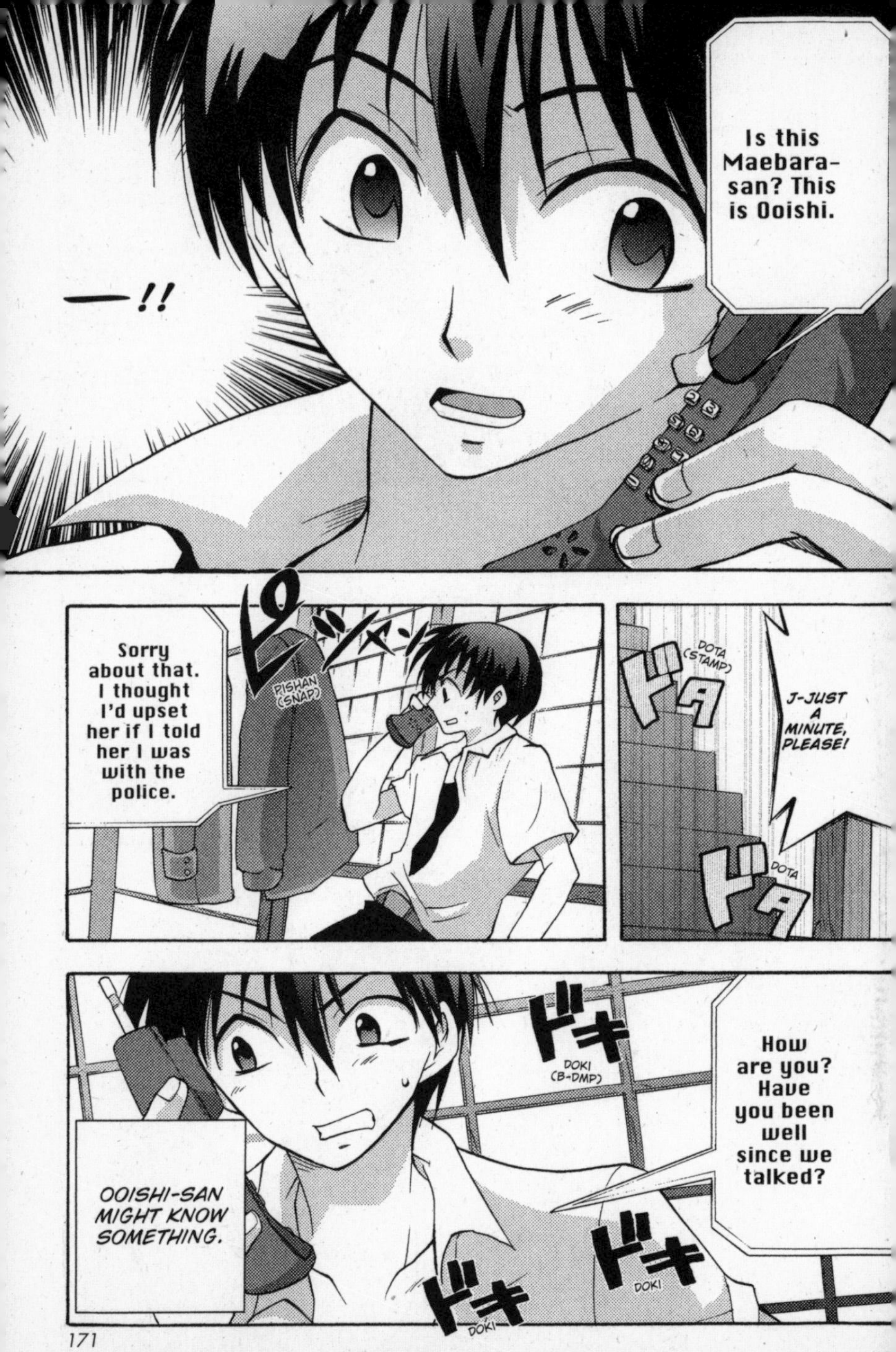
Is this Maebara-san? This is Ooishi.
—!!
DOTA (STAMP)
J-JUST A MINUTE, PLEASE!
DOTA
PISHAN (SNAP)
Sorry about that. I thought I'd upset her if I told her I was with the police.
How are you? Have you been well since we talked?
DOKI (B-DMP)
OOISHI-SAN MIGHT KNOW SOMETHING.
DOKI
DOKI

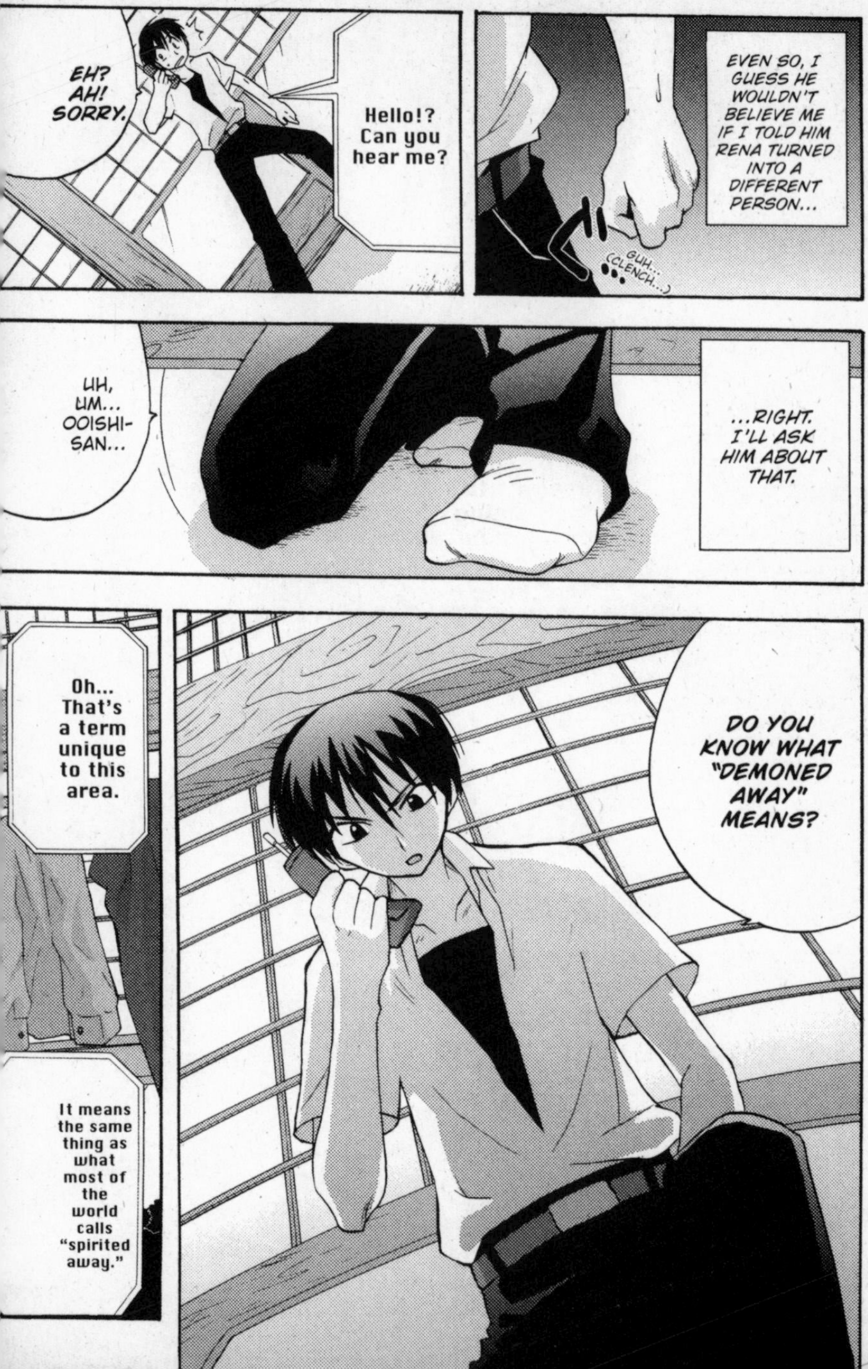
EVEN SO, I GUESS HE WOULDN'T BELIEVE ME IF I TOLD HIM RENA TURNED INTO A DIFFERENT PERSON...
GUH... (CLENCH...)
Hello!? Can you hear me?
EH? AH! SORRY.
...RIGHT. I'LL ASK HIM ABOUT THAT.
UH, UM... OOISHI-SAN...
DO YOU KNOW WHAT "DEMONED AWAY" MEANS?
Oh... That's a term unique to this area.
It means the same thing as what most of the world calls "spirited away."

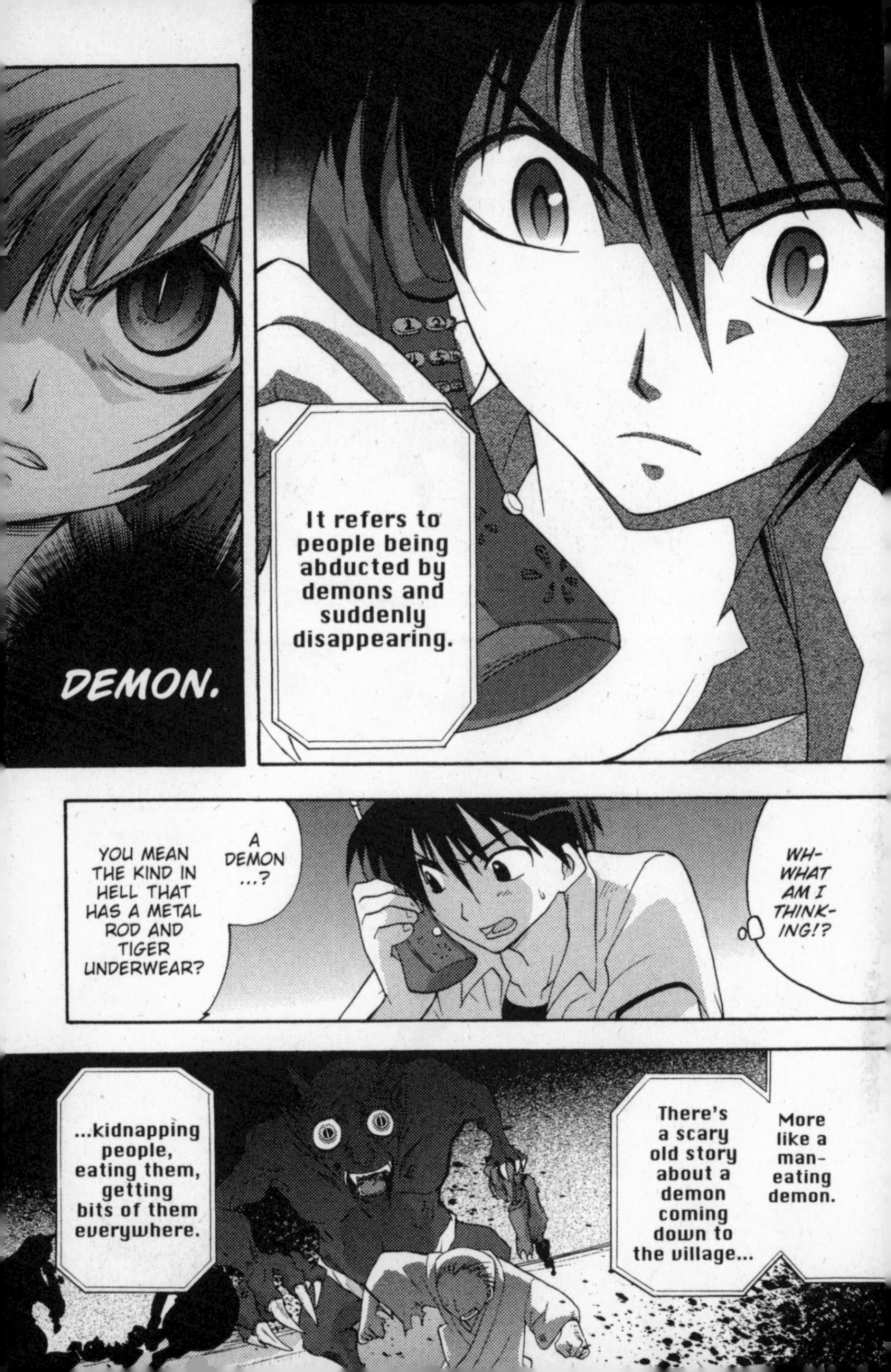
It refers to people being abducted by demons and suddenly disappearing.
DEMON.
WH-WHAT AM I THINKING!?
A DEMON ...?
YOU MEAN THE KIND IN HELL THAT HAS A METAL ROD AND TIGER UNDERWEAR?
More like a man-eating demon.
There's a scary old story about a demon coming down to the village...
...kidnapping people, eating them, getting bits of them everywhere.

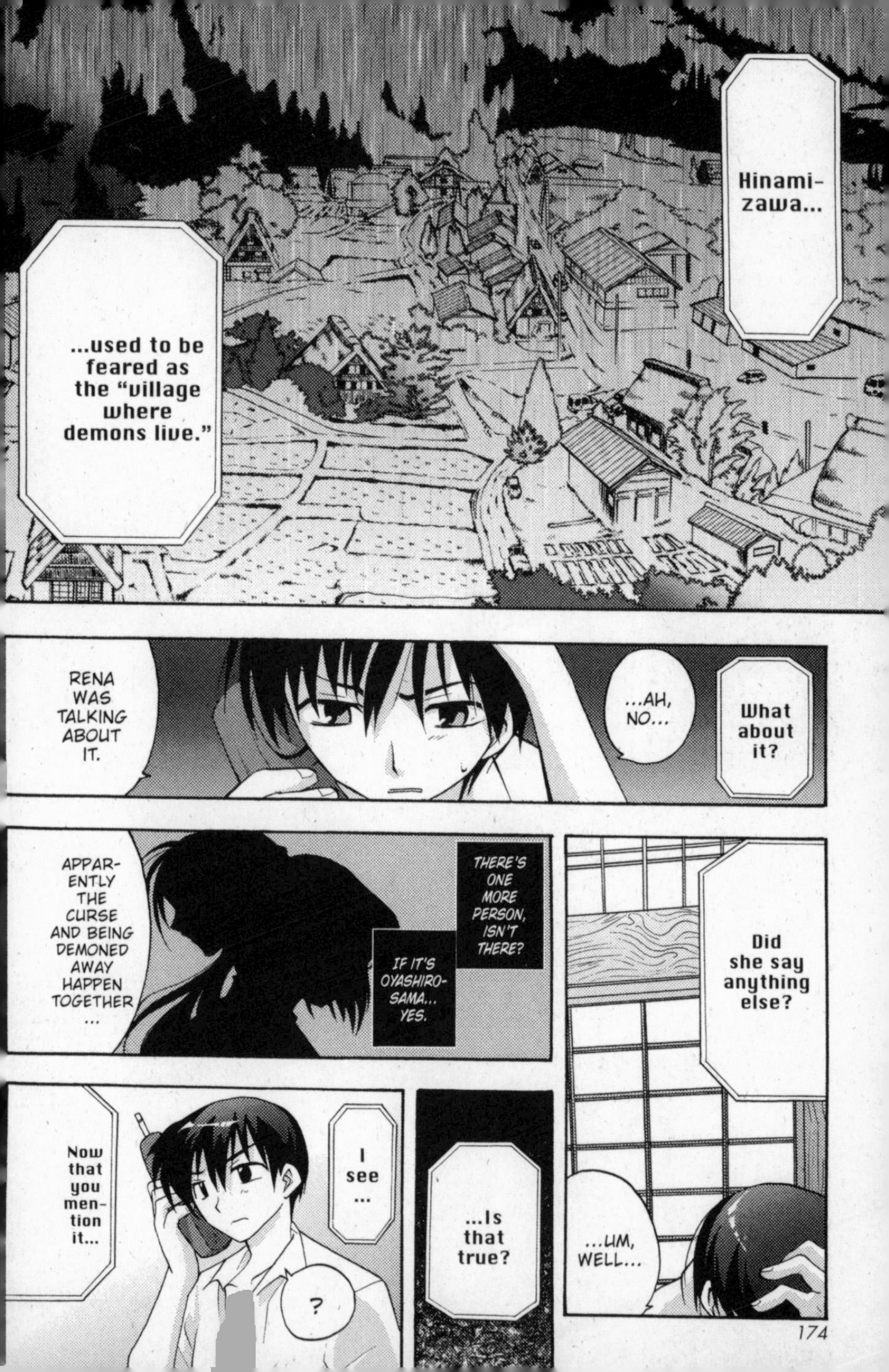
Hinami-zawa...
...used to be feared as the "village where demons live."
What about it?
...AH, NO...
RENA WAS TALKING ABOUT IT.
Did she say anything else?
...UM, WELL...
THERE'S ONE MORE PERSON, ISN'T THERE?
IF IT'S OYASHIRO-SAMA... YES.
APPARENTLY THE CURSE AND BEING DEMONED AWAY HAPPEN TOGETHER...
...Is that true?
I see...
Now that you mention it...
?

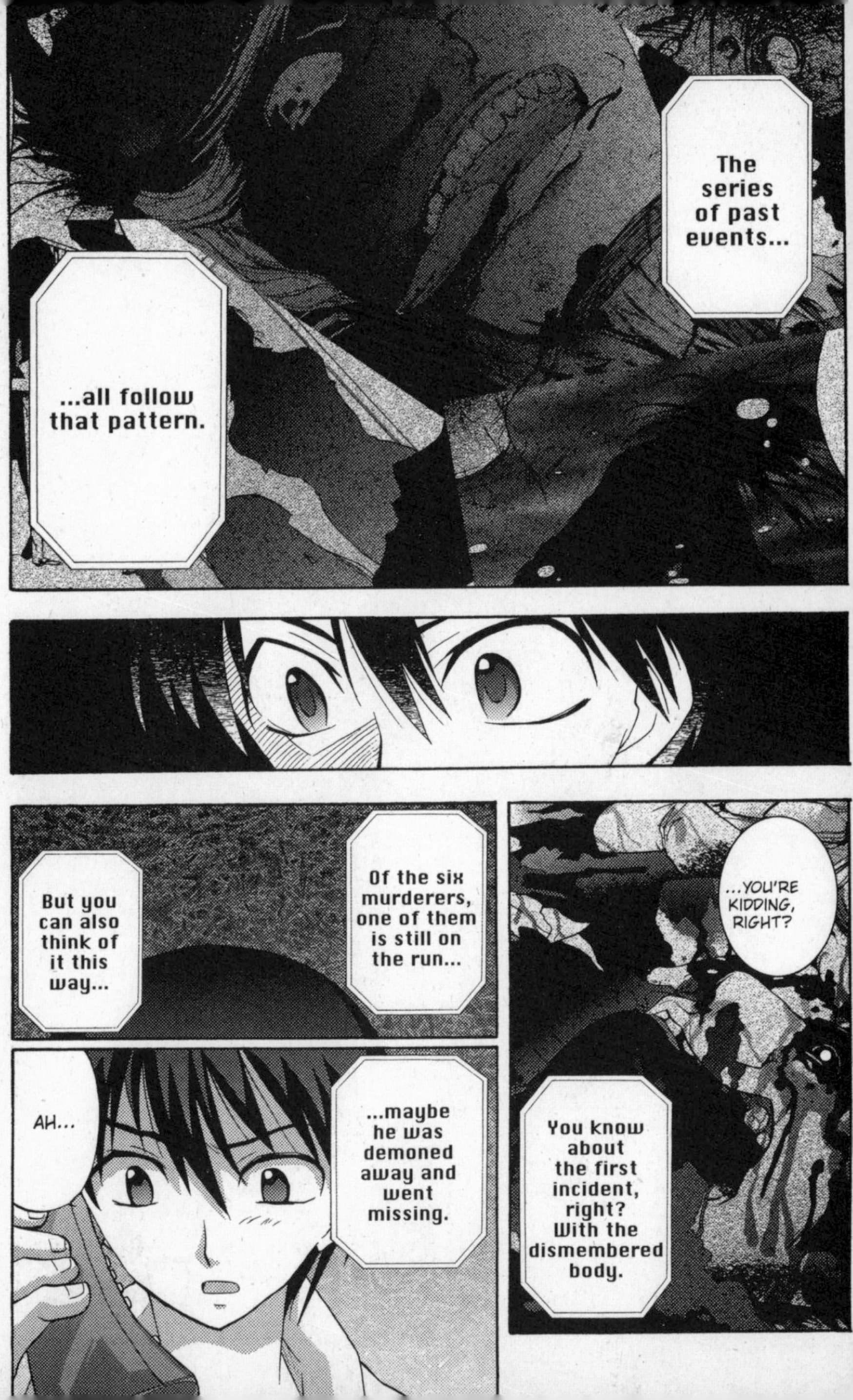
The series of past events...
...all follow that pattern.
...YOU'RE KIDDING, RIGHT?
You know about the first incident, right? With the dismembered body.
Of the six murderers, one of them is still on the run...
But you can also think of it this way...
...maybe he was demoned away and went missing.
AH...

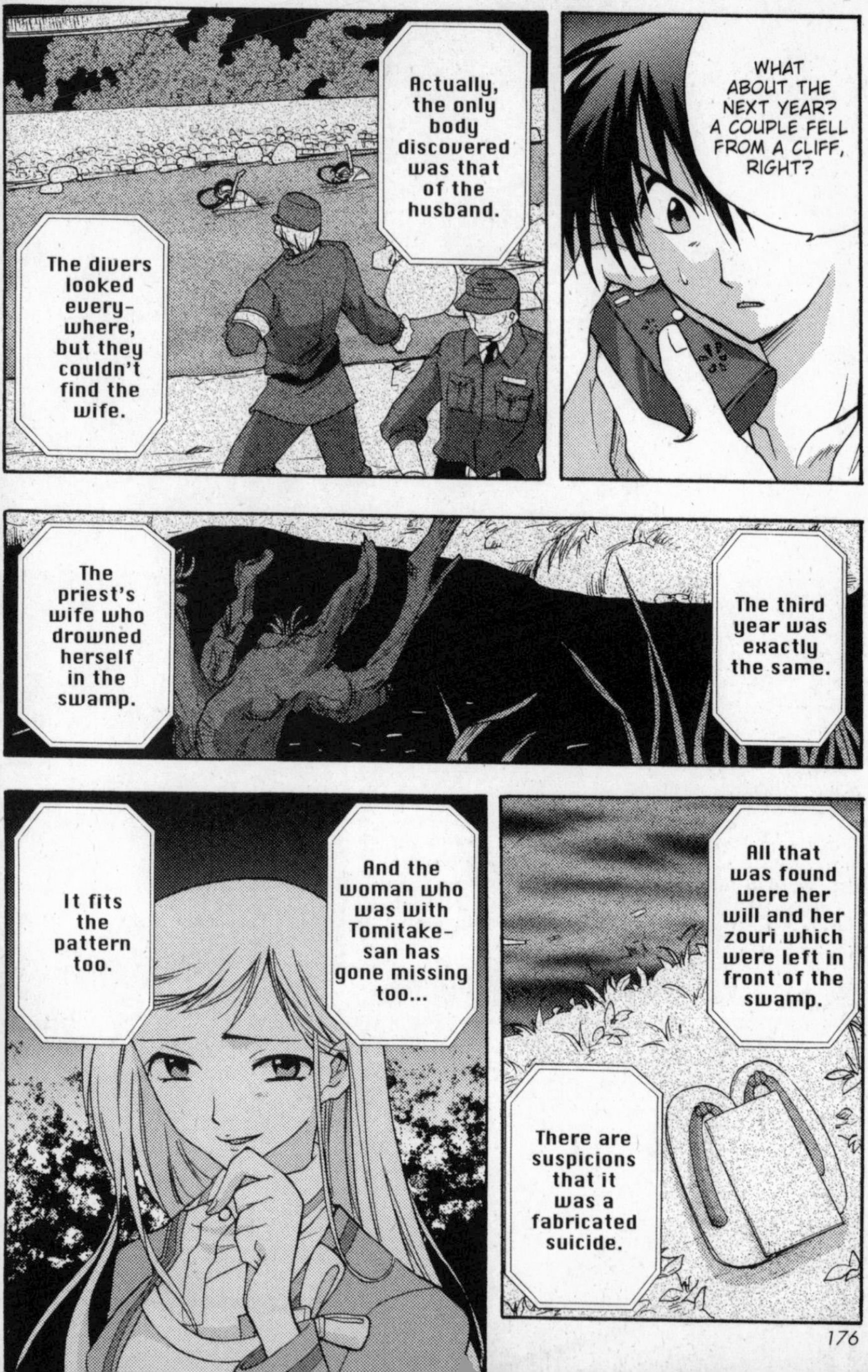
WHAT ABOUT THE NEXT YEAR? A COUPLE FELL FROM A CLIFF, RIGHT?
Actually, the only body discovered was that of the husband.
The divers looked every-where, but they couldn't find the wife.
The third year was exactly the same.
The priest's wife who drowned herself in the swamp.
All that was found were her will and her zouri which were left in front of the swamp.
There are suspicions that it was a fabricated suicide.
And the woman who was with Tomitake-san has gone missing too...
It fits the pattern too.

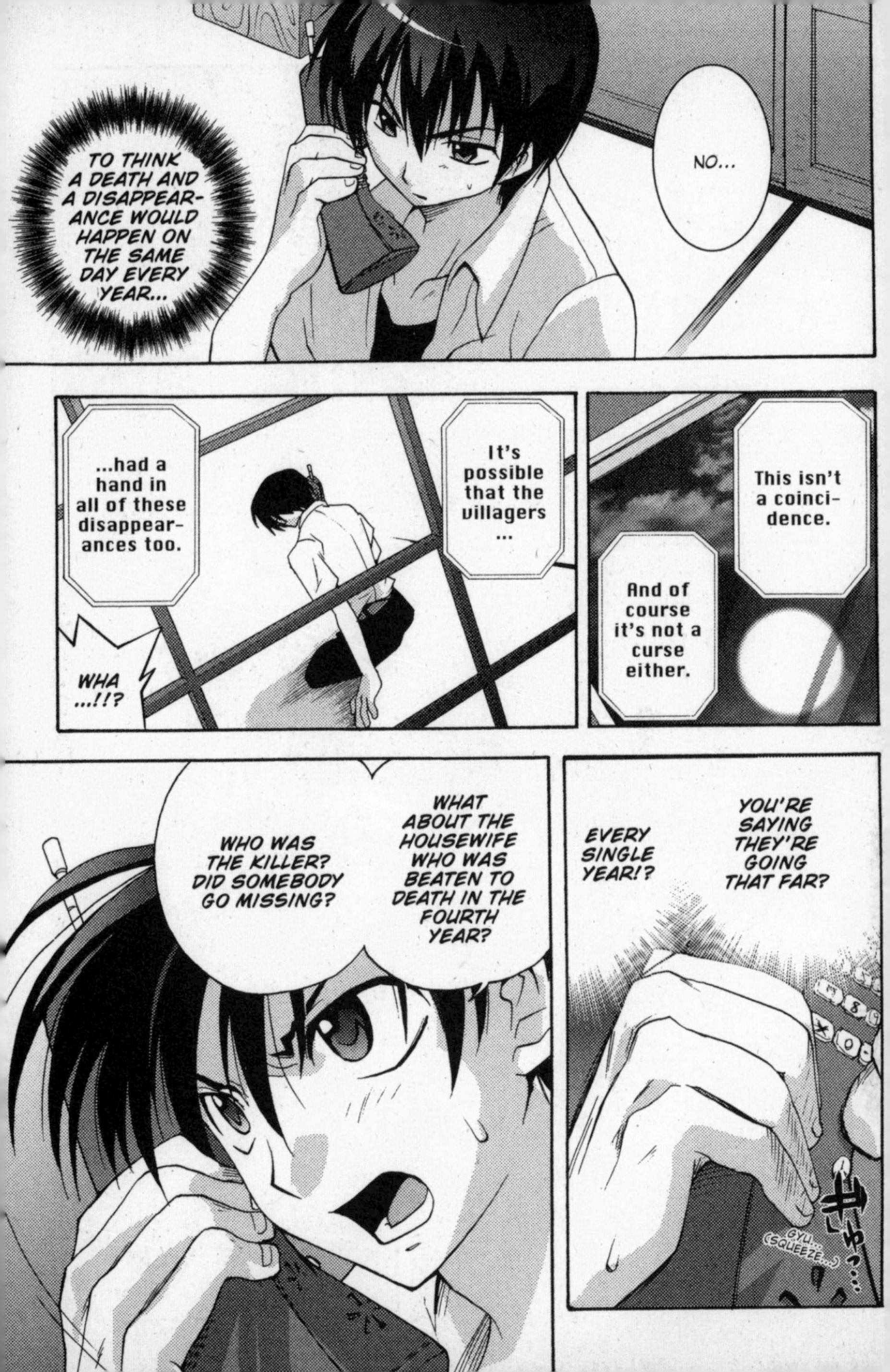
NO...
TO THINK A DEATH AND A DISAPPEARANCE WOULD HAPPEN ON THE SAME DAY EVERY YEAR...
This isn't a coincidence.
And of course it's not a curse either.
It's possible that the villagers ...
...had a hand in all of these disappearances too.
WHA ...!!?
YOU'RE SAYING THEY'RE GOING THAT FAR?
EVERY SINGLE YEAR!?
GYU... (SQUEEZE...)
WHAT ABOUT THE HOUSEWIFE WHO WAS BEATEN TO DEATH IN THE FOURTH YEAR?
WHO WAS THE KILLER? DID SOMEBODY GO MISSING?

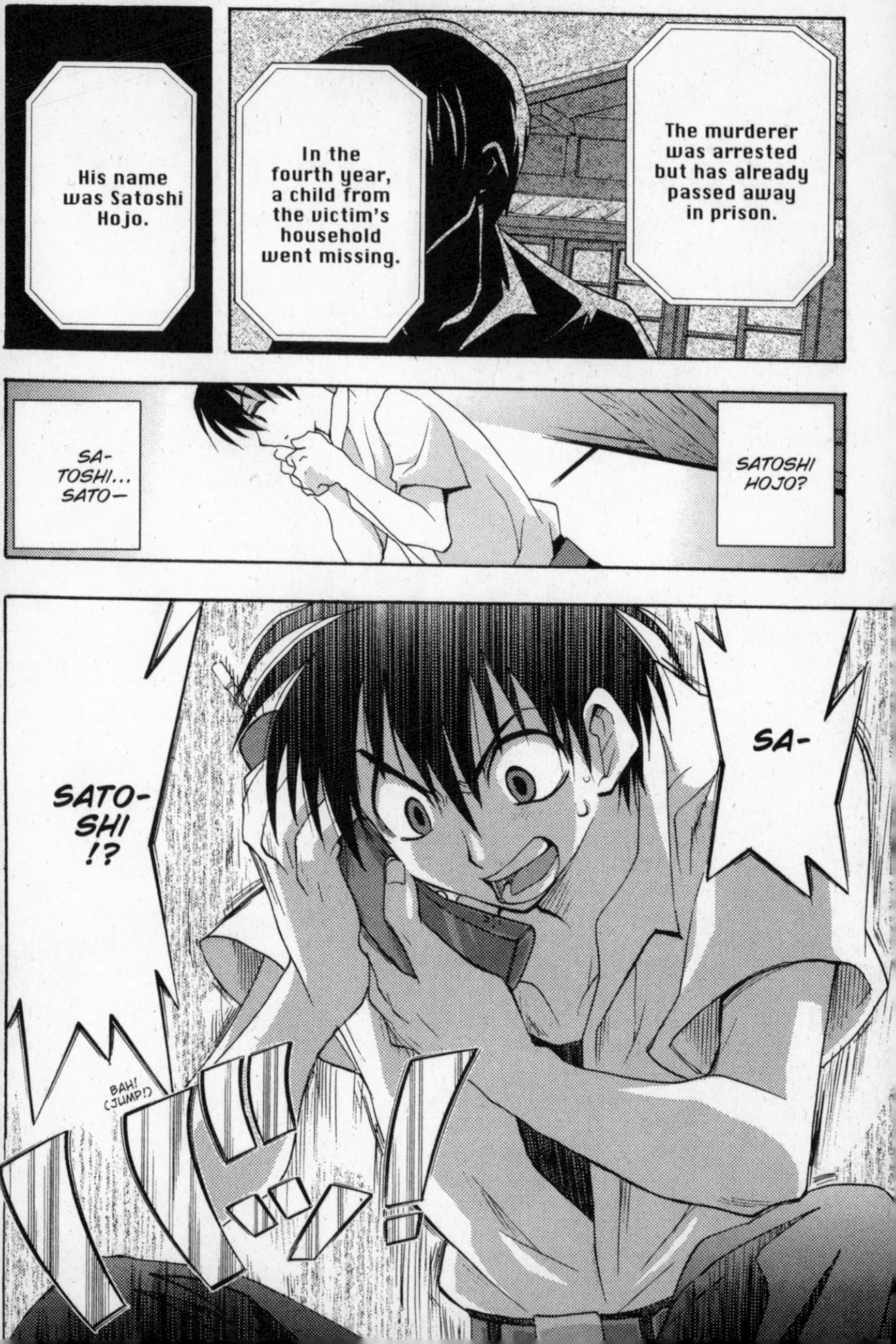
The murderer was arrested but has already passed away in prison.
In the fourth year, a child from the victim's household went missing.
His name was Satoshi Hojo.
SATOSHI HOJO?
SA-TOSHI... SATO—
SA-
SATO-SHI !?
BAH! (JUMP!)

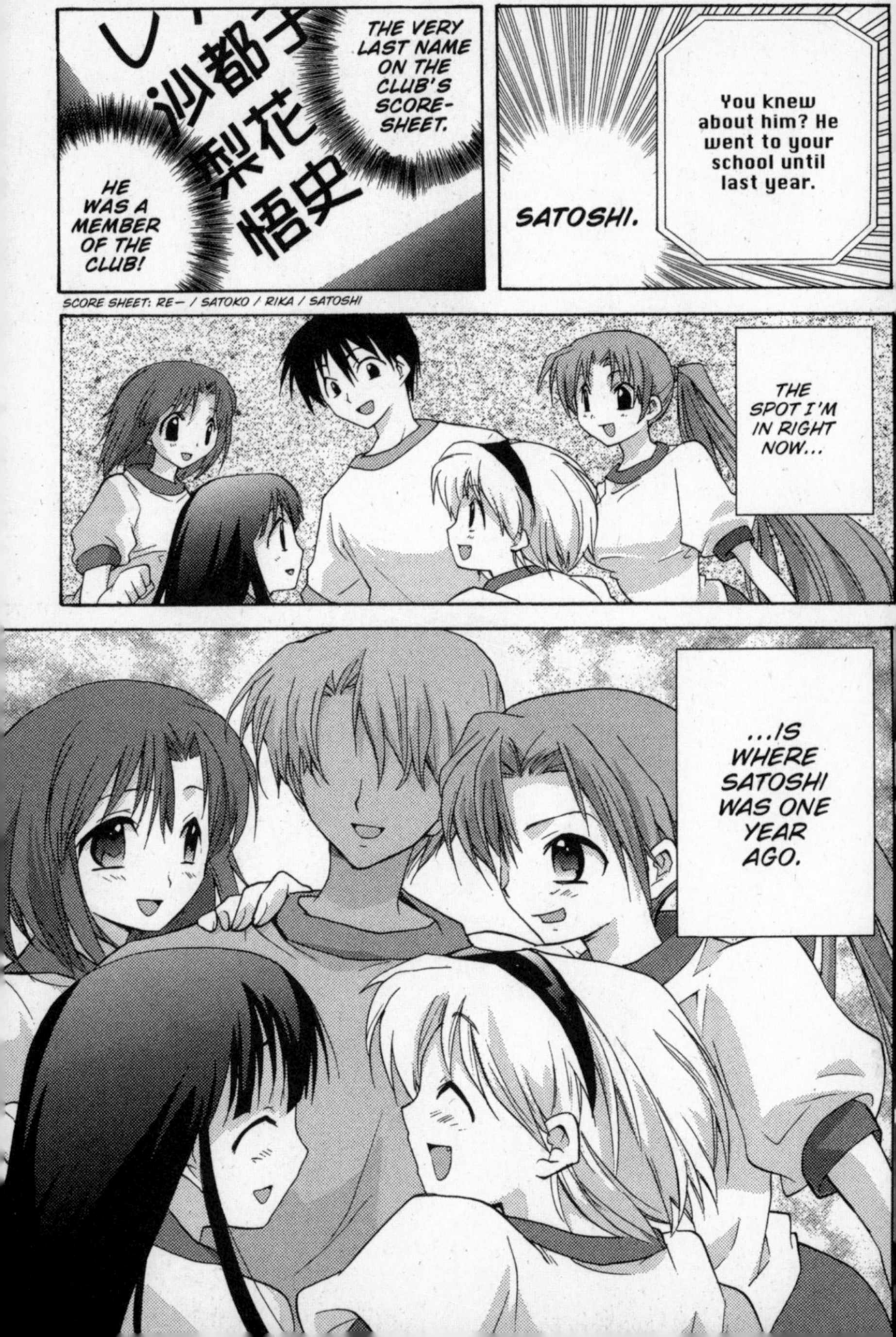
You knew about him? He went to your school until last year.
SATOSHI.
THE VERY LAST NAME ON THE CLUB'S SCORE-SHEET.
沙都子
梨花
悟史
HE WAS A MEMBER OF THE CLUB!
SCORE SHEET: RE— / SATOKO / RIKA / SATOSHI
THE SPOT I'M IN RIGHT NOW...
...IS WHERE SATOSHI WAS ONE YEAR AGO.

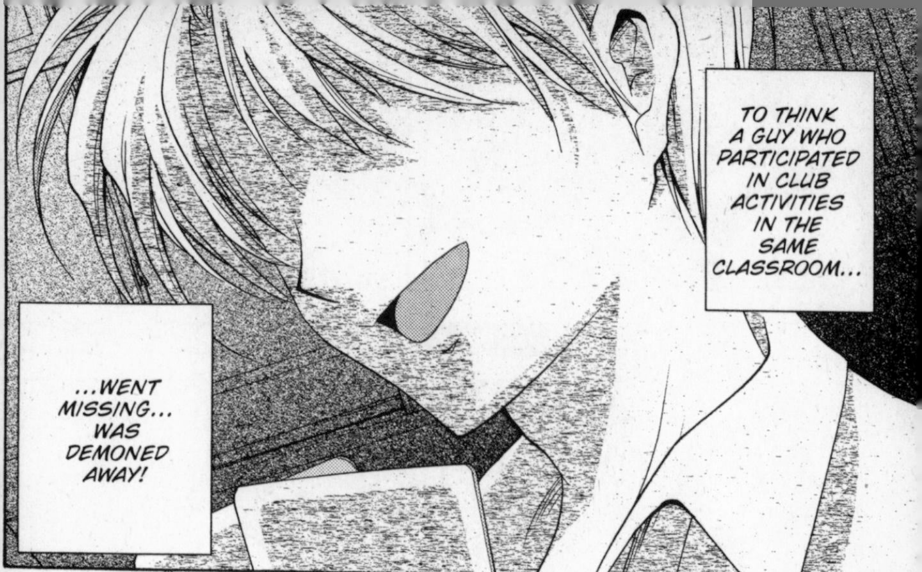
TO THINK A GUY WHO PARTICIPATED IN CLUB ACTIVITIES IN THE SAME CLASSROOM...
...WENT MISSING... WAS DEMONED AWAY!

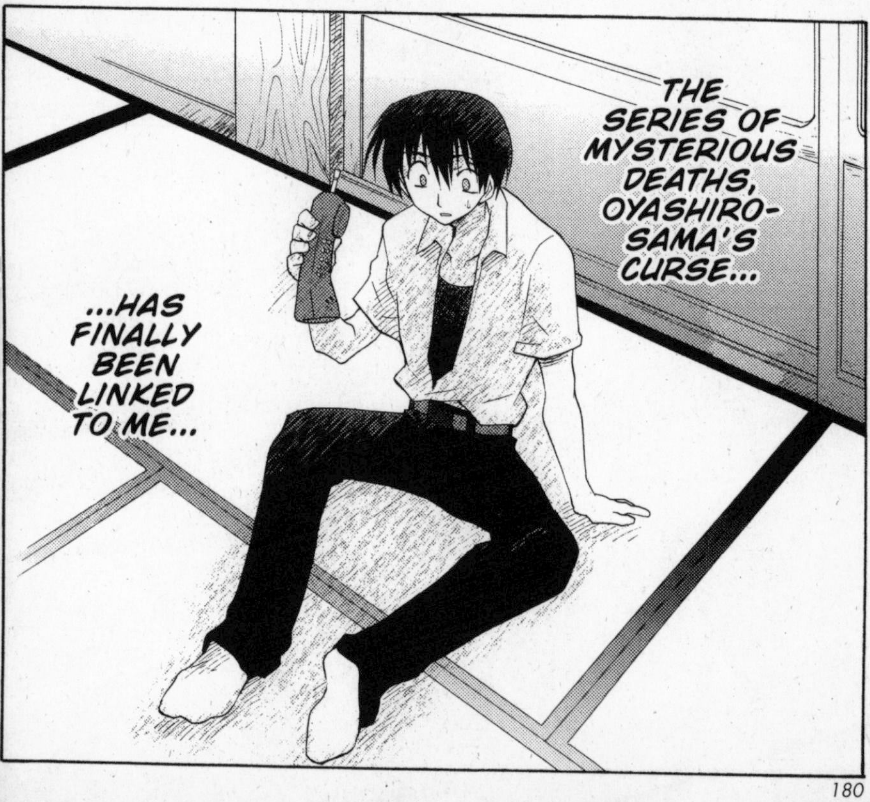
THE SERIES OF MYSTERIOUS DEATHS, OYASHIRO-SAMA'S CURSE...
...HAS FINALLY BEEN LINKED TO ME...

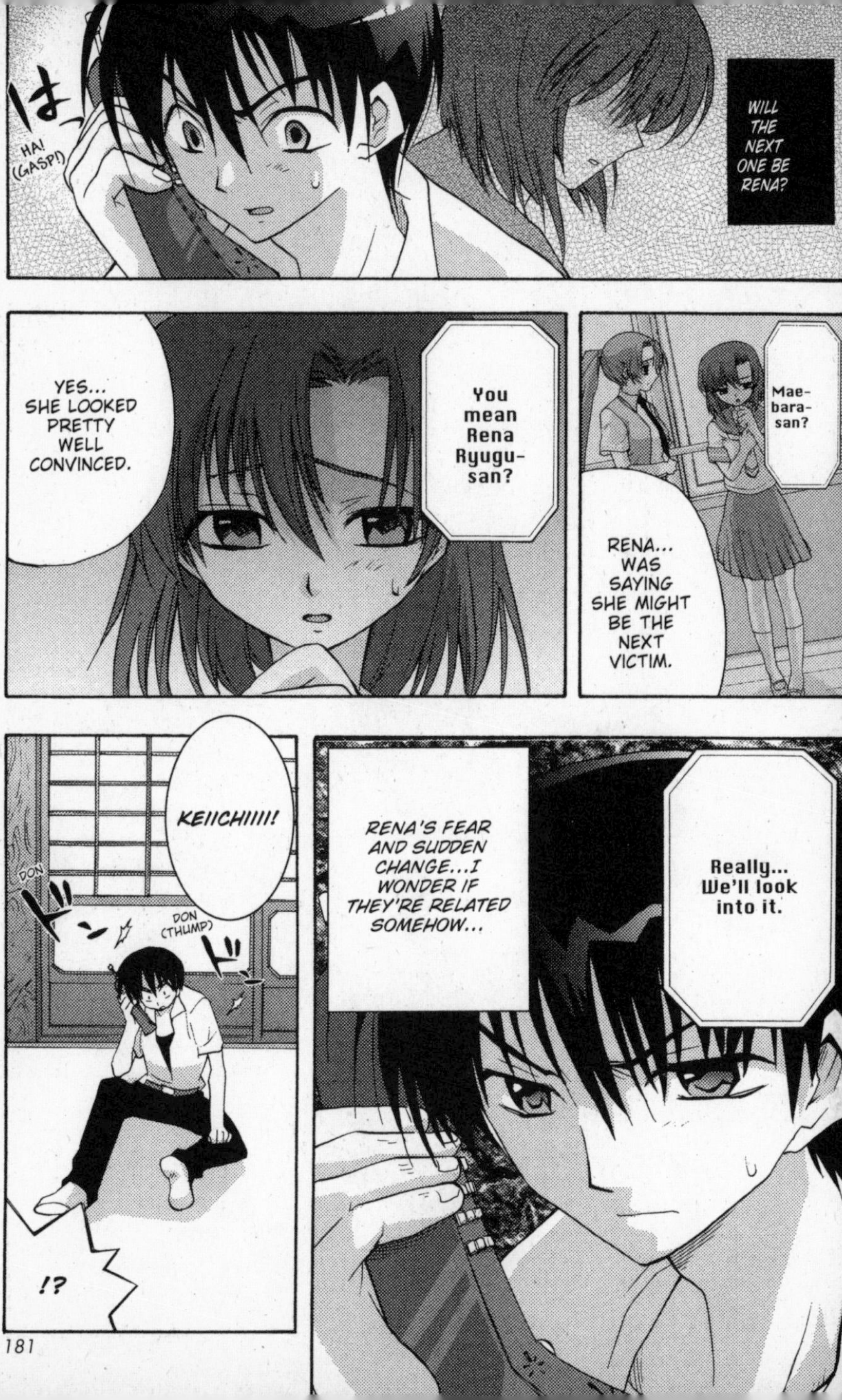
WILL THE NEXT ONE BE RENA?
HA! (GASP!)
Mae-bara-san?
RENA... WAS SAYING SHE MIGHT BE THE NEXT VICTIM.
You mean Rena Ryugu-san?
YES... SHE LOOKED PRETTY WELL CONVINCED.
Really... We'll look into it.
RENA'S FEAR AND SUDDEN CHANGE...I WONDER IF THEY'RE RELATED SOMEHOW...
KEIICHI!!!!!
DON (THUMP)
DON
!?

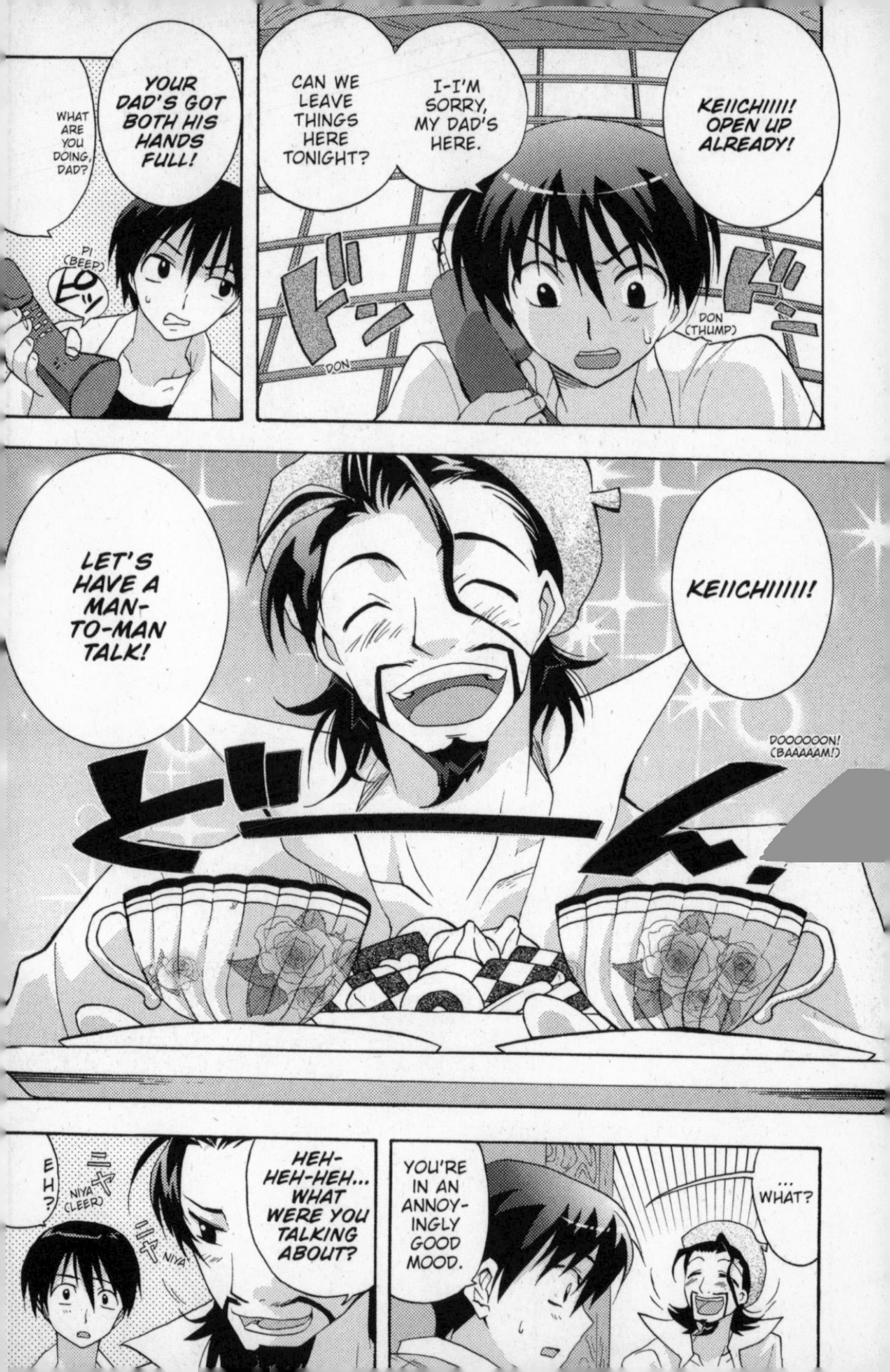
KEIICHIIIII! OPEN UP ALREADY!
DON (THUMP)
I-I'M SORRY, MY DAD'S HERE.
CAN WE LEAVE THINGS HERE TONIGHT?
DON
YOUR DAD'S GOT BOTH HIS HANDS FULL!
WHAT ARE YOU DOING, DAD?
PI (BEEP)
KEIICHIIIIII!
LET'S HAVE A MAN-TO-MAN TALK!
DOOOOOON! (BAAAAAM!)
...WHAT?
YOU'RE IN AN ANNOY-INGLY GOOD MOOD.
HEH-HEH-HEH... WHAT WERE YOU TALKING ABOUT?
NIYA
NIYA (LEER)
EH?

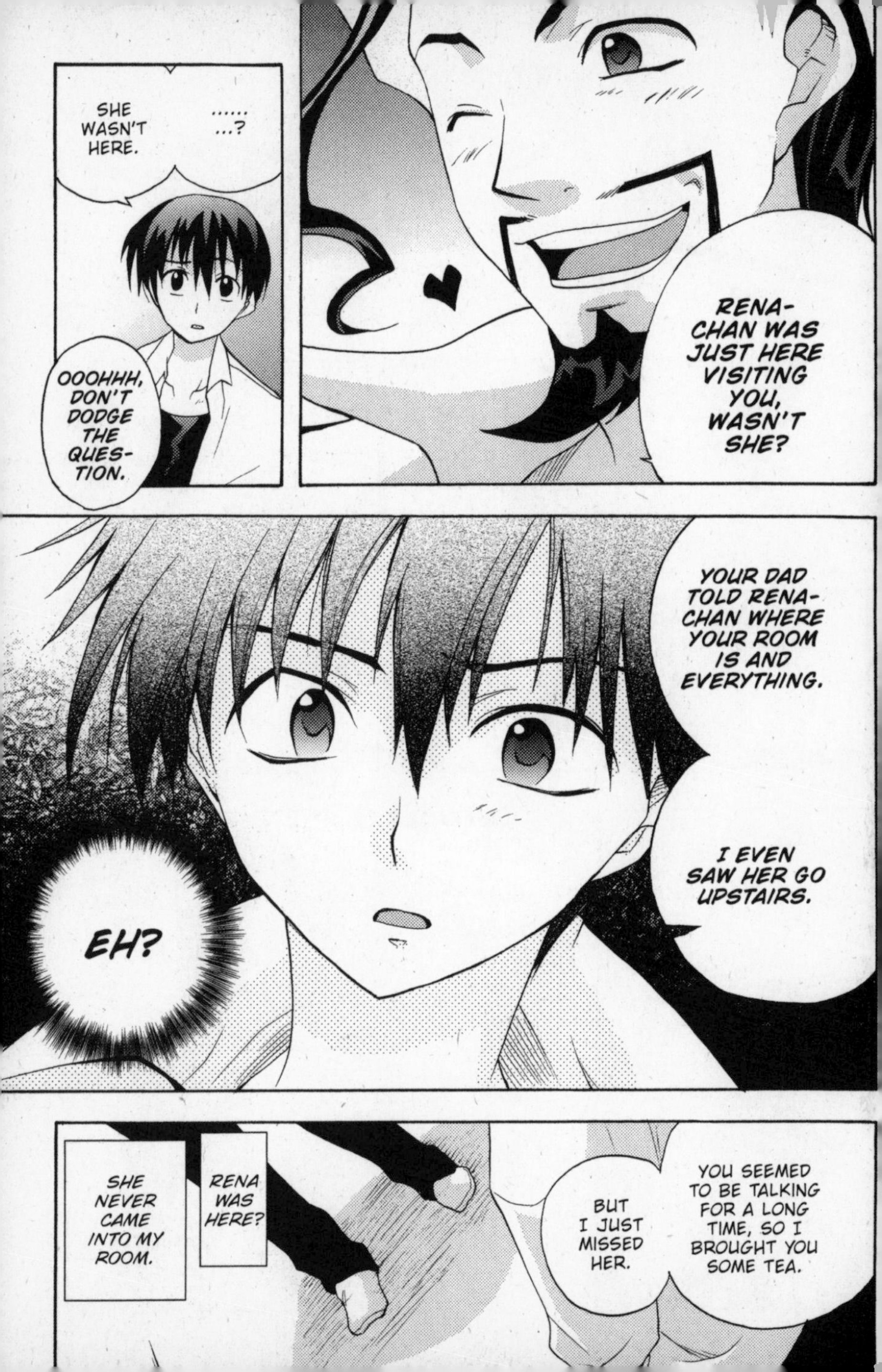
RENA-CHAN WAS JUST HERE VISITING YOU, WASN'T SHE?
......
...?
SHE WASN'T HERE.
OOOHHH, DON'T DODGE THE QUES-TION.
YOUR DAD TOLD RENA-CHAN WHERE YOUR ROOM IS AND EVERYTHING.
I EVEN SAW HER GO UPSTAIRS.
EH?
YOU SEEMED TO BE TALKING FOR A LONG TIME, SO I BROUGHT YOU SOME TEA.
BUT I JUST MISSED HER.
RENA WAS HERE?
SHE NEVER CAME INTO MY ROOM.

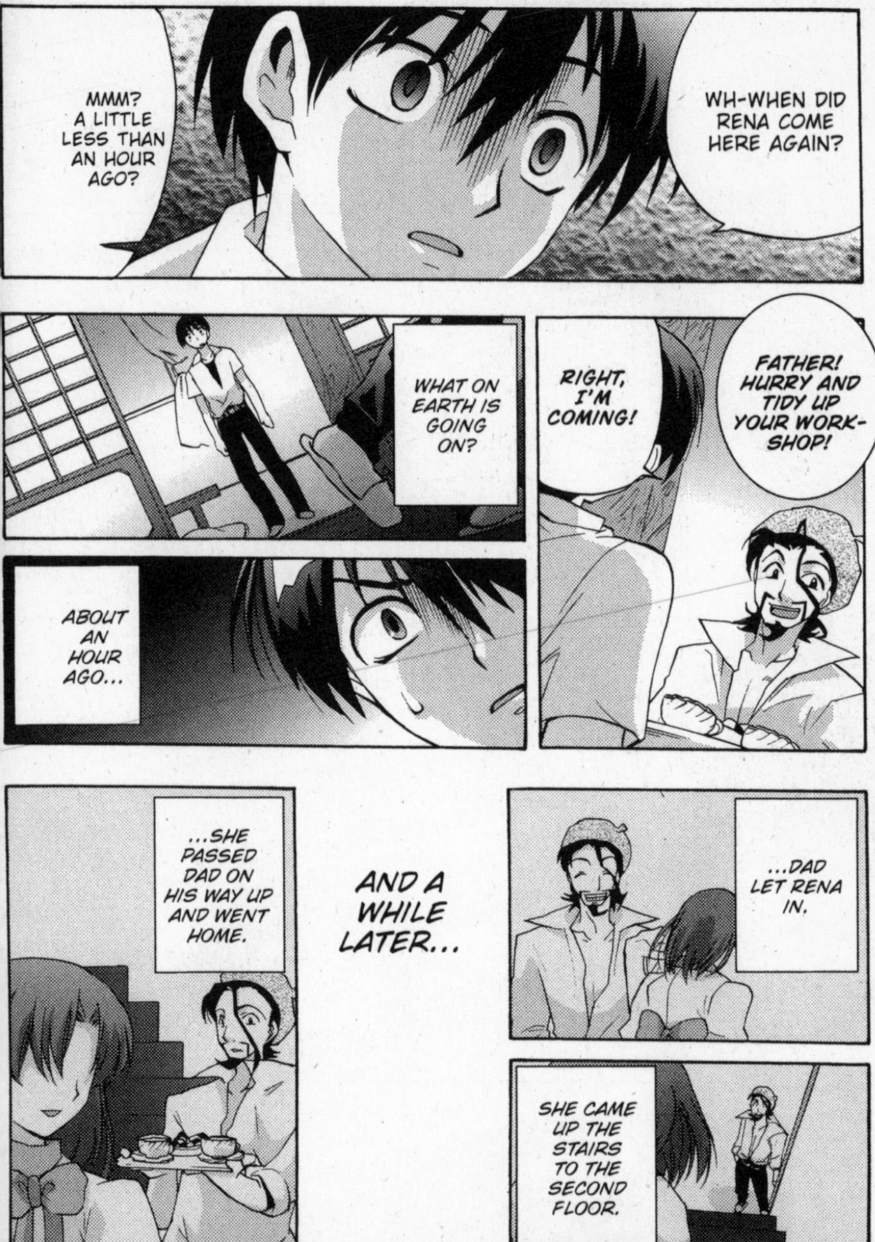
WH-WHEN DID RENA COME HERE AGAIN?
MMM? A LITTLE LESS THAN AN HOUR AGO?
FATHER! HURRY AND TIDY UP YOUR WORK-SHOP!
RIGHT, I'M COMING!
WHAT ON EARTH IS GOING ON?
ABOUT AN HOUR AGO...
...DAD LET RENA IN.
SHE CAME UP THE STAIRS TO THE SECOND FLOOR.
AND A WHILE LATER...
...SHE PASSED DAD ON HIS WAY UP AND WENT HOME.

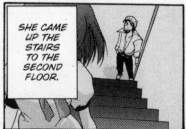

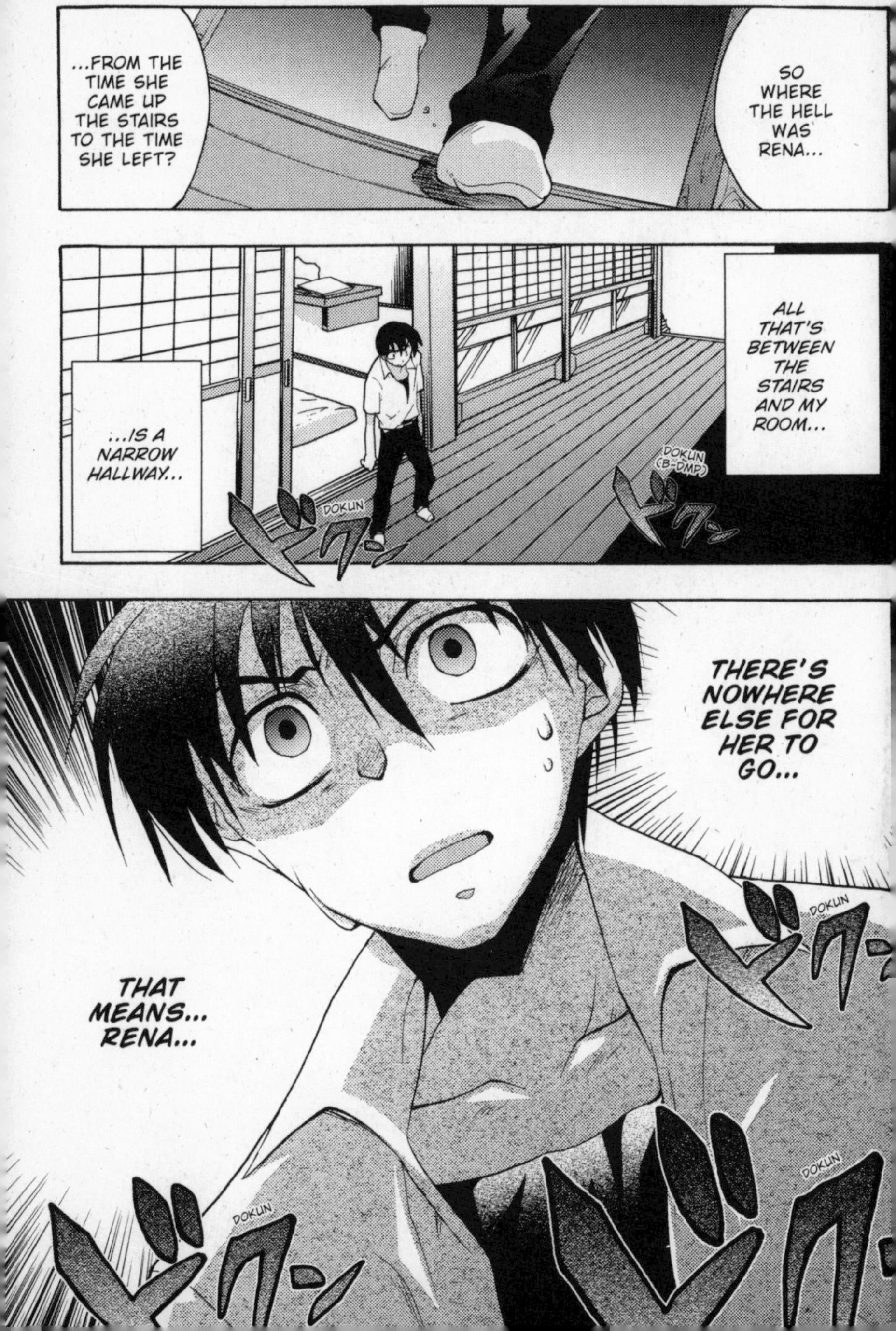
SO WHERE THE HELL WAS RENA...
...FROM THE TIME SHE CAME UP THE STAIRS TO THE TIME SHE LEFT?
ALL THAT'S BETWEEN THE STAIRS AND MY ROOM...
DOKUN (B-DMP)
...IS A NARROW HALLWAY...
DOKUN
THERE'S NOWHERE ELSE FOR HER TO GO...
DOKUN
THAT MEANS... RENA...
DOKUN
DOKUN

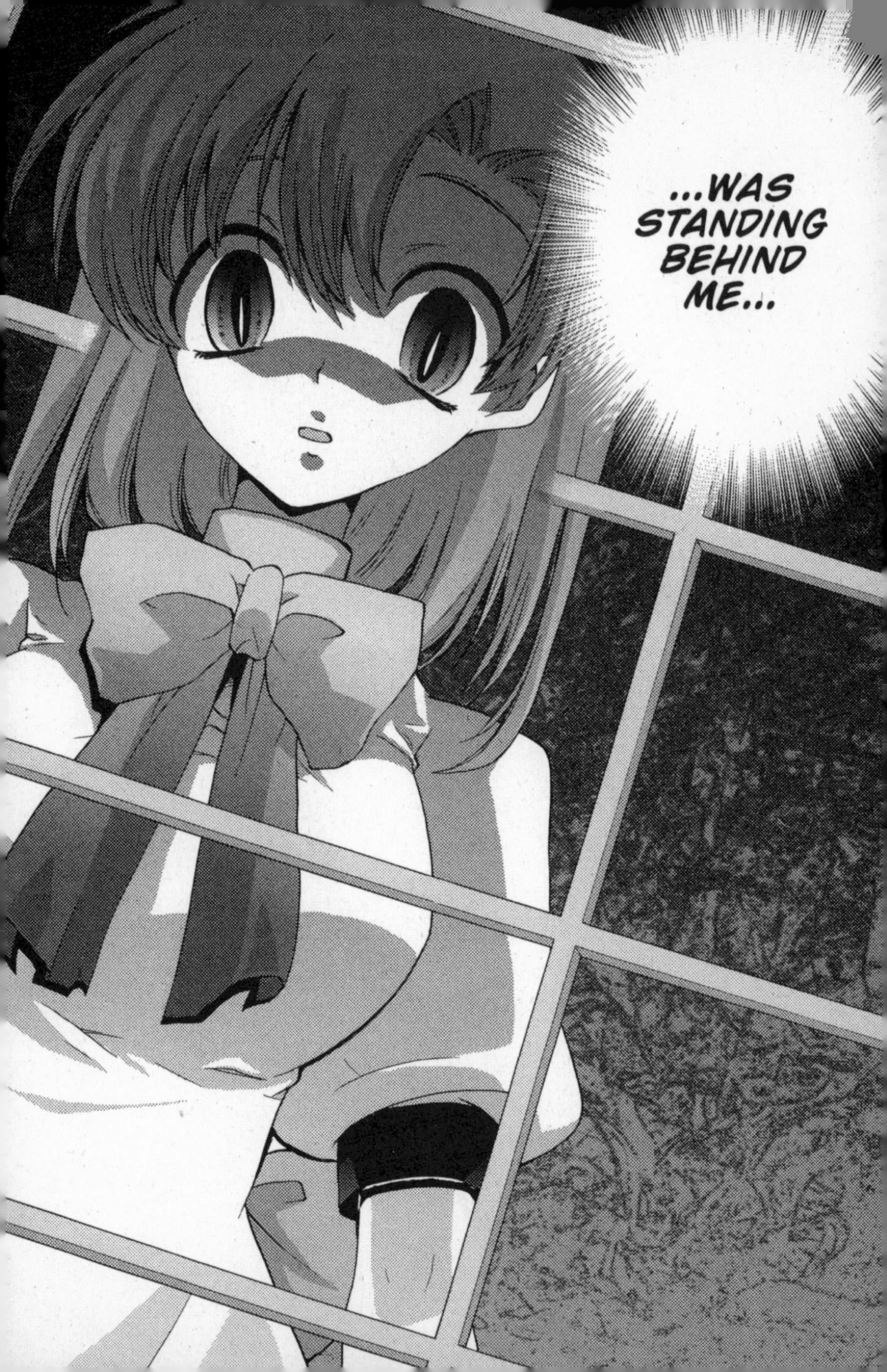
...WAS STANDING BEHIND ME...

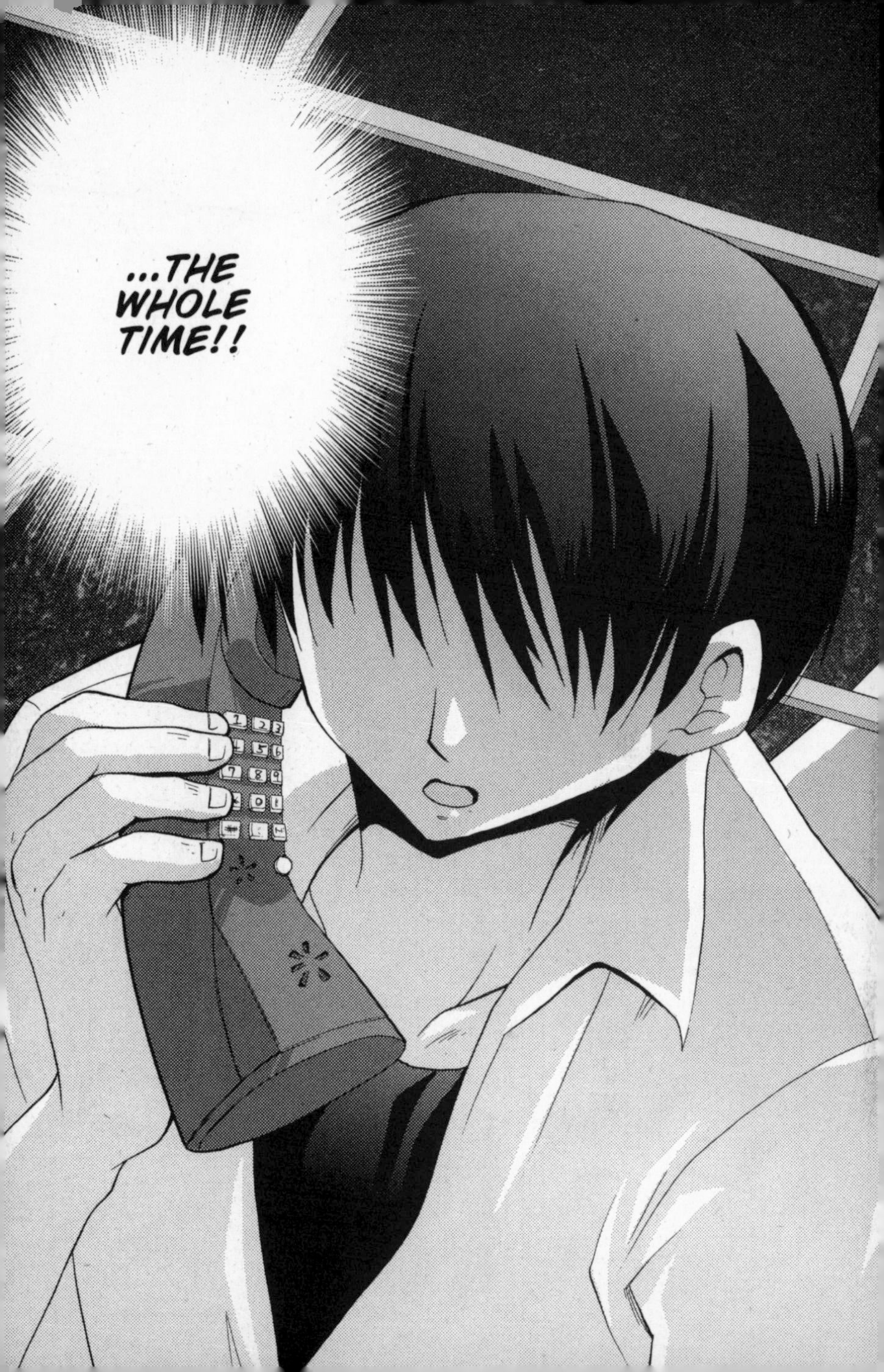
...THE WHOLE TIME!!

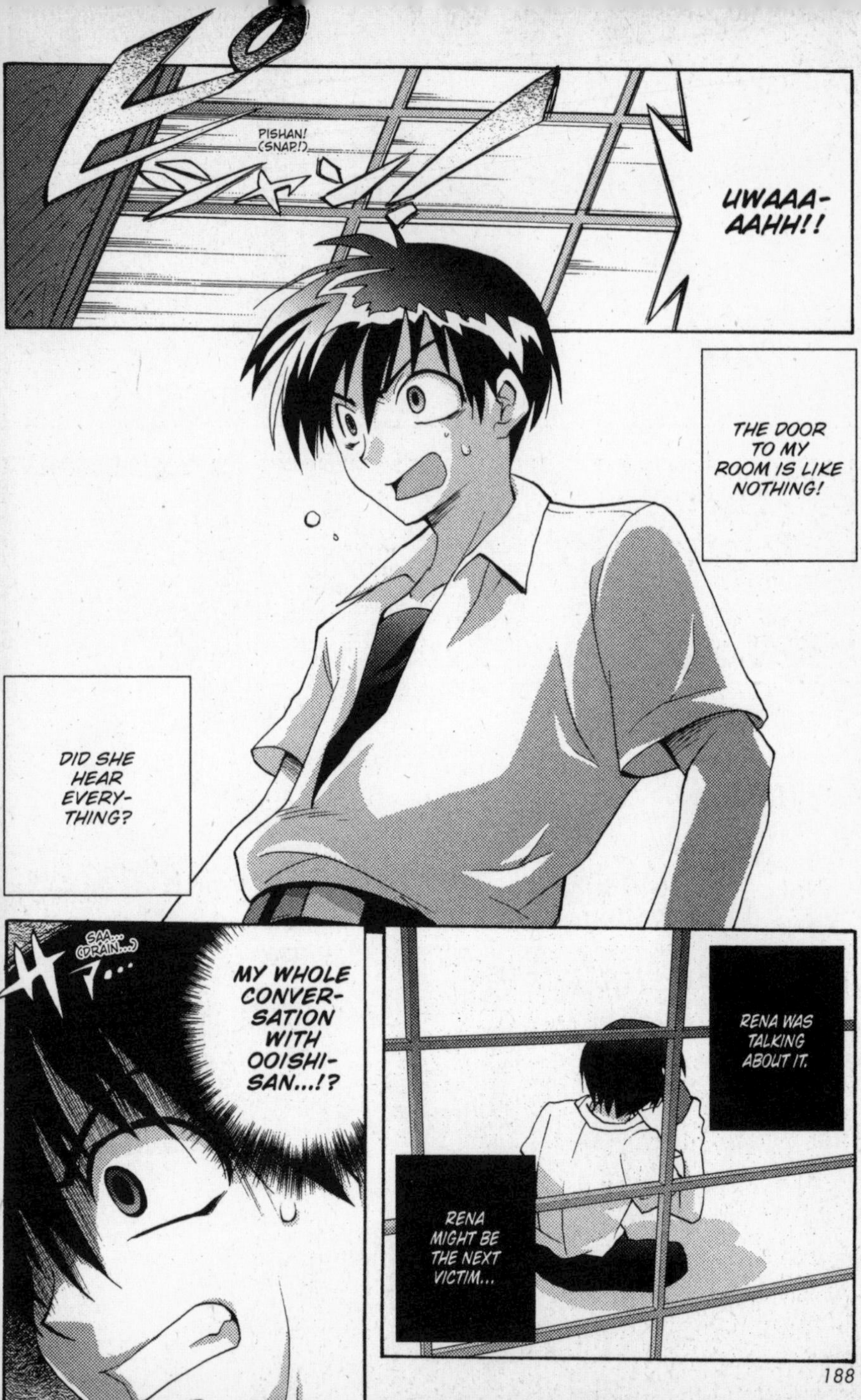
PISHAN! (SNAP!)
UWAAA-AAHH!!
THE DOOR TO MY ROOM IS LIKE NOTHING!
DID SHE HEAR EVERYTHING?
RENA WAS TALKING ABOUT IT.
RENA MIGHT BE THE NEXT VICTIM...
SAA... (DRAIN...)
MY WHOLE CONVERSATION WITH OOISHI-SAN...!?

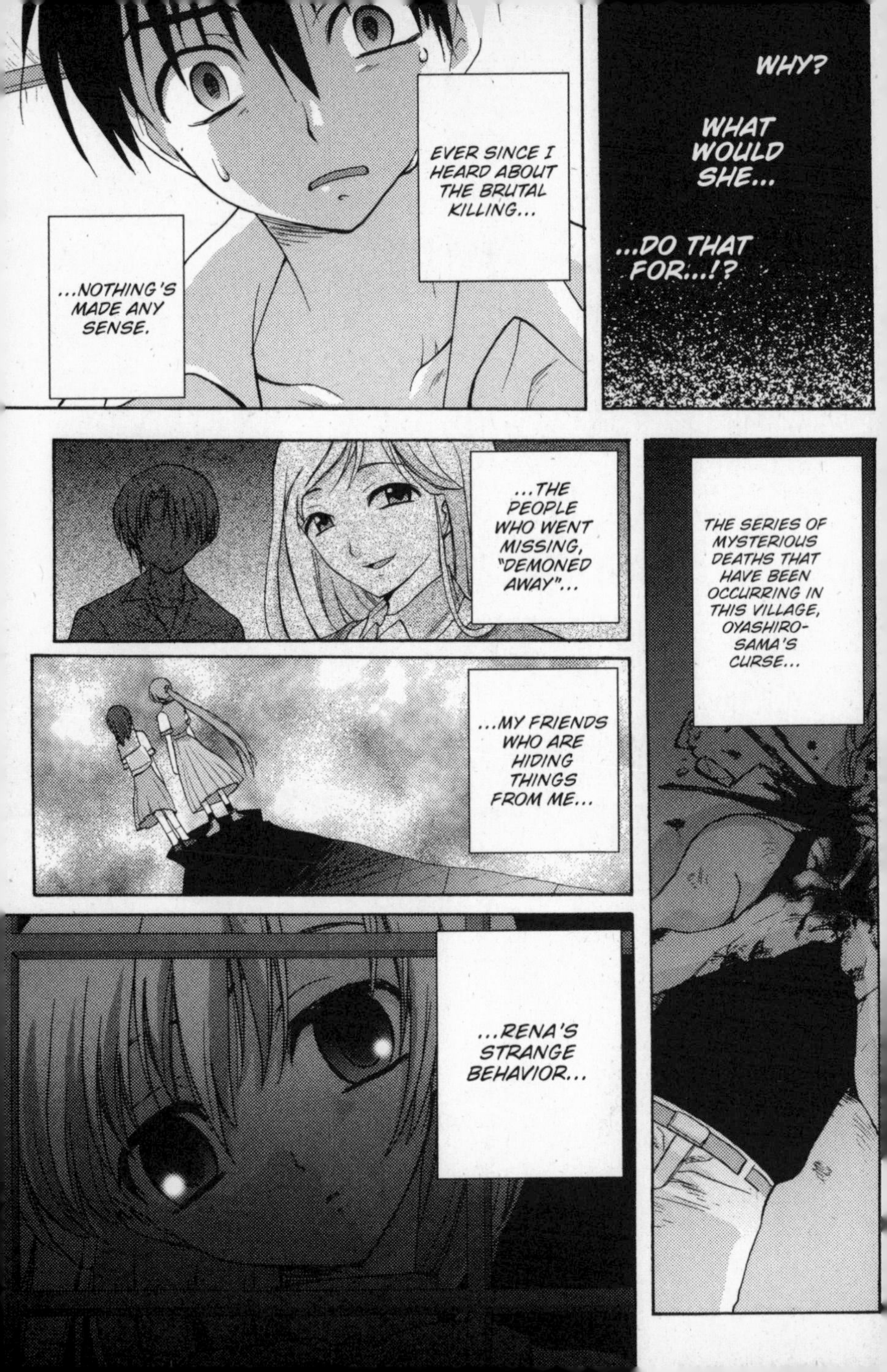
WHY?
WHAT WOULD SHE...
...DO THAT FOR...!?
EVER SINCE I HEARD ABOUT THE BRUTAL KILLING...
...NOTHING'S MADE ANY SENSE.
THE SERIES OF MYSTERIOUS DEATHS THAT HAVE BEEN OCCURRING IN THIS VILLAGE, OYASHIRO-SAMA'S CURSE...
...THE PEOPLE WHO WENT MISSING, "DEMONED AWAY"...
...MY FRIENDS WHO ARE HIDING THINGS FROM ME...
...RENA'S STRANGE BEHAVIOR...

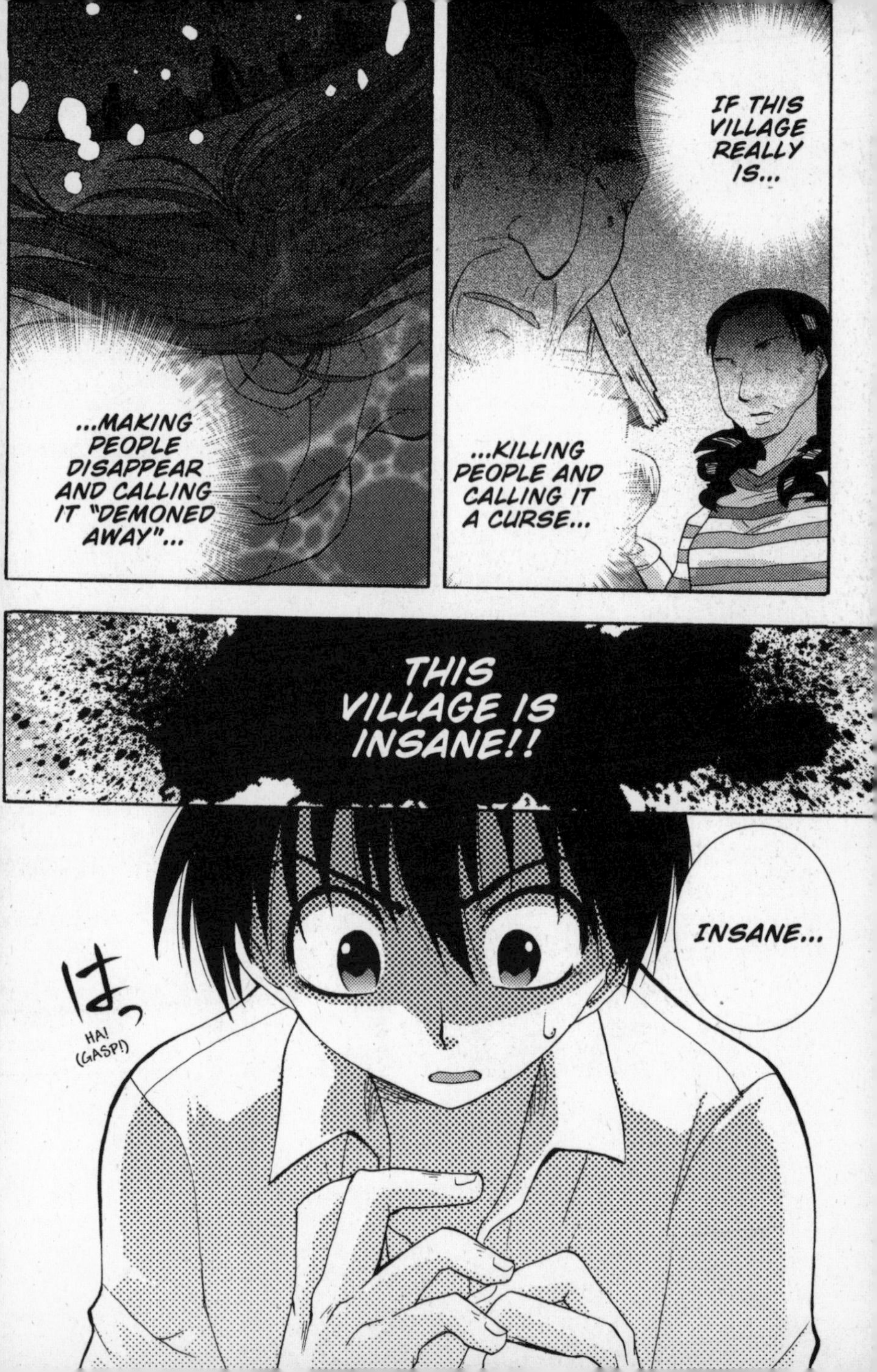
IF THIS VILLAGE REALLY IS...
...KILLING PEOPLE AND CALLING IT A CURSE...
...MAKING PEOPLE DISAPPEAR AND CALLING IT "DEMONED AWAY"...
THIS VILLAGE IS INSANE!!
INSANE...
はっ
HA! (GASP!)

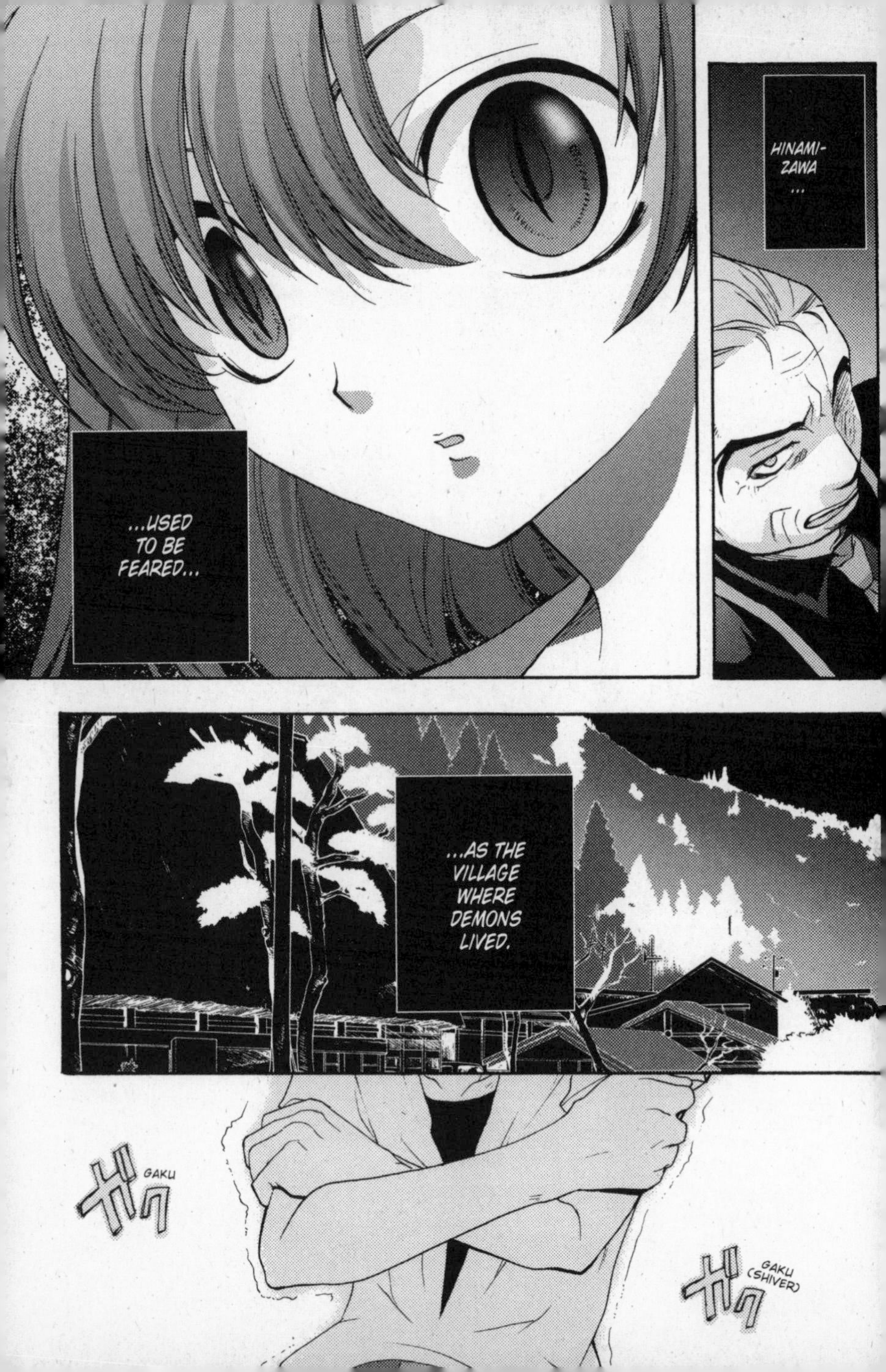
HINAMI-ZAWA ...
...USED TO BE FEARED...
...AS THE VILLAGE WHERE DEMONS LIVED.
GAKU (SHIVER)
GAKU

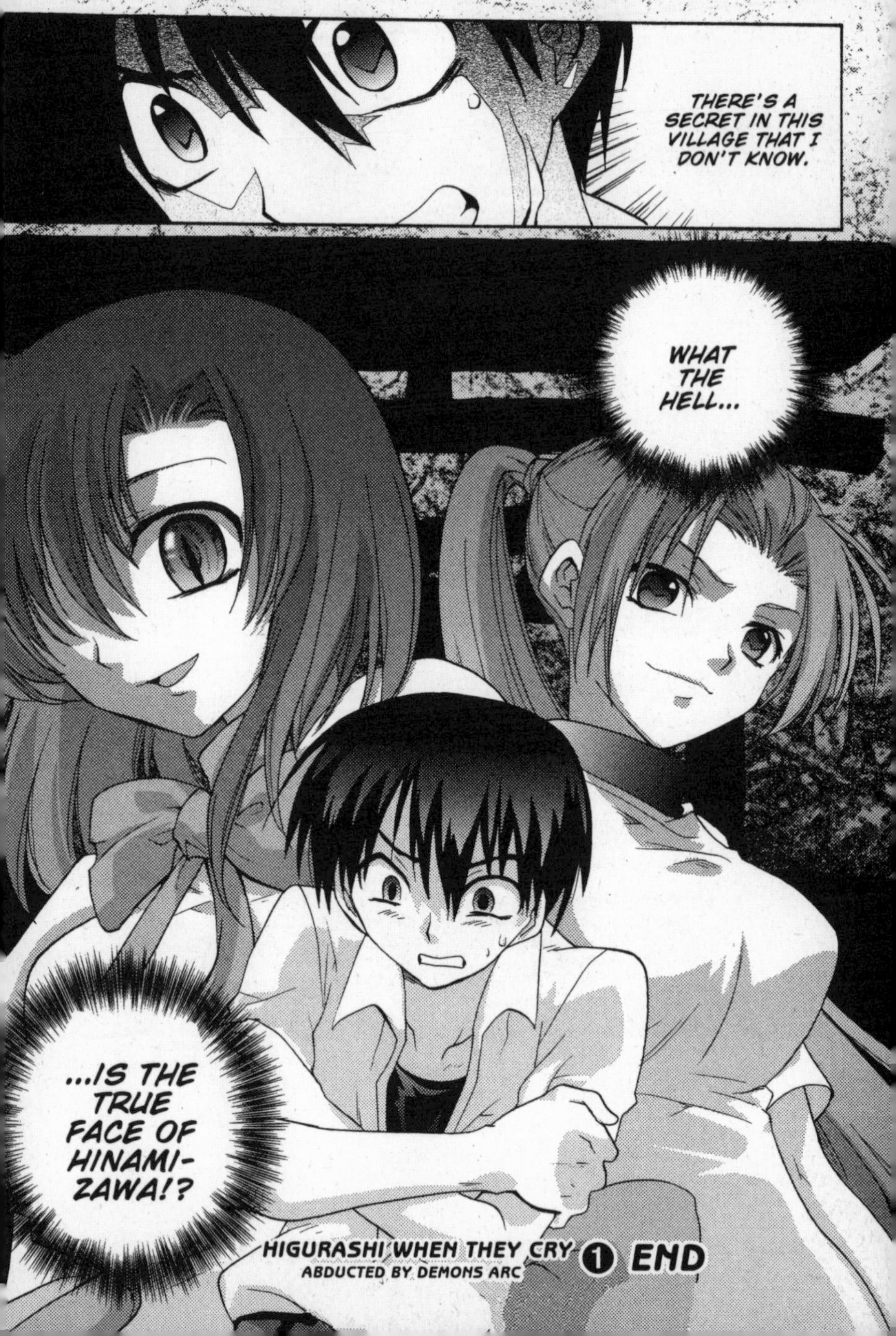
THERE'S A SECRET IN THIS VILLAGE THAT I DON'T KNOW.
WHAT THE HELL...
...IS THE TRUE FACE OF HINAMI-ZAWA!?
HIGURASHI WHEN THEY CRY 1 END
ABDUCTED BY DEMONS ARC

HIGURASHI WHEN THEY CRY

07th Expansion presents Volume 1: Abducted by Demons Arc
"WHEN THEY CRY."

ABOUT THE MANGA VERSION OF THE "ABDUCTED BY DEMONS ARC"

ORIGINAL STORY, SUPERVISOR:
RYUKISHI 07

HELLO, I AM RYUKISHI 07; I WROTE THE ORIGINAL STORY. I TRULY THANK YOU FOR PICKING UP "HIGURASHI WHEN THEY CRY: ABDUCTED BY DEMONS ARC" VOLUME ONE.

PARTIALLY BECAUSE THE ORIGINAL STORY "HIGURASHI WHEN THEY CRY" IS A NOVEL GAME, ALMOST ALL OF THE EXPRESSIONS ARE WRITTEN IN TEXT. SO THERE ARE MORE THAN A FEW PLACES WHERE I LEFT THEM TO THE READERS' IMAGINATIONS AND ONLY DEPICTED VAGUE EXPRESSIONS.

I AM TRULY THANKFUL TO SUZURAGI-SENSEI FOR PORTRAYING THE FUN AND HORROR OF THE ORIGINAL STORY SO WONDERFULLY IN MANGA FORM! JUST WHEN THEIR FUN DAILY LIFE HAS BEEN COMPLETELY MUTILATED, THERE'S THE SHOCKING SCENE WITH RENA, AND I COULDN'T HELP BUT BE IN AWE AT SUZURAGI-SENSEI'S BLOODCURDLING POWER!! THERE ARE MORE SCARY SCENES TO COME IN THE "ABDUCTED BY DEMONS ARC," SO I'M AFRAID (CAN'T WAIT) TO SEE THE ROUGH DRAFT!

THE "ABDUCTED BY DEMONS ARC" IS THE FIRST OF THE EIGHT STORY ARCS, AND I THINK ONE OF ITS HIGHLIGHTS IS THAT IT CLEARLY SHOWS THE LIGHT AND DARK SIDES OF THE STORY'S SETTING, HINAMIZAWA. I HOPE YOU ENJOY SEEING THE CONTRAST AS THE STORY COMPLETELY CHANGES FROM VOLUME ONE TO THE FUTURE VOLUME TWO.

WITH THE HELP OF VARIOUS PEOPLE, I'VE FINALLY MADE IT THIS FAR. I AM EXTREMELY GRATEFUL TO BE ALLOWED TO HAVE A HAND IN THE MANGA ADAPTATION OF THE FAMOUS WORK, "HIGURASHI WHEN THEY CRY." FURTHERMORE, PERSONALLY, I WAS ALLOWED TO STUDY MY OWN OBSESSION... (LAUGH)

RYUKISHI07-SAMA, WHO CHECKED THE ROUGH DRAFTS THOROUGHLY AND METICULOUSLY DESPITE BEING SO BUSY; MY EDITORS, KOIZUMI-SAMA AND KOUNO-SAMA, WHO PATIENTLY GAVE ME DETAILED ADVICE; HIKARU UZAKI-SAMA, NIWAKO-SAMA, YOSHI SAKANO-SAMA, MOYOMOSO-SAMA, WHO HELPED ME WHEN I NEEDED IT DURING THEIR HECTIC SCHEDULES. MY FAMILY, WHO WARMLY WATCHED OVER ME.

AND YOU, WHO READ THIS MANGA! REALLY, THANK YOU VERY MUCH!

"HIGURASHI WHEN THEY CRY: ABDUCTED BY DEMONS ARC - MANGA VERSION" WILL BE GOING ON TO VOLUME TWO. I WILL CONTINUE TO DO MY VERY BEST, SO PLEASE KEEP READING.

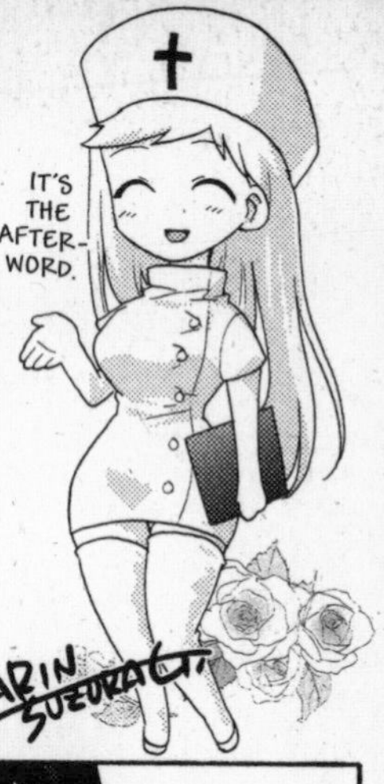
IT'S THE AFTER-WORD.
KARIN SUZURAGI

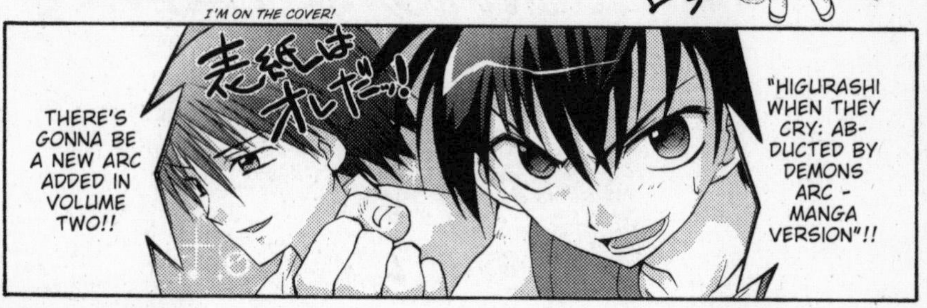
I'M ON THE COVER!
"HIGURASHI WHEN THEY CRY: ABDUCTED BY DEMONS ARC - MANGA VERSION"!!
表紙はオレだッ!
THERE'S GONNA BE A NEW ARC ADDED IN VOLUME TWO!!

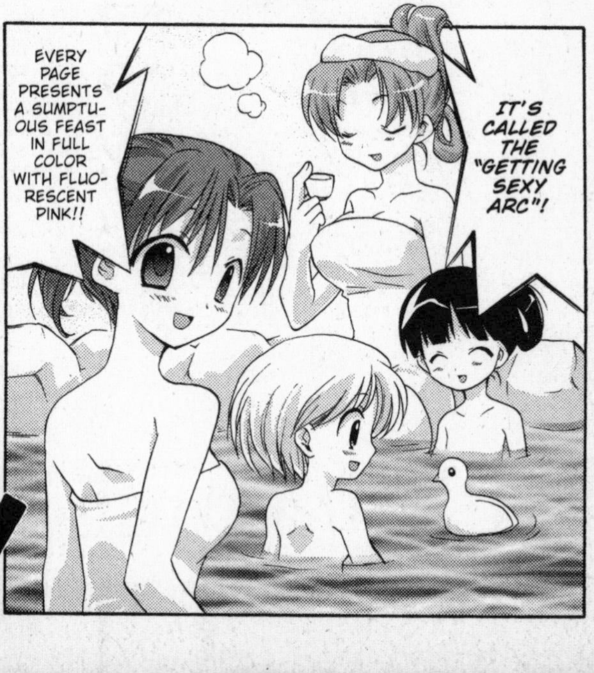
IT'S CALLED THE "GETTING SEXY ARC"!
EVERY PAGE PRESENTS A SUMPTUOUS FEAST IN FULL COLOR WITH FLUORESCENT PINK!!

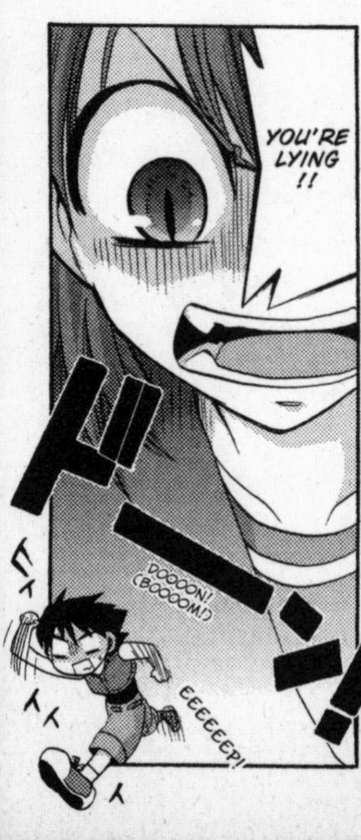
YOU'RE LYING!!
DOOOON! (BOOOOM!)
EEEEEEEP!

I, KEIICHI MAEBARA, AM IN DANGER OF LOSING MY LIFE. I DON'T KNOW WHO'S TRYING TO KILL ME OR WHY. THE ONE THING I KNOW IS THAT IT HAS SOMETHING TO DO WITH OYASHIRO-SAMA'S CURSE.

FROM A NOTE FOUND IN THE HOME OF THE SUSPECT, KEIICHI MAEBARA, AFTER THE TRAGEDY.

TRANSLATION NOTES

Pg. 46
Old geezer is a card game similar to Old Maid. Instead of using a joker, you pick another card to use in the joker's place.

Pg. 66
A **higurashi** is a variety of cicada, which sings in the early evening, just before nightfall. Higurashi literally means "day darkener," and its call is appropriately a sad and mournful one.

Pg. 76
A **lantern drifting**, or *tourou nagashi*, is a ceremony in which paper lanterns are set afloat down a river in mourning for the dead. It is often performed at the time of the Obon Festival, a Japanese festival honoring the dead.

Pg. 79
I know I'm inexperienced. As Keiichi comments, this is something commonly said by a new bride to her husband and/or his family, to apologize for being unfamiliar with the ways of being a good wife.

Okonomiyaki is loosely translated to "fried the way you like it." Okonomiyaki is kind of like a pizza and kind of like a pancake, made with all sorts of ingredients.

Pg. 84
Obatcha comes from *Obaachan*, which pretty much means "Grandma." Because Mion comes from such a small town, she says it with an accent, and it becomes "Obatcha."

Pg. 85
Takoyaki, meaning "octopus fry," are octopus dumplings, and can almost always be found at a Japanese festival.